PHENOMENOLOGY AND EXISTENTIALISM

Edited by

Robert C. Solomon

UNIVERSITY
PRESS OF
AMERICA

LANHAM • NEW YORK • LONDON

Copyright © 1980, 1972 by

Robert C. Solomon

University Press of America,™ Inc.

4720 Boston Way
Lanham, MD 20706

3 Henrietta Street
London WC2E 8LU England

ISBN (Perfect): 0-8191-0826-X
LCN: 79-66420

CONTENTS

for Frithjof,
  for getting me interested
for Izchak,
  for keeping me interested

PREFACE

Jean-Paul Sartre is the best known of the many philosophers who have referred to their work as "phenomenology." He is also the most articulate spokesman for the popular philosophy of "existentialism." As a result, commentators on recent European philosophy have bonded phenomenology and existentialism together in a common-law marriage of association. But on first examination, no two philosophies could appear more different. Phenomenology is often characterized as a philosophical method whose goal is to establish a "science" of philosophy and to demonstrate the objective validity of the foundation principles of mathematics and natural science, epistemology, and ontology. Phenomenology was christened if not wholly initiated by Edmund Husserl, a German philosophy professor who has left us volumes of austere and difficult academic lectures and manuscripts, most of which are still not published and few of which are easily understood even by professional philosophers who have not immersed themselves in Husserliana.

In contrast, the existentialists have rejected academic and professional philosophy, have rejected the idea that philosophy could ever become a science, have illustrated their ideas in novels and plays as often as arguing them in philosophical essays, and have ignored and even denied the importance and even the possibility of proofs of the "objective validity" of science and mathematics. Existentialism has its roots in the nineteenth century in the individualistic, irreverent, and "untimely" writings of Kierkegaard, Nietzsche, and Dostoyevsky. Existentialists have produced some of the most sensational literature, some of the most influential changes in Christian thought, and some of the most con-

troversial moral doctrines of the twentieth century. Because of
their scandalous reputations and their dramatic celebration of
the human condition, existentialists are still ignored and even
repudiated by many professional philosophers, including some
well-known phenomenologists.

Thus it must appear that Sartre has sanctioned an impossible marriage of professions. But he is not the only philosopher
who has joined together phenomenology and existentialism. Martin Heidegger before him, and Gabriel Marcel, Maurice Merleau-
Ponty, and Paul Ricoeur, his contemporaries, have also been
self-avowed phenomenologists and have been called, with good
reason, existentialists as well. The coupling of phenomenology
and existentialism is not a historical accident; there is a 'logic'
here that too-technical descriptions of phenomenology and too-
popular characterizations of existentialism tend to obscure. Both
movements have their basis in traditional European philosophy,
the tradition following Descartes that established the framework
within which Husserl, Heidegger, Sartre *et al.* support each other
and disagree. It is what we shall describe as the Cartesian starting
point that defines the position from which all theories, analyses,
objections, and methods derive their validity. Both phenomenology and existentialism are concerned with the relationship
that we may, gingerly at first, call "the relationship between
human consciousness and the world," and with the "foundations" or "essences" or "existential structures" that support this
relationship. In the work of Heidegger and Sartre, phenomenology becomes support for an existentialism derived from Nietzsche and Kierkegaard. This support is not, as it is often described, simply the support of a set of philosophical doctrines
by a philosophical method. (We shall show that it is a serious
mistake to see phenomenology merely as a philosophical method.) Phenomenology supports existentialism as an epistemological and ontological thesis is used to support a theory of human
action and freedom. Both begin with a special kind of description
of human consciousness. But while Husserl remains concerned
with human *knowledge* and *belief*, Heidegger and Sartre turn
their attention to problems of human *practice*. All remain within

respectable reach of traditional Cartesian philosophy, whatever the radical departure from this tradition that over-zealous defenders have so repeatedly claimed. Both movements can only be understood in the context of the problems and ambitions of Western philosophy as a whole, and the seemingly vast differences between the two movements can only be appreciated in a perspective from which the similarities and mutual dependencies are evident.

Because both phenomenology and existentialism are *movements* and not systems of catechisms, neither can be simply displayed by a small number of 'official' statements by leading proponents, e.g. Husserl and Sartre. Even within Husserl's writings, for example, doctrines and methods are perpetually under examination, frequently changing and subject to later rejection. To make matters worse, the key writings of phenomenology are for the most part disconnected "meditations" or "investigations" without beginning or conclusion, and the central works in existentialism are impossibly involuted systematic works or inexplicit illustrations of philosophical points in literary form. Moreover, phenomenology has been carried on in investigations of psychology, aesthetics, science, and virtually every human endeavor, and existentialists have spread their efforts just as widely. Thus, a reader on phenomenology and existentialism might include selections on virtually any topic whatever.

I have limited the selections in this book to philosophical writings that are more or less explicitly concerned with Husserl's phenomenology, problems developing within Husserl's phenomenology, and concerns developing from his philosophy that remain peculiarly philosophical problems. Husserl's philosophy will be our focal point, but Husserl's own writings and the writings of those who consider themselves orthodox phenomenologists will not be given exclusive attention. Several of the selections are taken from philosophers who are not at all of "phenomenological" persuasion. Some make Husserlian points in a different and sometimes less obscure idiom; others are introduced to manifest the significant differences between phenomenology and other contemporary schools of thought.

The selections from the existentialists do not pretend to give the movement its usual wide coverage, and I have offered only a taste of such exciting but tangentially philosophical writers as Albert Camus and Simone de Beauvoir. The existentialism treated here might better be considered as existential phenomenology; a brand of phenomenology rather than the controversial popular doctrines.

Because of the stylessness of much phenomenological writing and the systematized styling of the best existentialist writing, I have forced pieces of long works and closely edited snippits of interminably long "studies" and "meditations" into a more readable topical outline. I do not deny that this type of editing does not display the original works in their full glory, but I hope you will find that it does succeed in doing what volumes of phenomenological and existentialist literature have failed to do for themselves,—to present phenomenology and existentialism as a coherent pair of philosophical movements whose variety and characteristics can be understood by the uninitiated student of philosophy. I have tried to make this book adequate as a text book for courses in phenomenology and existentialism. Where more reading is desired, I would suggest pairing this book with either Husserl's _Ideas_ or _Cartesian Meditations_ and Sartre's _Being and Nothingness_.

R.C.S.

GENERAL INTRODUCTION
WHAT IS PHENOMENOLOGY?

Phenomenology is a philosophical movement that has received its most persuasive impetus, formulation, and defense
from the German philosopher Edmund Husserl during the first
three decades of this century. Husserl views Descartes and Kant
as his most important philosophical predecessors, and his phenomenology takes the Cartesian attention to the primacy of first-
person experience and the Kantian search for basic "a priori"
principles as its modus operandi. Phenomenology begins with
the study of human consciousness; it is an attempt to define the
"structures" that are essential to any and every possible experience. Phenomenology is ultimately a search for "foundations."
Husserl's own interest in philosophy began with an attempt to
explain the validity of the fundamental laws and concepts of
arithmetic. As his interests developed he came to seek not only
the foundations of arithmetic but the "a priori" principles of all
human "cognition" (i.e. all knowledge and belief). Ultimately
Husserl's phenomenology took the ambitious range of concerns
that occupied Kant in his *Critique of Pure Reason*—the identification and defense of the basic a priori principles of all human
experience and understanding. (1)[1]

The existential phenomenologists also begin from Descartes
and his "first-person standpoint," but they shift their attention
away from the foundations of knowledge to the foundations of
human *action.* According to the variations of phenomenology

---

[1] Numbers in parentheses refer to selection numbers in the text.

advanced by Heidegger, Sartre, and Merleau-Ponty, "consciousness" is not to be interpreted primarily as a *knowing* consciousness but as an acting, 'willing', deciding consciousness. It is not those experiences relating to knowing and reasoning that are the paradigm to be examined but rather the experiences of doing, participating, and choosing. For the existentialists, it is the Kant of the *Critique of Practical Reason* that serves as a historical model, for it is the nature of human freedom and not the nature of human knowledge that poses the fundamental problem. (32–34, 40–44). For Husserl the study of consciousness is essentially an epistemological study; for the existentialists, it is a means to understanding what it is to be a *person*. Of course, there are very important disagreements among the existentialists as they carry this analysis through, but their heretical deviation from Husserl can best be appreciated by understanding that Heidegger, Sartre, and Merleau-Ponty are only tangentially interested in the foundations of mathematics and science but fundamentally interested in the universal ("a priori," "essential," "existential," "ontological") presuppositions of human action.[2]

Although phenomenology, both Husserlian and existential, has a Cartesian starting point, there is no easy way to define this general philosophical approach. The details of method employed by Descartes himself—a rigid distinction between mind and body coupled with the presumption that we know the mind better than the body, and the tentative methodological supposition that everything we believe is false—these are all repudiated by every phenomenologist. Husserl characterized his phenomenology as a "return to the things themselves," where the things in question

---

[2] The existentialists are *not* to be characterized by their interest in the individual and their rejection of the universal, nor by their attention to the concrete and neglect of the concept, nor by their focus on *life* and their neglect of the transcendental. These glib and popular characterizations might be reinterpreted as the shift from knowledge to practice, from *Denken überhaupt* to individual perspective, but more often they simply provide a poor ground for wild claims about Existentialism. In the readings from the existentialists, it will be quite clear that they are making universal conceptual claims about all (possible) human beings.

are phenomena or intuitions. But it is not immediately clear how "phenomena" or "intuition" are to be analyzed. Phenomena are not to be identified with natural phenomena, and intuitions are not to be identified (in general) as "experiences." Husserl insists that phenomenology begins with a "suspension of the natural (everyday) standpoint." We must begin with the *ego cogito* instead of nature and take up the standpoint of "transcendental subjectivity." (45) But not only do all of these technical phrases need accounting for, some of them would be rejected as a fair characterization of phenomenology by a great many phenomenologists. Perhaps the most general characterization possible is the thesis that the phenomenologists begin with an analysis of "one's own consciousness of the world"; (13–18) but the complex concept "consciousness of the world" is analyzed in radically different ways by different phenomenologists. (cf. 13–18 and 32–44) One is rightly warned by practicing phenomenologists that one needs to develop a taste for phenomenology and some feeling for its workings before one is in a position to say what it is. This is not meant to make phenomenology sound mysterious; it is simply to remind us that phenomenology is a very loose-knit system of problems, philosophers, and philosophies, all of which are brought together only by the slack and ultimately vacuous insistence that a first-person description, without theoretical bias, of one's own consciousness of the world must precede all philosophical theorizing. Although we may expect phenomenology to emerge from our readings as a more or less distinct approach to philosophy, we must not demand too rigid a summary or definition of the phenomenological approach.

THE PRESUPPOSITIONS
OF PHENOMENOLOGY

Among the strongest claims for phenomenology made by Husserl and his followers is that phenomenology is "presuppositionless" and without theoretical bias—that the results of phenomenology, if properly attained, are unconditionally or "absolutely" true. But Husserl characterized himself as a "perpetual beginner," by which he means that no concept in his philosophy was immune to further criticism. He insisted that phenomenology consists solely of descriptions, and that it neither presupposes nor advances any philosophical theories (a claim made more recently by Ludwig Wittgenstein in his later work). Husserl denied that a philosophical theory is possible: theories always assert more than their data, and this something 'more' has no place in philosophy. (As with Wittgenstein, it is some of Husserl's closest followers who ignore this basic denial.)

Phenomenology is said to be presuppositionless and theory-free. Here we may distinguish two separate claims: phenomenology is presuppositionless because it demands that any concept and any proposition can be reassessed at any point; phenomenology may also be said to be presuppositionless in the much stronger sense that its descriptions neither presuppose nor involve any philosophical theory.

The demand that philosophy be without presuppositions (in both senses) is an attempt to guarantee that a philosophy will not be one more system of dogmatic assertions without ultimate philosophical support. Husserl is suspicious of the axiomatic philosophical systems of Descartes and Spinoza, and at the same time he is intolerant of the relativist claims of philosophers like Dilthey and Marx, who would deny any philosophy the claim of being absolutely true outside of a particular socio-intellectual context. Against the temptation to be dogmatic, Husserl demands that every philosophical proposition be constantly open to question. Against the temptation to give up the demand for absolute truth, Husserl insists that a presuppositionless philosophy will admit only those propositions which will be true and acceptable in any intellectual environment. Wary of having his philosophical vision distorted by preconceptions, Husserl devises a series of disciplines to assure that phenomenological descriptions are not philosophical theories in disguise. (His famous *epoché* is one of these disciplinary techniques.) For example, a description of consciousness is constantly endangered by the many metaphors and traditional philosophical theories that present an image of the mind as a mysterious container or stream ("all in your mind," "introspect," "stream of consciousness"). A philosophy that begins by taking these metaphors and theories seriously has, according to Husserl, based itself on presuppositions instead of pure description. Phenomenology must limit itself to reconfirmable descriptions of experience.

These good intentions give rise to problems and paradoxes. The two senses of "presuppositionless" which have been praised as the greatest merit of phenomenology have been roughly paralleled by two widespread and often persuasive criticisms of phenomenology. First, the demand that phenomenology continuously reassess all of its own concepts and propositions leads to the objection that the phenomenological enterprise is unavoidably circular. The concepts and claims of phenomenology can only be criticized and evaluated in terms of the concepts and claims of phenomenology. Secondly, the demand that phenomenology undergo constant reexamination leads to the objection that phenomenology will always be so obsessed with itself as method that it can never be productive. Hence a frequent challenge from both critics and proponents of phenomenology is to stop *talking about* phenomenology and to start *doing* phenomenology.

If we are to understand Husserl's phenomenology, we must first understand what is so very wrong with these objections. We must appreciate both the extent to which the demand is valid that phenomenology be presuppositionless and the extent to which it is hopelessly extravagant. The weaker demand for presuppositionless philosophy (that every concept and proposition be always open to reassessment) lies at the very heart of Husserl's philosophizing. This is not only evident in what Husserl says about his work; it is more persuasively obvious in what Husserl does. His writings are a remarkable model of philosophical integrity, whatever else one might say about them. Every idea is worked and reworked, altered and even rejected as his philosophy develops. If phenomenology appears to be presented dogmatically in Husserl's formidable writings, that is surely not the nature either of the discipline itself or of Husserl as philosopher.

But to defend Husserl's phenomenology as presupposition-less in this sense is not to accept it in the stronger sense, which may amount to a claim that phenomenology is the *only* correct approach to philosophy. What one does see is that phenomenology is a *distinct* philosophical approach. It employs concepts that other philosophies do not employ; it defends claims that other philosophies would reject. But if phenomenology is distinct as a philosophy, there must be something that distinguishes it from other philosophies. We have called it the "Cartesian starting point." Most likely we would not want to call this starting point a "theory" or even a "presupposition" in any ordinary sense. But isn't any such starting point or position already a delimitation of what a philosophy can describe, explain or argue? It may be that no philosophical principle is presupposed, whether formal, logical, material, or epistemological, and yet certain methodological procedures are employed from the outset. What is mistaken, of course, is the assumption that methodological procedures cannot prejudice results; as if an axiom is a presupposition but a rule of inference is not. It is clear that for Husserl, starting with "phenomena" does dictate certain results and deny others. Otherwise there would be no dispute between phenomenology and alternative philosophical approaches. But this separation of method from results raises more serious dangers, especially because of the frequent talk of phenomenology as a philosophical *method*. To distinguish methodological principles from doctrines in philosophy is to establish a set of principles that are immune to criticism. The role of this set of principles will go unchallenged during the production of a philosophy (e.g. Descartes's or Spinoza's "mathematico-deductive" methods and the empiricists' exhaustive distinction between "truths of reason" and "matters of fact"). But this is a flagrant violation of Husserl's insistence that there be no privileged principles, and Husserl's own works made it clear that those principles which might be called "methodological" are the very ones that are rethought and recast most often. There can be no distinction between method and result in Husserl's philosophy, and the acceptance of the weaker demand for presuppositionless philosophy entails a rejection of the stronger demand.

There is an apparent paradox in our introduction to Husserl. Very simply, it appears that we have presented phenomenology as a distinct philosophical approach while insisting that its every concept and proposition is always open to revision. In removing this paradox we can also show that the circular nature of phenomenology is not "vicious," and that it is simply false that phenomenology has become obsessed with method.

The solution to the paradox—and the answer to these two objections—is that there is no distinction in Husserl's philosophy between method and result. The claims that Husserl makes about the nature of consciousness, experience, and knowledge cannot be the results of any method that does not already have something to say about the nature of consciousness, experience, and knowledge. It does not make sense to call these claims "methodological" because these are the very claims that are generally recognized as the *fruits* of Husserl's phenomenology.

Deprived of any distinction between method and result, the objection that phenomenology has become obsessed with its own method is simply foolish. Phenomenologists have indeed continuously recast their propositions about the nature of consciousness, experience, knowledge, truth, and intentionality, but now we see that this is not a struggle with method, it is simply doing philosophy.

If phenomenology cannot analyze its concepts and defend its propositions except by appeal to its own concepts and principles, then it is in a dilemma no different from any other thoroughgoing philosophy. Because philosophy, unlike specific scientific disciplines, has no methodology to be distinguished from its substantial content, and because a philosophy presents itself as the source of ultimate appeal, there can be no escape from circularity. An empiricist insists that all knowledge comes from experience, but how does he defend *that* claim? He either defends it from experience or he gives up his claim as a piece of *knowledge*. Linguistic philosophers claim that philosophical insights can be obtained through an investigation of language, but the very notions central to the development of this claim, "meaning," "synonymy," "convention," "statement," and so on, have become central to their investigations. Yet it is not the case that these philosophers have become obsessed with their *method*. Instead, certain important initial insights generated a family of new philosophical problems, and not surprisingly, these problems turned out to be inseparably interrelated. Similarly, phenomenology has no alternative but to defend its claims and analyze its concepts in its own terms. It is in no worse and no better a position in this regard than any other philosophy.

Does this "turning back on itself" reduce phenomenology (or any other philosophy) to triviality? We might briefly answer this by appealing to a metaphor used by W. V. O. Quine. What one does in philosophy is like repairing a boat on the high seas. It is not a matter of formulating a method with clear concepts and then applying it, but a matter of keeping afloat. We may build and tear apart, but we must always keep the entire structure sufficiently intact. Phenomenology starts with the crude insight that philosophy must examine consciousness. Slowly it builds a theory of consciousness, all the while keeping the initial insight as its framework. When the theory is sufficiently developed, even the initial insight can be reworked, torn apart, and possibly even rejected. This is the course of Husserl's philosophy. It is ever self-contained and self-referring and yet it is neither trivial nor dogmatic. There are doctrines in Husserl's thought that remain more or less invariant throughout, e.g. the demand that philosophy pay attention to "phenomena." But his analysis of "phenomenon" changes continuously, as do his analyses of the central concepts of "intentionality," "constitution," "consciousness," and his theories of the role of the ego in consciousness. What distinguishes phenomenology from alternative philosophies, e.g. from traditional empiricism or from linguistic philosophy, is its use of this family of concepts, its general insistence on the role of intuition—special kinds of intuition—in knowing. At the same time, it neglects or denies a similar role to (empirical) experience and to language. There are no clear head-on confrontations between phenomenology and other philosophies, but neither do they differ only in vocabulary and learned societies.

THE "FOUNDATIONS"
OF KNOWLEDGE

Phenomenology has been referred to as both a "rationalism" and a "radical empiricism." Husserl's philosophy is rationalistic in that he believes there are a priori principles or "truths of reason"; but he does not agree with traditional rationalists that there is a faculty or special power of reason that will identify these truths. Rather, these a priori truths are to be located and defended in terms of a special sort of "seeing," and it is in this sense that Husserl claims to be a sort of empiricist. But his empiricism is not the traditional empiricism of Locke, Berkeley, Hume, and Mill. He maintains what they would never allow: that there are *necessary* truths which can be established *through intuition.* The fundamental doctrine of Husserl's phenomenology is the doctrine that he summarizes in the phrase "intuition of essences." With the rationalists, he maintains that we can and do have knowledge which is neither empirical nor trivial; with the empiricists, he maintains that all knowledge comes from intuition. But contrary to both traditional movements, he insists that intuition itself gives us necessary truths, that the empiricist notion of "experience" must be supplanted with a more general notion of "intuition," such that it is possible not only to have intuition of empirical facts ("the cat is on the mat") but to also have intuition of necessary truths ("2+3=5"). (29, 30, 31)

The "foundations" of knowledge are those necessary and a priori principles which constitute the presuppositions of any knowledge whatever. For example, the existence of the ("external") world is a presupposition of every law, theory, and hypothesis of every natural science. Similarly, a naturalized version of the principle of sufficient reason ("there is a sufficient natural explanation in terms of antecedent conditions and natural laws for everything that happens") is a presuppositition for every attempt at scientific explanation, and the basic principles of arithmetic and geometry are presupposed in every act of measuring, counting, calculating. But it is not enough to demonstrate that these presuppositions are necessary to carry out the endeavor in question (i.e. it is not enough to show that belief in the world is necessary to do physics and chemistry, and not sufficient to show that acceptance of arithmetic is necessary to count and calculate) ; it must also be demonstrated that these principles are necessary in that one could not but accept them. "Rationalist" philosophers from the ancients to Descartes, Leibniz, and Spinoza attempted to prove that reason assured us the truth of such principles; "empiricist" philosophers have attempted to show that such principles could be firmly anchored in experience. Some philosophers, notably David Hume, concluded from the failure of both of these approaches that no justification for these principles could be found, and while the fact of our belief in them had to be admitted, our *right* to them could not be defended. Subsequently, Kant made an elegant list of the fundamental a priori principles necessary for mathematics and science and attempted to prove their legitimacy by arguing that they were not only necessary to do mathematics and science but basic to the very nature of human consciousness. The existence of human consciousness alone was sufficient to establish their validity.

Before we examine Husserl's "radical" claim that the foundations or a priori principles he seeks to identify and defend can be found in an examination of a special sort of "intuition," we should look at the alternative attempts to provide the "foundations" of knowledge that Husserl rejected. Foremost among these is the doctrine referred to as *psychologism*, which is a species of a general philosophical approach called *naturalism*. (2–8) According to the naturalist, all concepts are abstractions from experience and all knowledge of the world is empirical knowledge; the only necessary truths are trivial and conventional truths, e.g. "every cat is an animal," "a rose is a rose." According to the psychologist, all nontrivial but apparently "necessary" truths are not necessary at all, but merely well-confirmed psychological truths, principles governing the way in which we do, as a matter of fact, think. The naturalist presses allegedly a priori principles into one or the other of these two categories: either they are abstract and very general empirical truths or subtle linguistic or logical conventions. Modern empiricists tend to push most of the problematic a priori principles, including all of mathematics, logic, and geometry, as well as the basic principles of natural science, into the class of conventions and linguistic truths. But the naturalist-psychologists of Husserl's time (including Husserl himself in his earliest works), tended to defend most of these a priori principles, including all of mathematics, logic, geometry, and most philosophical principles, as well-confirmed empirical generalizations. Thus the psychologist would argue that the laws of elementary arithmetic are empirical laws formulated on the basis of our experience of counting, and that the principle that every event has sufficient natural cause is an empirical law different only in its level of abstraction from "bronze statues turn green because copper is oxidized in the open air." The psychologist would explain the apparent necessity of mathematical proof and logical validity solely by appeal to psychological laws: The proof of the Pythagorean theorem would be translated from a list of axioms, postulates, previously proven theorems, and intermediate steps into a series of psychological laws to the effect that "if someone believes these axioms and postulates, then he will accept these intermediate steps and accept the Pythagorean theorem." Similarly, the logical law that states "if 'if P then Q,' is true and P is true, then Q is true" would be "justified" psychologically by establishing that if anyone believes both "if P then Q" and that P is true, then he will believe that Q is true.

As a student of Franz Brentano and an enthusiast for John Stuart Mill, Husserl had endorsed psychologism and written his dissertation and a book (*Philosophy of Arithmetic*) applying psychologism to the foundations of arithmetic. But Husserl's enthusiasm for psychologism was utterly destroyed by a review of his book by the great German mathematician Gottlob Frege. (5) Frege argued that mathematical concepts are not abstractions and mathematical laws are not generalizations. Psychological laws say what people in fact do think; mathematical laws state what is necessarily true whether or not anyone happens to think it. Psychological laws are at best probable; they are revisable every time we find someone who happens not to believe the law. But mathematical laws are necessarily true: a proof of a theorem by one person is a proof of that theorem for all persons. What is established in a mathematical proof is not a truth about people's having certain thoughts, but a truth about the thoughts themselves. (3, 4, 5, 6, 7)

Husserl's reaction to this onslaught was admirable. He was so impressed with Frege's critique that he altered the entire direction of his philosophy and tried to understand how a priori principles could be possible. (3)

The attack on psychologism and naturalism is the best known of Husserl's attacks against alternative philosophies, but it must be seen as one aspect of his general concern to understand necessary truth. It is not sufficient for him to argue that necessary truths are not psychological or empirical truths. Frege also asserted this, but went on to insist that necessary truths are *conventional* truths. There were other mathematicians too, who agreed with the attack on psychologism, but they went on to insist that mathematical truths were merely *formal* truths—truths concerning the manipulation of signs. Husserl's rejection of these two alternatives marked his most important deviation from the linguistic direction of philosophy influenced by Frege. Husserl rejected "linguisticism" and "formalism" along with psychologism, and in place of these current alternatives he suggested a thesis reminiscent of scholastic philosophy. What makes necessary truths true, he said, is the very structure of human consciousness and a peculiar class of objects called essences, which are not to be discovered in a study of psychology or in a study of the syntax and semantics of the language of necessary truth. The discovery of essences would demand a new and special discipline, and this discipline is, of course, phenomenology.

PHENOMENA
AND PHENOMENOLOGICAL
DESCRIPTION

What is described in phenomenology? The most obvious characterization of that which is described by phenomenologists is simply *phenomena*. But what are phenomena?

"Phenomena" are best characterized as that which can be described from the phenomenological standpoint, and the "phenomenological standpoint" is best characterized as that standpoint from which phenomena are described—but obviously we would have to bring in some other concepts to avoid vicious circularity. We have already pointed to those concepts, of course, in the phenomenological study of consciousness in general and intuition and in our mention of the Cartesian or first-person standpoint. We can give an independent characterization of "phenomena" by further characterizing the phenomenological description of consciousness. Then we can give an independent characterization of the "phenomenological standpoint" by characterizing the Cartesian standpoint and the nature of phenomenological reflection. The two studies will provide us with complementary analyses of both "phenomena" and "phenomenology."

It would not be correct to say that phenomena are experiences, even if we were to qualify this by adding that phenomena are *essential* experiences. The problem with all such "experience" talk is that it reinforces traditional philosophical dualisms that distinguish between experiences and the objects themselves. But Husserl's phenomenology and the phenomenology of the existential phenomenologists both reject this distinction. The concept of the "phenomenon" represents *both* something that is 'in' experience and something that is the object itself. Perhaps we can begin by stating that the phenomenon is an object as it is experienced. One might say that the phenomenon is what is *directly evident* (17) or what "immediately presents itself." (13, 18) To say that a phenomenon is directly evident is to say that the only justification for the proposition identifying that phenomenon is that one is conscious of the phenomenon. As Husserl says, "If we ask why the statement is justified, and ascribe no value to the reply 'I see that it is so,' we fall into absurdity." (*Ideas*, 76). Descartes tells us that "there is an earth" is a dubitable proposition because it is possible that I should believe there is an earth when in fact there is not. But, he insists, "I *think* there is an earth" is indubitable because I cannot think there is an earth and not think it. Descartes' distinction between what is indubitable and what is dubitable is a crude ancestor of the distinction between what is phenomenon and what is not. We must not put much stress on the clumsy notion of "indubitability" here, but the idea of "self-confirming" propositions will be a helpful approach to the analysis of phenomena.

It is still not clear to what extent a phenomenon is and is not an experience. Descartes's distinction is often cast in the form of a distinction between my knowledge of experience and my knowledge of physical objects. The phenomenon that Husserl talks about is not something other than a physical object, but it is not something other than experience either. To understand this complex analysis, we shall have to understand what Husserl calls the *"intentionality"* of experience, (19–23) and we shall have to understand what he calls the *"constitution* of objects in consciousness." (24–28)

A characterization of the phenomenological standpoint in terms of Cartesianism and refection might appear at first to be simply a return to the Cartesian insistence that one first examine one's intuitions. But talk of intuition need have no place in the characterization of the phenomenological standpoint. One of the disputes that most sharply distinguishes the existential phenomenologists from the Husserlian phenomenologists is the rejection by the existentialists of the idea that one can talk about intuitions or phenomena at all without at the same time talking about existent objects. The nature of this disagreement is too subtle to go into at this point, but it forces us to separate a characterization of phenomenology in terms of an examination of consciousness from a similar characterization in terms of the phenomenological standpoint. What makes the existentialists phenomenologists is their acceptance of the standpoint in spite of their rejection of key Husserlian doctrines concerning the nature of consciousness.

The phenomenological standpoint is marked by an insistence that one describe one's *world* (*not* one's experience) without any presumption that it is either real or imagined, or that it is shared with other persons or is private. This may sound like just another way of repeating the demand that phenomenology limit itself to describing phenomena. But since for Husserl these two characterizations are complementary, we should expect that the characterization of "phenomena" and the characterization of the "phenomenological standpoint" would complement each other. The misleadingly simple characterization of the phenomenological standpoint as the insistence that one simply describe the world is not the same as an insistence that one examine *consciousness*. Underlying this simple characterization is a complex of doctrines about the "world," about the sense in which one is "conscious" of the world, and about the extent to which some description of experience is involved in the description of the world. It is not altogether clear in what sense this Cartesian standpoint can be said to be a *first-person* standpoint. Husserl, like Descartes and Kant, usually argued that there must be a self or ego that "inhabits" consciousness and is in some sense responsible for consciousness of the world. According to his doctrine, the first-person standpoint might be characterized as a "self-examination," or as "egology" as Husserl sometimes put it. But some phenomenologists—notably the existential phenomenologists and even Husserl himself in one of his important early works—deny the existence of any such "inhabitant" of consciousness. There is no ego; there is just "consciousness-of-the-world." And this consciousness must be "impersonal"—not mine ("my ego's") or yours or ours. Thus it becomes puzzling how the phenomenological standpoint can be called a "first-person" standpoint—or for that matter, any "standpoint" at all. (11)

Husserl's phenomenology is the investigation of the nature of human consciousness with a view toward disclosing certain special intuitions that yield necessary truths. These special intuitions are called *"eidetic"* or *"essential"* intuitions and are to be distinguished from the traditional notion of "experience" which is limited to what Husserl calls *factual* or *empirical* intuition. Essential intuition is also identified as intuition of the universal, while empirical intuition is sometimes called *individual* intuition. Because Husserl seeks the a priori conditions of all experience and knowledge, his interest in empirical intuition is not an interest in the (empirical) contents of these intuitions but rather in their essential forms. Thus there are two questions here: What is essential intuition? and What is the essential form of any experience?

These questions are not equivalent, but pertain to different "realms" of consciousness. The first question is directed toward necessary truths of an "ideal" sort, such as the truths of mathematics. The second question is directed toward the nature of empirical experiences; it is the search for necessary truths regarding perception, like the Principles of Understanding in Kant's philosophy. Having mentioned before the marked similarities between Husserl and Kant—particularly in the search for a priori foundations of all experience and knowledge—we might point out have the very important differences between the two. Kant distinguishes between phenomena, which are given in intuition, and noumena, which lie "behind" intuition. Husserl collapses this distinction and insists that the phenomena *are* the things themselves. Moreover, Husserl rejects Kant's view of the "faculties" of sensibility and understanding. Not only does he reject the presupposition that there are any such distinct faculties, but more importantly, he holds that Kant's distinction between sensibility and understanding already precludes the basic thesis of phenomenology—namely, that what Kant called the a priori principles of understanding are given in intuition. Husserl's concept of "intuition" includes parts of *both* what Kant divided into sense and understanding. (13, 14, 29, 30, 31)

Husserl's insistence that phenomena simply be *described* is directed at eliminating the philosophical constructions that all philosophers impose upon their experience. This is not to deny that experience itself has structures that are imposed upon it by consciousness, but only that the theories philosophers use to explain their experience may not be an accurate description of these structures. How can one distinguish between those structures that are 'given' in any experience, those structures that are learned and imposed upon experience, and those structures that are imposed by philosophical reflection upon experience? For example, it seems to be 'given' that we see objects in Euclidean three-dimensional space. To what extent is this an essential feature of any experience whatever? There are non-Euclidean geometries which have been developed by mathematicians, and hypothetical many-dimensional worlds which have been described by writers. To what extent is the Euclidean world one that we have all learned to see and which now seems to us as the 'natural' way of seeing the world? To what extent is the Euclidean view actually imposed by centuries of philosophical thought? Husserl demands: Describe phenomena, don't superimpose theories on them and don't populate an imaginary "behind-the-phenomena" stage with unknowable "things-in-themselves." The description of phenomena must be one that is devoid of theory, devoid of prejudice or presupposition. But whether such a description is in fact possible is a major problem for phenomenology. (11, 15, 16, 18)

INTENTIONALITY
AND INTENTIONAL OBJECTS

Two of the problems we encounter in any attempt to explain the notion of "phenomena" is the temptation to reduce it to the empiricist notion of "experience" and the dialectically opposed compulsion to interpret the phenomena as if they are not to be distinguished from things-in-themselves, as whatever natural *objects* we experience. Analogously, the traditional philosophical analysis of "consciousness" has often either fallen into a treatment of consciousness as some mysterious and autonomous realm or substance (Descartes and the British empiricists) or it has come to deny consciousness altogether and simply talk in a persistently third-person if not behaviorist manner (e.g. Spinoza and Witt-

genstein). Husserl criticizes the empiricists for their "natural-
ization" of consciousness, which means, first, that they mistook
a priori truths about consciousness for empirical truths about
consciousness. (13, 29) Even so, they treated consciousness as a
medium or "stream" separate from nature and natural objects,
and at the same time incorporated into their analysis of consciousness a great many naturalistic concepts. The criticism that
empiricists separated consciousness from the world and yet confused the two has the effect of a two-pronged attack on the naive
view of consciousness that gives rise to many of the epistemological problems of the Cartesian tradition.

Descartes spoke seriously of the distinction between mental
and physical *substance,* and philosophers following him took
equally seriously the metaphorical distinction between "in the
mind" and "in the world." The views of the mind as a container
of ideas, as a stream of floating impressions, and as a blank
tablet that passively receives sensations, are at the very heart of
the epistemologies of many modern philosophers. Husserl argues
that such theories of mind are simply the product of careless
phenomenological description—a failure to look at what consciousness really is like. (20, cf. 23)

From his teacher Brentano (22) Husserl borrowed his central thesis: consciousness is *intentional.* This tells us, in a phrase,
that consciousness always takes an object. An act of consciousness is always directed towards something. When we love, we
love something; when we are afraid, we are afraid of something;
when we know, we know something. The object of an intentional
act need not be a real material object. One can be afraid of Communists under the bed when there are no Communists under the
bed; one can imagine a golden mountain when there is no
golden mountain; one can believe that there is no prime number
between 3 and 11 when the proposition that there is no prime
number between 3 and 11 is false. The intentional object can
be a material object, but it may also be an 'unreal' object, a
proposition, or an 'ideal object,' (e.g. a number).

The thesis that consciousness is intentional requires that we
distinguish between an *act* of consciousness and the intentional

object of consciousness. Intentional acts are of many kinds— loving, thinking, feeling, imagining, perceiving, calculating, asserting, doubting. There is a correlation between acts and objects; every act takes at least one object; every object is the object of at least one possible act. (20, 22)

We can see now what is wrong with traditional philosophical talk of "experience" or "consciousness" by itself, and we can understand our difficulties in understanding the notion of "phenomenon." "Experience" is equivocal between the intentional act (the *experiencing*) and the intentional object (the *experienced*). To say "experience is 'in' consciousness," or "we experience only experiences, not objects themselves," or "only I can have my experience," is to speak ambiguously. If we are talking about the *act*, it makes some sense to say that the act is "in" consciousness (i.e., it is an act of consciousness), and to say that only I can perform my *acts*, while it makes no sense at all to say "I experience nothing but my acts of experiencing." If we are talking about the intentional *objects*, all three statements are false or senseless. What I experience may or may not have existence apart from my experiencing of it, may or may not be experiencable by other people. If the object is a tree, it is an open question whether the object of my experience is an object of a perceptual act or an object of a hallucinatory act. If the object is the number 5 or the proof of the Pythagorean Theorem, it is surely available to anyone else. The number 5 is not an idea of mine, but a number, and if my proof is a proof at all, it is a proof for everybody. If the object in question is a proposition, i.e. "the cat is on the mat," it may be certain that I believe it, but it is an open question whether or not it is true. (7)

Insofar as the phenomenon is an intentional object of consciousness, therefore, it is not correct to say that it is simply an intuition, nor is it correct to say that it is simply an object. The phenomenon is an *object as intuited*. Whether the phenomenon is real or unreal (if it is the sort of object that can be perceived), whether it is true or false (if it is the sort of object that, like a proposition, can be asserted or denied), or whether it exists or not in some other sense (e.g. in the sense that a prime number between 7 and 13 exists) is a question which the analysis and description of the phenomenon itself (i.e. the intentional object) need not determine. Thus we can see how there is no distinction to be drawn between the phenomenon and the object-in-itself. If I perceive a real tree, then the tree as a phenomenon and the tree-in-itself are one and the same. But at the same time the phenomenon is inseparably connected to experience, for it is a phenomenon because it is an object as experienced. Thus we can also see how it will be possible to develop a phenomenology such that no mention at all need be made of *experience;* there are experiencing acts or act of intuition, and there are experienced objects or phenomena. If one wishes to insert an intermediate term such as "sense data," "sense," "immediate nonobjective experience," or "sensation appearances," this is something additional to the basic phenomenological project. (Husserl does supply us with an equivalent term of this sort, but he continuously argues that it has a merely secondary place in this analysis; he calls it *hylé,* the "matter" of experience. Merleau-Ponty's *Phenomenology of Perception* contains the best detailed phenomenological account of the concept of the "sensation" in perception.)

Phenomenology may thus be separated once again into two distinct but yet complementary investigations: there is the investigation of the conscious *act,* and the investigation of the intentional *object.* While the two cannot be completely separated, it is the latter investigation that will occupy most of our attention.

PHENOMENOLOGICAL REDUCTION

Husserl takes the phenomenological reduction or *epoché* (literally, *abstention*) to be his greatest "discovery." The nature of this reduction (or these reductions, as a number of them may be distinguished) can be stated summarily, provided that we keep in mind that the reduction is among the most controversial of all of the issues raised by Husserl's philosophy. Sartre and Heidegger explicitly reject the reduction in all of its forms;

Merleau-Ponty reinterprets it beyond recognition; (11, 40) and Husserl and other phenomenologists have offered several different and sometimes incompatible descriptions of it. (cf. 9, and 10)

The purpose of the reduction is to satisfy the demands that we have described as central to phenomenology: to guarantee the 'purity' of description and to aid in the discovery of the essences that are the key to Husserl's analysis of necessary truth. The reduction assures us that the object described by phenomenology will be the phenomenon, or intentional object of experience, and not something else—especially not a construction made by philosophers or scientists, or a transexperiential object that "common sense" teaches us to see. The reduction forces us to look at what we simply *see*, without the presupposition of interpretations *imposed* upon what we see. If I am asked to give a phenomenological description of the setting sun on a smogless night, for example, I cannot say that I see a gaseous ball of fire some 93,000,000 miles away which appears red because of the refraction of light through the earth's atmosphere. What I describe is a red disk, which might just as well be 200 yards away. In other words, my knowledge of the solar system and of the behavior of light in the earth's atmosphere is irrelevant to the description of what I *see*. The phenomenological reduction does not deny any of these scientific facts, it only suspends them so that we begin our philosophy only with what we see.

The reduction guarantees us purity of description by forcing us to describe only intentional objects or phenomena and forbidding us to describe "natural objects." A different way of putting it in Husserl's philosophy is to say that the reduction or *epoché* forces us to describe consciousness and its objects rather than the world and its objects. This can be misleading if we take this distinction to mark off the traditional realms of nature and mind. But this is not the purpose of the distinction. Rather, we want only to distinguish between objects as seen and objects as interpreted. There is only one world and one (indefinitely large) set of objects, but it can be seen from two viewpoints, the natural viewpoint and the phenomenological viewpoint. Phenomenology, we might say, is always a describing of objects *for consciousness* (i.e. as one sees them) rather than for science or for common sense. (13)

The phenomenological reduction also guarantees that we see essences and not just individuals. Husserl reminds us that our description of consciousness must be a description of the essence of consciousness, and our description of objects—either objects in general or particular kinds of objects—must be a description of essences of objects. The phenomenologist is not interested in the fact that he now sees a red-x; but he is interested in what it is to see a material object. He is not interested in the fact that he now sees A cause B, but he is interested in what it is to see something cause something. The purpose of the phenomenological reduction is to 'reduce' descriptions to descriptions of essences, to focus attention on the *meaning* of phenomena rather than on the peculiarities of particular experiences.

Finally, the reduction is intended to eliminate from philosophical investigation a number of puzzles that have plagued philosophers since Plato, problems that might be summarized as problems of existence. What is it for a material object to exist? Is there a difference between 100 real dollars and 100 nonexistent dollars? Is the number 5 as real as my typewriter? Does the concept of "cat" exist over and above all existent cats? Although Husserl has been indicted as a Platonist on several counts, he rejects not only Plato's postulation of a superworldly realm of Being but also the philosophical questions that lead Plato to make such a postulation. According to the phenomenological reduction, we do not ask whether something exists or not, is real or not. When we describe the essence of something, its existence is irrelevant. We can describe the essence of the minotaur without asking whether there are such beasts. We can ask the essence of the number 5 without puzzling ourselves whether numbers exist like mushrooms. We do not mean to say that the phenomenologist is not interested in the analysis of what it is for a material object or a number to be an object for consciousness—to exist in that sense. But a main function of the reduction, according to Husserl, is to "bracket out existence" for the purpose of phenomenology, to abstain from asking Does this thing exist?

Husserl often talks of *the* phenomenological reduction, as if a single methodological technique will assure us of all these ends. But there are several different reductions to be separated out in Husserl's philosophy. These reductions perform different functions and raise different issues.

The reduction does not appear in Husserl's philosophy until his mature works, and then it appears as the simple *epoché*, the "suspension of the natural standpoint" or "the bracketing of existence." (9) In Husserl's book *Ideas*, the *epoché* instructs us that we should "put out of action" our belief in the independent existence of the world we see. In the same work, we are introduced to a number of specific "phenomenological reductions": the suspension of our beliefs in the existence of our ego, in the existence of God, in the validity of the laws of logic, in the laws of natural science, and even in the existence of the phenomenologist himself. All of this is strongly reminiscent of Descartes' thorough-going methodological doubt, but with a most important difference. Where Descartes seriously (or mock-seriously) doubts all of those things and then insists on a proof of their derivation from some indubitable self-evident truth, Husserl does not doubt, and does not seek a proof, but only seeks to describe *what it is* to believe these things. In other words, the *epoché* is not a universal doubt, but a demand that we stop simply believing and start looking at our belief to see what it is for one to believe in his own existence, in the existence of the world, and in God.

In the same work again, Husserl introduces an *eidetic* reduction. As we may see in the very name, this is a reduction to *essences*. It is to be more or less distinguished from the *epoché*, or what is there called the "phenomenological reduction." The *epoché* assures us that we will describe only "pure consciousness"; the eidetic reduction assures us that we shall describe only the essence of consciousness and its objects.

In his later works (*Cartesian Meditations*) (10, 45), Hus-

serl continues to use the phrase *"phenomenological reduction,"*
but in this period the reduction becomes a *transcendental reduction*. There is a difficulty in that Husserl uses his old terminology
to describe something new, but it is clear that the transcendental
reduction is not meant to be added to the other reductions as
much as to replace them all. The transcendental reduction represents a step back toward Descartes, for it is no longer a reduction to pure consciousness so much as a reduction to the transcendental ego and a transcendental "realm." (10, 12, 14, 45) In
the earlier works, the *epoché* was a temporary methodological
device to allow us to perform our phenomenological tasks more
securely; in the later works the reduction becomes a permanent
performance, and the phenomenological standpoint is not a new
way of looking at things so much as a "new realm of transcendental subjectivity." With such drastic changes in the conception
of the reduction, we must avoid general claims about what it does
or does not do. But since it is surely a key feature of Husserl's
phenomenology, these wildly different conceptions of the function and results of the reduction will also lead to radically different conceptions of the phenomenological project.

MEANING AND CONSTITUTION

The central concept of "meaning" in Husserl's philosophy
is not to be identified with the linguistic analysts' notion of
"meaning." Husserl is concerned with the meaning of phenomena and the meanings of intentional acts; the meanings of
words and sentences, and what a person means when he says
something, are special instances of this more general concept
of meaning.

According to Husserl and most phenomenologists, the object of consciousness *is* its meaning. This locution may sound
strange to those who are unfamiliar with Continental philosophy,
but is used to convey a two-way implication: If an *act* has any
meaning, that meaning is its object, and if an act has any object,
that object is its meaning. Thus acts of perception, imagination, and feeling have their meanings in the objects perceived,

imagined, and felt. Acts of speech, of doubting, thinking, and believing have their meaning in the propositions expressed, doubted, thought, and believed. For phenomenologists, the analysis of meaning and the analysis of what it is for there to be an object are one and the same.

As we said before, talk about acts and talk about intentional objects must always be correlated. The analysis of the meaning of the intentional act and of that meaning as the intentional object must be carried out together. But this is not because of the simple equivalence between an act's having meaning and an act's having an object. It is not as if the object itself can be understood apart from the act that intends it. In Husserl's terminology, it is the intentional act that *constitutes* the object. Without the act there would be no object.

The idea that the intentional object is constituted in the intentional act has become the central confusion in Husserl's entire philosophy. On the one hand, Husserl does insist, particularly in his early works, upon the possibility and the necessity of investigating objects without regard for the activities that reflect upon them or whatever activities may have 'produced' them. This insistence is central to his refutation of psychologism, and the idea of the "investigation of phenomena" lies, almost tautologically, at the heart of phenomenology. Accordingly, Husserl's works carry the persistent theme (but more clearly in the earlier works again) that objects (phenomena) are *given* in intuition, that objects can be described independently of intentional acts but only *understood* in such acts. (24–28) Phenomenological reflection contributes nothing to the meaning or unity of the phenomenon or object, but describes it as it is. But there is a second picture of the nature of constitution which emerges throughout Husserl's writings and becomes dominant in his later works. Husserl continuously stresses the nature of the act of consciousness as "meaning-bestowing" or "signifying." His late works, e.g. *Cartesian Meditations*, stress the notion of the active constitution of objects by the ego. According to this second theme, constitution is not an already completed process that is *given* to the phenomenologist, but an always on-going *production* of the object. Quite literally, it is the act of conscious-ness that produces a phenomenon. As such, it is impossible for the phenomenologist to identify those aspects of the object which he creates in his reflection, and those aspects of the object which are produced by other acts simultaneous with the reflection, as distinct from those aspects of the object (if there are any) which are simply given. It is not to be supposed, however, that these two themes are completely separable: as in Kant's philosophy, the question of whether an object is given or not is a one for which there is no clear answer. The nature of the concept of "constitu-tion" changes throughout Husserl's writings, and the contrast between constitution and intuition changes accordingly. Husserl is always trying to reconcile the two, and his conceptions of the reduction, the transcendental ego, and the key notions of "phe-nomena" and "reflection" change as he attempts to reconcile these two theses. It is on the basis of this uncertainty about the possibility of distinguishing phenomenon from the reflective act, and the problem of ascertaining to what extent the object or phenomenon is given and to what extent it is literally produced, that most of the subsequent problems of phenomenology are born. The question whether phenomenology is a "realism" or an "idealism"—whether it maintains that consciousness simply finds objects before it or whether it actively creates these objects —is a manifestation of this unresolved attempt at synthesis throughout Husserl's works. The split between Husserl's tran-scendental phenomenology and the existentialists' phenomenol-ogy largely revolves around this intuition–constitution dispute. If one interprets Husserl as placing his emphasis wholly upon the production of phenomena by consciousness or by the ego, one has the picture of a total split between phenomenology and exist-entialism that one finds in Sartre's writings on Husserl. (36, 38, 46) But if one focuses rather upon Husserl's notions of "intui-tion," the 'givenness' of phenomena, and the notion of "inten-tionality," then the split between Husserl and existentialism ap-pears to be one of minor points of interpretation. It is such a reconciliation that one finds, for example, in Merleau-Ponty's reflections on Husserl. (37)

ESSENCES AND NECESSARY TRUTH

The phenomenologist is concerned with the description of what is essential in phenomena—what is necessary for there to be any experience whatever. He is concerned not only with essential aspects of empirical consciousness but also with the peculiarities of nonempirical consciousness. In his analysis of empirical consciousness, he separates the essential form of experience from the particular content of experience. But in his examination of certain kinds of intuition, for example, the intuitions of a mathematician (*qua* mathematician) he finds no empirical content because the contents of those intuitions are themselves essential. The objects of such intuitions are 'ideal' objects, *essences*.

In one sense, we might say that essences are the sorts of things that other philosophers have called "concepts" and "propositions." (Husserl, like many philosophers of that time, talked about words and sentences, concepts and propositions, without always distinguishing them.) Husserl warns us, however, against interpreting this equivalent sense of "concept" in a psychological fashion. Concepts are different from people's having concepts, as propositions are different from people's believing propositions. If we neglect this difference, we fall back into psychologism, the rejected thesis that items of logic are reducible to psychological entities. Concepts and propositions are what give meaning to all experience, what make it possible for us to see objects. For every particular object we see, we also intuit an essence. Every time I see a dog, I see *that* it is a dog (or if I misperceive, at least I see that it is an animal, or that it is an object). Essences are what make a thing "what it is." The essence of a dog is what makes it a dog; the essence of the number 5 is what makes 'it' the number 5.

The nature of an essence can be illustrated very simply by an appeal to a proof of geometry. If I prove that the interior angles of a (Euclidean) triangle are equal to 180°, I have proven this of all triangles, those that have never been or never will be drawn or imagined as well as all actual triangles. I may perform the proof by using a hastily sketched out triangle on a black-board, but the precise nature of that triangle is irrelevant to the proof. In fact, it is probably empirically false that the triangle drawn on the board has angles that total 180°. My proof of the theorem is not an observation about this particular triangle, but a proof about triangles in general. The triangle we have drawn is purely an instance of essential being, and "in accordance with the rubric '*in general*' " (*Ideas*, 48). Husserl is concerned with such objects 'in general', for they are the subject of philosophical investigation and the objects that lie at the foundation of the a priori disciplines such as mathematics, logic, and geometry.

Propositions that take essences as their subject-matter are necessary (essential) truths. "The interior angles of a triangle total 180°" is an essential truth because it is a proposition about the essence of triangle, not a proposition about a particular tri-angle. It is not even a proposition about *all triangles*, but about every possible triangle. Propositions that take essences as their subject-matter must be distinguished from propositions *about* essences; for example, 'triangle' means three-angled figure" is a proposition about essences, but its status as a necessary truth is much more debatable than "triangles have three angles." Our concern for essences and essential or necessary truths will be limited to propositions that take essences as their subjects. Essences are what make necessary propositions true and what make any experience at all possible. The problem Husserl faces is a Platonic one: How is it that we not only see particular objects but that we also see *kinds* of particular objects and *ideal* objects? Husserl rejects the Platonic solution that what we see as particulars are but shadows of Ideas or Forms that we do not see. Plato thought that essences occupy a peculiar world of Being and are separate from the particulars, which only "partici-pate" in them. Aristotle then objected on the ground that es-sences are inseparable from objects themselves—they are to be found in the forms of objects and in the world. Scholastic philos-ophers (e.g. William of Ockham), argued that the existence of essences was only in consciousness. But Husserl will take no sides in this classical dispute over "universals." To a phenomenologist who has already broken down the traditional distinctions between " 'in' consciousness" and "in the world," the Platonic-Aristotelean-Scholastic dispute makes no sense. Essences or Ideas (after Plato) are to be found in phenomena through phenomenological reflection. And this means that essences are neither 'in' consciousness nor in the world nor anywhere else. The *epoché* assures us that such bizarre questions of ontology can be avoided, and that one can describe the nature of essences and essential truth without dealing with the ontology of universals at all. (29–31)

EXISTENTIAL PHENOMENOLOGY

The existential phenomenologists shift the emphasis away from Husserl's question, "What is knowledge?" to the very different question, "What is it to be a person?" It is not to be thought that the existentialists leave Husserl far behind, however. His phenomenology is always the foundation of their investigations, and the existentialists' primary interest in what people are and do rather than what they can and do know is not a rejection of Husserl so much as a redirecting of his philosophy. In fact, Husserl's last work (40) *Crisis*, is already an anticipation of many of the major theses developed by existentialist philosophers.

The existentialists, like Husserl, are concerned with *foundations*, not the foundations of knowledge (essences) but "existential foundations," the a priori principles regarding what it is to be a man. This does not mean, as is so often suggested, that existentialism is concerned with the individual and the particular instead of the universal and the conceptual. Existential phenomenology is looking for the universal conceptual features that are necessary for anything to be a human being. The ability to think and to know is, as would be expected, one such set of features, but not the most significant. Equally important human characteristics, according to the existentialists, are man's abilities to act, to plan, to use language, to evaluate, and perhaps most important of all, to ask who he is and what he ought to *do*.

Heidegger's early formulation of the "question of Being" begins, if not ends, with this question of self-identity. Heidegger's notions of "authenticity" and "inauthenticity" (or "ownness" (*eigenlich*) and "un-ownness") as well as Sartre's central concepts of "bad faith" and "sincerity" are wholly concerned with the question of who one is.

The question of self-identity which is fundamental to existential phenomenology is directed both to the general problem, "What is it to be a person?" and to the particular question, "As a person, who am I?" One might think that both questions could be answered in the form "A person is something that has the following characteristics:————" and "I am the person who has————characteristics." For example, we might say that a person is, first of all, a slightly hairy biped, and that Charles is identifiable as having brown hair and being 5 feet 8 inches tall. But the existentialists' answer to the general question of self-identity rejects this formulation. They answer that the nature of man is such that there is no nature of man (cf. Sartre's celebrated slogans "man makes himself" and "human existence precedes essence.") In other words, to be a person is to be in a position to raise the question of who one is. But this is not a question of *knowledge*; one does not *find out* who he is. He decides, and acts upon his decision. He does not find that he is selfish; he makes himself selfish. He does not find mankind to be pitiful or glorious; he makes a decision that men are pitiful or glorious. In other words, the existentialist answer to the question "Who is man?" is, roughly, "whatever he decides to be." And the answer for each of us to the question "Who am I?" is: "whatever I make of myself." And since we *are* what we *do*, according to this philosophy, the questions of phenomenology, ontology, and ethics merge into a single set of problems. (36–37)

Although existentialism is best known for these ethical theses, the existentialist philosophers have not considered their own work as "ethics." Sartre does not take *Being and Nothingness* to be a work of ethics and he has never written the treatise on ethics that he promised at the end of that work. Heidegger has gone so far as to have claimed that ethics is impossible.

But this incredible divorce between the popular conception of existentialism as an ethics and the existentialists' own rejection of ethics is only apparent. Because their answer to the question "What is it to be a person?" is that a person is whatever he makes of himself, they cannot possibly go on to give a detailed account of specific principles that men ought to live by. They argue that there is no possible "given" answer to the question "Who am I," and so they must refuse to treat any ethical principles as "givens." But the existentialists have a great deal to say that bears on the nature of evaluation, action, freedom, choice, and reasons for choice. Although they do not and cannot dictate choices or courses of action to their readers, the existentialists do outline a theory of choice and action, one which sets the parameters for any possible choice and actions. (53–60) It is this theory and the phenomenological analysis that supports it that make the existentialists important philosophers. The ethical conclusions themselves, (e.g. "man makes himself") could be no more than trite grand-motherly 'wisdom' unless viewed in the perspective of their foundations. And these foundations begin with what at first appear to be innocent and merely technical variations on Husserl's phenomenology.

But Heidegger, Sartre, and Merleau-Ponty hardly confine themselves to a point-by-point critique of Husserl's work. Quite the opposite, they ignore Husserl's warnings against systematized philosophy and return in style to the ambitious systematic philosophy of Hegel. Heidegger's *Being and Time,* Sartre's *Being and Nothingness,* and Merleau-Ponty's *Phenomenology of Perception* each attempt a remarkable construction of a system of phenomenological descriptions. The key deviations from Husserl are not always presented as such and often are left implied as presuppositions for an analysis. Thus it would be highly misleading to isolate one or two points of disagreement with Husserl and mark them as the seeds from which these existentialist systems grew. It is also impossible for us to reconstruct in miniature a model of the theses, analyses, and systematic structures which they share with Husserl. Still there are some clearly identifiable elements in the existentialist revolt within phenomenology, and a brief mention of them should suffice as an introduction to existentialist thought.

1. Human action

The existential phenomenologists are as concerned as Husserl with the nature of our consciousness of the world. But they disagree with his description of consciousness. Fundamentally, we do not *know about* objects in the world; we *use* them, and the problem for the phenomenologist is to explain how it is that we can withdraw ourselves from our tools in order to look at them as *things*. Phenomenology cannot describe the objects of our world without paying attention to what we do with them as well as what we know about them. Husserl's mistake, according to the existentialists, was to suppose that our primary commerce with things was to know them, that our distinguishing and most essential ability was reflective thought, and that our relationship to the world was not first to *live* in it. The ideal of description of the "things themselves" must not be mistaken for a description of intentional objects without regard for the *person* who is conscious of them, and this means paying attention to those intentional acts which are not merely cognitive but also involve caring, desiring, and manipulating, and are tied up with moods, emotions, and simple feeling. (41–44)

2. The Epoché Reconsidered

The existential phenomenologists reject Husserl's phenomenological reduction in all its forms (although Merleau-Ponty attempts to reinterpret it in a harmless way). (11, 37) It is not possible, according to them, to suspend our belief in the world, nor is it possible to place oneself in any "realm" other than the natural world. This does not mean that they reject the phenomenological standpoint; what they reject is a particular technique supposedly applicable within that standpoint. A man is not a detachable consciousness who can abstract himself from the world around him. He is essentially "being-in-the-world"—an expression whose hyphenation indicates that its morphemic parts are not separable. The most important link among the existential phenomenologists—the philosophical key to their calling themselves "existential"—is their insistence that it is not possible to abstract oneself from involvement in the world. One cannot "bracket existence" as the *epoché* requires; our existence and the existence of the world around us are given together as the starting point of all phenomenological description. (36–37)

It might be questioned to what extent this celebrated difference between Husserl and the existentialists is a real difference. Husserl starts out by describing intentional objects or phenomena *as if* they were nothing more than objects *for* consciousness, but he soon argues that one cannot but describe them as natural objects; epistemological skepticism is absurd because the very nature of phenomena makes it necessary for us to interpret intended objects as the objects-themselves. Similarly, Merleau-Ponty tells us that the "most important lesson which the reduction teaches us is the impossibility of a complete reduction." (37) In some of Husserl's later work (e.g. *Cartesian Meditations*), he does maintain that the *epoché* is more than a *reductio ad absurdum* way of establishing the necessary nature of our knowledge of the 'external' (transcendental) world. But in his earlier and his very latest works, his position is not so far from the existentialists—as Sartre, at least, has claimed. (36, 46)

The rejection of the *epoché* leads Heidegger, followed by Sartre and Merleau-Ponty, to equate the practice of phenomenology with ontology. In other words, the study of phenomena and the study of the kinds of things in the world are not separable enterprises. (35) Once again, it may be questioned whether this in fact marks a more than technical difference with Husserl, since Husserl himself had argued that ontology could only be based on phenomenology and that phenomenology could not properly dispense with ontology.

But the rejection of the *epoché*, even if itself not a serious departure from Husserl, leads the existentialists to conclusions that are antithetical to Husserl's phenomenological outlook. Heidegger's introduction of the notion of "being-in-the-world" is not simply a clever Germanic neologism but one of the most radical moves in modern philosophy. What he rejects is not only the Husserlian *epoché* but the entire tradition of epistemological dualism for which Descartes is ceremoniously blamed. Husserl had rejected one traditional dualism between consciousness and nature—the one which began by distinguishing between objects of consciousness and objects-in-themselves—but he readily accepted another dualism, that between consciousness and its intentional objects. Heidegger rejects all such dualisms, and demands that philosophy begin with a single concept of "Being-in-the-world" which is not separable into consciousness on the one hand and objects (whether intentional or 'in-themselves') on the other. (35, 39, 41, 47) Sartre also begins with the existential concept of man-in-the-world, but then he distinguishes between pure consciousness ("being-for-itself") and objects ("being-in-itself")—the pair of terms coming from Hegel. (38) Merleau-Ponty rightfully accuses Sartre of falling back into the traditional dualistic traps. He remains more faithful to Heidegger's radical notion of "Being-in-the-world" by developing in detail a concept of "bodily consciousness' that further breaks down all traditional attempts to isolate consciousness from concrete worldly existence. (44)

3. Prereflective Consciousness

The existential emphasis on human practice and the rejection of the *epoché* come together in the recognition of an entire realm for investigation that Husserl neglected if not ignored. Husserl, like Descartes, began his philosophy from a *cogito*, an "I think," and took this *cogito* to be a basic starting point for phenomenological description and philosophical argument. The existentialists point out that the starting point of phenomenological description need not be this self-reflection or the reflection on our consciousness of objects. We can describe what we are doing as well as our *knowledge* of what we are doing, our knowing *how* to do something rather than our knowing *that* something is the case. Thus Heidegger distinguishes between *ontic* and *ontological* structures, i.e. those that exist before we are aware that they exist as opposed to those that come into existence only with reflection. Similarly, Sartre distinguishes between "prereflective" and "reflective consciousness," and Merleau-Ponty distinguishes "preconscious" and "conscious (i.e. knowing) intentionality." We have already observed that the existentialists pay attention primarily to description of human action rather than human knowledge. To this we may now add that they describe our preconscious or prereflective involvement in our actions rather than our reflections on our actions and our actions as they become reflected upon. Self-conscious reflection is not a detached observer of our actions but an active participant that changes what it 'observes'. (46)

4. The Rejection of the Self

Among the most treacherous distortions induced by description of *self*-consciousness is the idea that consciousness is *essentially* self-conscious. The *cogito* of Descartes, Kant, and Husserl falls into just this trap. (45) Sartre argues that while it is always possible for us to reflect on our experiences, wo do not *in fact* always do so. Consciousness is not always self-conscious. (46)

But the idea of "self-consciousness" is itself suspicious. What is this "self" of which we are conscious? In Descartes and Husserl, it appears as if the "self" is a peculiar internal object that "inhabits consciousness" or "lies behind it." But the self is no such peculiar object, argues Sartre, nor is it a transcendental or formal principle that unifies our experience, as Kant had argued. The self does not exist in prereflective consciousness, and it is only *created* in reflective consciousness. We become "selves" by looking at ourselves as other people look at us. The self is "an object in the world, like the self of an Other," according to Sartre. Similarly, Heidegger tells us that the self is not primitive (not necessary to consciousness) but develops only in the company of other persons. (47–52)

5. The "Ambiguity" of Human Existence

In our introduction to Husserl, we argued that he never resolves a conflict in his philosophy between the claim that objects are "given in intuition" and the opposing claim that

objects are "constituted by consciousness." According to the
first thesis, consciousness is at the mercy of whatever is given
to it; according to the second thesis, consciousness creates its
world. Husserl could never be satisfied with either thesis alone.
He maintained an uncomfortable if not inconsistent attempt to
hold the two together. The existentialists, influenced much more
than Husserl by the dialectics of Hegel and Marx, saw this conflict but did not think it necessary to resolve it. They accepted it
as a necessary peculiarity of human existence. This is not to say
that they held inconsistent theses or that existentialism condones
the occurence of contradictions as such. It is rather to say that
it is the nature of being a person that one can never ascertain
with confidence which features of our "situation" are given to us
and fixed from without (*facticity*) and which features of our
situation are created by us (*transcendence* or *possibility*). One
can never tell how much of what we see is there independently
of us, and how much of what we see is created by our viewpoint,
by our language, our prejudices and presuppositions. This is not
offered solely as a thesis about our perception of objects, however; it is more importantly applied to our evaluations and conceptions of ourselves. The questions "What is it to be a person?"
and "Who am I?" receive strange and disturbing answers. To be
a person is to be in a position of never being able to *know* what
is given and what one can produce, and this means there can be
no answer for a living man to the question "Who am I?" To
accept any answer to this question would be to accept a characterization of oneself as a "given," to make oneself inauthentic or
put oneself in bad faith. When Sartre offers his famous slogans
"man makes himself" and the "man's existence precedes his
essence," he means to make just this point. One cannot give a
characterization of oneself or of men generally, except to say
that man is that kind of being who has to decide who he is. (53–
56, 58–60)

6. Absolute Freedom

This begins to give us a clear view of the celebrated existentialist notion of "absolute freedom." Because one can never know

what is given (his facticity) and what is up to him to decide
(his transcendence), one can never settle for any characterization
of himself or of man generally. "Absolute freedom" means that
nothing is ever simply "given." But the existentialists do not
mean, as is often argued by unsympathetic critics, that a man is
always free to do anything he likes. It means at most that a man
has freedom to *decide* to do anything, though even this must be
tempered with Sartre's thesis that a man can decide to do only
what he believes he can actually try to do. I can decide to climb
the mountain, for example, even though I can't do it, but I
cannot decide to levitate since I do not have the faintest belief
that I could succeed if I tried. It is wrong, however, to concentrate only on the freedom or transcendence half of the existentialist ambiguity. One cannot ever accept anything as open to
choice either (by virtue of the same thesis), and so one is always
unsure about the limits of his situation and the restrictions on his
freedom. In Heidegger's dramatic terms, man is *thrown* into a
world and into a particular situation. Absolute freedom, Sartre
tells us, is free only within the confines of one's situation. But
one never knows where his situation stops and his freedom
begins. This is the source of the existential anxiety derived from
Kierkegaard's philosophy. Existentialism insists that men are
always in a position such that they must make choices; but we
must not forget that existentialism also insists that men are
always in a position such that there are any number of choices
that they do *not* have. And to make the entire thesis more problematic, they can never know which is which. (53–60)

7. Existential Ethics

It should be evident by now why the existentialists cannot
provide us with an ethics. Our situation consists not only of
tools for us to act with and physical obstacles for us to act
against, it consists also of any number of seemingly "given"
values—given by parents, society, God, conscience, and by
Nature. But we are in the same ambiguous position with regard
to values; one can never tell whether a value is truly a given
value, or whether it is something that one has chosen to accept.

There is always the temptation to proselytize a value as given (by God, by "Reason") when in fact it is a value that one has simply chosen and for which one has constructed a rationalization. Or one might try to shut his eyes to the problem and claim to be a "nihilist," e.g. Camus in the "Myth of Sisyphus" (57) and refuse to accept any values at all. But this Oedipal refusal to see is but one more version of "bad faith", for as Sartre reminds us, "not to choose is to *choose* not to choose."

All of these theses would require a volume apiece for adequate explanation, criticism, and defense, but this sketch must suffice as an introduction to the change in phenomenology that will be evident in the selections in this book.

Existentialism is often characterized as "irrational," as a "revolt against traditional Western philosophy." What will become clear in this anthology, I hope, is that the dramatic ethical doctrines and literary masterpieces of the existentialists are first the products of a serious and technical development within traditional Western epistemology and Husserl's phenomenology.

There is nothing that gives rise to knowledge of any object which does not even more certainly lead us to know our thought.
—René Descartes DISCOURSE ON METHOD

All our knowledge relates, in the end, to possible intuitions, for it is by them alone that an object can be given.
—Immanuel Kant CRITIQUE OF PURE REASON

. . . everything depends upon grasping and expressing the ultimate truth not as substance but as subject as well. At the same time we must note that concrete substantiality implicates and involves the universal or the immediacy of knowledge itself, as well as the immediacy which is being, or immediacy *qua* object *for* knowledge . . .
—Georg Wilhelm Friedrich Hegel PHENOMENOLOGY OF MIND

Phenomenology denotes a new, descriptive, philosophical method, which, since the concluding years of the last century, has established (1) an *a priori* psychological discipline, able to provide the only secure basis on which a strong empirical psychology can be built, and (2) a universal philosophy, which can supply an organum for the methodological revision of all the sciences.

—Edmund Husserl, "PHENOMENOLOGY"

The expression "phenomenology" signifies primarily a *methodological conception*. This expression does not characterize the what of the objects of philosophical research as subject-matter, but rather the *how* of that research. . . . Thus the term "phenomenology" expresses a maxim which can be formulated as "To the things themselves!" It is opposed to all free-floating constructions and accidental findings; it is opposed to taking over any conceptions which only seem to have been demonstrated; it is opposed to those pseudo-questions which parade themselves as "problems," often for generations at a time.
—Martin Heidegger BEING AND TIME

"It was in reaction against the inadequacies of psychology and psychologism that about thirty years ago a new discipline was constituted called phenomenology. Its founder, Husserl, was struck by this truth: essences and facts are incommensurable, and one who begins his inquiry with facts will never arrive at essences. . . . However, without giving up the idea of experience (the principle of phenomenology is to go to "things themselves" and the basis of these methods is eidetic intuition), it must be made flexible and must take into account the experience of essences and values; it must even recognize that essences alone permit us to classify and inspect the facts."

—Jean-Paul Sartre EMOTIONS

What is phenomenology? It may seem strange that this question has still to be asked half a century after the first works of Husserl. The fact remains that it has by no means been answered. Phenomenology is the study of essences, and according to it, all problems amount to finding definitions of essences: the essence of perception, or the essence of consciousness, for example. But phenomenology is also a philosophy which puts essences back into existence, and does not expect to arrive at any understanding of man and the world from any starting point other than that of their 'facticity'. . . . It is the search for a philosophy which shall be a 'rigorous science', but it also offers an account of space, time, and the world as we 'live' them.

—Maurice Merleau-Ponty PHENOMENOLOGY OF PERCEPTION

Taken alone the term "phenomenology" is not very illuminating. The word means science of appearances or of appearings. Thus any inquiry or any work devoted to the way anything whatsoever appears is already phenomenology. . . . Phenomenology becomes strict when the status of the appearing of things (in the broadest sense of the term) becomes problematical. . . . Phenomenology is a vast project whose expression is not restricted to one work or to any specific group of works. It is less a doctrine than a method capable of many exemplifications of which Husserl exploited only a few.

—Paul Ricoeur HUSSERL

Note:

In the course of this book, there will be repeated references to several works of Husserl, Heidegger, Sartre, Merleau-Ponty, and Frege. Such references will be incorporated in the text in parentheses, abbreviated as the following:

Husserl, *Erste Philosophie* (EP)
————, *Philosophy of Arithmetic* (PA)
————, *Logical Investigations* (LU)
————, *Ideas Towards a Pure Phenomenology* . . .
      (*Ideas*) (Volume I unless specified)
————, *Cartesian Meditations* (CM)
————, *Philosophy as a Rigorous Science* (PRS)
————, *Transcendental Phenomenology* (TP)
————, *The Crisis of European Science* . . . (Krisis)
————, *Phenomenological Psychology* (PPs)
————, *Formal and Transcendental Logic* (FTL)
Sartre, *Being and Nothingness* (BN)
Heidegger, *Being and Time* (BT)
Merleau-Ponty, *The Phenomenology of Perception* (PP)
Frege, *Philosophical Writings*, Black and Geach, eds. (BG)

All references to Husserl's works are to *sections*, not pages. References to Heidegger, Sartre, Merleau-Ponty, and Frege are to pages. All references are to original publications in the original language unless specified otherwise.

PART ONE

THE
PHENOMENOLOGY
OF EDMUND HUSSERL

INTRODUCTION

The Paris Lectures were delivered by Husserl at the Sorbonne in 1929. The lectures were later expanded into the *Cartesian Meditations.*

PARIS LECTURES

EDMUND HUSSERL

I am filled with joy at the opportunity to talk about the new phenomenology at this most venerable place of French learning, and for very special reasons. No philosopher of the past has affected the sense of phenomenology as decisively as René Descartes, France's greatest thinker. Phenomenology must honor him as its genuine patriarch. It must be said explicitly that the study of Descartes' *Meditations* has influenced directly the formation of the developing phenomenology and given it its present form, to such an extent that phenomenology might almost be called a new, a twentieth century, Cartesianism.

Under these circumstances I may have advance assurance of your interest, especially if I start with those themes in the *Meditationes de prima philosophia* which are timeless, and if through them I point out the transformations and new concepts which give birth to what is characteristic of the phenomenological method and its problems.

Every beginner in philosophy is familiar with the remarkable train of thought in the *Meditations*. Their goal, as we remember, is a complete reform of philosophy, including all the sciences, since the latter are merely dependent members of the one universal body of knowledge which is philosophy. Only through systematic unity can the sciences achieve genuine rationality, which, as they have developed so far, is missing. What is needed is a radical reconstruction which will *satisfy* the ideal of philosophy as being the *universal unity of knowledge* by means of a unitary and *absolutely rational foundation*. Descartes carries out the demand for reconstruction in terms of a subjec-

Reprinted from *Paris Lectures*, translated by P. Koestenbaum (The Hague, Netherlands: M. Nijhoff, 1964), by permission of the publisher.

tively oriented philosophy. This subjective turn is carried out in two steps.

First, anyone who seriously considers becoming a philosopher must once in his life withdraw into himself and then, from within attempt to destroy and rebuild all previous learning. Philosophy is the supremely personal affair of the one who philosophizes. It is the question of *his sapientia universalis,* the aspiration of *his* knowledge for the universal. In particular, the philosopher's quest is for truly scientific knowledge, knowledge for which he can assume—from the very beginning and in every subsequent step—complete responsibility by using *his* own absolutely self-evident justifications. I can become a genuine philosopher only by freely choosing to focus my life on this goal. Once I am thus committed and have accordingly chosen to begin with total poverty and destruction, my first problem is to discover an absolutely secure starting point and rules of procedure, when, in actual fact, I lack any support from the existing disciplines. Consequently, the Cartesian meditations must not be viewed as the private affair of the philosopher Descartes, but as the necessary prototype for the meditations of any beginning philosopher whatsoever.

When we now turn our attention to the content of the *Meditations,* a content which appears rather strange to us today, we notice immediately a *return to the philosophizing ego* in a second and deeper sense. It is the familiar and epoch-making return to the ego as subject of his pure *cogitationes.* It is the ego which, while it suspends all beliefs about the reality of the world on the grounds that these are not indubitable, discovers itself as the only apodictically certain being.

The ego is engaged, first of all, in philosophizing that is seriously solipsistic. He looks for apodictically certain and yet purely subjective procedures through which an objective external world can be deduced. Descartes does this in a well-known manner. He first infers both the existence and *veracitas* of God. Then, through their mediation, he deduces objective reality as a dualism of substances. In this way he reaches the objective ground of knowledge and the particular sciences themselves as well. All his inferences are based on immanent principles, *i.e.*, principles which are innate to the Ego.

So much for Descartes. We now ask, is it really worthwhile to hunt critically for the eternal significance of these thoughts? Can these infuse life into our age?

Doubt is raised, in any event, by the fact that the positive sciences, for which the meditations were to have served as absolutely rational foundation, have paid so very little attention to them. Nonetheless, and despite the brilliant development experienced by the sciences over the last three centuries, they feel themselves today seriously limited by the obscurity of their foundations. But it scarcely occurs to them to refer to the Cartesian meditations for the reformulation of their foundations.

On the other hand, serious consideration must be given to the fact that the meditations constitute an altogether unique and epochal event in the history of philosophy, specifically because of their return to the *ego cogito*. As a matter of fact, Descartes inaugurates a completely new type of philosophy. Philosophy, with its style now changed altogether, experiences a radical conversion from naive objectivism to *transcendental subjectivism.* This subjectivism strives toward a pure end-form through efforts that are constantly renewed yet always remain unsatisfactory. Might it not be that this continuing tendency has eternal significance? Perhaps it is a vast task assigned to us by history itself, invoking our collective cooperation.

The splintering of contemporary philosophy and its aimless activity make us pause. Must this situation not be traced back to the fact that the motivations from which Descartes' meditations emanate have lost their original vitality? Is it not true that the only fruitful renaissance is one which reawakens these meditations, not in order to accept them, but to reveal the profound truth in the radicalism of a return to the *ego cogito* with the external values that reside therein?

In any case, this is the path that led to transcendental phenomenology.

Let us now pursue this path together. In true Cartesian fashion, we shall become philosophers meditating in a radical sense, with, of course, frequent and critical modifications of the older Cartesian meditations. What was merely germinal in them must be freely developed here.

We thus begin, everyone for himself and in himself, with the decision to disregard all our present knowledge. We do not give up Descartes' guiding goal of an absolute foundation for knowledge. At the beginning, however, to presuppose even the possibility of that goal would be prejudice. We are satisfied to discover the goal and nature of science by submerging ourselves in scientific activity. It is the spirit of science to count nothing as really scientific which cannot be fully justified by the evidence. In other words, science demands proof by *reference to the things and facts themselves, as these are given in actual experience and intuition.* Thus guided, we, the beginning philosophers, make it a rule to judge only by the evidence. Also, the evidence itself must be subjected to critical verification, and that on the basis, of course, of further available evidence. Since from the beginning we have disregarded the sciences, we operate within our prescientific life, which is likewise filled with immediate and mediate evidences. This, and nothing else, is first given to us.

Herein arises our first question. Can we find evidence that is both immediate and apodictic? Can we find evidence that is primitive, in the sense that it must by necessity precede all other evidence?

As we meditate on this question one thing does, in fact, emerge as both prior to all evidence and as apodictic. It is the existence of the world. All science refers to the world, and, before that, our ordinary life already makes reference to it. *That the being of the world precedes everything is* so *obvious* that no one thinks to articulate it in a sentence. Our experience of the world is continuous, incessant, and unquestionable. But is it true that this experiential evidence, even though taken for granted, is really apodictic and primary to all other evidence? We will have to deny both. Is it not the case that occasionally something manifests itself as a sensory illusion? Has not the coherent and unified totality of our experience been at times debased as a mere dream? We will ignore Descartes' attempt to prove that, notwithstanding the fact of its being constantly experienced, the world's nonbeing can be conceived. His proof is carried out by a much too superficial criticism of sensory experience. We will keep this much: experiential evidence that is to serve as radical foundation for knowledge needs, above all, a critique of its validity and range. It cannot be accepted as apodictic without question and qualification. Therefore, merely to disregard all knowledge and to treat the sciences as prejudices is not enough. Even the experience of the world as the true universal ground of knowledge becomes an unacceptably naive belief. We can no longer accept the reality of the world as a fact to be taken for granted. *It is a hypothesis that needs verification.*

Does there remain a ground of being? Do we still have a basis for all judgments and evidences, a basis on which a universal philosophy can rest apodictically? Is not "world" the name for the totality of all that is? Might it not turn out that the world is not the truly ultimate basis for judgment, but instead that its existence presupposes a prior ground of being?

Here, specifically following Descartes, we make the great shift which, when properly carried out, leads to *transcendental subjectivity*. This is the shift to the *ego cogito*, as the apodictically certain and *last basis for judgment* upon which all radical philosophy must be grounded.

Let us consider: as radically meditating philosophers we now have neither knowledge that is valid for us nor a world that exists for us. We can no longer say that the world is real—a belief that is natural enough in our ordinary experience—; instead, it merely makes a claim to reality. This skepticism also applies to other selves, so that we rightly should not speak communicatively, that is, in the plural. Other people and animals are, of course, given to me only through sensory experience. Since I have questioned the validity of the latter I cannot avail myself of it here. With the loss of other minds I lose, of course, all forms of sociability and culture. In short, the entire concrete world ceases to have reality for me and becomes instead mere appearance. However, whatever may be the veracity of the claim to being made by phenomena, whether they represent reality or appearance, phenomena in themselves cannot be disregarded as mere "nothing." On the contrary, it is precisely the phenomena themselves which, without exception, render possible for me the very existence of both reality and appearance. Again, I may freely abstain from entertaining any belief about experience—which I did. This simply means that I refuse to assert the reality of the world. Nonetheless, we must be careful to realize that this epistemological abstention is still what it is: it includes the whole stream of experienced life and all its particulars, the appearances of objects, other people, cultural situations, etc. Nothing changes, except that I no longer accept the world simply as real; I no longer judge regarding the distinction between reality and appearance. I must similarly abstain from any other of my opinions, judgments, and valuations about the world, since these likewise assume the reality of the world. But for these, as for other phenomena, epistemological abstention does not mean their disappearance, at least not as pure phenomena.

This ubiquitous detachment from any point of view regarding the objective world we term the *phenomenological epoché*. It is the methodology through which I come to understand myself as that ego and life of consciousness in which and through which the entire objective world exists for me, and is for me precisely as it is. Everything in the world, all spatio-temporal being, exists for me because I experience it, because I perceive it, remember it, think of it in any way, judge it, value it, desire it, etc. It is well known that Descartes designates all this by the term *cogito*. For me the world is nothing other than what I am aware of and what appears valid in such *cogitationes*. *The whole meaning and reality of the world rests exclusively on such cogitationes.* My entire worldly life takes its course within these. I cannot live, experience, think, value, and act in any world which is not in some sense in me, and derives its meaning and truth from me. If I place myself above that entire life and if I abstain from any commitment about reality, specifically one which accepts the world as existing, and if I view that life exclusively as consciousness *of* the world, then I reveal myself as the pure ego with its pure stream of *cogitationes*.

I certainly do not discover myself as one item among others in the world, since I have altogether suspended judgment about the world. I am not the ego of an individual man. I am the ego in whose stream of consciousness the world itself—including myself as an object in it, a man who exists in the world—first acquires meaning and reality.

We have reached a dangerous point. It seems simple indeed to understand the pure ego with its *cogitationes* by following Descartes. And yet it is as if we were on the brink of a precipice, where the ability to step calmly and surely decides between philosophic life and philosophic death. Descartes was thoroughly sincere in his desire to be radical and presuppositionless. However, we know through recent researches—particularly the fine and penetrating work of Messrs. Gibson and Koyré—that a great deal of Scholasticism is hidden in Descartes' meditations as unarticulated prejudice. But this is not all. We must above all avoid the prejudices, hardly noticed by us, which derive from our emphasis on the mathematically oriented natural sciences. These prejudices make it appear as if the phrase *ego cogito* refers to an apodictic and primitive axiom, one which, in conjunction with others to be derived from it, provides the foundation for a deductive and universal science, a science *ordine geometrico*. In relation to this we must under no circumstances take for granted that, with our apodictic and pure ego, we have salvaged a small corner of the world as the single indubitable fact about the world which can be utilized by the philosophizing ego. It is not true that all that now remains to be done is to infer the rest of the world through correct deductive procedures according to principles that are innate to the ego.

Unfortunately, Descartes commits this error, in the apparently insignificant yet fateful transformation of the ego to a *substantia cogitans*, to an independent human *animus*, which then becomes the point of departure for conclusions by means of the principle of causality. In short, this is the transformation which made Descartes the father of the rather absurd transcendental realism. We will keep aloof from all this if we remain true to radicalism in our self-examination and with it to the principle of pure intuition. We must regard nothing as veridical except the pure immediacy and givenness in the field of the *ego cogito* which the *epoché* has opened up to us. In other words, we must not make assertions about that which we do not ourselves *see*. In these matters Descartes was deficient. It so happens that he stands before the greatest of all discoveries—in a sense he has already made it—yet fails to see its true significance, that of transcendental subjectivity. He does not pass through the gateway that leads into genuine transcendental philosophy.

The independent *epoché* with regard to the nature of the world as it appears and is real to me—that is, "real" to the previous and natural point of view—discloses the greatest and most magnificent of all facts: I and my life remain—in my sense of reality—untouched by whichever way we decide the issue of whether the world is or is not. To say, in my natural existence, "I am, I think, I live," means that I am one human being among others in the world, that I am related to nature through my physical body, and that in this body my *cogitationes,* perceptions, memories, judgments, etc. are incorporated as psychophysical facts. Conceived in this way, I, we, humans, and animals are subject-matter for the objective sciences, that is, for biology, anthropology, and zoology, and also for psychology. The life of the psyche, which is the subject-matter of all psychology, is understood only as the psychic life in the world. The methodology of a purified Cartesianism demands of me, the one who philosophizes, the phenomenological *epoché.* The *epoché* eliminates as worldly facts from my field of judgment both the reality of the objective world in general and the sciences of the world. *Consequently, for me there exists no "I" and there are no psychic actions, that is, psychic phenomena in the psychological sense.* To myself I do not exist as a human being, [nor] do my *cogitationes* exist as components of a psycho-physical world. But through all this I have discovered my true self. I have discovered that I alone am the pure ego, with pure existence and pure capacities (for example, the obvious capacity to abstain from judging). Through this ego alone does *the being of the world,* and, for that matter, any being whatsoever, make sense *to me* and has possible validity. The world—whose conceivable non-being does not extinguish my pure being but rather presupposes it—is termed *transcendent,* whereas my pure being or my pure ego is termed *transcendental.* Through the phenomenological *epoché* the natural human ego, specifically my own, is reduced to the transcendental ego. This is the meaning of the phenomenological reduction.

Further steps are needed so that what has been developed up to this point can be adequately applied. What is the philosophic use of the transcendental ego? To be sure, for me, the one who philosophizes, it obviously precedes, in an epistemological sense, all objective reality. In a way, it is the basis for all objective knowledge, be it good or bad. But does the fact that the transcendental ego precedes and presupposes all objective knowledge mean also that it is an epistemological ground in the ordinary sense? The thought is tempting. All realistic theories are guilty of it. But the temptation to look in the transcendental subjectivity for premises guaranteeing the existence of the subjective world evanesces once we realize that all arguments, considered in themselves, exist already in transcendental subjectivity itself. Furthermore, all proofs for the world have their criteria set in the world just as it is given and justified in experience. However, these considerations must not be construed as a rejection of the great Cartesian idea that the ultimate basis for objective science and the reality of the objective world is to be sought in transcendental subjectivity. Otherwise—our criticisms aside —we would not be true to Descartes' method of meditation. However, the Cartesian discovery of the ego may perhaps open up a *new concept of foundation, namely, a transcendental foundation.*

In point of fact, instead of using the *ego cogito* merely as an apodictic proposition and as an absolutely primitive premise, we notice that the phenomenological *epoché* has uncovered for us (or for me, the one who philosophizes), through the apodictic *I am,* a new kind and an endless sphere of being. This is the sphere of a new kind of experience: transcendental experience. And herewith also arises the possibility of both transcendental epistemology and transcendental science.

A most extraordinary epistemological situation is disclosed here. The phenomenological *epoché* reduces me to my transcendental and pure ego. I am, thus, at least *prima facie*, in a certain sense *solus ipse*, but not in the ordinary sense, in which one might say that a man survived a universal holocaust in a world which itself remained unaffected. Once I have banished from my sphere of judgments the world, as one which receives its being from me and within me, then I, as the transcendental ego which is prior to the world, am *the sole source and object capable of judgment* [das einzig urteilsmäBig Setzbare und Gesetzte]. And now I am supposed to develop an unheard-of and unique science, since it is one that is created exclusively by and inside my transcendental subjectivity! Furthermore, this science is meant to apply, at least at the outset, to my transcendental subjectivity alone. It thus becomes a transcendental-solipsistic science. It is therefore not the *ego cogito*, but a science about the ego—a pure *egology*—which becomes the ultimate foundation of philosophy in the Cartesian sense of a universal science, and which must provide at least the cornerstone for its absolute foundation. In actual fact this science exists already as the lowest transcendental phenomenology. And I mean the lowest, not the fully developed phenomenology, because to the latter, of course, belongs the further development from transcendental solipsism to transcendental intersubjectivity.

To make all this intelligible it is first necessary to do what was neglected by Descartes, namely, to describe the endless field of the ego's transcendental experience itself. His own experience, as is well known, and especially when he judged it to be apodictic, plays a role in the philosophy of Descartes. But he neglected to describe the ego in the full concretion of its transcendental being and life, nor did he regard it as an unlimited work-project to be pursued systematically. It is an insight central to a philosopher that, by introducing the transcendental reduction, he can reflect truthfully on his *cogitationes* and on their pure phenomenological content. In this way he can uncover all aspects of his transcendental being with respect to both his transcendental-temporal life and also his capabilities. We are clearly dealing with a train of thought parallel to what the world-centered psychologist calls inner experience or experience of the self.

One thing of the greatest, even decisive, importance remains. One cannot lightly dismiss the fact—even Descartes has so remarked on occasion—that the *epoché* changes nothing in the world. All experience is still his experience, all consciousness, still his consciousness. The expression *ego cogito* must be expanded by one term. Every *cogito* contains a meaning: its *cogitatum*. The experience of a house, as I experience it, and ignoring theories of perception, is precisely an experience of this and only this house, a house which appears in such-and-such a way, and has certain specific determinations when seen from the side, from near-by, and from afar. Similarly, a clear or a vague recollection is the recollection of a vaguely or clearly apprehended house. Even the most erroneous judgment means a judgment about such-and-such factual content, and so on. *The essence of consciousness, in which I live as my own self, is the so-called intentionality.* Consciousness is always consciousness of something. The nature of consciousness includes, as modes of being, presentations, probabilities, and non-being, and also the modes of appearance, goodness, and value, etc. Phenomenological experience as reflection must avoid any interpretative constructions. Its descriptions must reflect accurately the concrete contents of experience, precisely as these are experienced.

To interpret consciousness as a complex of sense data and then to bring forth gestalt-like qualities [*Gestaltqualitäten*] out of these—which are subsequently equated with the totality—is a sensualist invention. This interpretation is a basic error even from the worldly and psychological perspective, and much more so from the transcendental point of view. It is true that in the process of phenomenological analyses sense data do occur, and something is, in fact, disclosed about them. But what phenomenological analysis fails to find as primary is the "perception of an external world." The honest description of the unadulterated data of experience must disclose what appears first of all, *i.e.*, the *cogito*. For example, we must describe closely the perception of a house in terms of what it means as object and its modes of appearing. The same applies to all forms of consciousness.

When phenomenology examines objects of consciousness—regardless of what kind, whether real or ideal—it deals with these exclusively as objects of the immediate consciousness. The description—which attempts to grasp the concrete and rich phenomena of the *cogitationes*—must constantly glance back from the side of the object to the side of consciousness and pursue the general existing connections. For example, if I consider the perception of a hexahedron, then I notice in pure reflection that the hexahedron is given as a continuous and unitary object together with a many-formed and determinate manifold of modes of appearance. It is the same hexahedron, the same appearance, regardless of whether viewed from this side or that one, from this or that perspective, from close or from afar, with greater or with lesser distinctness and determinateness. Nonetheless, if we see any hexahedral surface, any edge or corner, any spot of color, in short, any aspect of the objective sense, then we notice the same thing in every case: it is the unity of a manifold with constantly changing modes of appearance, a unity of its particular perspectives and of the particular differentiations of the subjective here and there. If we look uncritically we find a color that is always identical and unchanging. But if we reflect on the mode in which it appears we recognize that the color is nothing other, nor can it be thought as anything other, than that which presents itself now as this and now as that shade of color. Unity is always unity of representations, which is the representation of the spontaneous presentation of color or the presentation of an edge. . . .

Intentional analysis is thus something altogether different from analysis in the ordinary sense. The life of consciousness is neither a mere aggregate of data, nor a heap of psychic atoms, nor a whole composed of elements united through gestalt-like qualities [*Gestaltqualitäten*]. This is true also of pure introspective psychology, as a parallel to transcendental phenomenology. *Intentional analysis is the disclosure of the actualities and potentialities in which objects constitute themselves as perceptual units.* Furthermore, all perceptual analysis takes place in the transition from real events to the intentional horizons suggested by them.

This late insight prescribes to phenomenological analysis and description an altogether new methodology. It is a methodology which goes into action whenever objects and meanings, questions about being, questions about possibilities, questions of origin, and questions of right are to be considered seriously. Every intentional analysis reaches beyond the immediately and actually [*reell*] given events of the immanent sphere, and in such a way that the analysis discloses potentialities—which are now given actually [*reell*] and whose horizons have been sketched—and brings out manifold aspects of new experiences in which are made manifest what earlier was meant only implicitly and in this way was already present intentionally. When I see a hexahedron I say, in reality and in truth I see it only from one side. It is nonetheless evident that what I now experience is in reality more. The perception includes a nonsensory belief through which the visible side can be understood to be a mere side in the first place. But how does this belief, that there is more, disclose itself? How does it become obvious that I mean more? It occurs through the transition to a synthetic sequence of possible perceptions, perceptions I would have—as indeed I can—were I to walk around the object. Phenomenology always explains meanings, that is, intentionality, by producing these sense-fulfilling syntheses. The tremendous task placed on description is to expound the universal structure of transcendental consciousness in its reference to and creation of meanings. . . .

The conceptual [*ideelle*] fixation of an intentional object-class leads, in intentional researches, as one soon recognizes, to an organization or order. In other words, transcendental subjectivity is not a chaos of intentional experiences, but it is a unity through synthesis. It is a many-levelled synthesis in which always new classes and individuals are constituted. However, every object expresses a *rule structured within transcendental subjectivity*. . . .

An object exists for me; that is to say, it has reality for me in consciousness. But this reality is reality for me only as long as I believe that I can confirm it. By this I mean that I must be able to provide usable procedures, that is, procedures which run through automatically, and other evidences, which lead me then to the object itself and through which I realize the object as being *truly there*. The same holds when my awareness of the object is a matter of experience, that is, when my awareness tells me that the object itself is already there, that the object itself is seen. This act of seeing, in turn, points to further seeing, that is, it points to the possibility of confirmation. Finally, it points to the fact that what has already once been realized as being can nonetheless be restored, again and again, to its previous condition of progressive confirmation.

Think about the tremendous importance of this remark, considering that we are on an egological foundation. We can see, from this ultimate point of view, that existence and essence have for us, in reality and truth, no other meaning than that of possible confirmation. Furthermore, these confirmation-procedures and their accessibility belong to me as transcendental subjectivity and make sense only as such.

True being, therefore, whether real or ideal, *has significance only as a particular correlate of my own intentionality,* actual or potential. Of course, this is not true of an isolated *cogito*. For example, the being of a real thing is not the mere *cogito* of an isolated perception that I now have. But the perception and its intentionally given object call to my attention, by virtue of the presumed horizon, an endless and open system of *possible* perceptions, perceptions which are not invented but which are motivated from within my intentional existence, and which can lose their presumed validity only when conflicting experience eliminates it. These possible perceptions are necessarily presupposed as *my* possibilities, ones which I can bring about—provided I am not hindered—by approaching the object, looking around it, etc.

Needless to say, the foregoing has been stated very crudely. Extremely far-reaching and complex intentional analyses are needed in order to explain the structure of these possibilities as they relate to the specific horizons belonging to every individual class of objects, and to clarify therewith the meaning of actual being. At the outset only one fact is evident and guides me, namely, that I accept as being only that which presents itself to me as being, and that all conceivable justification of it lies within my own self and is determined in my immediate and mediate intentionality, in which any other meaning of being is also to be determined.

THE
ATTACK
ON
PSYCHOLOGISM

Logic is the Quintessence of Cause and Effect
—D. H. Lawrence KANGAROO

INTRODUCTION

Husserl's first published work, *The Philosophy of Arithmetic* (after his dissertation at Halle, 1887), argued that the principles of arithmetic were essentially truths of psychology, hypotheses concerning our ideas about number. This is also presented in his early essay "On the Concept of Number." After the incisive critique of his book by Gottlob Frege in *Zeitschrift für Philosophie* (1894), Husserl himself turned against this thesis and initiated a sustained attack against this "psychologism" in his very important *Logical Investigations*. Included here are a summary of Husserl's early essay, the attacks by both Frege and Husserl on psychologism, a portion of Frege's essay "The Thought," in which he presents the philosophical basis for his alternative to psychologism, and a modern restatement of the psychologistic thesis and its problems by Roderick Chisholm, an influential American analytic philosopher who has much in common with Husserlian phenomenology.

ON THE CONCEPT OF NUMBER

EDMUND HUSSERL

Let us look once more, then, at the psychological foundation of the number concepts. *Two things constitute, in our view, the concept of number:* 1) *the concept of 'collective unification'* (Einigung) *and* 2) *the concept of 'something'. The abstraction of the former concept becomes possible in virtue of the fact that, in all cases where discrete contents are 'thought together', i.e., in a 'totality', there is present one and the same, constantly uniform act of collecting interest and noticing, which act separates each of the particular contents off to itself (as separately and specifically noticed), and simultaneously holds it together in a union with the others. It is with reference to this unifying act that we win the abstract representation of collective combination* (Verbindung). *As to the subsumption of any content under the concept of 'something', that requires reflection upon the act in which that content is represented.*

The two psychological constituents of the concept of number obviously are not independent of each other. We cannot conceive of a collective unification without united contents; and, if we wish to represent them *in abstracto,* then they must be thought of as 'something or other'. But if this is so, what, then, constitutes the distinction between the concepts *collective unification* and *multiplicity?* The answer is obvious. In the first case, interest rests exclusively upon the *combination* of the arbitrarily conceived contents; but in the latter, it rests upon the totality of

Reprinted from *Über den Begriff der Zahl* (Halle: Heynemann Beyer, 1887). Translated by Professor Dallas Willard of the Philosophy Department of the University of Southern California, who has kindly given his permission for inclusion in this volume. Copyright 1971 by Dallas Willard. This was Husserl's first published work.

those contents *as a whole,* i.e., upon *the elements* attended to *in* this their unification. So both concepts are equally essential to the concept of the multiplicity—the concept of 'something', and that of 'collective unification'. It is clear that the concept 'something' is related to a concrete content in exactly the same way as the concept 'number' is related to a totality of concretely given contents. However, the concept 'something' is the more primitive one. Without it there would be no number. The elementary fact which originally manifests itself in it, and essentially conditions it, is that which makes possible the concept of the collective unification.

LOGICAL INVESTIGATIONS: FORWARD

EDMUND HUSSERL

. . . . But in yet a wholly different direction I found myself involved in problems of general logic and epistemology. I had set out from the dominant persuasion that it was psychology from which the logic of the deductive sciences, as well as logic in general, must expect its philosophical clarification. In conformity with that persuasion, psychological investigations occupied a very large part of the first (and only published) volume of my *Philosophy of Arithmetic.* This psychological foundation was never fully satisfactory to me in certain respects. Where the issue was the origin of mathematical representations, or the (in fact psychologically determined) development of practical methods, the results of psychological analyses appeared clear and instructive to me. But as soon as attention is turned from the psychological relationships in the processes of thought to the logical unity of the thought *content* (the unity of theory), then

Reprinted from *Forward to Logische Untersuchungen,* 1st ed. (Halle: M. Niemeyer, 1900), Part I, Vol. I. Translated by Professor Dallas Willard of the Philosophy Department of the University of Southern California, who has kindly given his permission for inclusion in this volume. Copyright 1971 by Dallas Willard.

a proper continuity and clarity in *this* content is not to be obtained through such analyses. Therefore the fundamental doubt more and more disturbed me, as to how the objectivity of mathematics, and of all science in general, is consistent with logic having a psychological basis.

. . . . But as concerns the candid critique which I have exercised upon psychologistic logic and epistemology, I would like to recall, in Goethe's words, that "One is against nothing stronger than he is against those errors which he has just laid aside."

LOGICAL INVESTIGATIONS: PSYCHOLOGISM

EDMUND HUSSERL

CHAPTER THREE

Psychologism—Its Arguments and Its Position with Respect to the Common Counter-Arguments

Section 17. The Dispute about Whether or Not the Essential Theoretical Basis of Normative Logic Lies in Psychology

If we apply what was established in general in the last chapter to logic as a normative discipline, then the first and most important question that comes up is: Which theoretical sciences provide the essential basis of the theory of science? Thereto we immediately add the further question: Is it true that the theoretical truths which we find treated in the framework of traditional and modern logic—and especially those which belong to its essential basis—have their thoretical locus within sciences that are already delimited and independently developed?

Reprinted from *Logische Untersuchungen*, 1st ed. (Halle: M. Niemeyer, 1900), Part I, Vol. I. Translated by Professor Dallas Willard of the Philosophy Department of the University of Southern California, who has kindly given his permission for inclusion in this volume. Copyright 1971 by Dallas Willard.

Here we come upon the dispute about the relation between psychology and logic; for, to these questions raised, a school which is dominant right at this time has the following answer ready:—The essential theoretical basis of logic lies in psychology. According to theoretical content, the propositions which give logic its characteristic features belong in the domain of psychology. Logic is related to psychology like a branch of chemical technology is related to chemistry, or like surveying is related to geometry, and so on. For this school of thought there is here no occasion for laying out a new theoretical science—especially one which would deserve the name "logic" in a narrower and more profound sense. In fact, it is often implied that psychology provides the sole and sufficient theoretical basis for the logical *Kunstlehre*.[a] Thus, we read in Mill's attack on Hamilton: "Logic is not a science separate from and co-ordinate with psychology. So far as logic is a science at all, it is a part or branch of psychology, distinguished therefrom, on the one hand, as part from whole, and, on the other hand, as art from science. It owes its theoretical basis wholly to psychology, and involves so much of psychology as is necessary to ground its technical rules." According to Lipps it even appears as if logic is to be ranged within psychology as a mere constituent part. He says: "What with sufficient clarity distinguishes logic from psychology is precisely the fact that the former is a particular discipline within the latter."

Section 18. The Psychologistic Line of Argument

If we call for the justification of such views, there is offered to us a highly plausible argument which appears to cut off at the outset any further dispute. However one may define the logical *Kunstlehre*[a]—whether as *Kunstlehre* of thinking, judging, inferring, knowing (Erkennen), proving, knowing (Wissen), or

[a] A '*Kunstlehre*' in Husserl's sense is a theory (*Lehre*) of a technique or art (*Kunst*). It is a teaching about how to do something correctly. In the case of what is commonly taught as logic, Husserl supposed it best regarded as a practical theory about how to arrive at *knowledge*, as distinct from mere opinion or conjecture. (Translator's note)

as *Kunstlehre* of the directions taken by the understanding in the pursuit of truth or in the appraisal of proof procedures, and so on—we always find that psychical activities or products are designated as that which is to be practically regulated. And as, in general, the handling of a material by a technique presupposes knowledge of its properties, so also here where we are dealing specifically with psychological material. The scientific investigation of the rules according to which this material is to be dealt with will, obviously, lead to the scientific investigation of the relevant properties. Thus, psychology—or, more precisely, the psychology of recognition—provides the theoretical basis for the construction of a logical *Kunstlehre*.

This is also confirmed by every glance at the literature of logic. What is constantly discussed there? Why, concepts, judgments, inferences, deductions, inductions, definitions, classifications, and so on—all of its psychology, only selected and arranged in conformity with normative and practical points of view. However narrowly one may draw the limits of pure logic, one cannot remove from it the psychological element. It is already embedded in the concepts which are constitutive of the laws of pure logic: such concepts, for example, as truth and falsity, affirmation and denial, generality and particularity, ground and consequent, and the like.

Section 19. The Common Arguments Against Such a View, and How Psychologism Refutes Them

Curiously enough, those who oppose this view believe that they can ground a sharp cleavage between the two disciplines under discussion precisely upon the normative character of logic. Psychology, it is said, considers thinking as it is, while logic considers it as it should be. The former has to do with natural laws of thinking, and the latter has to do with its normative laws. So it is said in Jäsche's edition of Kant's logic lectures: "Some logicians indeed presuppose *psychological* principles in logic. But to bring such principles into logic is as absurd as to take moral principles from life. If we drew principles from psychology, i.e., from observations of our understanding, then we would merely see *how* thought actually proceeds, and how it *is* under the several subjective hindrances and conditions. But this would only lead to knowledge of merely *contingent* laws. However, in logic it is not a question of *contingent*, but rather of *necessary* rules—not of how we do think, but rather of how we should think. The rules of logic must, therefore, be drawn, not from any *contingent*, but rather from a *necessary* use of reason, which one finds in himself without recourse to any psychology. In logic we do not wish to know how the understanding is and thinks, and how it until now has proceeded in thinking. Rather we wish to know how it *should* proceed in thinking. Logic should teach us the correct use of the understanding, i.e., the use which is consistent with itself." Herbart takes a similar position by objecting—against the logic of his time and against "the would-be psychological histories of the understanding and the reason with which that logic begins"—that such procedure is just as bad an error as beginning a moral theory with a natural history of human inclinations, drives, and weaknesses. He too points to the normative character of logic, as of ethics, in order to found the distinction in question.

Such an argument gives the psychologistic logicians no pause at all. They reply:—The *necessary* understanding-function is just that, an *understanding*-function; and, along with the understanding itself, it belongs to psychology. Thinking as it should be is merely a special case of thinking as it is. Certainly psychology has to investigate the natural laws of thought, and, thus, the laws for all judgments whatsoever, whether true or false. But it would be absurd to interpret this in such a way as to make only those laws belong to psychology which, in most inclusive generality, refer to all judgments whatever, and thus to exclude specific laws of judging—such as those of correct judging—from psychology's domain. Or is this not the view advanced? Is it, rather, denied that the normative laws of thinking have the character of such specific laws? But this also will not do. The normative laws of thinking, it might be said, only mean to state how one has to proceed *presupposing* that he wants to think correctly. "In the material sense, we think correctly when we think of things as they are. But that things are certainly and indubitably such and such, that means, in our use, that, in virtue of the nature of our minds, we cannot think of them otherwise than in precisely *this* way. For in fact it does not need to be repeated, what has often enough been said, that obviously nothing, as it is independently of the way in which we must think of it, can be thought by us or be an object of our knowing; that, thus, whoever compares his thought of a thing with the thing itself can in fact only measure his contingent thinking, influenced by habit, tradition, inclination and disinclination, with that thinking which, free from such influences, hears no voice other than that of the lawfulness proper to it."

"But then the rules according to which one must proceed in order to think rightly are nothing other than rules according to which one must proceed in order to think as the peculiar character of the thinking—its specific nature—requires: in brief, these rules are identical with the natural laws of thinking itself. Logic is either the physics of thinking or it is nothing."

From the anti-psychologistic side it may be replied: Certainly the various species of representations, judgments, inferences, and so on, as psychic phenomena and dispositions, *also* belong to psychology. But psychology has, in regard to these, a different task than logic. Both investigate the laws of these activities, but "law" signifies something totally different for each. The task of psychology is to seek out the laws of the real (*realen*) connections within the processes of consciousness, as well as the laws which connect these *processes* with the correlative psychic *dispositions*, and with the related processes in the *bodily organism*. "Law" here means a formula comprehending a necessary and exceptionless linkage in the co-existence and succession of events. The linkage in question is a causal one. Quite of another nature is the task of logic. It does not inquire about the causal origins and consequences of intellectual activities, but rather about their truth content. It asks how such activities *should* be constituted and carried out, if the judgments thereby arrived at are to be true. Correct judgments and false ones, insightful ones and blind, come and go according to natural laws. Like all psychical phenomena, they have their causal antecedents and consequences. But the logician does not care about these natural connections. Rather he seeks for ideal connections, which he does not always—in fact only exceptionally—find realized in the actual course of thinking. Not a physics, but rather an ethics of thinking is his goal. Sigwart therefore rightly insists that, in the *psychological* account of thinking, "The antithesis true/false is of as little import . . ., as is the antithesis good/bad for the psychological study of human action."

The psychologist will reply: We are not to be satisfied with such superficialities. Certainly logic has a wholly different task than psychology. Who will deny it? To be exact, it is the technology of knowledge. But how, then, could it disregard the question about causal connections? And how could it seek for ideal connections without studying natural connections? "As if each *should* did not rest upon an *is;* and as if each ethics did not have to be at the same time a physics." "The question about what one should do is always reducible to the question of what one must do *if* he is to obtain a certain goal. This question, in turn, is the same as the question of how that goal *is actually obtained.*" That for psychology—in distinction from logic—the antithesis true/false is not considered "cannot mean that psychology passes these two different psychic facts off as the same, but only that it is equally concerned to render each of them intelligible." So, as theoretical, logic is related to psychology as part to whole. Its main goal is, specifically, to establish propositions of the form: —Just in *this* and no other way must mental activities—in general, or under determinately characterized circumstances—form, arrange, and point themselves, in order for the resulting judgments to acquire the character of *Evidenz,* or of knowledge in the full sense of the word. The reference to causal conditions is intelligible here. The psychological character of *Evidenz* is a causal consequence of certain antecedents. What is the nature of these antecedents? To investigate that is precisely the task. [cf. Mill, Sigwart, Wundt].

The following, oft-repeated argument has no better luck in shaking the psychologistic position: Logic, it is said, can rest upon psychology just as little as on any other science. For any science is such only *via* concord with the rules of logic, and thereby already presupposes the validity of those rules. Accordingly, it would be circular to try first to ground logic upon psychology.

The psychologists will answer:—The incorrectness of this argument is shown by the fact that from it follows the impossibility of any logic at all. Since, as a science itself, logic must proceed logically, it is caught in the same circularity. The validity of the rules which it presupposes must at the same time be established by it.

But let us take a closer look to see wherein the vicious circle is supposed to consist. In this, that psychology presupposes the logical laws to be valid? But one has to take into consideration the equivocality of "presupposition." That a science presupposes the validity of certain rules can mean that those rules are premisses in its proofs. But it can also mean that they are rules in conformity with which the science must proceed in order to be a science at all. The above argument treats the two meanings as one. To reason from premisses *in conformity with* logical rules, and to reason *from* logical rules as premisses, it treats as all the same. Yet it is only when they are reasoned *from* that the circularity arises. But just as so many artists create beautiful works without the slightest knowledge of aesthetics, so an investigator can construct proofs without ever having recourse to logic, which shows that logical laws could not be the premisses of the proofs. And what is thus true of single proofs holds also of entire sciences.

Section 20. A Hiatus in the Psychologistic Line of Argument

It is undeniable that these and related arguments seem to put the antipsychologist at a disadvantage. Not a few regard the dispute as settled beyond all doubt. They consider the rejoinders of psychologism to be absolutely decisive. Still, there is one thing here which may provoke the *philosopher* into his wonder: namely, the fact that there is any dispute at all, and that there *yet* is one, and that the same arguments are again and again brought up, the refutations of which are not acknowledged as binding. Were all really plain and clear, as the Psychologistic school assures us it is, then this state of affairs would not make sense, especially with unprejudiced, serious and intelligent thinkers standing in the opposition. May not the truth lie, once again, rich in the middle? And may not it be that each party has recognized a good portion of the truth, and has simply not been able to delimit its portion of the truth, and has simply not been able to delimit its portion with conceptual sharpness and to conceive of its portion precisely as *merely* a portion of the whole truth? Is it not, yet, possible that in the arguments of the anti-psychologist—involving many flaws of detail, which come clearly to light in the refutations—there remains something not resolved; that yet a true force resides in those arguments, one which turns up again and again in unprejudiced consideration of the relevant matters? For my part, I would like to answer those questions in the affirmative. What is more, it seems to me that the more important portion of the truth lies on the anti-psychologistic side; only there the decisive ideas are not appropriately worked out, and are clouded by many errors.

Let us turn back to the question about the essential theoretical basis of normative logic. Is this question really disposed of by the psychologistic line of argument? Here we immediately notice a weak point. Only one thing follows on that line: *viz.* that psychology *shares* in the founding of logic; but it is not shown that psychology *alone* has a share, or even that it predominates—i.e., that it is the '*essential basis*' of logic in the sense fixed by us in Section 16 above. The possibility remains open

that another science contributes to the founding of logic, and
does so in an incomparably more significant manner. And here
may be the place for that 'pure logic,' which, according to psychologism's opposition, is supposed to have its being independently of all psychology as a naturally delimited science,
complete in itself. We are glad to admit that what has been dealt
with under this title by the Kantians and Herbartians is not
wholly adapted to the character to which, according to the sus-
picions excited above (Section 13), it would have to conform.
Is not their talk always still of normative laws of thinking and,
in particular, of concept and judgment formation, and so on?
That is proof enough, one might say, that the respective subject
matter is neither theoretical nor foreign to psychology. But this
objection to 'pure' logic loses its force when, with closer inspection, the suspicion which came upon us above (3rd paragraph
from the end of Section 13) is confirmed:—namely, the suspicion that these schools were indeed unfortunate in their definition and construction of the intended discipline, but that yet
they came near to the truth. For they noted in the traditional
logic a plentitude of theoretically connected truths which neither
fell within psychology nor in any other particular science; and
so they had a presentiment of a properly distinct domain of
truths. And if it is just *these* truths to which every logical rule
is ultimately related, and of which one must, therefore, mainly
think where *logical* truths are concerned, then one could easily
come to see in them the essentials of the whole of logic, and to
call their theoretical unity 'pure logic'. I hope that I can show
that this, in fact, is a true picture of how things are.

CHAPTER FOUR

Empiricist Consequences of Psychologism

Section 21. Characterization and Refutation of Two Empiricist Consequences of the Psychologistic Point of View

Let us for the moment adopt the psychologistic view of
logic. Let us, thus, assume that the essential theoretical founda-

tions of logical rules lie in psychology. However psychology may be defined—whether as the science of psychic phenomena, or as the science of the facts of consciousness, of the facts of inner experience, or of experiences in their dependence upon the experiencing individual, or however else—everyone agrees that it is a science of facts, and is, consequently, a science drawn from experience. We also will encounter no opposition by adding that, yet today, psychology is lacking in more genuine (and hence more exact) laws, and that the propositions which it dignifies with the name "law" are indeed quite valuable, but are still only vague, empirical generalizations. These 'laws' are assertions about approximate regularities of co-existence and succession, which cannot at all claim to formulate with precise and infallible determinateness which things, under exactly stated circumstances, must exist together or succeed each other. Just take the laws of the association of ideas, to which Association Psychology would like to assign the position and importance of psychological *axioms,* as an example. As soon as one tries to give an adequate formulation of their empirically justified meaning, they immediately lose their ostensible character as laws. And this has consequences which give the psychologistic logician something to think about!

First of all, only vague rules can be grounded upon vague theoretical foundations. If psychological laws are devoid of exactitude, the same must be true of logical rules. Now, no doubt, many logical rules are infected with empirical vagueness. But precisely the laws called 'logical' in the full sense—those which we earlier acknowledged as constituting, as laws of proofs, the genuine core of all logic; i.e., the logical 'principles', the laws of the syllogism, and the laws of the various other sorts of inference (such as those in the logic of identity, or in the Bernoullian inference from n to n *plus 1,* and such as the principles involved in probability inferences, and so on)—are of absolute exactitude. Any interpretation which attributes empirical indeterminateness to them, and which makes their validity depend upon vague 'conditions', would modify their true sense from the ground up. It is obvious that they are genuine laws, and not 'merely empirical', i.e., approximate, rules.

If, as Lotze supposed, pure mathematics is only an independently developed branch of logic, then the inexhaustible plentitude of purely mathematical laws also belong within that domain of exact logical laws just referred to. In considering all further objections, along with that law domain we shall want to keep the domain of purely mathematical laws in view.

Second, should anyone try to dodge our first objection by denying the all-pervasive inexactness of psychological laws, and by seeking to ground norms of the sort just designated upon allegedly exact natural laws of thinking, little would be gained.

No natural law is *a priori*, i.e., knowable with insight. The only way in which such a law can be proven and justified is by induction over particular experienced facts. But induction does not show that a law obtains. Rather, it only shows the more-or-less high probability of it obtaining, hence yielding insight into the probability, but not into the law. So, on the move just suggested, the laws of logic also, without any exception, must have the rank of probabilities. But, to the contrary, nothing appears more obvious than this: that the laws of 'pure logic' are all valid *a priori*. They find their proof and justification, not through induction, but rather through apodictic Evidenz. What is justified through insight is not the mere probability of their obtaining (*Geltung*), but rather their obtaining or truth itself.

The principle of contradiction does not say that it is to be *conjectured* that of two contradictory judgments one is true and one is false. The mode "Barbara" does not say that, when "All *A's* are *B's*" and "All *B's* are *C's*" are true, it is to be *conjectured* that the corresponding proposition, "All *A's* are *C's*," is true. And so everywhere, even in the domain of purely mathematical propositions. Otherwise we leave open the *possibility* that the conjecture in question might be disconfirmed by the broadening of the range of experience, which always is only a limited one. But then perhaps our laws of logic are only 'approximations' to the truly valid laws of thinking, which for us are unattainable! With natural laws it is right to seriously consider such a possibility. Although the law of gravity is commended by the most extensive induction and verification, yet today no natural scientist takes it to be an absolutely valid law. Occasionally, new formulations of gravity are tried out. For example, it is proven that Weber's fundamental law of electrical phenomena could also function quite as well as the fundamental law of gravity. The factors which distinguish the two formulae from each other only condition differences in calculated values which do not go beyond the range of unavoidable error in observation. But an indefinitely large number of such factors as these can be conceived of. So we know *a priori* that indefinitely many laws can and must accomplish the same thing as Newton's law (which commends itself only by its peculiar simplicity). We know that, given the irremovable imprecision of observation, the very search here for 'the only true law' is silly. That is the way things are in the exact sciences of fact. But not in logic. What in the former is a legitimate possibility turns in the latter into an obvious absurdity. In fact, we have insight, not into the mere probability, but rather into the truth of the laws of logic. We intuitively grasp (*Wir sehen . . . ein*) the principles of syllogistic, of Bernoullian induction, of probability inferences, of general arithmetic, and the like. That is, we apprehend in them the truth itself. Consequently, the talk of a range of imprecision, of mere approximation, and so on, loses its possible meaning. But if the necessary consequence of psychologically grounding logic is absurd, then such a grounding is itself absurd.

Even the strongest of psychologistic arguments cannot prevail against truth itself insightfully grasped. Probability cannot do battle with truth, nor conjecture with insight. Those who remain caught up in discussions of generalities may be deceived by psychologistic arguments. A mere glance at any one logical law, at its true meaning and at the insightfulness with which it is grasped as a truth in itself, must make an end to that deception.

Yet, how plausible sounds that which the (so *very* seductive) psychologistic reflections aim to force upon us! The laws of logic

are laws of proofs. Proofs—what are they but particular trains
of human thought in which, under certain normal conditions, the
judgments turning up as the last members appear as imbued with
the character of necessary consequent. That character itself is
psychical, a certain phase of mental life, and nothing else. And
all of these psychic phenomena clearly do not stand in isolation,
but are threads in that vastly complicated web of psychic phenomena, psychic dispositions, and organic processes, which we
call 'human life'. And under such circumstances should we expect
some other result than empirical generalities? How could
psychology give more?

We reply: Certainly psychology gives no more. Precisely
because of that, it also cannot yield those apodictically evident
—and, consequently, supra-empirical and absolutely exact—laws
which constitute the core of all logic.

Section 22. The Laws of Thought as Alleged Natural Laws Which
            Causally Produce Rational Thinking When They Alone
            Influence Thought

This is also the place to take a position with reference to a
widely held view of logical laws, which defines right thinking
by means of its conformity to certain thought-laws (however
formulated), but which at the same time is inclined to psycho-
logistically interpret this conformity in the following manner:
—As this view holds 'thought-laws' to be just those *natural laws*
which express the peculiarity of our mind *as* one which thinks,
so the essence of the conformity which defines correct thinking
must lie in the *pure* efficacy of *these* 'thought-laws', unclouded by
any other sort of psychical influence (such as habit, inclination,
or tradition).

We will mention here only one of the dubious implications
of this theory. Thought-laws as causal laws, in conformity with
which knowledge comes about, could only be given in the form
of probabilities. Accordingly, no assertion whatsoever could be

judged as correct with certainty; for probability in the basic norm of all rightness must mark all knowledge with the stamp: 'mere probability'. So here we are confronting the most extreme probabilism. Even the assertion that all knowledge is only probable would be only probably true; and this new assertion, in turn, is only probable; and so on *in infinitum*. Since each subsequent level of probability sinks somewhat below the previous one, we must be gravely solicitous about the worth of all knowledge. But we can hope to be so fortunate that the degrees of probability in this infinite series will have the character of those in Cantor's 'basic series', so that the ultimate, limiting value for the probability of the knowledge to be appraised is always a real (*reelle*), absolute number greater than zero. Of course all of these disadvantages are avoided by regarding the thought-laws as insightfully given. But then, how are we supposed to have *insight* into *causal* laws?

And, even assuming that this difficulty did not exist, we could yet ask: Where in the world has it been *shown* that out of the pure efficacy of these alleged laws (or of whatever others) correct acts of thought arise? Where are the genetic analyses which justify our explaining the total phenomena of thought by means of two classes of natural laws: (1) the class of those laws which exclusively determine the process of such causation as lies at the root of *logical* thinking, and (2) the class of those laws which determine the causation at the root of *illogical* thinking—a causation which involves, along with other elements, the causes of logical thinking? Is the assessment of thinking by means of the laws of logic perhaps equivalent to the proof of its causal origin in conformity with those laws *as* natural laws?

At this point it appears that some seductive confusions have smoothed the way into the errors of Psychologism. In the first place, the laws of logic are confused with the judgments (acts of judgment) in which they may be known. Thus, the *laws* as 'judgment contents' are confused with the *judgments themselves*. The latter are real (*reale*) events which have their causes and effects. Specifically, judgments with a law as content frequently act as *thought-motives* which determine the course of our experience of thinking to proceed in conformity with what that content, the law of thought, prescribes. In such cases the real arrangement and connection of our experience of thinking is adequate to what is thought of in general in that act of law-knowledge which dominates the experience of thinking in question. I.e., such cases are concrete singular cases of the general laws. But if the law is confused with that judgment which is the knowing of the law—if, thus, the ideal is confused with the real—then the law appears as a force determining our thought process. It is, then, intelligible how easily a second confusion follows upon this first, namely, that between the *law as a term in a causal relation* and the *law as a principle of causation*. From another quarter, we are familiar with the myth that natural events are governed by the power of natural law—as if principles of causal connection could, in turn, themselves meaningfully function as causes, and so as terms in precisely the same type of connection. The grave confusion of such essentially different things was obviously favored in the case of our concern by the confusion between law and knowledge of the law, which had already been committed previously. The laws of logic appeared as being already present in thought as active agents. They causally regulate the course of thinking, it was supposed. Thus, they are the causal laws of thinking, and they express how, in consequence of *our* mind's nature, we must think. They essentially characterize the human mind insofar as it is a *thinking* mind, in the full sense. If occasionally we think otherwise than as these laws require, in the authentic sense we are not then 'thinking' at all. We then do not judge as the natural laws of thinking (or as the *character of our mind as* a thinking mind) require; but rather we judge as other laws—and, indeed, these too are causal laws—determine. We follow the muddling influences of habit, emotion, and the like.

Of course other motives also could have urged one to take this same view of the matter. The empirical fact that the investigator who is moderately competent in a certain sphere, e.g., the scientific, usually is logically correct in his judgments concerning its domain, appears to require, as its natural explanation, that the logical laws according to which the correctness of thinking is measured at the same time determine, in the manner of a causal law, the process of the respective thinking, whereas the sporadic deviations from the norm are easily accounted for in terms of those muddling influences from other psychological sources.

The following reflection suffices to show this wrong. Let us imagine an ideal man in whom *all* thinking proceeds as the laws of logic require. Of course the fact that it does so proceed has its explanatory ground in certain psychological laws which, in a certain manner, govern the course of psychic experiences in this creature, from certain initial 'collocations' on. I now ask: Would these natural laws and those logical laws be identical, given the condition assumed? The answer obviously must be negative. Causal laws according to which thinking must proceed in order to be justified by the ideal norms of logic, and these very norms themselves—here we have *two* things, not one. That there should be a creature so constituted, that it would not make contradictory judgments in a single context of thought, or that it can bring off no inference which offends against the moods of the syl-logism—this certainly does not mean that the principle of con-tradiction, the *modus Barbara*, and the like, are natural laws capable of explaining such a constitution. The example of the adding-machine makes the difference quite clear. The order and connection of the numbers which are inscribed by the machine are governed by natural laws in a way required by the meanings of arithmetical propositions. But in order to give a physical explanation of the machine's procedure, no one will invoke arithmetical laws instead of mechanical laws. The machine certainly does not think. It understands neither itself nor the significance of what it does. But, except for that one point, could not *our* 'thought machine' work in a way quite similar to the adding-machine, with the further exception that the real (*reale*) process of thinking can be recognized as correct only by means of insight into logical laws, which insight stands forth in a further act of thought? This further act of thought could be the work of the same 'thought machine', just as well as it could be the work of another one; but *evaluation* in terms of ideals and causal *explanation* always remain distinct. One also should not forget those 'initial collocations', which are indispensible for causal explanation, but which are irrelevant to evaluation in terms of ideals.

The psychologistic logicians misapprehend the essential and eternally irreconcilable distinction between ideal laws and real laws, between normative regulation and causal regulation, between logical and real (*realen*) necessity, between logical ground and real ground. In virtue of no conceivable graduated sequence can communion be established between the ideal and the real. It is indicative of the low state of pure-logical insight in our time, when an investigator of Sigwart's rank, precisely by reference to the fiction of an intellectually *ideal* creature such as was mentioned above, believes he may assume that, for such a creature, "logical necessity would also be real necessity, producing actual thinking," or when he uses the concept of thought-constraint to elucidate the concept of 'logical ground'. It indicates the same when a Wundt sees in the principle of Sufficient Reason "the fundamental law of the dependence of our acts of thought upon each other," and so forth. That what we have in these cases are actually fundamental logical errors, the course of subsequent investigations will, hopefully, bring to full certainty, even for those who are prejudiced on the matter.

Section 23. A Third Result or Implication of Psychologism, and Its Refutation

Third, did the source of our knowledge of logical laws lie in psychological *facts*—were, for example, logical laws normative applications of psychological *facts*, as our adversaries teach— then those laws would themselves have to have a psychological content. And, indeed, they would have to have it in two senses: They would have to be laws of psychic events, and, at the same time, would have to presuppose or involve the existence of psychic events. Now, that they are such can be proven false. No logical law implies a 'matter of fact', not even the existence of representations or judgments or other sorts of knowledge-phenomena. No logical law is—in its authentic sense—a law of the factualities of the psychic life. Thus, such a law is a law neither of representations (i.e., experiences of representing), nor of judgments (i.e., experiences of judging), nor of other sorts of psychic experiences.

Most psychologistic logicians stand too much under the influence of their general prejudice to think of verifying it by reference to the laws of logic lying right in front of them. If, for general reasons, these laws *must* be psychological, why bother with showing in detail that they really are such? It is not considered that a consistent Psychologism would be forced to interpret the laws of logic in a way foreign to their true sense from beginning to end. It is overlooked that those laws, naturally understood, do not presuppose, in their proof nor in their content, anything psychical (anything, thus, from the factualities of the mental life) ; and that, in any case, they do so no more than do the laws of pure mathematics.

Were Psychologism on the right track, then throughout the theory of inference only rules of the following sort could be expected: "Experience teaches that under circumstances C a conclusion of the form S, having the character of an apodictically necessary consequent, connects up with premises of the form P." So in order to infer 'correctly', i.e., in order to get by inferring to judgments having the character just indicated, one must proceed accordingly, and take care to realize the circumstances C, together with the respective premises. Psychical facts appear here as what is governed, and with one stroke the existence of such facts is both presupposed in the proof of the rules and is included in their content. But not a single law of inference is of this sort. What, for example, does the *modus Barbara* say? Only this: "It is true for any class terms A, B and C in general, that, if all A's are B's and all B's and C's, then all A's are C's." Again, *modus ponens,* when fully expressed, says: "For any propositions *A* and *B,* the law holds that if *A* is true, and *if A then B* is true, then *B* also is true." These and all similar laws are just as little psychological as they are empirical. Certainly in the traditional logic they are formulated with a view to the forming of judgmental activities. But is the existence of a single actual judgment, or of any other sort of psychic phenomenon, asserted *in* them? If anyone is of the opinion that it is, then we require of them a proof. What is asserted in a proposition must admit of derivation from that proposition by a valid mode of inference. But where are the forms of inference which permit the derivation of a fact from a pure law?

One cannot meet the above by replying that the talk of logical laws could never have occurred if we had never had representations and judgments in actual experience, and if we had not obtained the fundamental logical concepts involved in logical laws from these experiences by abstraction. Nor may it be said that in every act of understanding or assertion *of* these laws the existence of representations and judgments is implicit, and hence is, in turn, deducible therefrom. For it scarcely need be said that the consequence here is drawn, not from the logical law, but from the understanding and assertion of the law; and that the very same consequence would be derivable from any assertion whatever. Further, psychological presuppositions or ingredients of the *assertion* of a law must not be confused with the logical moments (*Momenten*) of its *content.*

'Empirical laws' have, *eo ipso,* a factual content. As 'laws' which are not genuine laws, they only assert, roughly expressed, that in the course of experience certain co-existences and successions customarily turn up in certain circumstances, or that they are to be expected with greater or less probability, depending upon the circumstances. Therewith it is said that such circumstances, and such co-existences or successions, *do in fact occur.* But even the rigorous laws of empirical science are not without factual content. They are not merely laws *about* facts. They also *imply* the *existence* of facts.

Yet greater precision is required on this point. *Exact* laws, in their normal formulation, certainly do present the character of *pure* laws. They contain no existential content at all. But when we consider the proofs out of which they draw scientific justification, it immediately becomes clear that they cannot be justified *as* the pure law which their normal formulation makes them out to be. The law of gravitation as enunciated by astronomy is not really the one which is proven. What is proven is, rather, only a proposition of this form:—According to the state of our present knowledge, there is a theoretically founded probability of the highest value that Newton's principle holds true for the range of experience attainable by presently available means—or, in general, that there holds true of that range one from the infinite multitude of mathematically conceivable laws which can differ from Newton's law only within the limits of unavoidable observational error. *This* truth is laden with factual content. It itself is, therefore, nothing less than it is a law in the genuine sense of the word "law." Also, it obviously includes several concepts of vague delimitation.

And thus all laws in the exact sciences of fact are indeed genuine laws; but, considered epistemologically, they are only idealizing fictions—albeit fictions *cum fundamento in re*. They fulfill the function of making possible theoretical sciences as ideals closely adequated to reality; and thus, the function of realizing the highest theoretical goal of all scientific investigation of fact—the ideal of explanatory theory, of unity issuing from law—insofar as the insurpassable limits of human knowledge allow. In place of absolute knowledge, which is denied to us, we first judiciously lift from the domain of empirical singulars and generalities those, so to speak, apodictic probabilities in which is included all attainable knowledge (*Wissen*) of reality. These we then reduce to certain exact propositions (*Gedanken*) which have the genuine character of law. Thus we succeed in constructing formally perfect systems of explanatory theories. But these systems (e.g. theoretical mechanics, theoretical acoustics, theoretical optics, theoretical astronomy, and so on) can in fact only be regarded as ideal possibilities *cum fundamento in re*, which do not rule out infinitely many other possibilities, but rather include them within determinate limits. Yet all this is of no further concern for us here, and still less is the discussion of the *practical* functions of these ideal theories in knowledge: *viz.*, their role in our successful prediction of future, and reconstruction of past, facts, and their role in the practical subjugation of nature. Therefore, we return to our proper subject.

If, as was just shown, genuine lawfulness remains a mere ideal in the area of factual knowledge, by contrast, it is realized in the area of 'purely conceptual' knowledge. In this latter sphere belongs our laws of pure logic, as also the laws of *Mathesis Pura*. The 'origin' or, more exactly stated, the justifying proof of such laws is not drawn from induction. Thus, they also do not have any of that existential content which infects all probabilities as such, even the highest and most valuable. What they assert holds good fully and completely. *They themselves*, in their absolute exactitude, are insightfully (*einsichtig*) proven, and not, in their stead, certain probability statements with obviously vague components. The particular law appears, not as one of innumerable theoretical possibilities of a certain domain factually delimited. It is the one and only truth which excludes any other possibility, and which, in content and in proof, keeps itself pure, as an *insightfully* known law, from all facts.

In the light of all this one sees how intimately the two halves of this third result or implication of Psychologism are related— *viz.* (i) that logical laws not merely involve existential assertions about psychic facts, but (ii) that they must also be laws *of* such facts. The refutation of the first half came first. Now that of the other half appears to be included in that of the first, according to the following argument: As any law which derives from experience and induction over singular facts is a law *of* facts, so, conversely, any law *of* facts is a law derived from experience and induction. Consequently, from such a law, as has been shown, assertions with existential content are inseparable.

Obviously we must not here include among laws of fact those general assertions which apply purely conceptual propositions to facts—i.e., propositions which present themselves, on the basis of pure concepts, as expressing universally binding relations. If 3 is greater than 2, then 3 books on this table are more than 2 books on that cupboard; and so for any arbitrary things in general. But pure number theorems say nothing about things. Rather they tell us about numbers—that *the* number 3 is greater than *the* number 2, for example. And they can be applied, not merely to individuals, but rather to 'general' objects as well, e.g., to species of color and tone, to types of geometrical figures, and so on.

If all of this be admitted, then the possibility of logical laws being (essentially) laws of psychic activities or products is naturally excluded.

Section 24. Continuation

Many will perhaps try to dodge our conclusion by the reply: —Not every fact-law is derived from experience and induction. Rather, a distinction must be made here. All knowledge of law is based on experience, but all does not arise from experience *via* induction, i.e., *via* that well known logical process which leads from singular facts, or from empirical generalities of a lower level, to general laws. Thus, specifically, the laws of logic are empirical, but not inductive, laws. In the *experience* of the psychical we abstract the basic concepts of logic, along with the purely conceptual relations given with them. What we find in front of us as a single case we immediately know to hold true in general, because it is grounded in the abstracted contents alone. Thus does experience bestow upon us a direct awareness of the lawfulness of our mind. And as we do not here require induction, the result we obtain also is not infected with the deficiencies of induction. Our result does not have the mere character of a probability. Rather it has that of apodictic certainty. It is not of vague, but is rather of exact, delimitation. Also, it in no way involves assertions of existence.

This reply, however, is not sufficient to turn back our conclusion. No one is questioning the fact that *knowledge* of the laws of logic, as a psychical act, presupposes experience of particulars, and that it has its foundation in concrete intuition. But *psychological* 'presuppositions' and 'foundations' of the *knowledge of law* must not be confused with *logical* presuppositions, grounds, or premisses of the *law*. Accordingly, psychological dependence (e.g., in the origination of law knowledge) must not be confused with logical proof and justification. The latter insightfully follows the objective relation of ground to consequence, whereas the former has reference to psychical connections of co-existence and succession. No one can seriously contend that the concrete, singular case (which, perhaps, is present to one, and on the 'ground' of which insight into the law occurs) has the function of logical ground, of premiss—as if the universality of the law were inferred from the existence of the singular. The intuitive apprehension of the law may psychologically require two steps: the viewing of the intuitive singulars, and then the related nomological insight (*gesetzliche Einsicht*). Logically, however, there is only one step involved. The content of the nomological insight is *not* logically derived from the singular.

All knowledge 'begins with experience', but it does not therefore 'arise out of' experience. What we maintain is that any law of facts arises *out of* experience, which simply means that such a law is to be proven only through induction over singulars. If there are insightfully known laws, then they, therefore, cannot be (direct) laws of facts. I do not mean to say that it is a flat absurdity to hold a law of fact to be directly knowable with insight. I just deny that it ever happens. Wherever such has been thought to happen, it has turned out, *either* that genuine laws of fact, i.e., laws of co-existence and succession, were confused with ideal laws, to which reference to the temporally determined is essentially foreign, *or* that the warm persuasion borne by familiar empirical generalities was taken for the insightfulness which we experience solely in the domain of the purely conceptual.

If even an argument of this sort cannot be decisive, it still can increase the force of other arguments. And we yet have one such other argument to add here.

It would be hard for anyone to deny that all of the laws of pure logic are of one and the same character. If we can, then, show of some such laws that it is impossible to conceive of them as laws of facts, the same must hold true of all of them. Now among those laws are found some which refer to truths in general, and in which, thus, truths are the governed 'objects'. For example, it holds true that, with reference to any truth *A*, its contradictory is no truth. For any pair of truths, *A* and *B*, it holds true that the conjunction of them and the disjunction of them are truths. For any three truths *A*, *B* and *C*, if they are so related that *A* is a ground of *B* and *B* is a ground of *C*, then *A* also is a ground of *C*. More such cases could be given. But it is absurd to designate laws which hold of truths as such as laws of facts. No truth is a fact, i.e., something temporally determined. Certainly a truth can *mean* that a thing exists, that a state of affairs obtains, that a change occurs, and so on. But the truth itself is something beyond all temporality. I.e., it makes no sense to ascribe temporal being, coming to be, or passing away to it. This is most clearly so in the case of the truths which themselves are laws of truth. As laws of reality (*Realgesetze*), they would be rules of the coexistence and succession of facts—more specifically, of 'truths'. And among these 'facts' which they regulate, they themselves—as truths—would have to belong. Here we would have a law prescribing the coming and going of certain facts called 'truths'; and among those facts there now would have to be—as one fact among all the others—that law itself! The law would come into being and pass out of being in accordance with itself. An obvious absurdity! It would also be absurd to try to interpret the law of truth as a law of *co-existence*—as a temporal particular and yet as a general rule normative for each and every temporal existent. Such absurdities are unavoidable when one does not take into account, or does not rightly understand, the fundamental distinction between real and ideal objects, and the corresponding distinction between real and ideal laws. We shall again and again see how this distinction is decisive for the controversy between psychologistic logic and pure logic.

CHAPTER SEVEN

Psychologism As Skeptical Relativism

Section 34. The Concept of Relativism and Its Specifications

For the purposes of a critique of psychologism, we still have to discuss the concept (also present in the metaphysical theory just discussed) of *subjectivism* or *relativism*. A more primitive concept of relativism is marked off by the Protagorian formula, "Man is the measure of all things," provided it is interpreted to mean that the individual man is the measure of all truth:—That truth is for each person what appears to *him* to be true. For one man *this,* for another just the opposite, is true, if it appears to him to be so. We could just as well here use the formula, "All truth (and knowledge) is relative—relative to whichever *subject* happens to be making a judgment." If, on the other hand, we take as the term of the relation—instead of the individual subject—the *species* of the being which happens to be judging, then we get a new form of relativism. The measure of all human truth is, thus, man *as such.* Any judgment rooted in the specific character of man, in the laws which constitute that character, is true—for us *men.* Insofar as such a judgment belongs to the general form of human subjectivity (of human 'consciousness in general'), one also speaks here of 'subjectivism' (of the subject as the ultimate knowledge-source, and the like). It is better, however, to use the term "relativism," and to then distinguish between individual and specific relativism. The delimiting reference to the human species then determines the latter as *Anthropologism.* Now we turn to the critique, the most careful execution of which is bidden by our interests.

Section 35. Critique of Individual Relativism

Individual scepticism is such an explicit and—I would almost like to say—impudent or 'fresh' scepticism that, if it has *ever* been seriously advocated, it has certainly not been so in modern times. The theory is already refuted by being formulated —but only for those who have insight into the objectivity of the logical. The subjectivist, as the express sceptic in general, cannot be convinced, if he lacks the disposition to see that axioms such as the principle of contradiction are ground in the mere nature (*Sinn*) of truth, and that, in conformance with them, the talk of a subjective truth, which for one is such and such, and for another is the opposite, must be regarded as just nonsense. The subjectivist also will not be convinced by the usual objection that in the act of asserting his position he raises the claim of being convincing to others, and that he thus presupposes that objectivity of truth which he *in thesi* denies. He, of course, will answer:—In my theory I express my viewpoint, which is true for me but need be true for no one else. Even the fact of his own subjective opining he will maintain to be true only for his own ego, but not in itself. But the question is not about the possibility of personally convincing the subjectivist, and bringing him to a confession of his errors. Rather it is one of the possibility of an objectively valid refutation of him. But refutation presupposes, as its lever, certain insightful and, hence, universally valid convictions. As such convictions, those trivial insights upon which all scepticism must run aground serve us normally constituted persons, insofar as it is by them that we know its doctrinal assertions to be absurd in the strongest and most literal sense:—The content of such assertions denies that which belong to the nature (*Sinn*) or content of every assertion whatsoever, and which, consequently, is obviously separable from no assertion.

Section 36. Critique of Specific Relativism and, in particular, of Anthropologism

It may be possible to doubt whether subjectivism has ever been seriously maintained. But modern and contemporary philosophy is inclined toward *specific* relativism, and more precisely, toward Anthropologism, to such a degree that only rarely does one find a thinker who has been able to avoid the errors of this theory. And yet, it too is a sceptical theory, in the sense (*Bedeutung*) spelled out above. Thus, it is infected with as great absurdities as one can conceive of in a theory. Also in it we find, only slightly veiled, an evident contradiction between the sense (*Sinn*) of its thesis and what is obviously inseparable from all theses as such. This is not hard to show in detail.

1. Specific relativism asserts that, for any species of judging being, that is true which, in conformity with the being's constitution and thought-laws, *has* to be regarded as true. Now this view is self-contradictory. For its meaning is that the same judgment-content (proposition) can be true for one being—specifically, a subject of the species *homo*—and false for another being—a subject of a species constituted differently than man. But the same judgment-content cannot be both true and false. This follows from the mere meaning of the words "true" and "false." If the relativist uses these words in their proper sense, then his thesis states what is contrary to its own meaning or nature.

It is clearly vain to try to dodge this point by saying: "The wording of the principle of contradiction here invoked, through which the meanings of the words 'true' and 'false' are displayed, is incomplete. What that principle is about is, precisely, the humanly true and the humanly false." Similarly, in fact, ordinary scepticism also could say: "To merely speak of the true and the false is imprecise. What is meant is that which is 'true or false for the individual subject'." And, of course, the answer to this is:—An evidently valid law cannot mean what is patently self-contradictory; and, in fact, this talk of truth *for* this person or that is self-contradictory. To hold open the possibility of the same judgment-content (we say, with dangerous looseness: 'the same judgment') being both true and false, depending upon who is judging, is an absurdity. Correspondingly, the answer to specific relativism will be:—'Truth for this or that species', e.g. for the human, is in the present context an absurdity. To be sure, the phrase can be used in a good sense; but then it means something totally different, namely, the range of truths which are accessible or knowable to men as such. What is true is absolutely true, is true 'in itself.' The truth is identically one, whether men or non-men, angels or gods, apprehend it in judgment. Of truth in this sense of an ideal unity, in contrast to the real multiplicity of races, individuals, and experiences, speak the laws of logic. And so speak we all, unless we perhaps share the relativistic delusion.

2. In the light of the fact that what the principles of contradiction and excluded middle assert is grounded in the mere senses of the` words "true" and "false," our objection can also be formulated in this manner:—If the relativist says that there could also be beings which are not bound by these principles (and it is easily seen that this assertion is equivalent to the relativist thesis formulated above), he means *either* that there could turn up in the judgings of these beings propositions and truths which do not conform with these principles, *or* that the process of judging as it occurs in these beings is not *psychologically* governed by these principles. As to the latter alternative, there is nothing at all odd about it; for we ourselves are such beings. (Recall here our objections—in chapters 5 and 6 above—to the psychologistic interpretation of the logical laws.) But as to the first alternative, we simply reply: *Either* those beings understand the words "true" and "false" in our sense, in which case

it is not intelligible to say that these principles do not hold true. (They in fact inhere in the mere sense of those words—as we understand it, of course. We would not 'call' anything true or false which was contrary to those principles.) *Or,* alternatively, those beings use the words "true" and "false" in a different sense; and then we have only a verbal disagreement. If, for example, they call 'trees' what we call 'propositions', then in that usage the assertions in which we formulate the logical principles will, of course, not be true. But then they *also* even lose the sense in which we assert them. So relativism winds up by totally changing the sense of the word "truth," but all the while claiming to speak of truth in the sense which is fixed by the logical principles, and which we all have exclusively in mind when we speak of truth. In one sense there is only one truth. But, of course, in the equivocal sense there are as many 'truths' as there are equivocations which one may wish to create.

3. Now the constitution of our species is a fact. From facts only other facts can be derived. To ground truth in a relation to the constitution of the species means also to give it the character of a fact. But that is absurd. Every fact is individual and, therefore, is temporally determined. As to truth, temporal determination makes sense only in reference to a fact posited by it (provided that it is a factual truth), but not in reference to the truth itself. It is absurd to think of truths as causes and effects. We have already discussed that. Should one wish to argue that, nonetheless, as with every judgment, so also the true ones arise out of the constitution of the being judging, and arise on the basis of the appropriate natural laws, we would reply:—Do not confuse the judgment as judgment-content, i.e., as ideal unity, with the particular, real (*realen*) *act* of judgment. The former is meant where we speak of *the* judgment 2×2 *is 4,* which is the same whoever makes it. Also, do not confuse the true judgment, as a *correct* act of judgment in conformity with truth, with the *truth* of this judgment or with the true judgment-content. My act of judging that 2×2 *is 4* is certainly causally determined, but the truth, 2×2 *is 4,* is not.

4. If, in the sense stated by Anthropologism, all truth had its exclusive source in the common, human constitution, then, *if no such constitution existed, there also would be no truth.* Now the thesis of the hypothetical assertion is inconsistent. For the proposition, *no truth exists,* is equivalent as to its sense with the proposition, *the truth that no truth exists exists.* The inconsistency of the thesis, now, requires the inconsistency of the hypothesis. But, as the denial of a true factual proposition, the hypothesis could indeed be false, but it could never be inconsistent. It has in fact not as yet occurred to anyone to reject as *absurd* the well-known theories of Geology and Physics which posit a temporal beginning and end to the human race. So the reproach of being inconsistent must fall upon the hypothetical assertion as a whole, since to an antecedent which is, in its very meaning, consistent or 'logically possible' it subjoins a consequent which is inconsistent or 'logically impossible'. That means that the very same reproach falls upon Anthropologism, and carries over, of course, *mutatis mutandis* to the more general form of Relativism.

5. According to Relativism, on the basis of the constitution of a species, the following 'truth', which would be true for that species, *could* arise: *The constitution of that species does not exist.* Should we, therefore, say that it does not exist in reality, or say that it exists, but only for us men? If, now, all men, and all species of judging beings except precisely the one presupposed, pass away, what then? Obviously we are afloat in absurdities. The idea that the non-existence of a specific constitution *could* have its ground in that very same constitution is a clear contradiction. The truth-grounding, and hence existing, constitution is to ground, along side other truths, the truth of its own non-existence!—The absurdity is not much less if we substitute "existence" for "nonexistence," and, correspondingly, take as our subject the human species, in place of our imagined species, which yet must be a possible species from the relativistic point of view. The clear contradiction just now elicited then dis-

appears, to be sure; but the other inconsistency, interwoven with that contradiction, does not disappear. The relativity of truth means that what we call truth is dependent upon the constitution of the species *homo*, and upon the laws which govern that species. This dependency is intended as, and can only be understood as, causal dependency. Therefore, the truth that this constitution and these laws exist would have to draw its real (*reale*) explanation out of the fact that they exist, in that the principles according to which the explanation would proceed would be identical with precisely these laws—nothing short of an absurdity! The constitution would be *causa sui*, upon the basis of laws which would cause themselves, upon the basis of themselves, etc. etc. *ad infinitum*.

6. The relativity of truth entails the relativity of the world's existence. For the world is only the total, objective unity which corresponds to, and is inseparable from, the ideal system of all factual truth. One cannot subjectivize the truth and leave its object (which *is* only in, and in virtue of, the truth) absolute or existing in itself. There would, therefore, be no world 'in itself', if the relativistic theory were true, but only a world for us, or for some other species of being. Now that will suit many people just fine; but it may well become dubious when we consider that the ego and the contents of its consciousness are also a part of the world. Even the "I am" and the "I experience such and such" would be false eventually:—namely, given that I were so constituted that I would *have* to deny these propositions in virtue of the constitution of my species. And there would not merely be no world *for* this or that species, but rather there would be no world at all, if no species of judging being were so fortunately constituted as to *have* to acknowledge a world (and that species itself, therein). But if we restrict ourselves to the sole species of which we actually have knowledge, the animal species, we find that a change in their world conditioned a change in the species constitution; so that, in conformity with generally accepted theory, the animal species are supposed to be evolutionary products of the world. So we would have a nice game going here:

From the world man develops, and from man comes the world; God creates man, and man creates God.

The essential point of this objection is: Relativism is also in obvious contradiction with the Evidenz of immediate, intuitional fact (*Daseins*), i.e. with the Evidenz of 'inner perception' in the legitimate, but then also indispensible, sense of the phrase. The Evidenz of judgments based upon intuition are justifiably contested so far as their intention reaches out beyond the content of the actual datum of consciousness. But judgments truly are evident where their intention is oriented upon that content itself, and in it, just as it is, finds fulfillment (*Erfullung*). This is not called into question by the vagueness of all such judgments (consider only the vagueness of temporal, and even local, determinations, which cannot be suppressed in any immediate judgment of intuition).

Section 37. General Remark. The Concept of Relativism in the Broad Sense

Our two forms of Relativism are specifications of Relativism in a certain widest sense of the word, as a theory that would somehow deduce the principles of pure logic from facts. Facts are 'contingent'. They could just as well also not be. They could be otherwise than they are. Hence, other facts, other laws of logic. These other laws would also be contingent, since they would be only *in relation to* the facts which are their ground. Against this, I do not aim merely to point to the apodictic Evidenz of the laws of logic, and to the other points made out in earlier chapters. Rather I want to make a different point, which at this juncture is more significant. I understand by "pure laws of logic," as you will gather from what has been said up to now, all ideal laws which are grounded solely in the sense (in the 'nature', the 'content') of the concepts *truth, proposition, object, property, relation, connection* (Verknupfung), *law, fact, etc.* Expressed more generally, such laws are grounded solely in the sense of the concepts which belong to the legitimate estate of *every* science, and so belong because they are the categories of the building blocks out of which science as such, according to its concept, is constituted. Laws of this sort must be offended by no theoretical assertion, no proof or theory. Not because such an assertion, proof or theory otherwise would be false—they would be this even by contradicting any arbitrary truth—but rather because they would then be self-contradictory. For example, an assertion whose content conflicts with principles which are grounded in the *nature* (*Sinne*) of truth as such 'cancels itself out'. For to assert is to state that such and such a content is true. Again, a proof which in its content conflicts with the principles which are grounded in the *nature* of the relation between ground and consequent cancels itself out. For to prove is, again, to state that such and such a relation of ground and consequent obtains. Etc. That an assertion 'cancels itself out', that it is 'logically absurd', that means:—Its peculiar content (sense, signification) contradicts that which the signification *categories* relevant to it universally require, or those truths which are universally grounded in the general types of significations which it involves. It is now clear that, in this pregnant sense, any theory is logically absurd which deduces the principles of logic from any sort of fact. Such a theory is in conflict with the general sense of the concepts, *logical principle* and *fact*. Or, to speak more precisely and more generally:—It is in conflict with the sense of the concepts, *truth grounded in the mere content of concepts*, and *truth about individual existence* (Dasein). It is also easily seen that the objections against the relativistic theories discussed above bear, in the main part, also upon Relativism in the most general sense discussed here.

Section 38. That Psychologism in All of Its Forms Is a Relativism

In combatting Relativism we have, of course, had Psychologism in mind. In fact, Psychologism, in all of its variations and individual forms, is nothing other than Relativism; but this is not always recognized and expressly admitted. And it is Psychologism all the same, whether it supports itself upon a 'transcendental psychology' and, as formal idealism, believes itself able to save the objectivity of knowledge, or whether it supports itself upon empirical psychology and assumes Relativism as an unavoidable fact.

Any theory which either, in the *Empiricist* style, conceives of the laws of pure logic as laws of empirical psychology, or, in the style of the *Apriorist,* more or less mythically reduces them to certain 'primitive forms' or 'modes of functioning' of the (human) understanding (to 'consciousness in general' as (human 'generic reason', to the 'psycho-physical constitution' of man, to the *'intellectus ipse'* which, as an innate (and generically human) disposition, precedes actual thinking and all experience, and to the like things)—any such theory is *eo ipso* relativistic, and, indeed, is of a kind with specific Relativism. All objections which we have raised against specific Relativism must also strike such a theory. But obviously, in order for this to be so, the somewhat scintillating shibboleths of *Apriorism,* e.g., "understanding," "reason," "consciousness," must be taken in that natural sense which confers upon them an essential relation to the human species. It has been the curse of the theories here examined that they have given to these shibboleths, now such and such a real (*reale*) signification, and now an ideal signification, and that they have thus concocted an intolerable jumble of partly true, and partly false propositions. In any case, we may also count the *aprioristic* theories among the Relativist theories, in so far as they do give space to relativistic motives. Certainly, when one of the Kantians sets aside a few logical axioms as principles of the 'analytic judgment', he also restricts his Relativism (i.e. to the domains of mathematics and knowledge of nature). But he does not thereby escape the sceptical absurdities. He still continues, in the narrower range, to derive truth from the generically human, and, thus, to derive the ideal from the real: more specifically, the necessity of law from the contingency of facts.

Review of Husserl's

PHILOSOPHIE DER ARITHMETIK

GOTTLOB FREGE

I. ON IMAGINATION AND THOUGHT

. . . Thus we have a blurring of the distinction between image and concept, between imagination and thought. Everything is transformed into something subjective. But just because the boundary between the subjective and the objective is obliterated, what is subjective acquires in its turn the appearance of objectivity. People speak, e.g., of such-and-such a mental image, as if it could be in public view, detached from the imagining mind. And yet a man never has somebody else's mental image, but only his own; and nobody even knows how far his image (say) of red agrees with somebody else's; for the peculiar character of the image I connect with the word 'red' is something that I cannot convey. In order to be able to compare one man's mental images with another's, we should have to have united them into one and the same state of consciousness, and to be sure that they had not altered in the process of transference. It is quite otherwise for thoughts; one and the same thought can be grasped by many men. The constituents of the thought, and *a fortiori* things themselves, must be distinguished from the images that accompany in some mind the act of grasping the thought—images that each man forms of things.

Originally published in *Zeitschrift für Philosophie und Philosophische Kritik*, 103 (1894), 22–41. Reprinted from M. Black and P. Geach, translated in *The Philosophical Writings of Gottlob Frege* (BG) (Oxford: B. Blackwell, 1960), pp. 79, 84–85, by permission of the publisher.

II. ON DEFINITIONS

. . . it is easy to understand the author's way of judging the value of definitions. An example from elementary geometry may illustrate it. The usual definition given there is: 'A right angle is an angle equal to its adjacent angle.' The author would probably comment on this as follows: 'The idea (*Vorstellung*) of a right angle is a simple one; so it is a wholly mistaken procedure to try to define it. Relation to another, adjacent, angle is in no way involved in our idea of a right angle.

. . . .

VI. ON ABSTRACTION

The author himself finds a difficulty about the abstraction that provides the general concept of the collective. He says: 'The peculiarities of the individual contents that are collected . . . must be completely abstracted from, but at the same time their connexion must be maintained. This seems to involve a difficulty if not a psychological impossibility. If we take the abstraction seriously, then the individual contents vanish, and so, naturally, does their collective unity, instead of remaining behind as a conceptual extract. The solution is obvious. To abstract from something simply means: not to attend to it specially.'

The kernel of this explanation is obviously to be found in the word 'specially'. Inattention is a very strong lye; it must be applied at not too great a concentration, so that everything does not dissolve, and likewise not too dilute, so that it effects a sufficient change in the things. Thus it is a question of getting the right degree of dilution; this is difficult to manage, and I at any rate have never succeeded.

. . . .

[Detaching our attention] is particularly effective. We attend less to a property, and it disappears. By making one characteristic after another disappear, we get more and more abstract concepts. . . . Inattention is a most efficacious logical faculty; presumably this accounts for the absentmindedness of professors. Suppose there are a black and a white cat sitting side by side before us. We stop attending to their colour, and they become colourless, but are still sitting side by side. We stop attending to their posture, and they are no longer sitting (though they have not assumed another posture), but each one is still in its place. We stop attending to position; they cease to have place, but still remain different. In this way, perhaps, we obtain from each one of them a general concept of Cat. By continued application of this procedure, we obtain from each object a more and more bloodless phantom. Finally we thus obtain from each object a *something* wholly deprived of content; but the *something* obtained from one object is different from the *something* obtained from another object—though it is not easy to say how. . . . On my view, bringing an object under a concept is just recognition of a relation that was there already; here, objects are essentially altered by abstraction, so that objects brought under one concept become more alike.

from FOUNDATIONS OF ARITHMETIC

GOTTLOB FREGE

In the enquiry that follows, I have kept to three fundamental principles:

always to separate sharply the psychological from the logical, the subjective from the objective;

never to ask for the meaning of a word in isolation, but only in the context of a proposition;

Reprinted from *Foundations of Arithmetic,* translated by J. L. Austin (Oxford: B. Blackwell, 1953), x^e, by permission of the publisher.

never to lose sight of the distinction between concept and object.

In compliance with the first principle, I have used the word "idea" always in the psychological sense, and have distinguished ideas from concepts and from objects. If the second principle is not observed, one is almost forced to take as the meanings of words mental pictures or acts of the individual mind, and so to offend against the first principle as well. As to the third point, it is a mere illusion to suppose that a concept can be made an object without altering it.

from THE THOUGHT

GOTTLOB FREGE

. . . Without wishing to give a definition, I call a thought something for which the question of truth arises. So I ascribe what is false to a thought just as much as what is true. So I can say: the thought is the sense of the sentence without wishing to say as well that the sense of every sentence is a thought. The thought, in itself immaterial, clothes itself in the material garment of a sentence and thereby becomes comprehensible to us. We say a sentence expresses a thought.

.   .   .   .

Even an unphilosophical person soon finds it necessary to recognize an inner world distinct from the outer world, a world of sense-impressions, of creations of his imagination, of sensations, of feelings and moods, a world of inclinations, wishes and decisions. For brevity I want to collect all these, with the exception of decisions, under the word 'idea'.

Reprinted from "The Thought," translated by Anthony and Marcelle Quinton, *Mind*, 65 (1956), pp. 289–311, with the permission of the translators and the editor of *Mind*, Gilbert Ryle.

Now do thoughts belong to this inner world? Are they ideas? They are obviously not decisions. How are ideas distinct from the things of the outer world? First:

Ideas cannot be seen or touched, cannot be smelled, nor tasted, nor heard.

I go for a walk with a companion. I see a green field, I have a visual impression of the green as well. I have it but I do not see it.

Secondly: ideas are had. One has sensations, feelings, moods, inclinations, wishes. An idea which someone has belongs to the content of his consciousness.

The field and the frogs in it, the sun which shines on them are there no matter whether I look at them or not, but the sense-impression I have of green exists only because of me, I am its bearer. It seems absurd to us that a pain, a mood, a wish should rove about the world without a bearer, independently. An experience is impossible without an experient. The inner world presupposes the person whose inner world it is.

Thirdly: ideas need a bearer. Things of the outer world are however independent.

My companion and I are convinced that we both see the same field; but each of us has a particular sense-impression of green. I notice a strawberry among the green strawberry leaves. My companion does not notice it, he is colour-blind. The colour-impression, which he receives from the strawberry, is not noticeably different from the one he receives from the leaf. Now does my companion see the green leaf as red, or does he see the red berry as green, or does he see both as of one colour with which I am not acquainted at all? These are unanswerable, indeed really nonsensical, questions. For when the word 'red' does not state a property of things but is supposed to characterize sense-impressions belonging to my consciousness, it is only applicable within the sphere of my consciousness. For it is impossible to compare my sense-impression with that of someone else. For that it would be necessary to bring together in one consciousness a sense-impression, belonging to one consciousness, with a sense-impression belonging to another consciousness. Now even if it were possible to make an idea disappear from one consciousness and, at the same time, to make an idea appear in another consciousness, the question whether it were the same idea in both would still remain unanswerable. It is so much of the essence of each of my ideas to be the content of my consciousness, that every idea of another person is, just as such, distinct from mine. But might it not be possible that my ideas, the entire content of my consciousness might be at the same time the content of a more embracing, perhaps divine, consciousness? Only if I were myself part of the divine consciousness. But then would they really be my ideas, would I be their bearer? This oversteps the limits of human understanding to such an extent that one must leave its possibility out of account. In any case it is impossible for us as men to compare another person's ideas with our own. I pick the strawberry, I hold it between my fingers. Now my companion sees it too, this very same strawberry; but each of us has his own idea. No other person has my idea but many people can see the same thing. No other person has my pain. Someone can have sympathy for me but still my pain always belongs to me and his sympathy to him. He does not have my pain and I do not have his sympathy.

Fourthly: every idea has only one bearer; no two men have the same idea.

For otherwise it would exist independently of this person and independently of that one. Is that lime-tree my idea? By using the expression 'that lime-tree' in this question I have really already anticipated the answer, for with this expression I want to refer to what I see and to what other people can also look at and touch. There are now two possibilities. If my intention is realized when I refer to something with the expression 'that lime-tree' then the thought expressed in the sentence 'that lime-tree is my idea' must obviously be negated. But if my intention is not realized, if I only think I see without really seeing, if on that account the designation 'that lime-tree' is empty, then I have gone astray into the sphere of fiction without knowing it or wanting to. In that case neither the content of the sentence 'that lime-tree is my idea' nor the content of the sentence 'that lime-tree is not my idea' is true, for in both cases I have a statement which lacks an object. So then one can only refuse to answer the question for the reason that the content of the sentence 'that lime-tree is my idea' is a piece of fiction. I have, naturally, got an idea then, but I am not referring to this with the words 'that lime-tree'. Now someone may really want to refer to one of his ideas with the words 'that lime-tree'. He would then be the bearer of that to which he wants to refer with those words, but then he would not see that lime-tree and no-one else would see it or be its bearer.

I now return to the question: is a thought an idea? If the thought I express in the Pythagorean theorem can be recognized by others just as much as by me then it does not belong to the content of my consciousness, I am not its bearer; yet I can, nevertheless, recognize it to be true. However, if it is not the same thought at all which is taken to be the content of the Pythagorean theorem by me and by another person, one should not really say 'the Pythagorean theorem' but 'my Pythagorean theorem', 'his Pythagorean theorem' and these would be different; for the sense belongs necessarily to the sentence. Then my thought can be the content of my consciousness and his thought the content of his. Could the sense of my Pythagorean theorem be true while that of his was false? I said that the word 'red' was applicable only in the sphere of my consciousness if it did not state a property of things but was supposed to characterize one of my sense-impressions. Therefore the words 'true' and 'false', as I understand them, could also be applicable only in the sphere of my consciousness, if they were not supposed to be concerned with something of which I was not the bearer, but were somehow appointed to characterize the content of my consciousness. Then truth would be restricted to the content of my consciousness and it would remain doubtful whether anything at all comparable occurred in the consciousnes of others.

If every thought requires a bearer, to the contents of whose consciousness it belongs, then it would be a thought of this bearer only and there would be no science common to many, on which many could work. But I, perhaps, have my science, namely, a whole of thought whose bearer I am and another person has his. Each of us occupies himself with the contents of his own consciousness. No contradiction between the two sciences would then be possible and it would really be idle to dispute about truth, as idle, indeed almost ludicrous, as it would be for two people to dispute whether a hundred-mark note were genuine, where each meant the one he himself had in his pocket and understood the word 'genuine' in his own particular sense. If someone takes thoughts to be ideas, what he then recognizes to be true is, on his own view, the content of his consciousness and does not properly concern other people at all. If he were to hear from me the opinion that a thought is not an idea he could not dispute it, for, indeed, it would not now concern him.

So the result seems to be: thoughts are neither things of the outer world nor ideas.

A third realm must be recognized. What belongs to this corresponds with ideas, in that it cannot be perceived by the senses, but with things, in that it needs no bearer to the contents of whose consciousness to belong. Thus the thought, for example, which we expressed in the Pythagorean theorem is timelessly true, true independently of whether anyone takes it to be true. It needs no bearer. It is not true for the first time when it is discovered, but is like a planet which, already before anyone has seen it, has been in interaction with other planets.[1]. . .

So, it seems to me, the matter becomes intelligible. If man could not think and could not take something of which he was not the bearer as the object of his thought he would have an inner world but no outer world. But may this not be based on a mistake? I am convinced that the idea I associate with the words 'my brother' corresponds to something that is not my idea and about which I can say something. But may I not be making a mistake about this? Such mistakes do happen. We then, against our will, lapse into fiction. Indeed! By the step with which I secure an environment for myself I expose myself to the risk of

[1] One sees a thing, one has an idea, one apprehends or thinks a thought. When one apprehends or thinks a thought one does not create it but only comes to stand in a certain relation, which is different from seeing a thing or having an idea, to what already existed beforehand.

error. And here I come up against a further distinction between my inner and outer worlds. I cannot doubt that I have a visual impression of green but it is not so certain that I see a lime-leaf. So, contrary to widespread views, we find certainty in the inner world while doubt never altogether leaves us in our excursions into the outer world. It is difficult in many cases, nevertheless, to distinguish probability from certainty here, so we can presume to judge about things in the outer world. And we must presume this even at the risk of error if we do not want to succumb to far greater dangers.

In consequence of these last considerations I lay down the following: not everything that can be the object of my under-standing is an idea. I, as a bearer of ideas, am not myself an idea. Nothing now stands in the way of recognizing other people to be bearers of ideas as I am myself. And, once given the possi-bility, the probability is very great, so great that it is in my opinion no longer distinguishable from certainty. Would there be a science of history otherwise? Would not every precept of duty, every law otherwise come to nothing? What would be left of religion? The natural sciences too could only be assessed as fables like astrology and alchemy. Thus the reflections I have carried on, assuming that there are other people besides myself who can take the same thing as the object of their consideration, of their thinking, remain essentially unimpaired in force.

Not everything is an idea. Thus I can also recognize the thought, which other people can grasp just as much as I, as being independent of me. I can recognize a science in which many people can be engaged in research. We are not bearers of thoughts as we are bearers of our ideas. We do not have a thought as we have, say, a sense-impression, but we also do not see a thought as we see, say, a star. So it is advisable to choose a special expression and the word 'apprehend' offers itself for the purpose. A particular mental capacity, the power of thought, must correspond to the apprehension[2] of thought. In thinking

2 The expression 'apprehend' is as metaphorical as 'content of con-sciousness.' The nature of language does not permit anything else. What I hold in my hand can certainly be regarded as the content of my hand

we do not produce thoughts but we apprehend them. For what I have called thought stands in the closest relation to truth. What I recognize as true I judge to be true quite independently of my recognition of its truth and of my thinking about it. That someone thinks it has nothing to do with the truth of a thought. 'Facts, facts, facts' cries the scientist if he wants to emphasize the necessity of a firm foundation for science. What is a fact? A fact is a thought that is true. But the scientist will surely not recognize something which depends on men's varying states of mind to be the firm foundation of science. The work of science does not consist of creation but of the discovery of true thoughts. The astronomer can apply a mathematical truth in the investigation of long past events which took place when on earth at least no one had yet recognized that truth. He can do this because the truth of a thought is timeless. Therefore that truth cannot have come into existence with its discovery.

Not everything is an idea. Otherwise psychology would contain all the sciences within it or at least it would be the highest judge over all the sciences. Otherwise psychology would rule over logic and mathematics. But nothing would be a greater misunderstanding of mathematics than its subordination to psychology. Neither logic nor mathematics has the task of investigating minds and the contents of consciousness whose bearer is a single person. Perhaps ther task could be represented rather as the investigation of the mind, of the mind not of minds.

The apprehension of a thought presupposes someone who apprehends it, who thinks. He is the bearer of the thinking but not of the thought. Although the thought does not belong to the contents of the thinker's consciousness yet something in his consciousness must be aimed at the thought. But this should not be confused with the thought itself. Similarly Algol itself is different from the idea someone has of Algol.

The thought belongs neither to my inner world as an idea nor yet to the outer world of material, perceptible things. . . .

---

but is all the same the content of my hand in quite a different way from the bones and muscles of which it is made and their tensions, and is much more extraneous to it than they are.

SCEPTICISM AND PSYCHOLOGISM

RODERICK M. CHISHOLM

Theodore Lipps wrote, in 1880, that "logic is either the physics of thought or nothing at all" and he tried to show that the truths of logic are, in fact, truths about the ways in which people think[1] This is the view that was called "psychologism" and it was applied generally to the subject matter of the truths of reason.

A psychologistic interpretation of "Necessarily, being red excludes being blue" might be: "Everyone is so constituted psychologically that if he thinks of a thing as being red then he cannot help but think of it as not being blue." And a psychologistic interpretation of the logical truth "For any propositions p and q, if p is true and p implies q, then q is true" might be: "Everyone is so constituted psychologically that if he believes that p is true, and if he believes that p implies q, then he cannot help but believe that q is true."

But obviously, these psychological sentences do not at all convey what is intended by the sentences they are supposed to translate. The psychological sentences are empirical generalizations about the ways in which people think, and as such, they can be supported only by extensive psychological investigation. Thus, Gottlob Frege said, in connection with the psychologistic interpretation of mathematics: "It would be strange if the most exact

[1] *"Die Aufgabe der Erkenntnistheorie," Philosophische Monatshefte,* Vol. XVI, (1880) ; quoted by Husserl, in *Logische Untersuchungen,* Vol. I (Halle: Max Niemeyer, 1928). In his *Philosophie der Arithmetik* (Leipzig: C. E. M. Pfeffer, 1891), Husserl defended a version of "psychologism," but he criticizes that view in the *Logische Untersuchungen.*

Reprinted from Roderick M. Chisholm, *Theory of Knowledge* © 1966 (Englewood Cliffs, N.J.: Prentice-Hall, 1966), pp. 79–82. Reprinted by permission of Prentice Hall, Inc., Englewood Cliffs, New Jersey.

of all the sciences had to seek support from psychology, which is still feeling its way none too surely." *The Foundations of Arithmetic* (Oxford: Basil Blackwell, 1950), p. 38; Frege's work was first published in 1884. Cf. Philip E. B. Jourdain, *The Philosophy of Mr. B*rtr*nd R*ss*ll* (London: George Allen & Unwin, 1918), p. 88: "The psychological founding of logic appears to be not without analogy with the surprising method of advocates of evolutionary ethics, who expect to discover what *is* good by inquiring what cannibals have *thought* good. I sometimes feel inclined to apply the historical method to the multiplication table. I should make a statistical inquiry among schoolchildren, before their pristine wisdom has been biased by teachers. I should put down their answers as to what 6 times 9 amounts to, I should work out the average of their answers to six places of decimals, and should then decide that, at the present stage of human development, this average is of the value of 6 times 9." And being empirical generalizations, the psychological sentences are probable at best and are at the mercy of contrary instances. The existence somewhere of one unreasonable individual—one man who believed that some things are both red and blue, or one man who believed that a certain proposition *p* is true and also that *p* implies *q*, and who yet refused to believe that *q* is true—would be sufficient to insure that the psychological sentence is false. And we know, all too well, that there are such men. Their existence, however, has no bearing upon the truths expressed by "Necessarily, being red excludes being blue" and "Necessarily, for any propositions *p* and *q*, if *p* is true and if *p* implies *q*, then *q* is true."

In the face of such difficulties, the proponent of psychologism is likely to modify his view. He will say of sentences expressing the laws of logic and the other truths of reason, that they really express *rules of thought*, and that they are not descriptive sentences telling us how people actually do think. But to see the hopelessness of this approach we have only to consider the possible ways of interpreting the sentence "The laws of logic are rules of thought."

(1) One interpretation would be: "The laws of logic are

ethical truths pertaining to our duties and obligations with respect to thinking." In this case, the problem of our knowledge of the laws of logic is transferred to the (more difficult) problem of our knowledge of the truths (if any) of ethics.

(2) "The laws of logic are imperatives commanding us to think in certain ways—and imperatives are neither true nor false." This way of looking at the matter leaves us with the problem of distinguishing between valid and invalid imperatives. For there is a distinction between "Do not believe, with respect to any particular thing, both that it is red and that it is blue" and "Do not believe, with respect to any particular thing, that that thing is either red or not red." The former imperative, surely, is correct or valid, and the latter incorrect or invalid. If we are not to fall back into scepticism, we must also say that the former is known to be valid and the latter is known to be invalid. Moreover, it is not possible to construe all of the statements of logic as imperatives. For the logician can also tell us nonimperatively such things as: If you believe that p, and if you believe that p implies q, and if you conform to the imperative, modus ponens, then you will also believe that q. This statement is a necessary truth. (A manual of chess, similarly, may give us certain rules in the form of imperatives: "Move the king only one square at a time." And possibly these imperatives are neither valid nor invalid. But whether or not they are valid, the chess manual will also contain true indicative sentences—sentences which are not themselves imperatives but which tell us what will happen when, in accordance with the imperatives that the manual lays down, we move the pieces into various positions. "It is impossible, if white is in such and such a position, for black to win in less than seven moves." And these statements are also necessary truths.)

(3) "The laws of logic tell us which ways of believing will lead to truth and which will lead to falsehood." According to this interpretation, our two examples might be thought of as telling us respectively: "A necessary condition of avoiding false beliefs is to refrain from believing, with respect to any particular thing, both that that thing is red and also that it is blue" and "A

necessary condition of avoiding false beliefs is to refrain from believing, at one and the same time, with respect to any propositions p and q, that p is true, that p implies q, and that q is false." To see that this way of formulating psychologism leaves us with our problem, let us compare it with a similar psychologistic interpretation of some other subject matter, say, astronomy. We may say, if we like, that what the statement "There are nine planets" really tells us is that if we wish to avoid error with respect to the number of planets, it is essential to refrain from believing that there are not nine planets; it also tells us that if we wish to arrive at the truth about the number of planets, it is essential to believe that there *are* nine planets. It is not likely that in so spinning out what is conveyed by "There are nine planets," we can throw any light upon what the astronomer thinks he knows. In any case, our problem reappears when we compare our new versions of the statements of logic with those of the statements of astronomy. The former, but not the latter, can be prefixed by "It is necessary that," and unless we give in to scepticism (which it was the point of psychologism to avoid) we must say that the result of such a prefixing is also a statement we can know to be true.[2]

[2] Cf. the criticism of psychologism in Husserl's *Logische Untersuchungen*, I, 154ff., and Rudolf Carnap, *The Logical Foundations of Probability* (Chicago: University of Chicago Press, 1950), pp. 37–42.

THE
PHENOMENOLOGICAL
REDUCTIONS

Only those objects should engage our attention, to the sure and indubitable knowledge of which our mental powers seem to be adequate.

—René Descartes RULES FOR THE DIRECTION OF THE MIND (Rule II)

The most important lesson which the reduction teaches us is the impossibility of a complete reduction.

—Maurice Merleau-Ponty THE PHENOMENOLOGY OF PERCEPTION, Preface

INTRODUCTION

Husserl takes the phenomenological reduction to be his greatest contribution to philosophy. The first selection is his now classic introduction to this reduction or *epoché* from Chapter 3 of *Ideas*. The second selection is a later statement of the reduction from *Cartesian Meditations* in which the reduction leads the way to the transcendental ego. The selections by Maurice Merleau-Ponty, one of the most prominent French existential phenomenologists, and Richard Schmitt, a sensitive American interpreter of phenomenology, are both critical of the reduction.

THE THESIS OF THE NATURAL STANDPOINT AND ITS SUSPENSION

EDMUND HUSSERL

30.

We emphasize a most important point once again in the sentences that follow: I find continually present and standing over against me the one spatio-temporal fact-world to which I myself belong, as do all other men found in it and related in the same way to it. This "fact-world," as the world already tells us, I find to *be out there,* and also *take it just as it gives itself to me as something that exists out there.* All doubting and rejecting of the data of the natural world leaves standing the *general thesis of the natural standpoint.* "The" world is as fact-world always there; at the most it is at odd points "other" than I supposed, this or that under such names as "illusion," "hallucination," and the like, must be struck *out of it,* so to speak; but the "it" remains ever, in the sense of the general thesis, a world that has its being out there. To know it more comprehensively, more trustworthily, more perfectly than the naïve lore of experience is able to do, and to solve all the problems of scientific knowledge which offer themselves upon its ground, that is the goal of the *sciences of the natural standpoint.*

31. RADICAL ALTERATION OF THE NATURAL THESIS "DISCONNEXION," "BRACKETING"

Instead now of remaining at this standpoint, we propose to alter it radically. Our aim must be to convince ourselves of the possibility of this alteration on grounds of principle.

The General Thesis according to which the real world about me is at all times known not merely in a general way as something apprehended, but as a fact-world *that has its being out there*, does *not* consist of course *in an act proper*, in an articulated judgment *about existence*. It is and remains something all the time the standpoint is adopted, that is, it endures persistently during the whole course of our life of natural endeavour. What has been at any time perceived clearly, or obscurely made present, in short everything out of the world of nature through experience and prior to any thinking, bears in its totality and in all its articulated sections the character "present" "out there," a character which can function essentially as the ground of support for an explicit (predicative) existential judgment which is in agreement with the character it is grounded upon. If we express that same judgment, we know quite well that in so doing we have simply put into the form of a statement and grasped as a predication what already lay somehow in the original experience, or lay there as the character of something "present to one's hand."

We can treat the potential and expressed thesis exactly as we do the thesis of the explicit judgment. A procedure of this sort, *possible at any time*, is for instance, *the attempt to doubt everything* which *Descartes*, with an entirely different end in view, with the purpose of setting up an absolutely indubitable sphere of Being, undertook to carry through. We link on here, but add directly and emphatically that this attempt to doubt everything should serve us *only as a device of method*, helping us to stress certain points which by its means, as though secluded in its essence, must be brought clearly to light.

The attempt to doubt everything has its place in the realm of our *perfect freedom*. We can *attempt to doubt* anything and everything, however convinced we may be concerning what we doubt, even though the evidence which seals our assurance is completely adequate.

Let us consider what is essentially involved in an act of this kind. He who attempts to doubt is attempting to doubt "Being" of some form or other, or it may be Being expanded into such predicative forms as "It is," "It is this or thus," and the like. The attempt does not affect the form of Being itself. He who doubts, for instance, whether an object, whose Being he does not doubt, is constituted in such and such a way doubts *the way it is constituted*. We can obviously transfer this way of speaking from the doubting to the *attempt* at doubting. It is clear that we cannot doubt the Being of anything, and in the same act of consciousness (under the unifying form of simultaneity) bring what is substantive to this Being under the terms of the Natural Thesis, and so confer upon it the character of "being actually there" (*vorhanden*). Or to put the same in another way: we cannot at once doubt and hold for certain one and the same quality of Being. It is likewise clear that the *attempt* to doubt any object of awareness in respect of it *being actually there necessarily conditions a certain suspension (Aufhebung) of the thesis;* and it is precisely this that interests us. It is not a transformation of the thesis into its antithesis, of positive into negative; it is also not a transformation into presumption, suggestion, indecision, doubt (in one or another sense of the word); such shifting indeed is not at our free pleasure. *Rather is it something quite unique. We do not abandon the thesis we have adopted, we make no change in our conviction,* which remains in itself what it is so long as we do not introduce new motives of judgment, which we precisely refrain from doing. And yet the thesis undergoes a modification—whilst remaining in itself what it is, *we set it as it were "out of action," we "disconnect it," "bracket it."* It still remains there like the bracketed in the bracket, like the disconnected outside the connexional system. We can also say: The thesis is experience as lived (*Erlebnis*), *but we make "no use" of it,* and by that, of course, we do not indicate privation (as when we say of the ignorant that he makes no use of a certain thesis); in this case rather, as with all parallel expressions, we are dealing with indicators that point to a definite but *unique form of consciousness,* which clamps on to the original simple thesis (whether it actually or even predicatively *posits* existence or not), and transvalues it in a quite peculiar way. *This transvaluing is a concern of our full freedom, and is opposed to all cognitive attitudes* that would set themselves up as co-ordinate with the *thesis,* and yet within the unity of "simultaneity" remain incompatible with it, as indeed it is in general with all attitudes whatsoever in the strict sense of the word.

In *the attempt to doubt* applied to a thesis which, as we presuppose, is certain and tenaciously held, the "disconnexion" takes place in and with a modification of the antithesis, namely with the *"supposition"* (*Ansetzung*) *of Non-Being*, which is thus the partial basis of the attempt to doubt. With Descartes this is so markedly the case that one can say that his universal attempt at doubt is just an attempt at universal denial. We disregard this possibility here, we are not interested in every analytical component of the attempt to doubt, nor therefore in its exact and completely sufficing analysis. *We extract only the phenomenon of "bracketing" or "disconnection,"* which is obviously not limited to that of the attempt to doubt, although it can be detached from it with special ease, but can appear *in other contexts also,* and with no less ease *independently.* In relation to every thesis and wholly uncoerced we can use this *peculiar εποχη,* (*epokhe*—abstention), *a certain refraining from judgment which is compatible with the unshaken and unshakable because self-evidencing conviction of Truth.* The thesis is "put out of action," bracketed, it passes off into the modified status of a "bracketed thesis," and the judgment *simpliciter* into "*bracketed judgment.*"

Naturally one should not simply identify this consciousness with that of "mere supposal," that nymphs, for instance, are dancing in a ring; for thereby *no disconnecting* of a living conviction that goes on living takes place, although from another side the close relation of the two forms of consciousness lies clear. Again, we are not concerned here with supposal in the sense of *"assuming"* or *taking for granted,* which in the equivocal speech of current usage may also be expressed in the words: "I suppose (I make the assumption) that it is so and so."

Let us add further that nothing hinders us *from speaking bracketing correlatively* also, in respect of *an objectivity to be posited,* what ever be the region or category to which it belongs. What is meant in this case is that *every thesis related to this objectivity* must be *disconnected* and changed into its bracketed counterpart. On closer view, moreover, the "bracketing" image

is from the outset better suited to the sphere of the object, just
as the expression "to put out of action" better suits the sphere
of the Act or of Consciousness.

32. THE PHENOMENOLOGICAL εποχη

We can now let the universal εποχη, (*epokhe*—abstention)
in the sharply defined and novel sense we have given to it step
into the place of the Cartesian attempt at universal doubt. But
on good grounds we *limit* the universality of this εποχη. For
were it as inclusive as it is in general capable of being, then
since every thesis and every judgment can be modified freely to
any extent, and every objectivity that we can judge or criticize
can be bracketed, no field would be left over for unmodified
judgments, to say nothing of a science. But our design is just to
discover a new scientific domain, such as might be won precisely
through the method of bracketing, though only through a de-
finitely limited form of it.

The limiting consideration can be indicated in a word.

*We put out of action the general thesis which belongs to the
essence of the natural standpoint*, we place in brackets whatever
it includes respecting the nature of Being: *this entire natural
world therefore* which is continually "there for us," "present to
our hand," and will ever remain there, is a "fact-world" of which
we continue to be conscious, even though it pleases us to put it
in brackets.

If I do this, as I am fully free to do, I do *not* then *deny*
this "world," as though I were a sophist, *I do not doubt that
it is there* as though I were a sceptic; but I use the "phenomenological" εποχη, which *completely bars me from using any judgment that concerns spatio-temporal existence* (*Dasein*).

Thus *all sciences which relate to this natural world*, though
they stand never so firm to me, though they fill me with wondering admiration, though I am far from any thought of objecting
to them in the least degree, *I disconnect them all, I make absolutely no use of their standards, I do not appropriate a single
one of the propositions that enter into their systems, even though
their evidential value is perfect, I take none of them, no one of*

them serves me for a foundation—so long, that is, as it is understood, in the way these sciences themselves understand it, as a truth *concerting the realities* of this world. *I may accept it only after I have placed it in the bracket.* That means: only in the modified consciousness of the judgment as it appears in disconnexion, and *not as it figures within the science as its proposition, a proposition which claims to be valid and whose validity I recognize and make use of.*

The εποχη here in question will not be confined with that which positivism demands, and against which, as we were compelled to admit, it is itself an offender. We are not concerned at present with removing the preconceptions which trouble the pure positivity (*Sachlichkeit*) of research, with the constituting of a science "free from theory" and "free from metaphysics" by bringing all the grounding back to the immediate data, nor with the means of reaching such ends, concerning whose value there is indeed no question, What *we* demand lies along another line. The whole world as placed within the nature-setting and presented in experience as real, taken completely "free from all theory," just as it is in reality experienced, and made clearly manifest in and through the linkings of our experiences, has now no validity for us, it must be set in brackets, untested indeed but also uncontested. Similarly all theories and sciences, positivistic or otherwise, which relate to this world, however good they may be, succumb to the same fate.

THE WAY TO THE TRANSCENDENTAL EGO

EDMUND HUSSERL

3. THE CARTESIAN OVERTHROW AND THE GUIDING FINAL IDEA OF AN ABSOLUTE GROUNDING OF SCIENCE

Reprinted from *Cartesian Meditations*, translated by D. Cairns, (The Hague: M. Nijhoff, 1960), section 15, pp. 7, 17–18, 27–29, by permission of the publisher.

And so we make a new beginning, each for himself and in himself, with the decision of philosophers who begin radically: that at first we shall put out of action all the convictions we have been accepting up to now, including all our sciences. Let the idea guiding our meditations be at first the Cartesian idea of a science that shall be established as radically genuine, ultimately an all-embracing science. . . .

7. THE EVIDENCE FOR THE FACTUAL EXISTENCE OF THE WORLD NOT APODICTIC; ITS INCLUSION IN THE CARTESIAN OVERTHROW

The question of evidences that are first in themselves can apparently be answered without any trouble. Does not the *existence of the world* present itself forthwith as such an evidence? The life of everyday action relates to the world. All the sciences relate to it: the sciences of matters of fact relate to it immediately; the apriori sciences, mediately, as instruments of scientific method. More than anything else the being of the world is obvious. It is so very obvious that no one would think of asserting it expressly in a proposition. After all, we have our continuous experience in which this world incessantly stands before our eyes, as existing without question. But, however much this evidence is prior in itself to all the <other> evidences of life (as turned toward the world) and to all the evidences of all the world sciences (since it is the basis that continually supports them), we soon become doubtful about the extent to which, in this capacity, it can lay claim to being apodictic. And, if we follow up this doubt, it becomes manifest that our experiential evidence of the world lacks also the superiority of being the absolutely primary evidence. Concerning the first point, we note that the universal sensuous experience in whose evidence the world is continuously given to us beforehand is obviously not to be taken forthwith as an apodictic evidence, which, as such, would absolutely exclude both the possibility of eventual doubt whether the world is actual and the possibility of its non-being. Not only can a particular experienced thing suffer devaluation as an illusion of the senses; the whole unitarily surveyable nexus, experienced throughout a period of time, can prove to be an illusion, a coherent dream. We need not take the indicating of these possible and sometimes actual reversals of evidence as a sufficient criticism of the evidence in question and see in it a full proof that, in spite of the continual experiencedness of the world, a non-being of the world is conceivable. We shall retain only this much: that the evidence of world-experience would, at all events, need to be criticized with regard to its validity and range, before it could be used for the purposes of a radical grounding of science, and that therefore we must not take that evidence to be, without question, immediately apodictic. It follows that denying acceptance to all the sciences given us beforehand, treating them as, for us, inadmissible prejudices, is not enough. Their universal basis, the experienced world, must also be deprived of its naïve acceptance.

12. THE IDEA OF A TRANSCENDENTAL GROUNDING OF KNOWLEDGE

Our meditations now require a further development, without which what has already been discovered cannot yield the right profit. As one who is meditating in the Cartesian manner, what can I do with the transcendental ego philosophically? Certainly his being is, for me, prior in the order of knowledge to all Objective being: In a certain sense he is the underlying basis on which all Objective cognition takes place. But can this priority rightly signify that the transcendental ego is, in the usual sense, the knowledge-basis on which all Objective knowledge is grounded? Not that we intend to abandon the great Cartesian thought of attempting to find in transcendental subjectivity the deepest grounding of all sciences and even of the being of an Objective world. If we were to abandon that thought, we should not be following Cartesian paths of meditation at all; our divergencies would be more than modifications prompted by criticism. But perhaps, with the Cartesian discovery of the transcendental ego, *a new idea of the grounding of knowledge* also becomes disclosed: the idea of it as a transcendental grounding. And indeed, instead of attempting to use *ego cogito* as an apodictically evident premise for arguments supposedly implying a transcendent subjectivity, we shall direct our attention to the fact that phenomenological epoché lays open (to me, the meditating philosopher) *an infinite realm of being of a new kind,* as the sphere of a new kind of experience: transcendental experience: When we take it into consideration that, for each kind of actual experience and for each of its universal variant modes (perception, retention, recollection, etc.), there is a corresponding pure phantasy, an "as-if experience" with parallel modes (as-if perception, as-if retention, as-if recollection, etc.), we surmise that there is also an apriori science, which confines itself to the realm of pure possibility (pure imaginableness) and, instead of judging about actualities of transcendental being, judges about [its] apriori possibilities and thus at the same time prescribes rules a priori for actualities.

But admittedly, when we let our thoughts hasten on in this manner, to the conception of a phenomenological science destined to become *philosophy,* we immediately run into the already-mentioned difficulties raised by the fundamental methodological demand for an apodictic evidence of the ego. For, as we have already seen, no matter how absolute the apodictic evidence of the ego's existence may be for him, still it is not necessarily evidence for the existence of the manifold data of transcendental experience. On the other hand, though the *cogitationes* given to me, in the attitude that effects transcendental reduction,—given as perceived, recollected, or otherwise experience *cogitationes*— must not yet be declared absolutely indubitable with respect to their present or past existence, still it may be possible to show that the absolute evidence of the *ego sum* does, after all, necessarily extend into those manifolds of self-experience in which the ego's *transcendental life* and *habitual properties* are given, even if there are limits that define the range of these evidences (the evidences of recollection, retention, etc.). More precisely stated: The bare identity of the "I am" is not the only thing given as indubitable in transcendental self-experience. Rather

there extends through all the particular data of actual and possible self-experience—even though they are not absolutely indubitable in respect of single details—a *universal apodictically
experiencable structure* of the Ego (for example, the immanent
temporal form belonging to the stream of subjective processes).
Perhaps it can also be shown, as something dependent on that
structure, and indeed as part of it, that the Ego is *apodictically
predelineated*, for himself, as a concrete Ego existing with an
individual content made up of subjective processes, abilities, and
dispositions—horizontally predelineated as an experienceable
object, accessible to a possible self-experience that can be per-
fected, and perhaps enriched, without limit.

THE PHILOSOPHER AND HIS SHADOW

MAURICE MERLEAU-PONTY

Take for example the theme of phenomenological reduction,
which we know never ceased to be an enigmatic possibility for
Husserl, and one he always came back to. To say that he never
succeeded in ensuring the bases of phenomenology would be to
be mistaken about what he was looking for. The problems of
reduction are not for him a prior step or preface to phenomenology; they are the beginning of inquiry. In a sense, they are
inquiry, since inquiry is, as he said, a continuous beginning.
We must not imagine Husserl hamstrung here by vexatious
obstacles; locating obstacles is the very meaning of his inquiry.
One of its "results" is the realization that the movement of return
to ourselves—of "re-entering ourselves," St. Augustine said—is
as if rent by an inverse movement which it *elicits*. Husserl re-
discovers that identity of "re-entering self" and "going-outside
self" which, for Hegel, defined the absolute. To reflect (Husserl

Reprinted from *Signs*, translated by R. McCleary (Evanston, Ill.:
Northwestern University Press, 1964), pp. 161–166, by permission of the
publisher.

said in *Ideen I*) is to unveil an unreflected dimension which is at a distance because we are no longer it in a naive way, yet which we cannot doubt that reflection attains, since it is through reflection itself that we have an idea of it. So it is not the unreflected which challenges reflection; it is reflection which challenges itself. For by definition its attempt to revive, possess, internalize, or make immanent has meaning only with respect to an already given terminus which withdraws into its transcendence beneath the very gaze which has set out in search of it in this attempt.

So it is not through chance or naiveté that Husserl assigns contradictory characteristics to reduction. He is saying what he means here, what is imposed by the factual situation. It is up to us not to forget half the truth. Thus on the one hand reduction goes beyond the natural attitude. It is not "natural" (*natural*). [*Ideen II*] This means that reduced thought no longer concerns the Nature of the natural sciences but in a sense the "opposite of Nature." [*Ibid*] In other words, reduced thought concerns Nature as the "ideal meaning of the acts which constitute the natural attitude" [*Ibid*] Nature becomes once more the noema it has always been, Nature reintegrated to the consciousness which has always constituted it through and through. In the realm of "reduction" there is no longer anything but consciousness, its acts, and their intentional object. This is why Husserl can write that Nature is relative to mind, and that Nature is relative and mind absolute. [*Ibid*]

But this is not the whole truth. The fact that there is *no* Nature *without* mind, or that Nature may be *done away with* in thought *without* doing way with mind, does not mean that Nature is produced by mind, or that any combination (even a subtle one) of these two concepts suffices to give the philosophical formula of our situation in being. Mind without Nature can be thought about and Nature without mind cannot. But perhaps we do not have to think about the world and ourselves in terms of the bifurcation of Nature and mind. The fact is that phenomenology's most famous descriptions go in a direction which is not that of "philosophy of mind." When Husserl says that reduction goes beyond the natural attitude, he immediately adds that this going beyond preserves "the whole world of the natural attitude." The very transcendence of this world must retain a meaning in the eyes of "reduced" consciousness, and transcendental immanence cannot be simply its antithesis. From *Ideen II* on it seems clear that reflection does not install us in a closed, transparent milieu, and that it does not take us (at least not immediately) from "objective" to "subjective," but that its function is rather to unveil a third dimension in which this distinction becomes problematic. There is indeed an I which makes itself "indifferent," a pure "knower," in order to grasp all things without remainder—to spread all things out before itself—and to "objectify" and gain intellectual possession of them. This I is a purely "theoretical attitude" which seeks to "render visible the relationships which can provide knowledge of being as it comes to be." [*Ibid*] But it is just this I which is not the philosopher, just this attitude which is not philosophy. It is the science of Nature, or in a deeper sense, a certain philosophy which gives birth to the natural sciences and which comes back to the pure I and to its correlative, "things simply as things" (*blosse Sachen*), stripped of every action-predicate and every value-predicate. From *Ideen II* on Husserl's reflections escape this tête-à-tête between pure subject and pure things. They look *deeper down* for the fundamental. Saying that Husserl's thought goes in another direction tells us little. His thought does not disregard the ideal correlation of subject and object; it very deliberately goes beyond it, since it presents it as relatively founded, true derivatively as a constitutive result it is committed to justifying in its proper time and place.

But what is the starting point for this new turn in Husserl's thought, and what is the deeper urgency behind it? What is false in the ontology of *blosse Sachen* is that it makes a purely theoretical or idealizing attitude absolute, neglecting or taking as understood a relation with being which founds the purely theoretical attitude and measures its value. Relative to this scientific *naturalism*, the *natural* attitude involves a higher truth that we must regain. For the natural attitude is nothing less than naturalistic. We do not live naturally in the universe of *blosse Sachen*.

Prior to all reflection, in conversation and the practices of life, we maintain a "personalist attitude" that naturalism cannot account for, and here things are not nature in itself for us but "our surroundings." [*Ibid*] Our most natural life as men intends an ontological milieu which is different from that of being in itself, and which consequently cannot be derived from it in the constitutive order.

Even when our knowledge of things is concerned, we know far more about them in the natural attitude than the theoretical attitude can tell us—and above all we know it in a different way. Reflection speaks of our natural relationship to the world as an "attitude," that is, as an organized totality of "acts." But this is a reflection which presupposes that it is in things and which sees no farther than itself. At the same time Husserl's reflection tries to grasp the universal essences of things, it notes that in the unreflected there are "syntheses which dwell this side of any thesis." [*Ibid*] The natural attitude really becomes an attitude—a tissue of judicatory and propositional acts—only when it becomes a naturalist thesis. The natural attitude itself emerges unscathed from the complaints which can be made about naturalism, because it is "prior to any thesis," because it is the mystery of a *Weltthesis* prior to all theses. It is, Husserl says in another connection, the mystery of a primordial faith and a fundamental and original opinion (*Urglaube, Urdoxa*) which are thus not even in principle translatable in terms of clear and distinct knowledge, and which—more ancient than any "attitude" or "point of view"—give us not a representation of the world but the world itself.

Reflection cannot "go beyond" this opening to the world, except by making use of the powers it owes to the opening itself. There is a clarity, an obviousness, proper to the zone of *Weltthesis* which is not derived from that of our theses, an unveiling of the world precisely through its dissimulation in the chiaroscuro of the doxa. When Husserl insistently says that phenomenological reflection begins in the natural attitude (in *Ideen II* he repeats it in order to relate the analysis he has just made of the corporeal and intersubjective implications of the *blosse*

Sachen [*Ibid*] to the realm of constituted phenomena), this is not just a way of saying that we must necessarily begin with and go by way of opinion before we can attain knowledge. The doxa of the natural attitude is an Urdoxa. To what is fundamental and original in theoretical consciousness it opposes what is fundamental and original in our existence. Its rights of priority are definitive, and reduced consciousness must take them into account.

The truth is that the relationships between the natural and the transcendental attitudes are not simple, are not side by side or sequential, like the false or the apparent and the true. There is a preparation for phenomenology in the natural attitude. It is the natural attitude which, by reiterating its own procedures, seesaws in phenomenology. It is the natural attitude itself which goes beyond itself in phenomenology—and so it does not go beyond itself. Reciprocally, the transcendental attitude is still and in spite of everything "natural" (*natürlich*). [*Ibid*] There is a truth of the natural attitude—there is even a secondary, derivative truth of naturalism. "The soul's reality is based upon corporeal matter, not the latter upon the soul. More generally, within the total objective world, the material world is what we call Nature, a self-contained and particular world which does not require the support of any other reality. On the contrary the existence of mental realities and a real mental world is tied to the existence of a nature in the first sense of the term, to the existence of a material nature, and it is so linked not for contingent reasons of principle. Whereas the *res extensa*, when we examine its essence, contains neither anything which arises from mind nor anything which mediately (*über sich hinaus*) requires connection with a real mind; we find on the contrary that a real mind, according to its essence, can only exist tied to materiality as the real mind of a body." [Husserl, *Ideen III*] We quote these lines only to provide a counterpoise to those which affirmed the relativity of Nature and the non-relativity of mind, and demolished the sufficiency of Nature and the truth of the natural attitudes that are here reaffirmed. In the last analysis, phenomenology is neither a materialism nor a philosophy of mind. Its proper work is to unveil the pre-theoretical layer on which both of these idealizations find their relative justification and are gone beyond.

How will that infrastructure, that secret of secrets this side of our theses and our theory, be able to turn to rest upon the *acts of* absolute consciousness? Does the descent into the realm of our "archeology" leave our analytical tools intact? Does it make no changes at all in our conception of noesis, noema, and intentionality—in our ontology? After we have made this descent, are we still entitled to seek in an analytics of acts what upholds our own and the world's life without appeal? We know that Husserl never made himself too clear about these questions. A few words are there like indicators pointing to the problem— signaling unthought-of elements to think about. To begin with, the element of a "pre-theoretical constitution," [*Ideen II*] which is charged with accounting for "pre-givens," [*Ibid*] those kernels of meaning about which man and the world gravitate. We may with equal truth say of these pre-givens (as Husserl says of the body) either that they are always "already constituted" for us or that they are "never completely constituted"—in short, that consciousness is always behind or ahead of them, never contemporaneous. Husserl was undoubtedly thinking of these singular beings when in another connection he evoked a constitution which would not proceed by grasping a content as an exemplification of a meaning or an essence (*Auffassungsinhalt-Auffassung-als* . . .), an operating or latent intentionality like that which animates time, more ancient than the intentionality of human *acts*. There must be beings for us which are not yet kept in being by the centrifugal activity of consciousness: significations it does not spontaneously confer upon contents, and contents which participate obliquely in a meaning in the sense that they indicate a meaning which remains a distant meaning and which is not yet legible in them as the monogram or stamp of thetic consciousness. In such cases we do still have a grouping of intentional threads around certain knots which govern them, but the series of retro-references (*Rückdeutungen*) which lead us ever deeper could not possibly reach completion in the intellectual possession of a noema. There is an ordered sequence of steps, but it is without end as it is without beginning. Husserl's thought is as much attracted by the haecceity of Nature as by the vortex of absolute consciousness. In the absences of explicit theses about the relationship of one to the other, we can only examine the samples of "pre-theoretical constitution" he offers us and formulate—at our own risk—the unthought-of elements we think we see there. There is undeniably something between transcendent Nature, naturalism's being in itself, and the immanence of mind, its acts, and its noema. It is into this interval that we must try to advance.

TRANSCENDENTAL PHENOMENOLOGY: MUDDLE OR MYSTERY?

RICHARD SCHMITT

Phenomenology is the descriptive science of the transcendental realm. [Husserl, *Ideas* III, 141]. The realm is accessible only by way of the phenomenological reduction. No one who has not understood what this reduction consists of, who does not know how to perform it and has, in fact, performed it can understand what phenomenology is and how to work in it. The fact that the terms employed by Husserl, for instance the word "transcendental", are familiar must not mislead us as to the novelty of the phenomenological project. More than once Husserl surveyed the history of philosophy in considerable detail to show that earlier philosophers were groping for the insights embodied in the phenomenological programme but failed to achieve them. [Husserl, Krisis 202–203].

Commentators have, on the whole, written about Husserl as if they had found no serious difficulty in understanding the

Reprinted from *The Journal of British Society for Phenomenology*, Vol. 2, (January 1971), by permission of *The Journal of British Society for Phenomenology* and the author and publisher.

transcendental-phenomenological reduction. For myself, I have
never been so fortunate. This paper is an attempt to articulate my
hesitations and uncertainties about Husserl's repeated discussion
of the epoché and reduction. I will argue that the descriptions of
the epoché and the claims made for it presuppose the distinction
between the mundane and the transcendental domain. This distinction, we shall find, cannot be 'made clear because it arises
from a series of confusions. Husserl's great discovery is a
muddle.

I

In the phenomenological epoché we abstain from all affirmation and negation with respect to a large range of objects.
"Affirmation and negation" refers not only to explicit acts of
affirming or denying but to all those mental acts in which some
beliefs are ingredients. [Husserl, *Ideas* I 256ff.]

This kind of abstention is an important ingredient in the
transition from straightforward thinking to reflection. Husserl's
description of the epoché thus is a description of the transition
from a non-reflective to a reflective attitude. Husserl is aware of
that. The phenomenological epoché is the transition from non-
reflective to reflective thinking of a very particular sort, namely
to a universal reflection. Phenomenological reflection differs
from ordinary, mundane reflection in its scope. It is not just
reflecting about this or that particular subject. It is reflection
about everything. [Husserl, EP II 154–155; Id I 119]

But how are we to understand this? While it seems clear
that reflection, in the sense under discussion, requires a partial
suspension of affirmation or negation, it would seem that a complete suspension of all such acts, past, present and future would
make any reflection following this change of attitude impossible.

Reflection requires a subject matter. That subject matter
must be identified and it must remain the same in the course of
the reflection and unless I am at least prepared to assert that I
am reflecting about . . . and that the different stages of my reflection are about one and the same subject, reflection is impossible.
If the case about which I am reflecting is purely suppositious, I

must at least be prepared *to assert* that I suppose to the case under consideration to have . . . features. Reflection, moreover, is a process in which I do not merely entertain disconnected propositions but I connect propositions in various ways with each other and I must be prepared to assert some logical connections between these propositions even if each of them begins with "Suppose that . . .". In order to make such assertions about the logical connections between my suppositions, I must be prepared to make other assertions about the meanings of the propositions connected with each other and that may involve talking about truth conditions of these propositions. But these truth conditions of what I suppose to be the case are not themselves suppositious. I must be willing and able to assert them, if I am to engage in anything that could possibly be called "reflection".

Husserl is aware of this difficulty and provides a clear-cut solution. The university of the epoché is qualified. Specifically, it is restricted to the world of the "natural attitude" [Husserl, *Ideas* I, 67]. What is that distinction? Husserl more than once speaks of "transcendental experience" which we are enabled to have once the transcendental-phenomenological epoché has been performed. The subject matter of this transcendental experience is said to be "transcendental subjectivity" with "transcendental, immanent experience." This is the domain of "my pure life with all its pure, immanent experiences . . . the universe of *phenomena.*" [Husserl, CM 58–61] But are we as practicing phenomenologists in a position to make any affirmations or negations concerning these experiences and the ego and immanent experience etc.? It seems clear in the light of what I said before about reflection that we do make affirmations and negations in the phenomenological attitude. All we abstain from is affirming or denying anything concerning the mundane objects and their existence. It is *their* existence that is bracketed, not that of the transcendental domain and whatever is in it. It is ordinary experience and the judgments it involves that is suspended and not transcendental experience. It is clear at this point that Husserl operates with an implicit distinction between two senses of "to exist", two senses of "experience", two senses of "immanent experience", of "self" and of other concepts. For each of them we must distinguish the transcendental from the mundane sense of that term. We can understand and practice the epoché only if we understand that distinction. The epoché is legitimate only if the distinction between the mundane and the transcendental domain is legitimate.

It is clearer now what question needs to be asked and what occasions the difficulty in understanding Husserl's descriptions. The difficulties hinge on the difficulty we may have in understanding the distinction between the transcendental and the mundane. We have thereby discovered a central issue in Husserlian phenomenology: the claim that there is a transcendental domain. This claim will require a good deal of discussion.

II

An essential ingredient in Husserl's support for the existence of a transcendental realm is the argument from the possible "destruction of the world:"

. . . the being of consciousness, of any stream of immanent experience, would of course necessarily be modified by a destruction of the world of things, but would not be affected in its existence [Husserl, *Ideas* I 115].

The expression "destruction of the world" refers to one's experience becoming chaotic. The change is not one from experience of the world to experience of an utter void, but one from ordered to disrupted experience.

At the heart of this argument to support the existence of a transcendental realm is a claim about the central feature of consciousness which Husserl, following Brentano, calls "intentionality". Conscious acts are said to be such that a true description of any act does not entail that the object of the act exists or has the properties attributed to it in the description. It follows from this that the object of any given act of consciousness cannot justifiably be asserted to exist (except in rare cases) unless there are other acts which support that assertion. Thus it is possible that acts as they follow one another fail completely to give evidential support to one another. But in that situation the individual acts, Husserl tells us here, remain intact and can be described. What thus remains, Husserl seems to suggest, is the transcendental realm. The present argument for the mundane-transcendental distinction, namely that if experience became chaotic, there would still remain the individual intentional acts, thus rests directly on Husserl's views about intentionality.

It is obvious however that this concept of intentionality will not by itself yield the distinction between the transcendental and the mundane. It does not follow from Husserl's analysis of intentional acts that intentional acts are not psychological and therefore 'mundane'. We may admit that Husserl's statements about intentional acts are not empirical psychological statements but are, instead, analyses of the concepts of intentionality and of evidence. None of this implies that the acts themselves and their concatenation in actual sequences are anything but contingent events that are properly studied by the empirical methods of the psychologist. Eidetic reflection about intentional acts and evidence may yield the analyses that Husserl provides. But this no more implies that individual intentional acts are transcendental rather than mundane occurrences which are to be studied in empirical psychology than that the possibility of making philosophic points about the concept of nature implies that there is no empirical natural science or that nature is a "transcendental" domain.

III

One question recurs, with slight variations, again and again in Husserl's writing:

How are we to understand the fact that the 'in itself' of objectivity can become 'idea' and even be 'grasped' in knowledge and thus, ultimately, becomes subjective again . . . [LU II, 8].

. . . we do not understand what sense a being can have which is in itself and nevertheless is known [LU 30].

Whatever meaning it [i.e., the world] has for us . . . is meaning
which is formed in our subjective genesis; every claim to existence is validated by us . . . ; that applies to the world in every
respect, of course also in the self-evident one that whatever
belongs to it is "in and for itself" whether I or whoever else
happen to be aware of it or not [*Encyclopedia Brittanica*, 14th
ed., "Phenomenology," 288]

It is not terribly clear what the problem is that Husserl
raises here. But the question raised seems central to any understanding of Husserl's distinction of the mundane from the transcendental. For that distinction is offered as a solution of the
puzzle concerning the relation of what is "in itself" and what is
"for us" pointed to in the passages cited. It is thus absolutely
necessary for any more detailed understanding of Husserlian
phenomenology that we try to state clearly the problem that
Husserl only hints at.

Reference to a further problem, that occupied Husserl, will
make it easier to throw at least some light on this one. Throughout his career, Husserl was concerned to avoid positions which
he thought would lead to scepticism. In the *Logical Investigations*
of 1900 he devotes a good deal of time to a position which he
called "psychologism", the doctrine that logical laws depend on
psychological facts. He regarded psychologism as a species of
scepticism. [Husserl, LU I 110ff.] The problem of scepticism is
raised again in a series of lectures given in 1907, *The Idea of
Phenomenology*. In 1910 he published a long paper, "Philosophy
as Strict Science," in which he attacks psychologism once more
but now extends the earlier polemic to the views of men like
Dilthey—views which Husserl brands "historicism." The objection to these views is also that they lead to sceptical conclusions.
[PRS 323 ff.]. In his later writings, Husserl associates his own
work closely with that of Descartes, specifically with the attempt
to end sceptical doubts once and for all by means of systematic
doubt and he repeatedly describes it as the goal of phenomenology to find an "Archimedean Point" [Husserl, Krisis 82],
an absolutely unshakeable starting point for the philosophical
enterprise.

Does the distinction between the mundane and the transcendental realm resolve sceptical doubts once and for all or at least contribute to such a solution? If we are to answer that question we need to take a closer look at what Husserl calls "scepticism". In one fairly typical passage Husserl recognizes that Descartes uncovered the transcendental ego but criticizes him for misunderstanding that discovery. The source of the misunderstanding, Husserl thinks, is Descartes' failure to get a good grasp on the problem raised by the sceptics. There is a "frivolous" brand of scepticism which denies that we can know anything at all, on the grounds that we can never be sure that we have adequate evidence for any given knowledge claim. Such scepticism is indeed refuted by Descartes' discovery of the indubitable existence of the thinking self, for here we have at least one knowledge claim which is not open to challenge by the "frivolous" sceptic. Husserl regards this brand of scepticism as frivolous because he thinks that we are perfectly well able to discriminate true statements from those that are false [Husserl, EP I 54].

Descartes, however, thinking mistakenly that it needed to be shown that we can tell true from false statements, interpreted the cogito as one instance of indubitable knowledge. As a consequence, Husserl seems to suggest, he [Descartes] missed the properly transcendental nature of the thinking self. We begin to grasp this transcendental character of the ego only if we understand what Husserl thinks is the real problem raised by the sceptics, namely whether there is a distinction between "objective" and "subjective" truths and whether we are able to draw that distinction [Husserl, EP I 61–62].

Here we encounter again the difficulty with which this section opened, one that involves centrally the distinction between what is 'for us' or 'subjective' and what is 'in itself' or 'objective'. In some way Husserl is worrying about the concept of objectivity and about the objectivity of our knowledge.

But what shall we make of this worry? Specifically, what shall we make of his distinction between "objective truth" and "subjective truth" [EP I, 62]? It is not by any means unreasonable to say that the expression "subjective truth" is incoherent unless it means only "what someone (mistakenly) believes to be true." But if that is all that Husserl means by that phrase, his worry about scepticism is exactly that of Descartes. Here is one more formulation of Husserl's question:

> Evidence, the rational insight, which gives preference to scientific judgments over the vague and blind judgments of everyday life, is itself a subjective occurrence in consciousness. What entitles us to give this subjective characteristic the status of a criterion for a truth which is valid in itself, which may claim validity independently of subjective, immanent experience? [Husserl, EP I, 65].

After the refutation of psychologism was completed, that is after Husserl had argued that true propositions are objectively true, that their truth value is logically independent of the psychological or linguistic facts about the person asserting a true proposition, Husserl now feels uncertain as to whether we are justified in claiming to know such true propositions. What he seems to have in mind is something of this sort: We assert propositions either because they are immediately evident to us or because they are entailed by or supported by immediately evident propositions. Our beliefs and knowledge claims thus always rest on evident propositions and we *experience* that a proposition is evident [Husserl, LU I 13]. Are we entitled to take what is experienced as true to be true in itself? (The experience of truth yields, I suspect, what Husserl calls "subjective truth".) We have fairly complex criteria to separate true from false propositions. Suppose a given proposition satisfies all criteria. We shall certainly regard it as true. If it is true by our criteria, are we also entitled to call it true "in itself" that is, outside the context of human inquiry, inference and criteria? It is conceivable, is it not, that our criteria do not discriminate objective truth from objective falsity, but only discriminate what is true for us from what is false for us. The worry here is no longer whether there might not be further evidence bearing on any belief we have which would show this belief to be mistaken. The worry is not even that a corresponding mistake may have crept into the formulation of our criteria of adequate evidence. Presumably Husserl is satisfied that there are some statements which are true by our standards of truth and is also satisfied that at least some of the criteria we employ can be formulated in statements which can be shown to be valid. The worry is rather that the criteria of truth which we apply in all these cases may, although valid "for us", not be valid "in themselves."

One may object to these reflections, that they possess specious plausibility only due to misuse of language. The meaning of "true" and "false," the objection points out, is tied closely to our criteria of truth and falsity. The supposition that anything could be called "true" or "false" without conforming to our criteria for the use of these terms would therefore be incoherent. Husserl agrees. He recognizes that the words "true" and "false" can only mean what they mean for us now. Distinctions of this sort, as also the distinction between what is 'in itself' and what is 'for us' are, after all distinctions which we draw [EP I, 67]. All of these terms, 'true', 'false', 'in itself', 'for us' are terms in our language. The criteria employed for the use of these terms are built into our language. This however, once again, suggests to Husserl that the objectivity of what we know is compromised.

But this suggestion is the product of a confusion. On the one hand, Husserl seems prepared to recognize that words like "true" and "objective" mean what they mean in the usage of the most informed and thoughtful users of our language. On the other hand he wants to say that, therefore, our explications of these terms are valid only relative to us, i.e. that their objectivity is compromised. Such a claim implies that there is a sense to be given to "true" and to "objective" which is independent of our usage, our language and of the distinctions which we draw. But this claim is clearly inconsistent with the admission that "objective" and "true" means what *we* mean by [them]. He seems to hold that the meaning to be given to our concepts, e.g. to the concept of objectivity, is that which we would give it after careful and exhaustive reflection and, at the same time, that these concepts have meanings independent of our usage so that we may ask whether what *we* call "objective" is objective by this other standard. But if we recognize this other standard, then the real meaning of terms is not relative to us, but only what we *think* is the meaning of terms and thus we would only be able to raise the sort of sceptical question that Husserl imputes to Descartes and calls "frivolous." As applied to statements about the meanings of concepts, this scepticism would counter all explications of concepts, however careful and exhaustive with the question whether continued reflection about any given concept would not tend to show the explication given to be mistaken. If, on the other hand, we recognize only the distinctions which we draw, then only what we call "objective" *is* objective and then the fact that we draw the distinction between what is objective and what is not does not compromise the objective validity of the explication of these two concepts.

It seems now that Husserl's worries about the relativity of our knowledge spring from using terms, particularly "objective", in two different senses, thereby generating a version of scepticism different from that of Descartes, which he [Husserl] regards as "frivolous". But like the distinction between two different versions of scepticism, [it] is confused. That distinction will therefore not do the job that Husserl claimed for it: it will not throw light on the peculiar transcendental character of the thinking subject discovered by Descartes.

We shall see, in the final section, some further considerations that tended to obscure the confusions from which spring the apparent problem of the relativity of knowledge to ourselves. But first we must draw some other distinctions, not drawn by Husserl, which lend some plausibility, however specious to the distinction between the mundane and the transcendental subject.

IV

The central claim of Husserl's transcendental phenomenology is contained in this passage:

The objective world, which is, was or will be for me, with all its objects, derives, I said, its entire meaning and its claim to existence from me, as the transcendental ego, which first comes to light in the transcendental-phenomenological epoché [Husserl, CM 65].

What meaning can we give to this concept of a transcendental ego and to the claim that the world is constituted by it?

One interpretation can be derived from Husserl's extensive and often extremely interesting analyses of intentional acts [See e.g., Husserl, *Ideas* I 174–375].

1. All acts of consciousness are intentional.
2. What makes an act intentional is a particular structure. Every act has a subject, an act-quality or 'noesis', and act-matter or 'noema', and an actual or merely intended object.
3. The objective world is constituted in complex series of intentional acts.

The sort of case that Husserl has in mind here is examplified by seeing a material object, say, a red sphere and looking at it from different sides. The initial impression that we are seeing a red sphere may be confirmed by looking further at the thing. But it may also be disappointed. We may find out that the backside is green and concave. Our expectations are disappointed and we alter the initial description. [Cf. Husserl, PRS 25 ff.] There is no reason to believe that the relations between the noemata of different acts cannot be put in perfectly familiar logical terms. We may identify the noemata of different acts or recognize that they are different. In fact Husserl uses the term "*Satz* (proposition)" to describe a central core of the noema, and although this proposition is not, precisely, a linguistic entity it has all the essential characteristics of what are usually called propositions [Husserl, *Ideas* I 324]. Noemata are in a strict sense consistent or inconsistent with one another or entail each other. The relations between these noemata can thus, as far as we can tell, be formalized. The same, Husserl thinks, can be expected with respect to noeses [Husserl, *Ideas* I, 325 ff.].

On this account of constitution as the logical concatenation of noemata and noeses, we can draw an intelligible distinction between an empirical ego and a transcendental ego. In any given experience I perform a series of intentional acts. I may walk around the red sphere in different ways, or if it is small enough, pick it up etc. There are alternative sequences of acts that may yield the same result. But all of these series must, if they yield a correct result, instantiate certain general formal rules about the correct concatenations of noemata and noeses. We may say then that the term "empirical ego" refers to the actual sequence which may acts follow, a sequence which could be other than it is without affecting the outcome of the perceptual series and that the term "transcendental ego" refers to my series of acts insofar as they instantiate formal rules for doing this sort of thing correctly. There are passages to support such an interpretation. [See e.g. Husserl, CM 61–66]

But if the term "transcendental ego" refers to these rules, it is extremely misleading to refer to the set of them as an "ego". In the first place, this suggests, as Husserl clearly believes, that there are many egos. But there is only one set of formal rules, although many instantiations of them. Besides, egos are someone's. They belong to persons or are individual persons. But a set of formal rules does not belong to anyone, nor is it an individual person.

It would similarly be misleading to apply the word "constitution" to the way in which the formal rules determine the actual construction of knowledge and experience. The transcendental ego, in the present interpretation of that concept, no more constitutes the world (in any reasonable sense of "constitutes") than logic constitutes mathematics or, for that matter, traffic regulations constitute traffic flow.

More seriously, the conception of the transcendental ego as the formal rules instantiated in inference and other mental acts is clearly different from the transcendental ego described in the passage with which this section opens. It is simply false that "the objective world . . . derives its entire meaning and its claim to existence . . ." from a transcendental ego that is no more than a set of formal rules.

Husserl's failure to see that his account of the transcendental ego is not coherent was encouraged by further confusions.

The dependence of the world on the transcendental ego is often expressed in statements like these:

> Experience is the performance (*Leistung*) in which experienced being is there as it is, for me who has the experience . . . [Husserl, FTL 206].
>
> There is no being or being-thus-and-so, whether as actuality or possibility, unless it is as valid (*geltend*) for me [Husserl, FTL 207].

If we were to rewrite this and similar statements in the formal mode, it would come to this: Whatever truth claims I make about the world or about myself, the evidence I provide for these claims will contain at least some first-person statements. What is more, these first-person statements are of different sorts and appear in different contexts. The most obvious examples are statements in support of empirical claims. I support

"There is a phenomenologist in the attic"

by detailing a series of fairly complex observations and inferences from these observations. Observation statements and inferences if challenged will be further backed up by saying "I saw . . ." and "From *p* I inferred *q*." Different first person statements will come up in the conversation if my criteria for knowing are challenged. Suppose you accept my observations and the inference but believe that the evidence I have produced does not entitle me to claim that I know that there is a phenomenologist in the attic. I may reply "I call it knowing if . . ."

These observations are, I think, unobjectionable. This is in fact what lends considerable plausibility to Husserl's gropings, that his starting points are impeccable. Thus most epistemologists would certainly be willing to say that certain first-person statements, for instance, are the court of last resort if someone's observation statements are challenged. Usually this presents certain problems to the epistemologist, precisely because he has to make clear the nature of the transition from the report "I saw a . . ." to a valid claim of the form "There was (is) an . . ."

But it is not usually taken to imply that there is a transcendental ego on which the world and our knowledge of it are dependent. It is not too difficult to see, however, how Husserl is led to these opinions.

Husserl does not speak of first-person observation statements, he speaks, instead, of perceptual acts. [There are good reasons for using the act vocabulary in contexts of this sort, for speaking say of evidencing acts rather than of evidence statements: not all experiences, observations, sensings are put in words. But it is what we experience, observe, sense that is evidence for empirical knowledge claims, not just what we *say* we experience, observe or sense.] He also uses the act vocabulary to talk about the merely formal features of inferences. [See e.g. Husserl, CM 111ff.; *Ideas* I 371 & 377ff.; FTL 171ff.] Both the sensing which validates reports of observations as well as the formal rules that validate inferences are said to be acts. Both sorts of acts establish the validity of our beliefs. Acts, moreover, are always acts of an agent, a subject. Thus we find ourselves with a notion of a subject whose acts support both our perceptual reports and our more general claims about the world. Once we accept this notion, it is not implausible to say that the validity of our knowledge claims depend on this subject. Since the formal rules which are one of the performances of this subject are not empirical rules it is, furthermore, not implausible to speak of it as a "pure" subject, i.e., one which is not known empirically.

But, of course, Husserl ascribes quite diverse functions to the transcendental ego and its acts. He ascribes to it the rules by which we validate series of acts, rules of formal logic and rules of evidence, and he ascribes to it the first-person statements which give last ditch support to observation statements. The former are plausibly said to be nonempirical but cannot really be said to be "mine" or "yours". The latter are clearly mine or yours but cannot be plausibly said to be nonempirical. But both serve to validate, in different ways, my empirical claims about the world. Husserl's notion of the transcendental ego seems to confuse these two very different ways of validating empirical claims because he is not clear about the very different entities, referred to by 'act'. Once we let this confusion pass, it is easy to speak of an individual that is not empirical which provides these validations.

V

One further confusion must be noted. It throws additional light on the genesis of Husserl's concept of the transcendental ego. It also helps to clarify further the earlier problem, how things can be both 'in themselves' and 'for us'.

Husserl uses the term "act" in two radically distinct senses. He tells us, on the one hand, that "act" is not to be construed as "action":

> As regards the talk about acts, on the other hand, one may, of course, not think here of the original meaning of *actus;* any idea of activity must remain completely excluded [Husserl, LU II 379].

A footnote to this passage makes some suggestion as to what sort of distinction Husserl has in mind when he differentiates acts from actions.

> We completely agree with Natorp (*Introduction to Psychology*, p. 21) when he objects that we must not take talk of mental acts seriously as actions of consciousness or of the ego: "Consciousness seems to be a doing and its subject a doer only because it is often or always accompanied by striving." We reject the mythology of actions, we define 'acts' not as mental activities but as intentional, immanent experiences [*ibid*].

The term 'action' refers to a doing, to the sort of thing which involves striving or trying, and thus, presumably, success or failure. Actions bring something about, if they succeed, or fail to do so. None of this is true of 'acts'.

The adoption of a second sense of act as action is quite explicit in a later passage, written in the mid 1920's:

When we speak of producing in other contexts we have reference to the domain of the real. We mean the producing of real things or processes by doing. . . . In our case we have non-real (*irreale*) objects before us which we treat and shape by acting in this way or that, being all the while directed towards them and not towards psychological realities. . . . We may now weaken [the claim] that what takes place here is seriously a doing that shapes, an activity. . . . Indeed, judging (and in its originality, of course, in a special way judging which yields knowledge) is also a case of acting . . . in judging something non-real is constituted intentionally [Husserl, FTL 149].

Here the difference between acts in the psychological and the phenomenological sense is no longer a difference between action as full-fledged doing, that takes time and brings something about and an act of which neither of these is true, but is rather a difference between the objects brought about. In the psychological sphere they are real objects (i.e. spatio-temporally located objects) whereas that is not true in the phenomenological sphere. But in both cases we speak, apparently without shift of meaning or metaphorical usage, of an action, a doing, which may also be called "constituting" and thus sounds very much like making.

Husserl thus gives two quite distinct meanings to the word "act." In the sense which the term takes in the early writings, acts differ from one another as seeing differs from imagining for instance. These differences presumably can be expressed as *purely logical differences* between what is in one case seen and in the other imagined i.e., as different logical features of the contents of these acts. There is e.g., an oddity in "I saw a unicorn but unicorns do not exist" whereas there is no oddity in "I imagined a unicorn but unicorns do not exist." No more is meant by "act" than that. There is no implication of something being done, of something being produced. Yet all of this is what is meant by 'act' as Husserl uses it in *Ideas* in 1913 and later, in 1929, in *Formal and Transcendental Logic*.

Husserl never seems to notice that the word "act" is used in these utterly diverse senses. If we fail to draw this necessary distinction, it becomes easy to find the objectivity of our knowledge problematic. For if we use "act" in the sense of "action," specifically of "making," what we know and experience is made by us and is, in this way, dependent on or relative to us. That relativity extends to everything, including concepts like "objectivity". But if we then move surreptitiously to the earlier concept of act, where act differences are purely logical differences, our acts do not affect what is known and experienced and thus knowledge and experience can claim objectivity in a sense devoid of all dependence on or relativity to a subject. Using the two senses of act interchangeably further encourages use of two sorts of meaning ascribed to "objectivity" (noted previously in section III) and thus gives added support to the pressing, albeit confused, worry about the relativity of the world to ourselves as subjects.

Once this confusion has been let by, it is easier to speak of a transcendental ego as a genuinely individuated subject which, in addition, is in some sense numerically identical with the empirical ego [EP I 340]. For the failure to separate different senses of act goes hand in hand with failure to differentiate corresponding different senses of 'subject'. The subject of an action is, like this action itself, at least partially individuated by its position in space and time. Actions occur at particular places and times, and thus the agent must be locatable in space and time. If, on the other hand, we mean by 'act' certain formal features of actions, reference to acts does involve reference to subjects, but since acts, as purely formal features are neither in space nor in time, the corresponding subject is also not spatio-temporally located. Given the confusion of two senses of "act" we very conveniently get the notion of a subject that performs full-blooded actions—it senses, observes, believes and infers—and yet is, as subject of formal features of acts, not located in space and time. Thus we can ascribe actual mental actions to a 'pure subject'.

In this way we can understand some of the sources of Husserl's notion of the transcendental ego and of the relativity of our knowledge—a problem resolved by the discovery of the transcendental ego. Both problem and solution, we have seen, are irremediably confused. Our persistent uneasiness about the transcendental-phenomenological reduction thus turns out to be justified. That methodological move, we saw, is only intelligible if the mundane-transcendental distinction is already available. If, as it now turns out, that distinction cannot be drawn, the transcendental-phenomenological reduction cannot be performed. This does not mean, of course, that there cannot be philosophical reflection about concepts. But it does mean that Husserl's injunction to perform universal reflection is not intelligible.

VI

If one argues for an interpretation of a given philosophic text one must make heavy use of arguments to show that alternative interpretations would make the text come out self-contradictory. On the assumption that the author of the text did not contradict himself one can reject a number of interpretations which seem plausible at first because they seem to fit specific passages. Without this appeal to the consistency of the author interpreted it is more difficult to defend a reading of a philosophic text. The interpretation which I have given in the preceding sections obviously cannot use this appeal since the claim here is precisely that Husserl's writings are shot through with inconsistencies. This makes it hard to defend this interpretation against other readers of Husserl who agree in general that Husserl is inconsistent but find the inconsistencies in different places.

But the preceding arguments have built up a strong case against those readers of Husserl who want to hold that the discussion of the transcendental-mundane distinction is intelligible and can be made clear. For the preceding arguments constitute a challenge to those readers to show that the difficulties I have found in Husserl are readily resolved and that the questions I have raised have answers. I can see no way of escaping the conclusion that Husserl's transcendental phenomenology is a big muddle. Should this conclusion be false, I have at least shown that, so far, it is a mystery.

PHENOMENA AND PHENOMENOLOGICAL REFLECTION

THE PRINCIPLE OF ALL PRINCIPLES: No theory we can conceive can mislead us in regard to the *principle of all principles:* that every primordial dator Intuition is a source of authority for knowledge, that whatever presents itself in 'intuition' is primordial form . . . is simply to be accepted as it gives itself out to be, though only within the limits in which it then presents itself.

—Edmund Husserl IDEAS

Self-evident data are patient, they let theories chatter about them, but remain what they are.

—Edmund Husserl IDEAS

Husserl's famous slogan, "Back to the Things Themselves," emphasizes the aim of dealing only with what is given in direct experience.

—Marvin Farber THE AIMS OF PHENOMENOLOGY

INTRODUCTION

What is left after the phenomenological reduction? What are the "phenomena" that phenomenology describes? In the first two selections Husserl is attempting to describe the "phenomenological residuum" (from *Ideas*) and the peculiar transcendental attitude one adopts in phenomenology (from CM). Frank Tillman, an American interpreter of phenomenology, attempts to analyze the concept of "phenomenological reflection." Eugene Gendlin, an American psychologist with both phenomenological and existentialist sympathies, argues a revised conception of phenomenological inquiry which does not presuppose Husserl's notion of an assumption-free "given." Roderick Chisholm provides an analytic argument for the idea of the "given," and Wilfrid Sellars, one of the most important of contemporary analytic philosophers, offers a sharp critique of the same notion.

EXPERIENCE AND PURE CONSCIOUSNESS

EDMUND HUSSERL

(19)

Immediate "seeing" (*Sehen*), not merely the sensory seeing of experience, but *seeing in general as primordial dator consciousness of any kind whatsoever,* is the ultimate source of justification for all rational statements. It has this right-conferring function only because and in so far as its object-giving is primordial. If we see an object standing out in complete clearness, if purely on the basis of the seeing, and within the limits of what we grasp through really seeing, we have carried out processes of discrimination and conceptual comprehension, if then we see (as a new way of "seeing") how the object is constituted, the statement faithfully expressing this has then its justification. If we ask why the statement is justified, and ascribe no value to the reply "I see that it is so," we fall into absurdity, as will later become clear to us. Moreover, this does not exclude the possibility, as we may here add so as to prevent misconstructions that may arise, that under certain circumstances one "seeing" can very well conflict with another, and likewise one *legitimate* statement with another. For the implication in this case is not that seeing is no ground of legitimacy, any more than the outweighing of one force by another means that it is no force at all. What it does tell us is that perhaps in a certain category of intuitions (those of sensory experience would just fit the suggestion), seeing in its very essence is "imperfect": it can on lines of principle be strengthened or weakened, and hence an assertion which has

Reprinted with permission of the Macmillan Company from *Ideas*, by Edmund Husserl, translated by W. R. Boyce-Gibson, pp. 75–77, 101–103. First Collier Books Edition, 1962. Copyright 1931 by Crowell Collier and Macmillan, Inc., New York.

an immediate and therefore a genuine ground of legitimacy in
experience must none the less be given up in the course of experience under the pressure of a counterclaim which exceeds
and annuls it.

(20)

Thus for "experience" (*Erfahrung*) we substitute the more
general "intuition," therefore decline to identify science in general and science of experience. Moreover, it is easy to see that he
who supports this identification and contests the validity of pure
eidetic thinking is led into a scepticism which, genuine, cancels
itself through its own absurdity. [Cf. Husserl, LU] It is sufficient to question empiricists concerning the source of the
validity of their general thesis (e.g., that "all valid thought has
its ground in experience as the sole object-giving intuition") to
get them involved in demonstrable absurdities. Direct experience
gives only singular elements and no generalities, and is thus
insufficient. It can make no appeal to the intuition of essence,
since it denies such intuition; it must clearly rely on induction,
and so generally on the system of mediate modes of inference
through which the science of experience wins its general propositions. How fares it now, we ask, with the truth of mediated
conclusions, be these deductively or inductively inferred? Is this
truth (indeed, we could even say, the truth of a singular judgment) itself something experienceable, and thus in the last resort
perceptible?

33. INTIMATION CONCERNING "PURE" OR "TRANSCENDENTAL CONSCIOUSNESS" AS PHENOMENOLOGICAL RESIDUUM

We have learnt to understand the meaning of the phenomenological επσχη (*epokhe*—abstention), but we are still quite in
the dark as to its serviceability. In the first place it is not clear
to what extent the limitation of the total field of the επσχη, as
discussed in the previous pages, involves a real narrowing of its

general scope. *For what can remain over when the whole world is bracketed, including ourselves and all our thinking (cogitare)?*

Since the reader already knows that the interest which governs these "Meditations" concerns a new eidetic science, he will indeed at first expect the world as fact to succumb to the disconnexion, but not *the world as Eidos,* nor any other sphere of Essential Being. The disconnecting of the world does not as a matter of fact mean the disconnecting of the number series, for instance, and the arithmetic relative to it.

However, we do not take this path, nor does our goal lie in its direction. That goal we could also refer to as *the winning of a new region of Being, the distinctive character of which has not yet been defined,* a region of *individual* Being, like every genuine region. We must leave the sequel to teach us what that more precisely means.

We proceed in the first instance by showing up simply and directly what we see; and since the Being to be thus shown up is neither more nor less than that which we refer to on essential grounds as "pure experiences *(Erlebnisse)*" "pure consciousness" with its pure "correlates of consciousness," and on the other side its "pure Ego," we observe that it is from *the Ego, the* consciousness, *the* experience as given to us from the natural standpoint, that we take our start.

I, the real human being, am a real object like others in the natural world. I carry out *cogitationes,* "acts of consciousness" in both a narrower and a wider sense, and these acts, as belonging to this human subject, are events of the same natural world. And all my remaining experiences *(Erlebnisse)* likewise, out of whose changing stream the specific acts of the Ego shine forth in so distinctive a way, glide into one another, enter into combinations, and are being incessantly modified. Now in its *widest connotation* the expression *"consciousness"* (then indeed less suited for its purpose) includes *all* experiences *(Erlebnisse),* and entrenched in the natural standpoint as we are even in our scientific thinking, grounded there in habits that are most firmly established since they have never misled us, we take all these data of psychological reflexion as real world-events, as the ex-

periences (*Erlebnisse*) of animal beings. So natural is it to us
to see them only in this light that, though acquainted already
with the possibility of a change of standpoint, and on the search
for the new domain of objects, we fail to notice that it is from
out of these centres of experience (*Erlebnisse*) themselves that
through the adoption of the new standpoint the new domain
emerges. Connected with this is the fact that instead of keeping
our eyes turned towards these centres of experience, we turned
them away and sought the new objects in the ontological realms
of arithmetic, geometry, and the like, whereby indeed nothing
truly new has to be won.

Thus we fix our eyes steadily upon the sphere of Consciousness and study what it is that we find immanent in *it*. At first,
without having yet carried out the phenomenological suspen-
sions of the element of judgment, we subject this sphere of
Consciousness in its essential nature to a systematic though in
no sense exhaustive analysis. What we lack above all is a certain
general insight into the essence of *consciousness in general,* and
quite specially also of consciousness, so far as in and through
its essential Being, the "natural" fact-world comes to be known.
In these studies we go so far as is needed to furnish the full insight at which we have been aiming, to wit, *that Consciousness
in itself has a being of its own which in its absolute uniqueness
of nature remains unaffected by the phenomenological disconnexion.* It therefore remains over as a *"phenomenological residuum,"* as a region of Being which is in principle unique, and
can become in fact the field of a new science—the science of
Phenomenology.

Through this insight the "phenomenological" ε$\pi\sigma\chi\eta$ will for
the first time deserve its name; to exercise it in full consciousness
of its import will turn out to be the necessary operation which
*renders "pure" consciousness accessible to us, and subsequently
the whole phenomenological region.* And thus we shall be able
to understand why this region and the new science attached to
it was fated to remain unknown. From the natural standpoint
nothing can be seen except the natural world. So long as the
possibility of the phenomenological standpoint was not grasped,

and the method of relating the objectivities which emerge therewith to a primordial form of apprehension had not been devised, the phenomenological world must needs have remained unknown, and indeed barely divined at all.

We would add yet the following to our terminology: Important motives which have their ground in epistemological requirements justify us in referring to "pure" consciousness, of which much is yet to be said, also as *transcendental consciousness*, and the operation through which it is acquired as *transcendental* εποχη. On grounds of method this operation will split up into different steps of "disconnexion" or "bracketing," and thus our method will assume the character of a graded reduction. For this reason we propose to speak, and even preponderatingly, of *phenomenological reductions* (though, in respect of their unity as a whole, we would speak in unitary form of *the* phenomenological reduction). From the epistemological viewpoint we would also speak of transcendental reductions. Moreover, these and *all* our terms must be understood exclusively in accordance with the same which *our* presentations indicate for them, but not in any other one which history or the terminological habits of the reader may favour.

NATURAL AND TRANSCENDENTAL REFLECTION

EDMUND HUSSERL

For the sake of further clarification, however, it should be added that we must distinguish *"straightforwardly" executed* grasping perceiving, remembering, predicating, valuing, purposing, etc., from the *reflections* by means of which alone, as grasping acts belonging to a new level, the straightforward acts

Reprinted from *Cartesian Meditations*, translated by D. Cairns (The Hague, Netherlands: M. Nijhoff, 1960), section 15, pp. 33–37, by permission of the publisher.

become accessible to us. Perceiving straightforwardly, we grasp, for example, the house and not the perceiving. Only in reflection do we "*direct*" ourselves to the perceiving itself and to its perceptual directedness to the house. In the "*natural reflection*" of everyday life, also however in that of psychological science (that is, in psychological experience of our own psychic processes), we stand on the footing of the world already given as existing —as when, in everyday life, we assert: "I see a house there" or "I remember having heard this melody." In *transcendental-phenomenological reflection* we deliver ourselves from this footing, by universal epoché with respect to the being or non-being of the world. The experience as thus modified, the *transcendental experience*, consists then, we can say, in our *looking at* and describing the particular transcendentally reduced *cogito*, but without participating, as reflective subjects, in the natural existence-positing that the originally straightforward perception (or other *cogito*) contains or that the Ego, as immersing himself straightforwardly in the world, actually executed. Therewith, to be sure, an essentially changed subjective process takes the place of the original one; accordingly it must be said that this reflection *alters* the original subjective process. But that is true of every reflection, including natural reflection. Natural reflection alters the previously naïve subjective process quite essentially; this process loses its original mode, "straightforward", by the very fact that reflection makes an object out of what was previously a subjective process but not objective. The proper task of reflection, however, is not to repeat the original process, but to consider it and explicate what can be found in it. Naturally the transition to this considering yields a new intentional process, which, with its peculiarity of "relating back to the earlier process", is awareness, and perhaps evident awareness, of just that earlier process itself, and not some other. Precisely thereby an experiential knowing (which at first is descriptive) becomes possible, that experiential knowing [*Erfahrungswissen*] to which we owe all conceivable cognizance [*Kenntnis*] and cognition [*Erkenntnis*] of our intentional living. This continues to hold, then, for transcendental-phenomenological reflection. The reflecting Ego's non-participation in the "positing" (believing, taking a position as to being) that is part of the straightforward house-perception in no wise alters the fact that his *reflecting* experiencing is precisely an *experiencing* experiencing of the ˌhouse-perception with all its moments, which belonged to it before and are continuing to take shape. And among these, in our example, are the moments of the perceiving itself, as the flowing subjective process, and the moments of the perceived "house", purely as perceived. There is lacking neither, on the one side, the existence-positing (perception belief) in the mode of certainty, which is part of—normal—perceiving, nor, on the other side (that of the appearing house), the character of simple "factual existence". The non-participating, the abstaining, of the Ego who has the phenomenological attitude is *his* affair, not that of the perceiving he considers reflectively, nor that of the naturally perceiving Ego. We may add that it is itself accessible to an appropriate reflection; and only by means of this do we know anything about it.

We can describe the situation also in the following manner. If the Ego, as naturally immersed in the world, experiencingly and otherwise, is called *"interested" in the world,* then the phenomenologically altered—and, as so altered, continually maintained—attitude consists in a *splitting of the Ego:* in that the phenomenological Ego establishes himself as *"disinterested on-looker",* above the naïvely interested Ego. That this takes place is then itself accessible by means of a new reflection, which, as transcendental, likewise demands the very same attitude of looking on *"disinterestedly"*—the Ego's sole remaining interest being to see and to describe adequately what he sees, purely as seen, as what is seen and seen in such and such a manner.

Then all occurences of the life turned toward the world, with all their simple and founded positings of being and with the correlative modes of being (such as certainly existing, being possible, being probable, also being beautiful and being good, being useful, etc.), pure of all accompanying and expectant meanings on the observer's part, become accessible to description. Only in this purity, indeed, can they become themes of a universal *criticism of consciousness,* such as our aiming at a philosophy necessarily demands. We recall the radicalness of the Cartesian idea of philosophy, as the idea of the all-embracing science, grounded to the utmost and apodictically. This idea demands an absolute universal criticism, which, for its part, by abstention from all positions that already give anything existent, must first create for itself a *universe of absolute freedom from prejudice.* The universality of transcendental experience and description does this by inhibiting the universal "prejudice" of world-experience, which hiddenly pervades all naturalness (the belief in the world, which pervades naturalness thoroughly and continuously), and then—within the sphere that remains unaffected, the absolute sphere of egological being, as the sphere of meanings reduced to an unalloyed freedom from prejudice—striving for a universal description. This description is then called on to be the foundation for a radical and universal criticism. Naturally everything depends on strictly preserving the absolute "unprejudicedness" of the description and thereby satisfying the principle of pure evidence, which we laid down in advance. That signifies restriction to the pure data of transcendental reflection, which therefore must be taken precisely as they are given in simple evidence, purely "intuitively", and always kept free from all interpretations that read into them more than is genuinely seen.

If we follow this methodological principle in the case of the dual topic, *cogito—cogitatum* (*qua cogitatum*), there become opened to us, first of all, the general descriptions to be made, always on the basis of particular *cogitationes,* with regard to each of the two correlative sides. Accordingly, on the one hand, descriptions of the intentional object as such, with regard to the determinations attributed to it in the modes of consciousness concerned, attributed furthermore with corresponding modalities, which stand out when attention is directed to them. (For example: the "modalities of being", like certainly being, possibly or presumably being, etc.; or the "subjective"-temporal modes, being present, past, or future.) This line of description is called *noematic.* Its counterpart is *noetic* description, which concerns the modes of the *cogito* itself, the modes of consciousness (for example: perception, recollection, retention), with the modal differences inherent in them (for example: differences in clarity and distinctness).

We now understand that, by our universal epoché with respect to the being or non-being of the world, we have not simply lost the world for phenomenology; we retain it, after all, *qua cogitatum*. And not only with respect to the *particular* realities that are meant (and *as* they are meant) in some set or other of separate acts of consciousness—or, stated more distinctly: that are meant selectively. For indeed their particularity is particularity within a unitary *universe*, which, even when we are directed to and grasping the particular, goes on "appearing" unitarily. In other words, there is always co-awareness of it, in the unity of a consciousness that can itself become a grasping consciousness, and often enough does. This consciousness is awareness of the world-whole in its own peculiar form, that of spatiotemporal endlessness. Throughout every change in consciousness the universe—changeable in its experienced (and otherwise selectively meant) particulars, but still the one and only universe—remains as the existing background of our whole natural life. Thus, when phenomenological reduction is consistently executed, there is left us, on the noetic side, the openly endless life of pure consciousness and, as its correlate on the noematic side, the meant world, purely as meant. Accordingly, not only in respect of particulars but also *universally*, the phenomenologically meditating Ego can become the "non-participant onlooker" at himself—including furthermore every Objectivity that "is" for him, and *as* it is for him. Obviously it can be said that, as an Ego in the natural attitude, I am likewise and at all times a transcendental Ego, but that I know about this only by executing phenomenological reduction. Only by virtue of this new attitude do I see that all the world, and therefore whatever exists naturally, exists for me only as accepted by me, with the sense it has for me at the time—that it exists for me only as *cogitatum* of my changing and, while changing, interconnected *cogitationes;* and I now accept it solely as that. Consequently I, the transcendental phenomenologist, have *objects* (singly or in universal complexes) as a theme for my universal descriptions: *solely as the intentional correlates of modes of consciousness of them.*

PHENOMENOLOGY

FRANK A. TILLMAN

One of the greatest difficulties in understanding Husserl's transcendental, phenomenological method is the language Husserl uses to describe it. He very often makes it appear highly esoteric and quite unrelated to anything in ordinary practice. And as Mr. Natanson rehearses it, it seems to bear no similarity to analytic practice. Yet the first step, the development of a reflective attitude, is a perfectly ordinary practice which has been turned into a methodological device. And as a device, it is an indispensable condition for the practice of both analytic philosophy and phenomenology. Later, I want to show that there is a counterpart in analytic philosophy for a number of stages of Husserl's method. At present, I will try to describe aspects of his method in standard English.

When I am engaged in common commerce with the world, whatever I am involved in doing engages my attention almost entirely: while I am engaged, I have little opportunity to reflect on myself as engaged—whatever I am doing narrows my concern to what is immediately relevant to what engages me. If I am searching for a long pointed red pencil I remember leaving on my desk, not only do I not reflect on myself as engaged in searching, but my field of vision is generally structured so that only long objects with the properties of being pointed and red stand out. And so it is with all practical task-oriented activities. But

Reprinted from a symposium on "Phenomenology As a Rigorous Science" with J. Edie and M. Natanson, from *The International Philosophical Quarterly* (1967), pp. 33–37, by permission of the author and the *International Philosophical Quarterly.*

suppose in the course of looking for my pencil I become aware that my search is not successful. For the first time, I may be led to make my activity of searching itself an object of reflection. What I gave no notice to *now* becomes prominent. I am now in the position of questioning what I was doing and how I was going about it. But, also, my world, once narrowed to just the awareness of red and pointed objects, may be expanded. Just this kind of wrenching myself away from my natural involvement in the world is the ordinary counterpart of the preliminary step to the phenomenological method.

But between this ordinary approximation of disinterested reflection and a fully realized phenomenological attitude there are crucial differences.

1. I made searching itself an object of reflection in order to improve my search. No such practical end motivates phenomenological reflection. The attitude of disinterestedness is cultivated in order to let whatever appears present itself just as it appears.[1] In ordinary circumstances, to have a pencil as the object of my search is also to believe in the existence of the pencil. But when I make searching the object of a phenomenological investigation, I am not trying to find the pencil, and I need not believe that a particular pencil exists. The act of searching remains phenomenologically interesting without such a belief. For I am now concerned with the question, "What is it for anything to be a case of searching?" rather than the questions, "Where is the object I am searching for?" or "Is this particular case a case of searching?" The latter are factual questions; the former is a question about meaning. This particular aspect of

---

[1] Husserl uses the technical term "phenomena" to designate whatever it is that presents itself. The name covers both perceptual and cognitive objects such as the objects of belief and knowledge. Thus, when Husserl uses perceptual verbs such as 'see' or 'inspect' he intends them to span both perceptual and cognitive uses. The sense of "seeing" phenomena is the sense of seeing something directly before us, the sense in which there is no room for doubt. Thus, our experiences of phenomena have a superior certainty which we do not associate with anything that is inferred or derived from experience.

phenomenological investigation Husserl calls "bracketing": in effect, it is a temporary suspension of belief in the existence of the objects of investigation.

2. The suspension of belief in existence makes it possible to concentrate on an essential trait of searching, or for that matter, any cognitive or perceptual act like knowing, believing, or perceiving. Searching is object-directed in that searching is always searching *for* something. But what is special to searching, in contrast to believing, is the belief in the object of search. It is a necessary truth that nothing is a case of searching unless the person searching believes in the existence of that for which he searches. This is hardly a profound insight. But it illustrates what Husserl calls "eidetic reduction" and shows why he distinguished pure phenomenology from phenomenological psychology. Phenomenology is pure in the sense that such studies are not dependent on empirical or statistical investigation. Just as I do not have to inspect a large number of cases of intersecting lines to see that a line can intersect another line at only one point in a plane, neither do I have to subject searching to an empirical study to know what is essential to it.

3. There is yet another way phenomenological reflection differs from ordinary reflection. What is essential to all acts of consciousness is a directedness toward objects, a characteristic which Husserl, following the tradition, calls "intentionality." Although the act of searching differs from acts of consciousness in that searching requires the existence of the object of search, these acts are on a par once we suspend belief in existence. Recall the example of searching: what becomes evident to me on phenomenological reflection was lost to me while I searched. While I was engaged in searching, what I saw was the world *as* I structured it. What I did not see[2] was *that* I had structured it. I did not see that the world was invested with my intent, nor did I see that these figments of my intent had their source in me. When all consciousness is made the object of phenomenological inquiry,

---

[2] In the sense of "see" that spans both perceptual and cognitive objects called "phenomena."

then every meaning-giving act and meant object comes within my purview, including the "I" to whom meaning is present and who is the source of meaning.

The technique of phenomenological reduction provides a critical tool for revealing biases not only of ordinary task-related activities, but the seldom acknowledged beliefs and theories that are buried in all practical and theoretical disciplines.

From the phenomenological point of view, the attitude of scientific neutrality itself reveals its bias. A psychologist may scrutinize me with the hope that my behavior will eventually reveal regularities on the basis of which he may predict my future behavior. But to my phenomenological gaze the object of his study, my behavior, and the results of his investigations, regularities pertaining to me, are like artifacts from an alien culture.

Phenomenological investigation also purports to be constructive. In revealing the often unacknowledged assumptions of the special sciences, and in subjecting them to eidetic reduction, Husserl hoped to supply the rationally certain basis of all the sciences. And in studying lived experience, Husserl also hoped to reveal the simpler preverbal experiences and constructive principles which the mind uses to build up more complex concepts and operations.

In concentrating on what is directly given in lived experience, Husserl and other phenomenologists have gained an incredibly rich field of investigation. It staggers the academic imagination and it brings the poignancy of life to philosophy. From the phenomenological standpoint we may study all those phenomena that are vested with our purposes, our hopes, wishes, longings, imaginings. This is the stuff that novels and dreams are made of. . . .

The difficulty here is the problem phenomenologists themselves avow as the problem of the intersubjectivity of evidence. Husserl's insistence on directly inspecting phenomena is the source of highest hope for the phenomenologist and of the deepest despair for the analytic philosopher. This is the place where the most entrenched dogmatic stances reveal themselves.

But here is a question.

How is it possible to know whether one person's phenomenological performance gives the same results as another's? How can I ever count on knowing that I am experiencing what Mr. Natanson designates by the term "weight"? Where one of us cannot determine whether he is wrong, is there really any sense in saying that we are both right? Perhaps this is congenial to Mr. Natanson, for he may be saying that it doesn't matter. In that case, all one can do is to speak for oneself. But this conclusion is hardly consistent with Husserl's conception of phenomenology as a science. For any conception of science the criterion of correctness can never be entirely one's own.

EXPERIENTIAL EXPLICATION

EUGENE GENDLIN

In a previous paper I tried to show that phenomenological description cannot be assumption-free. ["Expressive Meanings" in *Invitation to Phenomenology* (Chicago: Quadrangle Books 1965.)] I cited the preconceptual, preobjective, prereflective, preontological character of phenomena: that phenomena are not made of the units and patterns which description uses. Therefore, any description of phenomena cannot help but import assumption systems, structures, and forms that are not characteristic of preconceptual phenomena as such.

But then, I asked, is there anything left to phenomena and phenomenology? Are they nothing except what we formulate? If our appeal to "phenomena" cannot help us justify or ground the formulations and assumptions always involved in saying anything, isn't "phenomenological grounding" merely an invalid

Reprinted from the *Journal of Existentialism*, 22 (1965), by permission of the *Journal of Existentialism*. Presented at the Third Annual Meeting of the Society for Phenomenology and Existential Philosophy, Yale University, October 23, 1964.

claim to special privileges for one's unexamined schematic assumptions?

There is a relationship between formulations and the experiencing (phenomena) on which we try to "base" them. I gave this relationship of "basing on" the name "explication." What an "explication" statement says cannot be equated with experience; yet it is not just *arbitrarily* imposed on experience. We are working with a relationship between formulation and direct experience which is neither one of correspondence (which would assume that out schematic patterns are already in, read in, posited into experience), nor are our formulations just arbitrary. In explication there is a connection, but the connection isn't an equation between experience and something said of it. Rather, speaking, understanding, and attention are themselves experiential processes, and they carry forward the very experiencing they explicate. Therefore, phenomena don't ground description by being copied or "read off." How, then, do they ground description?

TWO CRITERIA

This relationship of "based on" can be characterized by two conditions which show that what one says of a phenomenological datum is not merely a creature of one's assumption systems. A concrete experential "this" datum has two independent powers (independent of the assumption systems one uses):

First, there is *independent access* to the datum, even without the formulation.

We often see, sense, and feel such a datum first, quite without formulation. For example, we listen to a discussion, then we have something to say. We "know" what we are about to say even without reciting words to ourselves. If we are distracted, we may lose hold of what we were going to say. (And, after groping directly into the concrete felt sense we still have, we can sometimes "get it back": "Oh!" we say, "I've got it back! Just a moment. . . ." We have again what we were about to say, still without words.) We have independent access to an experiential datum that never had formulation.

More often a formulation (description) must first lead us to a phenomenon. The formulation must first "lift out" the phenomenon and make us sense it concretely and specifically. Since we needed the formulation to lead us to it, the then noticed phenomenon seems to be the creature of the formulation. But no: even then, the phenomenon permits independent access. We can reject the formulation—perhaps it has inconsistencies, bothers us, is wrong for some purposes, or now seems an insufficient description of the very phenomenon to which it led us. We can say: "I know what you are getting at, but I don't agree with your formulation." We can try a different formulation, or even go a while without any that we accept. Still, we do not *un*notice the directly noticed phenomenal aspect we were led to. Thus, although a formulation may first have to lead us to a phenomenon, we can then directly notice or feel it; it is then independent of the formulation. We have access to the directly noticed aspect, even if we then drop or shelve the formulation that led us to the phenomenon.

Secondly, the directly noticed phenomenon has a power which I called *response*. What we directly sense or feel "responds" differently to different sentences (and to different nonverbal symbols, as well).

In our earlier example, not just any sentences will say what we just recalled we were about to say. Only just certain words will do that. Most other words would not let us feel that we are saying it. How can we tell, considering we never had what we were about to say in words? We can tell because certain words have the directly felt effect I term *response*. These words carry forward our experiencing. They release, relieve our felt sense of being about to say something. They do not leave this felt datum unchanged. We cannot—in words—copy, represent, or picture what we concretely had as felt meaning. (What would be a picture or representation of that feeling of being about to say something?) Rather, to explicate is always a further process of experiencing. It carries forward what we directly felt.

Now, of course, "carrying forward" is not just any and all

sorts of change. It is a very peculiar and specific type of change, and on this fact rests the possibility of a problem of truth. (If any kind of change were a "carrying forward," anything could be said equally well of any experience.)

Independent access and response enable us to know when sentences do carry forward—that is, engender an explication process—and when they do not. But if explication changes the datum it explicates, have we not lost the possibility of truth? Or does carrying forward have a definable truth of its own?

Explication is a process of steps. As we describe some directly felt experiential aspect, our felt experiencing is thereby released, carried forward (if we are lucky enough to find a sentence which brings about the response). This felt response is a shift in feeling, in experiencing, in how we are in the world. A moment later, new aspects of this new experiencing can be explicated. The statement which was previously so true may now be contradicted. The next step of explicating may again bring a felt response as experiencing is further carried forward; yet the new statement may seem to contradict the previous statement.

Thus, propositions as such are no longer true or false in themselves. Instead, there is a characteristic role they may have in the explication process.

Not any and all statements—just a very few—will be true in this sense of felt response and independent access to new facets of experiencing as it is carried forward. There is no problem here about recognizing which statements genuinely function in this way, as compared to the thousands of possible statements that would bring about no response in the directly felt datum, lift out nothing new, and leave everything unchanged.

Thus, we have a distinctly recognizable role which statements perform when they function (as "true" in this new sense) to bring about the steps of an explication process.

CORRECTING THE ERRONEOUS PHENOMENOLOGY

If we take into account that explication is a process of steps in which a datum can be directly accessible and can respond differentially in being carried forward, we will not fall into the following common misunderstandings of phenomenology:

1. Description Is Not Neutral

As I have already said, we can clear up the erroneous claim of "neutral" description (as though one insisted that one's assumption schemes are the very objects of the preobjective, the very themes of prethematic experience). Our criteria make the independent power of phenomena recognizable. We can tell whether or not they are functioning as bases of explication. Therefore, we need not lose phenomena by naïvely equating them with our formulations, the relativity and variety of which then seem to evaporate phenomena altogether.

2. The Unconscious

Phenomenology has seemed unable to handle the common undeniable observations of the so-called unconscious. We cannot solve the problem by simply throwing everyone's observations away. (For example, the observation common to everyone, that we *now* feel something which we insist we really felt earlier without then knowing it; that now we are saying in words what we earlier were about to say, although then we did not know in words what it was; or the insistent conviction that what we specifically lift out to notice now really *was* part of what we sensed then, only not separately as such.) Neither can we accept the theory of the unconscious. That theory is really again the same false assertion that the formulated results of explicating were already "there," before the process of explication occurred; it is much like the error of asserting that the explicit description was in the phenomena before we described [it].

What is later explicated was not all "there" earlier, but neither is the present moment totally new and unrelated to the earlier. What I now feel and assert was not all there then; but we are not always mistaken when we insist that what we now assert is somehow "based on" what we felt then. Each moment is not without any past determinants of personality, culture, and situation. Explication moves through experiential steps, by means of the effect of explicating upon the directly felt. To miss the process of steps in explicating is to lose all continuity, all grounding in experiencing. It leads to that helpless phenomenology which is rooted only in momentary awareness as it is momentarily construed. It is that erroneous phenomenology so widely taken as "limited to awareness." We rightly reject the hidden inner *entities*. But if the steps of explication are also left out, one has only momentary awareness; as someone construes something now, that is all that it is. From one moment to the next everything becomes arbitrary. There is no truth, no ethics, no value, no better or worse, no error, no chain of thought or feeling superior to each man's momentary seeming.

• • •

Thus, as Heidegger said, phenomena are mostly buried, and it is just for that reason that we need phenomenology. Far from staying rooted at what someone *momentarily* construes or feels, phenomenology is *a process* (a hermeneutic), steps of interplay between a "responding" felt concreteness and our explicative words of action.

• • •

6. Phenomena Are Not Internal

There is no fundamental difference between feeling-in-the-world and action-in-the-world. Feeling is our "possibilities" for action in the world (the situations we are in). It is an error to locate feelings "inside" and situation "outside" (out there, separate from us, as though definable apart from us). Then it becomes mysterious why feeling is our being in the situations, why we "interrogate" our feelings to see what we might do. Feelings are how we are in situations. A feeling might, at first, seem to be a dull ache-like things within. But when we *explicate* it, a feeling always turns out to be all about our living in situations. It is always at, toward, about, or with. A feeling is always like: "I am tense because I might get angry at him because he did such-and-such to me in front of so-and-so, which means to me that I am not as I wanted to seem, and that matters because if I'm not, then I'll have to attempt such-and-such instead, which I know I can't do because I would incur such-and-such, which would be bad because . . ." etc. Does it seem mysterious how such a complex explicated texture about living in situations emerges out of what seemed to be just one dull ache-like thing "inside" me? That is what feeling is—our bodily sentient living in the environment. Only very few aspects of our environment are ever separated out and explicated in words. Most of it is felt. Words and behavior carry it forward. Neither words nor acts paint pictures of what is "in" feelings, because feeling is a concrete living process, a living-in-situations, not a container of picturable contents.

Because feeling is already our complex living-in-situations, only certain words and actions can carry feeling forward (and lead to further ongoing feeling). Thereby new aspects can be explicated because there is *now* a *further* living-in-situation in which new aspects are felt, newly differentiable, accessible.

The new alternatives must be "true"; they must succeed in leading us (in the concrete situation) to what we wish (our felt wishing already involves the situation) in the recalcitrant facts we are up against. Feeling is already them—insofar as they mean anything to me. To explicate feeling is to explicate the situations I am up against. And since one does not just sit still and think words, but one also acts, therefore steps of explication include what is newly incurred at each step of thought and action.

Feeling seems "subjective" or "within" only so long as we don't explicate it. Then we might just take a drug or a drink to dull the inward ache. If we explicate it, we find that it is not at all "within"; we find it is at once in, about, and at, situational aspects and other people. When we look away from feeling, when we limit ourselves only to the few aspects of the situation we have already defined and can think clearly about—*then* we are being "subjective," stuck in our own few concepts and leaving out of account the whole sentient mesh of our concrete and complex situations.

Thus, our "criteria" of truth directly include the recalcitrant facts. We are organized living bodies made more complex by culture and learning. Therefore, we are and feel the facts around us. Therefore, not any and all sentences can carry a feeling forward. Only just these precise words will do it (more often than not we fail to find such words). Only just this action will carry forward (more often than not we try and fail to devise such an action). Words or actions that do carry forward sometimes require genius, because feeling already includes so very many givens, and so many facets of what we wish, must avoid, etc.

We are now a long way from that oversimplified misunderstanding of phenomenology which is only a person's arbitrary way of construing, from moment to moment, lacking past or present determinants, neither true nor false, neither good nor bad, authentic only by caprice and in oblivion of facts.

All this arbitrariness entered because existentialism rightly asserts that reality (phenomena) is not already fashioned according to some scheme, some ultimate code of values, set of truths or presuppositions, representations or laws. As Sartre says, there can be consciousness of laws, but not laws of consciousness—that is, the concrete, living, sentient, felt ongoing process is always more basic than any conceptual pattern. Living humans fashion laws, laws do not determine living humans. For existentialism, laws, forces, entities, principles, values, etc., are only some man's assumption system. But if everything is not to become arbitrary, phenomenology must be a systematic interplay between concretely felt, lived given experience (without read-in assumptions) on the one hand, and philosophy, formulation, words, concepts, forms, and action, on the other. This systematic interplay is explications: we use concepts and experience felt directly in a step-by-step carrying forward.

Thus the given is lived and shaped as it is explicated. I am not saying that it has no organization—anything living and sentient is always highly organized, highly meaningful, and symbolized. The organism living in situations is the most complexly organized system we know of—but it is living and that means that it is an order which evolves as it exists. Truth, for explication, cannot be described simply as accuracy. By our "criteria" the accurate explication *changes* the experienced concreteness, carries it forward, enables us to lift out something new, something that could not have been described before. And the proposition describing what we now, newly, lift out may contradict that earlier statement, whose effect carried us to this new step.

THE DIRECTLY EVIDENT

RODERICK M. CHISHOLM

STATES THAT PRESENT THEMSELVES

The following quotation from Leibniz points to what is directly evident:

> Our direct awareness of our own existence and of our own thoughts provides us with the primary truths *a posteriori*, the primary truths of fact, or, in other words, our primary experiences, just as identical propositions constitute the primary truths *a priori*, the primary truths of reason, or, in other words, our primary insights. Neither the one nor the other is capable of being demonstrated and both can be called *immediate*—the former, because there is no mediation between the understanding and its objects, and the latter because there is no mediation between the subject and the predicate.[1]

Thinking and believing provide us with paradigm cases of the directly evident. Consider a reasonable man who is thinking about Albuquerque, or who believes that Albuquerque is in New Mexico, and suppose him to reflect on the philosophical question "What is my justification for counting it as evident, or for thinking that I know, that I am thinking about Albuquerque, or that

---

[1] *New Essays Concerning Human Understanding*, Book IV, Chap. 9.

Reprinted from Roderick M. Chisholm, *Theory of Knowledge*, © 1966 (Englewood Cliffs, N.J.: Prentice Hall, 1966), pp. 27–34. Reprinted by permission of Prentice Hall, Inc., Englewood Cliffs, New Jersey.

I believe that Albuquerque is in New Mexico?" (He is *not* asking "What is my justification for thinking that Albuquerque is in New Mexico?") He could reply in the following way: "My justification for counting it as evident that I am thinking·about Albuquerque, or that I believe that Albuquerque is in New Mexico, is simply the fact that I *am* thinking about Albuquerque, or that I *do* believe that it is in New Mexico." And this reply fits our formula for the directly evident:

> What justifies me in counting it as evident that *a* is *F* is simply the fact that *a* is *F*.

The man has justified a proposition merely by reiterating it, and this type of justification is *not* appropriate in connection with the questions that were previously discussed. To the question "What justification do you have for counting it as evident that there can be no life on the moon?" it would be inappropriate—and impertinent—simply to reiterate "There can be no life on the moon." But we can state our justification for certain propositions about our *beliefs,* and certain propositions about our thoughts, merely by reiterating those propositions. They may be said, therefore, to pertain to what is directly evident.

Borrowing a technical term from Meinong, let us say that what is directly evident to a man is always some state of affairs that "presents itself to him." Thus, my believing that Socrates is mortal is a state of affairs that is "self-presenting" to me. If I do believe that Socrates is mortal, then, *ipso facto*, it is evident to me that I believe that Socrates is mortal; the state of affairs is "apprehended through itself."[2]

Other states that may be similarly self-presenting are those

---

[2] See A. Meinong, *Über emotionale Präsentation* (Vienna: Alfred Hölder, 1917), Sec. 1. Cf. Franz Brentano, *Psychologie vom empirischen Standpunkt* (Leipzig: Felix Meiner, 1924), Chap. 2. Sec. 2; Bertrand Russell, *An Inquiry into Meaning and Truth* (New York: W. W. Norton & Company, Inc., 1940) chaps. 9–11; Ledger Wood, *The Analysis of Knowledge* (Princeton: Princeton University Press, 1941), Chap. 5; and C. J. Ducasse, "Propositions, Truth, and the Ultimate Criterion of Truth," *Philosophy and Phenomenological Research,* IV (1944), 317–40.

described by "thinking that one remembers that . . ." or "seeming to remember that . . ." (as distinguished from "remembering that . . ."), and "taking" or "thinking that one perceives" (as distinguished from "perceiving"). Desiring, hoping, wondering, wishing, loving, hating may also be self-presenting. These states are what Leibniz intended by the term "thoughts." But the area of what is self-presenting may be somewhat wider than that of our thoughts, if we take the latter term in its ordinary sense.

It has been suggested, for example, that our own actions can be known "without observation"—that a man can know directly and immediately what it is that he is doing at any particular time without observing his actions by means of any of the senses.[3] However, it might be more accurate to say that a man can know directly and "without observation" what it is that he means or intends to be doing—what it is that he is trying or undertaking to do. For where his action is an overt, bodily action, he cannot know "without observation" what it is that he is succeeding in doing; he cannot know, without observation, what the actual effects of his trying or undertaking happen to be. The fact remains, however, that trying or undertaking is more than merely thinking and that trying or undertaking is also "self-presenting." We may say, therefore, that Leibniz was mistaken in restricting the "primary truths of fact" to "our direct awareness of our own existence and of our own thoughts." Statements about what a man is trying or undertaking to do at any particular time are not, strictly speaking, statements about his "thoughts," but they are statements which do express what is directly evident to him at that time.

AN ALTERNATIVE DESCRIPTION

But surely, one may object, it makes no sense whatever to ask "What is your justification for thinking you know that you believe that Socrates is mortal?"

---

[3] Cf. G. E. M. Anscombe, *Intention* (Oxford: Basil Blackwell, 1957), pp. 49–50.

To one who feels that such questions "make no sense," we need not reply by trying to show him that they do. It is enough to make two points: (1) If he is right, then such propositions as "I believe that Socrates is mortal" and "I am thinking about the moon" differ in one very important respect from such propositions as "Socrates is mortal" and "There can be no life on the moon." The former propositions, if our critic is right, are such that it "makes no sense" to ask, with respect to them, "What is my justification for thinking I know that they are true?" (2) Yet they resemble propositions which *are* known to be true in that they may function as *evidence.* My evidence that you and I think alike with respect to the mortality of Socrates cannot consist solely of the evidence I have concerning *your* beliefs about Socrates. It must also consist of the fact that *I* believe that Socrates is mortal. And these two points provide us with an alternative way of characterizing the directly evident.

We could say paradoxically that a proposition is *directly evident* to a man provided (1) that it makes no sense to say of him that he knows the proposition to be true, and (2) that the proposition is evidence for him of something else.

If we use our original characterization of the directly evident, we might think of the directly evident as that which "constitutes its own evidence," and therefore, in the terms of Sextus Empiricus, as that which is "apprehended through itself." But if we use the alternative characterization, we may think paradoxically of the directly evident as being that which is "evidence but not evident."[4] In the one case, we are reminded of the prime mover that moves itself, and in the other, of the prime mover unmoved.

---

[4] The second method of characterization is in the spirit of the following observations by Ludwig Wittgenstein: (1) "It can't be said of me at all (except perhaps as a joke) that I *know* I'm in pain" and (2) "Justification by experience comes to an end. If it did not it would not be justification." *Philosophical Investigations* (Oxford: Basil Blackwell, 1953), pp. 89e, 136e. From the fact that it can't be said of me that I know that I'm in pain, it will not follow, of course, that it *can* be said of me that I do not know—i.e., that I am ignorant of the fact—that I am in pain.

It will be convenient to continue with the terms of our original characterization, but what we shall say can readily be translated into those of the second.

We have yet to consider the most interesting—and controversial—examples of the directly evident.

SEEMING AND APPEARING

In the second of his *Méditations*, Descartes offers what he takes to be good reasons for doubting whether, on any occasion, he sees light, hears noise, or feels heat, and he then observes: "Let it be so; still it is at least quite *certain that it seems to me that* I see light, that I hear noise and that I feel heat."[5] This observation about seeming should be contrasted with what St. Augustine says, in his *Contra Academicos*, about appearing.

> I do not see how the Academician can refute him who says: "I know that this appears white to me, I know that my hearing is delighted with this, I know that this has an agreeable odor, I know that this tastes sweet to me, I know that this feels cold to me." . . . I say this that, when a person tastes something, he can honestly swear that he knows it is sweet to his palate or the contrary, and that no trickery of the Greeks can dispossess him of that knowledge.[6]

These two passages remind us that such words as "seem" or "appear" have different uses in different contexts.

Thus, Descartes' expression, "It seems to me that I see light," when uttered on any ordinary occasion, might be taken to be performing one or the other of two quite different functions. (1) The expression might be used simply to report one's belief; in such a case, "It seems to me that I see light" could be replaced by "I believe that I see light." Taken in this way, the "seems"

[5] E. S. Haldane and R. T. Ross, eds., *The Philosophical Works of Decartes*, I (London: Cambridge University Press, 1934), 153; my italics.

[6] *Against the Academicians* (*Contra Academicos*), trans. and ed. Sister Mary Patricia Garvey (Milwaukee: Marquette University Press, 1942), para. 26, p. 68 of translation.

statement expresses what is directly evident, but since it is equivalent to a belief statement it does not add anything to the cases we have already considered. (2) "It seems to me"—or better, "It seems to *me*"—may be used not only to report a belief, but also to provide the speaker with a way out, a kind of hedge, in case the statement prefixed by "It seems to me" should turn out to be false. This function of "It seems" is thus the contrary of the performative function of "I know" to which J. L. Austin has called attention. In saying "I know," I give my hearers a kind of guarantee and, as Austin says, stake my reputation; but in saying "It seems to *me*," I play it safe, indicating to them that what I say carries no guarantee at all and that if they choose to believe what I say they do so entirely at their own risk.[7] "It seems to me," used in this way, cannot be said to describe what is directly evident, for it cannot be said to describe anything at all.

But the word "appear" as it is used in the translation from St. Augustine—"This appears white to me"—performs still another function. (3) It may be used to describe a certain state of affairs which is not itself a belief. When "appear" is used in this descriptive, "phenomenological" way, one may say consistently and without any incongruity, "That thing appears white to me in this light, but I know that it is really gray." One may also say, again, consistently and without any incongruity, "It appears white to me in this light and I know that, as a matter of fact, it *is* white."

The latter statement illustrates two points overlooked by many contemporary philosophers, the first being that in such a statement, "appear" cannot have the hedging use just referred to, for if it did, the statement would be incongruous (which it is not). The second part ("I know that it is white") would provide a guarantee which the first part ("This appears white") withholds. The second point is that the descriptive, phenomenological use of "appears" is not restricted to the description of *illusory experiences*.

---

[7] Austin discussed this use of "seems" in considerable detail in his posthumous *Sense and Sensibilia* (Oxford: The Clarendon Press, 1962).

The following translation from Sextus Empiricus reminds us that "seems," as well as a number of other verbs, has this descriptive, phenomenological use:

> The same water which feels very hot when poured on inflamed spots seems lukewarm to us. And the same air seems chilly to the old but mild to those in their prime, and similarly the same sound seems to the former faint, but to the latter clearly audible. The same wine which seems sour to those who have previously eaten dates or figs seems sweet to those who have just consumed nuts or chickpeas; and the vestibule of the bathhouse which warms those entering from the outside chills those coming out.[8]

Sextus is here using certain appear-words to indicate a fact about our experience that is familiar to us all—namely, the fact that by varying the state of the subject or perceiver, or of the intervening medium, or of other conditions of observation, we may also vary the ways in which the objects that the subject perceives will appear to him. Sextus' appear-statements are simply descriptive of experience.

Some of these descriptive "appear"- and "seem"-statements may describe what is self-presenting, and when they do, what they express is directly evident. We can single out such a class of directly evident "appear"-statements by referring to what Aristotle called the "proper objects" of the various senses and to what he called the "common sensibles."[9] The "proper objects" may be illustrated by the following: visual characteristics such as blue, green, yellow, red, white, black; auditory characteristics such as sounding or making a noise; somesthetic characteristics such as rough, smooth, hard, soft, heavy, light, hot, cold; gustatory characteristics such as sweet, sour, salt, bitter; and olfactory characteristics, such as fragrant, spicy, putrid, burned. The "common sensibles" are those characteristics such as movement, rest, number, figure, and magnitude, which, as Aristotle says, "are not peculiar to any one sense, but are common to all."

[8] *Outlines of Pyrrhonism*, Book 1. Chap. 14; abridged from Vol. I of *Sextus Empiricus*, The Loeb Classical Library, pp. 55, 63, 65. Cf. K. Lykos, "Aristotle and Plato on 'Appearing,'" *Mind*, LXXIII (1964), 496–514.

[9] See Aristotle's *De Anima*, Book II, chaps. 6 and 7.

If for any such characteristic *F*, I can justify a claim to knowledge by saying of something that it *appears F* (by saying of the wine that it now *looks* red, or *tastes* sour, to me), where the verb is intended in the descriptive, phenomenological sense just indicated, then the *appearing* in question is self-presenting and my statement expresses what is directly evident. The claim that I thus justify, by saying of something that it appears *F*, may be the claim that the thing *is F*, but as we have seen, it may also be some other claim. To the question "What justification do I have for thinking I know, or for counting it as evident, that something now *looks* red to me, or *tastes* sour?" I could reply only by reiterating that something does now look red or taste sour.[10]

Strictly speaking, "The *wine* tastes sour to me" and "*Something* looks red to me" do not express what is directly evident in our sense of this term. For the first statement implies that I am tasting *wine* and the second that there is a certain thing that is appearing red to me, and "I am tasting wine" and "There is a certain physical thing that is appearing red to me" do not express what is directly evident. What justifies me in counting it as evident that I am tasting wine is *not* simply the fact that I am tasting wine, and what justifies me in counting it as evident that a certain physical thing is appearing red to me (and that I am not, say, merely suffering from an hallucination) is not simply the fact that a certain thing *is* appearing red to me. To arrive at what is directly evident in these cases, we must remove the reference to wine in "The wine tastes sour to me" and we must remove the reference to the appearing thing in "That thing appears red to me." This, however, is very difficult to do, since our language was not developed for any such philosophical purpose.

---

[10] Or if the directly evident is to be viewed in analogy with the prime mover unmoved instead of with the prime mover that moves itself, I could say (1) that it "makes no sense" to say "It is evident to me that something now looks red or tastes sour" and (2) that "Something now looks red" or "Something now tastes sour" may yet formulate my *evidence* for something else.

Many philosophers and psychologists would turn verbs into substantives, saying in the one case, "I have a sour taste," and in the other, "I am experiencing a red appearance." Such a procedure has the advantage of enabling us to assimilate these seemings and appearings to other types of sensuous experience—to feelings, imagery, and the sensuous content of dreams and hallucinations, all of which may be "self-presenting" in the sense we have described. But in introducing the substantive "appearance," we may seem to be multiplying entities beyond necessity; for now we seem to be saying that *appearances*, as well as fences and houses, may be counted among the entities that are red. "I have a sour taste" may suggest, similarly, that *tastes*, like wine and fruit, are among the entities that may be sour. It is clear that we must proceed with great care if we are to employ this substantival terminology.[11]

Let us consider another way of describing these self-presenting states. In our examples, "appear" requires a grammatical subject and thus requires a term that purports to refer not merely to a way of appearing, but also to a thing that is said to appear in that way. However, we may eliminate the reference to the thing that appears if we convert our appear-sentences: Instead of saying "Something appears white to me," we may say, more awkwardly, "I am appeared white to by something." We may then eliminate the substantival "something" by merely dropping the final clause, saying, "I am appeared white to."[12] The verbs "tastes" and "sounds" do not allow a similar conversion of "This tastes sour" and "That sounds loud," but "is appeared to" could

[11] One of the first philosophers to note the pitfalls which this substantival, or "sense datum," terminology involves was Thomas Reid; see his *Inquiry into the Human Mind* (1764), Chap. 6, Sec. 20, and *Essays on the Intellectual Powers* (1785), Essay II, Chap. 16 Cf. H. A. Prichard, *Kant's Theory of Knowledge* (Oxford: The Clarendon Press, 1909), and "Appearance and Reality," *Mind* (1906); the latter is reprinted in *Realism and the Background of Phenomenology*, ed. Roderick M. Chisholm (New York: Free Press of Glencoe, Inc., 1960).

[12] But the substantival "I" remains. Recall the beginning of our quotation from Leibniz: "Our direct awareness of our own existence and of our thoughts provides us with the primary truths *a posteriori* . . ."

replace such verbs: We could say "I am appeared loud to" and "I am appeared sour to," just as we have said "I am appeared white to." The words "loud," "'sour," and "white," in these sentences, do not function as adjectives; the sentences do not say, of any entity, that that entity *is* loud, sour, or white. The words are used here to describe *ways* of appearing, or of being appeared to, just as "swift" and "slow" may be used to describe ways of running. They function as adverbs and our sentences would be more correct, therefore, if they were put as: "I am appeared sourly to," "I am appeared whitely to," and "I am appeared loudly to."

The awkwardness of the "appears to" terminology could be avoided if, at this point, we were to introduce another verb, say, "sense," using it in a technical way as a synonym for "is appeared to." In this case, we would say "I sense sourly," "I sense whitely," and "I sense loudly." But even this procedure will introduce ambiguities, as the third example suggests.

Once these terminological difficulties have been removed, is there ground for doubt concerning the directly evident character of what is expressed by statements about appearing? Doubts have been raised in recent years and we should consider these briefly. . . .

THE MYTH OF THE GIVEN

WILFRED SELLARS

DOES EMPIRICAL KNOWLEDGE HAVE A FOUNDATION?

32. One of the forms taken by the Myth of the Given is the idea that there is, indeed *must be,* a structure of particular matter

Reprinted from "Empiricism and the Philosophy of Mind," in W. Sellars, *Science, Perception and Reality* (New York: Humanities Press, 1963), pp. 164–170 by permission of the publisher and Routledge & Kegan Paul.

of fact such that (*a*) each fact can not only be non-inferentially known to be the case, but presupposes no other knowledge either of particular matter of fact, or of general truths; and (*b*) such that the noninferential knowledge of facts belonging to this structure constitutes the ultimate court of appeals for all factual claims—particular and general—about the world. It is important to note that I characterized the knowledge of fact belonging to this stratum as not only noninferential, but as presupposing no knowledge of other matter of fact, whether particular or general. It might be thought that this is a redundancy, that knowledge (not belief or conviction, but knowledge) which logically presupposes knowledge of other facts *must* be inferential. This, however, as I hope to show, is itself an episode in the Myth.

Now, the idea of such a privileged stratum of fact is a familiar one, though not without its difficulties. Knowledge pertaining to this level is *noninferential,* yet it is, after all, *knowledge.* It is *ultimate,* yet it has *authority.* The attempt to make a consistent picture of these two requirements has traditionally taken the following form:

Statements pertaining to this level, in order to 'express knowledge' must not only be made, but, so to speak, must be worthy of being made, *credible,* that is, in the sense of worthy of credence. Furthermore, and this is a crucial point, they must be made in a way which *involves* this credibility. For where there is no connection between the making of a statement and its authority, the assertion may express *conviction,* but it can scarcely be said to express knowledge.

The authority—the credibility—of statements pertaining to this level cannot exhaustively consist in the fact that they are supported by *other* statements, for in that case all *knowledge* pertaining to this level would have to be inferential, which not only contradicts the hypothesis, but flies in the face of good sense. The conclusion seems inevitable that if some statements pertaining to this level are to express *noninferential* knowledge, they must have a credibility which is not a matter of being supported by other statements. Now there does seem to be a class of statements which fill at least part of this bill, namely such statements as would be said to *report observations*, thus, 'This is red.' These statements, candidly made, have authority. Yet they are not expressions of inference. How, then, is this authority to be understood?

Clearly, the argument continues, it springs from the fact that they are made in just the circumstances in which they are made, as is indicated by the fact that they characteristically, though not necessarily or without exception, involve those so-called token-reflexive expressions which, in addition to the tenses of verbs, serve to connect the circumstances in which a statement is made with its sense. (At this point it will be helpful to begin putting the line of thought I am developing in terms of the *fact-stating* and *observation-reporting* roles of certain sentences.) Roughly, two verbal performances which are tokens of a non-token-reflexive sentence can occur in widely different circumstances and yet make the same statement; whereas two tokens of a token-reflexive sentence can make the same statement only if they are uttered in the same circumstances (according to a relevant criterion of sameness). And two tokens of a sentence, whether it contains a token-reflexive expression—over and above a tensed verb—or not, can make the same *report* only if, made in all candour, they express the *presence*—in *some* sense of 'presence'—of the state of affairs that is being reported; if, that is, they stand in that relation to the state of affairs, whatever the relation may be, by virtue of which they can be said to formulate observations of it.

It would appear, then, that there are two ways in which a sentence token can have credibility: (1) The authority may accrue to it, so to speak, from above, that is, as being a token of a sentence type *all* the token of which, in a certain use, have credibility, e.g. '2+2=4.' In this case, let us say that token credibility is inherited from type authority. (2) The credibility may accrue to it from the fact that it came to exist in a certain way in a certain set of circumstances, e.g. 'This is red.' Here token credibility is not derived from type credibility.

Now, the credibility of *some* sentence type appears to be *intrinsic*—at least in the limited sense that it is *not* derived from other sentences, type or token. This is, or seems to be, the case with certain sentences used to make analytic statements. The credibility of *some* sentence types accrues to them by virtue of their logical relations to other sentence types, thus by virtue of the fact that they are logical consequences of more basic sentences. It would seem obvious, however, that the credibility of empirical sentence types cannot be traced without remainder to the credibility of other sentence types. And since no empirical sentence type appears to have *intrinsic* credibility, this means that credibility must accrue to *some* empirical sentence types by virtue of their logical relations to certain sentence tokens, and, indeed, to sentence tokens the authority of which is not derived, in its turn, from the authority of sentence types.

The picture we get is that of their being two ultimate modes of credibility: (1) The intrinsic credibility of analytic sentences, which accrues to tokens as being tokens of such a type; (2) the credibility of such tokens as 'express observations', a credibility which flows from tokens to types.

33. Let us explore this picture, which is common to all traditional empiricisms, a bit further. How is the authority of such sentence tokens as 'express observational knowledge' to be understood? It has been tempting to suppose that in spite of the obvious differences which exist between 'observation reports' and 'analytic statements', there is an essential similarity between the ways in which they come by their authority. Thus, it has been claimed not without plausibility, that whereas *ordinary* empirical statements can be *correctly* made without being *true*, observation reports resemble analytic statements in that being correctly made is a sufficient as well as necessary condition of their truth. And it has been inferred from this—somewhat hastily, I believe—that 'correctly making' the report 'This is green' is a matter of "following the rules for the use of "this", "is", and "green".'

Three comments are immediately necessary:

(1) First a brief remark about the term 'report'. In ordinary usage a report is a report made *by* someone *to* someone. To make a report is to *do* something. In the literature of epistemology, however, the word 'report' or *'Konstatierung'* has acquired a technical use in which a sentence token can play a reporting role (*a*) without being an *overt* verbal performance, and (*b*) without

having the character of being 'by someone to someone'—even oneself. There is, of course, such a thing as 'talking to oneself'— *in foro interno*—but, as I shall be emphasizing in the closing stages of my argument, it is important not to suppose that all 'covert' verbal episodes are of this kind.

(2) My second comment is that while *we* shall not assume that because 'reports' *in the ordinary sense* are actions, 'reports' in the sense of *Konstatierungen* are also actions, the line of thought we are considering treats them as such. In other words, it interprets the correctness of *Konstatierungen* as analogous to the rightness of actions. Let me emphasize, however, that not all *ought* is *ought to do*, nor all correctness the correctness of *actions*.

(3) My third comment is that if the expression 'following a rule' is taken seriously, and is not weakened beyond all recognition into the bare notion of exhibiting a uniformity—in which case the lightning—thunder sequence would 'follow a rule'—then it is the knowledge or belief that the circumstances are of a certain kind, and not the mere fact that they *are* of this kind, which contributes to bringing about the action.

34. In the light of these remarks it is clear that *if* observation reports are construed as *actions, if* their correctness is interpreted as the correctness of an *action,* and *if* the authority of an observation report is construed as the fact that making it is 'following a rule' in the proper sense of this phrase, *then* we are face to face with givenness in its most straightforward form. For these stipulations commit one to the idea that the authority of *Konstatierungen* rests on nonverbal episodes of awareness— awareness *that* something is the case, e.g. *that this is green*— which nonverbal episodes have an intrinsic authority (they are, so to speak, 'self-authenticating') which the *verbal* performances (the *Konstatierungen*) properly performed 'express'. One is committed to a stratum of authoritative nonverbal episodes ('awarenesses'), the authority of which accrues to a superstructure of *verbal actions*, provided that the expressions occurring in these actions are properly *used*. These self-authenticating episodes would constitute the tortoise on which stands the elephant on

which rests the edifice of empirical knowledge. The essence of the view is the same whether these intrinsically authoritative episodes are such items as the awareness that a certain sense content is green or such items as the awareness that a certain physical object looks to oneself to be green.

35. But what is the alternative? We might begin by trying something like the following: An overt or covert token of 'This is green' in the presence of a green item is a *Konstatierung* and expresses observational knowledge if and only if it is a manifestation of a tendency to produce overt or covert tokens of 'This is green'—given a certain set—if and only if a green object is being looked at in standard conditions. Clearly on this interpretation the occurrence of such tokens of 'This is green' would be 'following a rule' only in the sense that they are instances of a uniformity, a uniformity different from the lightning–thunder case in that it is an acquired causal characteristic of the language user. Clearly the above suggestion, which corresponds to the 'thermometer view' criticized by Professor Price, and which we have already rejected, won't do as it stands. Let us see, however, if it cannot be revised to fit the criteria I have been using for 'expressing observational knowledge'.

The first hurdle to be jumped concerns the *authority* which, as I have emphasized, a sentence token must have in order that it may be said to express knowledge. Clearly, on this account the only thing that can remotely be supposed to constitute such authority is the fact that one can infer the presence of a green object from the fact that someone makes this report. As we have already noticed, the correctness of a report does not have to be construed as the rightness of an *action*. A report can be correct as being an instance of a general mode of behaviour which, in a given linguistic community, it is reasonable to sanction and support.

The second hurdle is, however, the decisive one. For we have seen that to be the expression of knowledge, a report must not only *have* authority, this authority must *in some sense* be recognized by the person whose report it is. And this is a steep hurdle indeed. For if the authority of the report 'This is green' lies in the fact that the existence of green items appropriately related to the perceiver can be inferred from the occurrence of such reports, it follows that only a person who is able to draw this inference, and therefore who has not only the concept *green*, but also the concept of uttering 'This is green'—indeed, the concept of certain conditions of perception, those which would correctly be called 'standard conditions'—could be in a position to token 'This is green' in recognition of its authority. In other words, for a *Konstatierung* 'This is green' to 'express observational knowledge', not only must it be a *symptom* or *sign* of the presence of a green object in standard conditions, but the perceiver must know that tokens of 'This is green' *are* symptoms of the presence of green objects in conditions which are standard for visual perception.

36. Now it might be thought that there is something obviously absurd in the idea that before a token uttered by, say, Jones could be the expression of observational knowledge, Jones would have to know that overt verbal episodes of this kind are reliable indicators of the existence, suitably related to the speaker, of green objects. I do not think that it is. Indeed, I think that something very like it is true. The point I wish to make now, however, is that if it *is* true, then it follows, as a matter of simple logic, that one could not have observational knowledge of *any* fact unless one know many *other* things as well. And let me emphasize that the point is not taken care of by distinguishing between *knowing how* and *knowing that*, and admitting that observational knowledge requires a lot of 'know how'. For the point is specifically that observational knowledge of any particular fact, e.g. that this is green, presupposes that one knows general facts of the form *X is a reliable symptom of Y*. And to admit this requires an abandonment of the traditional empiricist idea that observational knowledge 'stands on its own feet'. Indeed, the suggestion would be anathema to traditional empiricists for the obvious reason that by making observational knowledge *presuppose* knowledge of general facts of the form *X is a reliable symptom of Y*, it runs counter to the idea that we come to know general facts of this form only *after* we have come to

know by observation a number of particular facts which support the hypothesis that X is a symptom of Y.

And it might be thought that there is an obvious regress in the view we are examining. Does it not tell us that observational knowledge at time t presupposes knowledge of the form *X is a reliable symptom of Y*, which presupposes *prior* observational knowledge, which presupposes *other* knowledge of the form *X is a reliable symptom of Y,* which presupposes still other, and *prior,* observational knowledge, and so on? This charge, however, rests on too simple, indeed a radically mistaken, conception of what one is saying of Jones when one says that he *knows* that-p. It is not just that the objection supposes that knowing is an *episode;* for clearly there are episodes which we can correctly characterize as knowings, in particular, *observings.* The essential point is that in characterizing an episode or a state as that of *knowing,* we are not giving an empirical description of that episode or state; we are placing it in the logical space of reasons, of justifying and being able to justify what one says.

37. Thus, all that the view I am defending requires is that no tokening by S *now* of 'This is green' is to count as 'expressing observational knowledge' unless it is also correct to say of S that he *now* knows the appropriate fact of the form *X is a reliable symptom of Y,* namely that (and again I oversimplify) utterances of 'This is green' are reliable indicators of the presence of green objects in standard conditions of perception. And while the correctness of this statement about Jones requires that Jones could *now* cite prior particular facts as evidence for the idea that these utterances *are* reliable indicators, it requires only that it is correct to say that Jones *now* knows, thus remembers,[1] that these particular facts *did* obtain. It does not require that it be correct to say that at the time these facts did obtain he *then* knew them to obtain. And the regress disappears.

Thus, while Jones's ability to give inductive reasons *today*

---

[1] (Added 1963) My thought was that one can have direct (noninferential) knowledge of a past fact which one did not or even (as in the case envisaged) *could* not conceptualize at the time it was present.

is built on a long history of acquiring and manifesting verbal habits in perceptual situations, and, in particular, the occurrence of verbal episodes, e.g. 'This is green', which is superficially like those which are later properly said to express observational knowledge, it does not require that any episode in this prior time be characterizeable as expressing knowledge.

38. The idea that observation 'strictly and properly so-called' is constituted by certain self-authenticating nonverbal episodes, the authority of which is transmitted to verbal and quasi-verbal performances when these performances are made 'in conformity with the semantical rules of the language', is, of course, the heart of the Myth of the Given. For the *given*, in epistemological tradition, is what is *taken* by these self-authenticating episodes. These 'takings' are, so to speak, the unmoved movers of empirical knowledge, the 'knowings in presence' which are presupposed by all other knowledge, both the knowledge of general truths and the knowledge 'in absence' of other particular matters of fact. Such is the framework in which traditional empiricism makes its characteristic claim that the perceptually given is the foundation of empirical knowledge.

Let me make it clear, however, that if I reject this framework, it is not because I should deny that observings are *inner* episodes, nor that *strictly speaking* they are *nonverbal* episodes. It will be my contention, however, that the sense in which they are nonverbal—which is also the sense in which thought episodes are nonverbal—is one which gives no aid or cómfort to epistemological givenness. In the concluding sections of this paper I shall attempt to explicate the logic of inner episodes, and show that we can distinguish between observations and thoughts, on the one hand, and their verbal expression on the other, without making the mistakes of traditional dualism. I shall also attempt to explicate the logical status of *impressions* or *immediate experiences,* and thus bring to a successful conclusion the quest with which my argument began.

One final remark before I begin this task. If I reject the framework of traditional empiricism, it is not because I want to say that empirical knowledge has *no* foundation. For to put it this way is to suggest that it is really 'empirical knowledge so-called', and to put it in a box with rumours and hoaxes. There is clearly *some* point to the picture of human knowledge as resting on a level of propositions—observation reports—which do not rest on other propositions in the same way as other propositions rest on them. On the other hand, I do wish to insist that the metaphor of 'foundation' is misleading in that it keeps us from seeing that if there is a logical dimension in which other empirical propositions rest on observation reports, there is another logical dimension in which the latter rest on the former.

Above all, the picture is misleading because of its static character. One seems forced to choose between the picture of an elephant which rests on a tortoise (What supports the tortoise?) and the picture of a great Hegelian serpent of knowledge with its tail in its mouth (Where does it begin?). Neither will do. For empirical knowledge, like its sophisticated extension, science, is rational, not because it has a *foundation* but because it is a self-correcting enterprise which can put *any* claim in jeopardy, though not *all* at once.

INTENTIONALITY

"Every mental phenomenon is characterized by what the Scholastics of the middle ages called the intentional (or mental) (in)existence of an object, and what we, although with not entirely unambiguous terms, would call the reference to a content, a direction towards an object. . . .
—Franz Brentano
PSYCHOLOGIE VOM EMPIRISCHEN STANDPUNKTE

[Brentano] has earned the epoch-making advantage of making phenomenology possible. He presented to the modern era the idea of Intentionality. . . .
—Edmund Husserl IDEEN III

INTRODUCTION

The thesis of intentionality maintains that (1) every 'act' of consciousness is directed toward an 'object', but that (2) this object need not exist. The first selection is a brief summary of the "Theory of Objects" of the Austrian philosopher Alexius Meinong. His theory had considerable influence on Husserl and phenomenology as well as a notorious negative influence on Bertrand Russell and logical analysis. Then there is a brief characterization of the distinction between "transcendence" and "immanence," which is central to the concept of "object" in the intentionality thesis, as it appears in the first of Husserl's writings that he considered truly phenomenological, *The Idea of Phenomenology*. The essay by Hubert Dreyfus, an American phenomenologist most sympathetic with the philosophy of Merleau-Ponty, attempts to develop Husserl's early notion of "intentionality" in relation to his central concept of "meaning" (*Sinn*). The next selection is a letter ot Husserl from Franz Brentano, his teacher, from whom he adopted the doctrine of intentionality (although there is considerable dispute as to what extent Brentano himself held this doctrine). Finally there is a critique from the distinguished Oxford philosopher Gilbert Ryle, who at one point was a sympathetic follower of the phenomenological movement.

MEINONG'S THEORY OF OBJECTS

Meinong's theory of objects is rooted in the psychology of Brentano. According to Brentano, a characteristic feature of mental phenomena is 'intentionality' or directedness towards an object. If one sees, one sees something; if one hears, smells, tastes, one hears, smells, or tastes some object. If one opines, supposes, knows, or believes, one opines, supposes, knows, or believes something. Meinong is thus led to see the possibility of a new science or field of knowledge, the theory of objects, for it is evident that there are among existing sciences none 'within which we could attempt a theoretical consideration of the object as such, or from which we could at least demand this'.[1]

But is not metaphysics precisely the discipline we are looking for? Metaphysics takes as its field the study of 'being qua being'. Surely it is in this discipline that we can find a study of objects as such. But, according to Meinong, in spite of the immense reach of metaphysics, it is still not universal enough to encompass the general science of objects. The reason is that metaphysics is confined to what exists. 'However, the totality of what exists, including what has existed and will exist, is infinitely small in comparison with the totality of the objects of knowledge.[2]

This may easily go unnoticed, says Meinong, because we have a 'prejudice in favour of the actual'. Led by this prejudice, we suppose that what is not real is a 'mere nothing'. We therefore conclude that the non-real is something for which science has no

[1] 'The Theory of Objects', in *Realism and the Background of Phenomenology* (ed.), by R. Chisholm, Free Press, 1960, p. 78.
[2] *Ibid.*, p. 79, all quotations from Meinong are taken from this source.

Reprinted from *Referring* (New York: Humanities Press, 1968), chap. 2, pp. 12–16, by permission of the publisher and Routledge & Kegan Paul.

application 'or at least no application of any worth'. That this view is mistaken can be shown by a consideration of 'ideal objects'. Ideal objects do indeed subsist (*bestehen*), but they do not exist (*existieren*). Consequently, they are not, in any sense, real (*wirklich*). The relations of similarity and difference are examples of ideal objects. They may subsist between realities but they are not 'part of reality' themselves. Our ideas, judgments, and assumptions are often concerned with such objects. Numbers are examples of ideal objects, they do not exist in addition to what is numbered (if what is numbered exists). Sometimes, of course, what is numbered does not exist, for example, we can count the mythological gods on Olympus.

In the new science of objects one important distinction which will be observed and investigated is the distinction between objects 'in the strict sense' and objectives (*objective*). Though all mental acts are directed towards objects, the objects of cognitive acts (knowing, believing, supposing) are of a special kind called 'objectives'.

What we see is an object in 'the strict sense', for example, a cat. But we 'judge' or 'assume' not a cat but, for example, *that the cat is on the mat*, or as Meinong sometimes puts it, we 'judge' *the being of the cat on the mat*. There is, then, besides objects in the strict sense, a special class of objects like *the being of the cat on the mat* or *the non-being of the cat on the mat* which are objects of cognitive acts. If what is judged is true, then the objective of the judgment subsists. The cat and the mat exist, but the objective *the being of the cat on the mat* (*that the cat is on the mat*) does not exist, it subsists.

In a certain sense the objective itself 'can assume the function of an object in the strict sense'. If I judge 'It is true that the antipodes exist' the objective *that the antipodes exist* is related to the objective of my judgment in the same way that the cat and the mat are related to the objective of my judgment 'the cat is on the mat'. 'Truth is ascribed not to the antipodes, but to the objective "that the antipodes exist".' This objective can subsist, but unlike the antipodes themselves, it cannot exist. This is true of all objectives, 'so that every cognitive act which has

an objective as its object represents thereby a case of knowing
something which does not exist'.

An important contention of Meinong's is formulated in what
he calls 'the principle of the independence of so-being (*Sosein*)
from being (*Sein*)'. An object's having such and such characteristics is independent of its existence. The round square is
round and square, though it does not exist. We may make true
or false assertions about what does not exist, e.g., Zeus or
Pegasus or the golden mountain. It would be false to say that
Pegasus is a duck and true to say he is a horse. But if this is so,
the so-being (*Sosein*) of Pegasus must be independent of his
being (*Sein*). Pegasus has the characteristic of being a horse
independently of whether he exists.

> Any particular thing that isn't real (*Nichtseiendes*) must at
> least be capable of serving as the object for those judgments
> which grasp its *Nichtsein*. . . . In order to know that there is no
> round square, I must make a judgment about the round square.
> . . . Those who like paradoxical modes of expression could very
> well say: 'There are objects of which it is true to say that there
> are no such objects.' (Es gibt Gegenstande, von denen gilt, dass
> es dergleichen Gegenstande nicht gibt).

Meinong's doctrine of the '*Aussersein* of the pure object' is
one of his most difficult, but it is also from the point of view
of this book, one of his most interesting and important notions:

> If I say, 'Blue does not exist', I am thinking just of blue,
> and not at all of a presentation and the capacities it may have.
> It is as if the blue must have being in the first place, before we
> can raise the question of its being (*Sein*) *or non-being* (*Nicht-
> sein*). . . . . Blue or any other object whatsoever, is somehow
> given prior to our determination of its being nor non-being, in a
> way that does not carry any prejudice to its non-being. . . . If
> I should be able to judge that a certain object is not, then I
> appear to have had to grasp the object in some way beforehand,
> in order to say anything about its non-being, or more precisely,
> in order to affirm or to deny the ascription of non-being to the
> object.

We have here the idea which is at the root of one of the principal problems about reference presented in our first chapter. Whatever we can talk about must in some sense *be* something, for the alternative is to talk about nothing. Meinong's theory of 'the *Aussersein* of the pure object' is in fact an attempt to provide a solution to that problem about reference. The solution, in effect, is that chimeras, round squares, etc., etc., are objects though non-real objects; objects 'beyond being and non-being'. This way of putting things is recognized by Meinong himself as 'pretentious'. It can easily be misunderstood. Russell, for example, thought that Meinong was committed to the view that Pegasus both exists and does not exist. But nothing could be a greater misunderstanding of Meinong's position. He is very careful to make it clear that he is not asserting the existence of round squares and chimeras.

The doctrine that the 'pure object' is 'indifferent to being' (*ausserseiend*) is best viewed as simply recognizing in a rather 'pretentious' way such things as that the subject term of a subject-predicate proposition may very well denote something that does not exist, e.g., Santa Claus. That some propositions about Santa Claus are true and some false is obvious. For example, 'Santa Claus lives at the South Pole' is false. Still, it is a proposition about Santa Claus. Meinong's doctrine of *aussersein* seems to me best interpreted as a recognition of such facts as these: That Santa Claus is denoted by the subject term of the above proposition, that Santa Claus is not Paul Bunyan though neither Santa Claus nor Paul Bunyan exists. The doctrine of the independence of *Sein* from *Sosein* recognizes the fact that some propositions about Santa Claus and Paul Bunyan are true and some false, though neither Santa Claus nor Paul Bunyan exists.

One of the problems about reference presented in the first chapter becomes, in Meinong's hands, an argument to show that the pure object is *ausserseiend*, beyond being and non-being. The argument is as follows. That A is not (the *Nichtsein* of A) is an objective, as much an objective as the being of A (the *Sein* of A). The degree of certainty which we are justified in having in asserting that A 'is not' is equal to the degree of certainty which we are justified in having that the objective '*Nichtsein* of *A*' has *Sein* (that it has subsistence). An objective can be an objective of being (*Seinsobjektiv*) or an objective of non-being (*Nichtseinsobjektiv*). 'Pegasus exists' asserts an objective-of the first kind and 'Pegasus does not exist' an objective of the second kind. Each of these objectives stands in a certain relation to its object, Pegasus. A natural view (a mistaken one according to Meinong) is that the relation of the objective to its object is that of whole to part. The difficulty is that if the whole has being, so must its parts. If we follow the analogy, then we could conclude from the being of the objective, *that Pegasus does not exist* (the non-being of Pegasus), that Pegasus has being. Now there is nothing wrong with this conclusion so long as we do not confuse being with existence. So long as what is asserted is merely that Pegasus has being in some sense or other, though not existence, there is nothing wrong. What Meinong, at one time, was inclined to say was that this argument showed that the object had some third order of being, neither subsistence like the objective nor existence like Plato. This third order of being would belong to every object 'as such'.

Now this third order of being would be different from either subsistence or existence in a special way. Existence is opposed to non-existence. Santa Claus does not, in fact, exist, but he could not subsist. Only ideal objects, numbers, objectives, can subsist. Just as existence is opposed to non-existence, so subsistence is opposed to non-subsistence. The objective *that Santa Claus does not exist,* subsists, but the objective *that Santa Claus exists,* does not subsist. The peculiarity of this third order of being is that it is opposed to nothing. No object can fail to have it. For suppose that there was some variety of non-being opposed to this kind of being, as there is something of the same type as existence and subsistence opposed to them. Then for us to judge that an object had this kind of non-being we would have to ascribe a fourth kind of being to the object, by the same argument used above. We would then be led into an infinite hierarchy of kinds of being. This regress can be stopped by supposing that the object (as such) has a kind of being opposed to nothing. 'The term "Quasisein" seemed to me,' says Meinong, 'for a while to be a completely suitable expression for this rather oddly constituted type of being.' Meinong was himself clearly dissatisfied with this notion of a third kind of being 'in principle unopposed by non-being', whether it was called *'Quasisein', Pseudoexistenz'*, or *'Quasitranszendenz'* (all alternatives which he used at one time or another). In his essay 'The Theory of Objects' he thought it best to say that objects 'as such' are *'ausserseind'*, 'beyond being and non-being'. Some of the things which Meinong says here are obscure, but it is certain that Russell's view of Meinong as a man who had embraced chimeras and golden mountains, spirits and round squares, as things which exist in another shadow world is far from true.

from THE IDEA OF PHENOMENOLOGY

EDMUND HUSSERL

I said that the cognitions with which the critique of cognition must begin must contain nothing doubtful or questionable. They must contain none of that which precipitates epistemological confusion and gives impetus to the critique of cognition. We have to show that this holds true of the sphere of the *cogitatio*. For this we need a more deeply probing reflection, one that will bring us substantial advantages.

If we look closer at what is so enigmatic and what, in the course of subsequent reflection on the possibility of cognition, causes embarrassment, we will find it to be the transcendence of cognition. All cognition of the natural sort, and especially the prescientific, is cognition which makes its object transcendent. It posits objects as existent, claims to reach matters of fact which are not "strictly given to it," are not "immanent" to it.

Reprinted from *The Idea of Phenomenology*, translated by W. Alston and G. Nakhnikian (The Hague: The Netherlands, M. Nijhoff, 1964), pp. 27–28, by permission of the publisher.

But on closer view, this *transcendence* is admittedly *ambiguous*. One thing one can mean by transcendence is that the object of cognition is not genuinely (*reell*) contained in the cognitive act so that one would be meaning by "being truly given" or "immanently given" that the object of the cognitive act is genuinely contained in the act: the cognitive act, the *cogitatio*, has genuine abstract parts genuinely constituting it: but the physical thing which it intends or supposedly perceives or remembers, etc., is not to be found in the *cogitatio* itself, as a mental process; the physical thing is not to be found as a genuine (*reell*) concrete part (*Stück*), not as something which really exists within the *cogitatio*. So the question is: how can the mental process so to speak transcend itself? *Immanent here means then genuinely (reell) immanent in the cognitive mental process.*

But there is still *another transcendence* whose opposite is an altogether different immanence, namely, *absolute* and *clear givenness, self-givenness in the absolute sense*. This givenness, which rules out any meaningful doubt, consists of a simply immediate "seeing" and apprehending of the intended object itself as it is, and it constitutes the precise concept of evidence (*Evidenz*) understood as immediate evidence. All cognition which is not evident, which though it intends or posits something objective yet *does not see it itself*, is transcendent in this second sense. In such cognition we go beyond what at any time *is truly given*, beyond what can be *directly "seen"* and *apprehended*. At this point we may ask: How can cognition posit something as existing that is not directly and truly given in it?

At first, before we come to a deeper level of critical epistemological reflection, these two kinds of immanence and transcendence run confusedly into each other. It is indeed clear that whoever raises the first question about the possibility of genuine (*reell*) transcendence is at the same time really also raising the second question: namely, how can there be transcendence beyond the realm of evident givenness? In this there is the unspoken supposition that the only actually understandable, unquestionable, absolutely evident givenness is the givenness of *the abstract part genuinely (reell) contained* within the cognitive act, and this is why anything in the way of a cognized objectivity that is not genuinely (*reell*) contained within that act is regarded as a puzzle and as problematic. We shall soon hear that this is a fatal mistake.

One may now construe transcendence in one sense or the other, or, at first even ambiguously, but transcendence is both the initial and the central problem of the critique of cognition. It is the riddle that stands in the path of cognition of the natural sort and is the incentive for new investigations. One could at the outset designate the solution to this problem as being the task of the critique of cognition. One would thereby delimit the new discipline in a preliminary fashion, instead of generally designating as its theme the problem of the essence of any cognition whatever.

SINN AND INTENTIONAL OBJECT

HUBERT L. DREYFUS

The sixth *Logische Untersuchung* is Husserl's first attempt at a phenomenological analysis of perception. We must begin, however, with a brief resumé of certain basic concepts used by Husserl in the first *Logische Untersuchung* in the analysis of linguistic expressions, for it is Husserl's attempt to generalize these notions, originally worked out on the conceptual level, to perception which leads to a new theory of perception and also to the difficulties and reformulations which we will be tracing through Husserl's works.

The first investigation treats expression and meaning (*Ausdruck* and *Bedeutung*). According to Husserl, the physical manifestation of a linguistic expression would merely be a sound or

Reprinted with permission of Hubert L. Dreyfus from his doctoral dissertation, *Husserl's Phenomenology of Perception: From Transcendental to Existential Phenomenology*, Ch. 1, pp. 1–17. (Harvard University, 1963) Soon to be published by Northwestern University Press.

some marks but for the act of consciousness which gives it meaning. Moreover, granted such an expression has meaning, it may
still fail to have an object unless the act which confers meaning
can be accompanied by an act of intuition. These observations
give rise to a threefold distinction, basic to Husserl's position,
between the physical manifestation of an expression, the meaning-conferring act (*bedeutungsverleihende Akt*) and the mean-
ing-filling acts (*bedeutungerfüllende Akte*). [Husserl, LU 38]

Turning to an analysis of the meaning-conferring, or what
Husserl elsewhere calls the "signifying acts," we note that such
acts have a meaning or sense whether they have a filling or not.
It is by virtue of this sense that the expression intends or means
(*meint*) an object, regardless of whether the object meant
(*gemeint*) is actually present in our experience. Even if the
object does not exist, even if it is unimaginable like a square
circle, each time I conceive of the object or understand a reference to it, I do so by virtue of the meaning correlated with my
act. Since the meaning does not depend on the existence of
anything which is beyond the act itself, the meaning is called the
content (*Inhalt*) of the act. And since this content is objective,
i.e., intersubjective and repeatable, but it is not physically real,
it is called ideal. The ideal content of sense-conferring acts Husserl calls the *Bedeutung*.

> It is unmistakable that what are called *Bedeutungen* comprise
> strictly ideal unities which are expressed in a plurality of ex-
> pressions and thought in a plurality of acts, but which must
> nonetheless be distinguished from the accidental experiences of
> the thinker as well as from the accidental expressions. [Husserl,
> LU 92]

This ideal content, Husserl declares, does not belong to the
real world of changing individuals nor even to our stream of
consciousness, since this too belongs to the "temporal sphere."
Rather, the meanings form a "class of concepts in the sense of
'universal objects' " which, like all concepts, are not in space
and time. [Husserl, LU 101]

The need for this distinction between the real object and the ideal content of the act will become clear, Husserl claims, when we notice that an expression may be true of several objects, as in the case of general terms, and that, more strikingly, several expressions may have different meanings (*Bedeutung*) and all have the same object (*Gegenstand*). [Husserl, LU 47] To conceptualize these relationships we must distinguish in a threefold way: the meaning-conferring act, the meaning of the act, and the object meant. The object meant may itself be an ideal entity as in the case of mathematical objects, or it may be a material object in space and time. If we restrict our discussion to perception so that the only objects under consideration are material objects, which Husserl calls real, [Husserl, LU 399] we can state Husserl's threefold distinction as follows: the act is *reell*, the meaning *ideal*, and the object *real*.

This trichotomy exactly parallels Frege's distinction between idea, sense and reference, in his article *"Sinn und Bedeutung."* [Frege, BG 59] This is no coincidence. Husserl's first book, *The Philosophy of Arithmetic*, was criticized by Frege for being too psychologistic, i.e., for "blurring the distinction between image and concept, between imagination and thought." Images, Frege, had argued, are psychic events confined to each man's mind, whereas "it is quite otherwise for thoughts: one and the same thought can be grasped by many men." [Frege, BG 79] For Frege, the meaning or the sense of an expression was universal and timeless.

> . . . . One need have no scruples in speaking simply of *the* sense, whereas in the case of an idea one must, strictly speaking, add to whom it belongs and at what time. [Frege, BG 60]

Husserl accepted Frege's threefold distinction between psychic events (including both states and acts) which are private and momentary, their meanings which are universal and non-temporal, and the objects to which these meanings refer.

> My act of judging is a transient experience, which arises and passes away. But this is not the case with what the expression

expresses, the content. . . . As often as I or anyone else utter the same expression in the same sense, a judgment is made. The acts of judging are different in each case, but that which is judged, that which is asserted in the statement, is always the same. It is, in the strictest sense of the word, identical. . . . [Husserl, LU 44]

We see the essence of the *Bedeutung* not in the experience which confers the meaning but in the 'content' of the experience, which poses an identical intentional unity over against the scattered manifold of actual or possible experiences of speakers and thinkers. [Husserl, LU 96–97]

The only change Husserl made in Frege's analysis was terminological. Husserl proposes to use "object (*Gegenstand*) for "reference" (*Bedeutung*), and *Bedeutung* and *Sinn* interchangeably for "sense" (*Sinn*), since "this is closer to German usage" and "it is convenient to have parallel terms in an investigation of this sort where it is precisely the meaning of *Bedeutung* which is being studied." [Husserl, LU 52–53]

The meaning of *Bedeutung* or *Sinn* and their function in knowledge is indeed the subject of all of Husserl's work, and our task will be to follow it through its many variations. The first use Husserl makes of the notion of meaning, here where it is introduced, is to note that a meaning-conferring act is essentially correlating with a meaning, whether it is correlated with a filling act or not.

One thing is certain, every expression whether or not it has an epistemological function (that is, whether its intention is or can be filled in a corresponding intuition) has its meaning (*Meinung*) . . . and that the *Bedeutung* constitutes the specific unified character of this Meinung. [Husserl, LU 45]

This observation can be used to bolster Husserl's philosophical preconception, viz., the doctrine of intentionality which he took over from his teacher Franz Brentano. Husserl quotes with approval Brentano's dictum that: "In perception something is perceived, in imagination something is imagined, in an expression something is expressed, in love something is loved, . . . etc.", and adds that "what can be seen in common in such examples is what Brentano had in mind when he said: 'Every psychic phenomenon is characterized by what the medieval scholastics called the intentional (or mental) inexistence of its object, and what we would call . . . the reference to a content, the directedness toward an object (which does not mean something real) or immanent objectivity (*Gegenstandlichkeit*)'." [Husserl, LU 366–367]

Husserl follows his teacher in viewing "the intentional relation . . . as an essential determination of all psychic acts," i.e., he takes Brentano's definition of acts as "those phenomena which contain in themselves an intentional object" to be an "essential definition." [Husserl, LU 368]

> If a conscious act is present, then *eo ipso*, and this lies, I stress, in its essence, the intention 'relation to an object' is consummated and *eo ipso* an object is 'intentionally present . . .' [Husserl, LU 372]

But what is the object which every act essentially has? Is it the *Sinn?* We have defined the *Sinn* as the necessary content or correlate of each act but not as its object. The *Sinn* is the *Meinung* not the *Gemeint*. Still, we are seeking an *intentional* object and the rules for what counts as an *intentional* object are by no means clear.

> The word *intentional,* as one would expect from its formation, can be applied to the *sense* as well as to the reference of the intention. Thus the intentional unity does not necessarily mean the intended unity, that of the objects. [Husserl, LU 97n.]

In one sense, then, the object which is "intentionally present" is the reference, the actual or real object meant (*gemeint*), but in another sense the object intentionally present is the *Bedeutung.*

If one wished to defend a theory of intentionality according to which every act has an object, one would be free to utilize this indeterminacy of the notion of intentional object, and to identify the sense of the act with its intentional object. "Intentional object" would then mean the same as what we have been calling the ideal correlate of the act, and the essential correlation of act and object demanded by the intentionalist thesis would be assured. Husserl, however, does not exploit this ambiguity. For the sake of clarity and presumably because in the case of an intentional act which has an object, the object before our mind is the reference and not the sense, he modifies Brentano's usage and uses the expression "intentional *correlate*" or "intentional object *as such*" to refer to the *Bedeutung*, and the expression "intentional *object*" to refer to the reference rather than the sense. He is not altogether consistent in this usage but this is the only way one can understand such otherwise confusing utterances as the following: "One need only say it and everyone must admit: the intentional object of a presentation is the selfsame (*Derselbe*) as its real outer object [Husserl, LU 424–425]

In order to express the fact that the same reference can be the intentional object of acts with different meanings, Husserl is then obliged to introduce a new distinction, between the "object *as it is* intended" and "the object *which is* intended." Both are the reference but the object *as it is* intended is the object from the point of view of the person doing the intending. In Frege's case of the morning star, the evening star, and the planet Venus, the object as it is intended would be the morning star or the evening star. The object which is intended is the object which can be viewed in these and other ways, e.g., also as the planet Venus. Husserl thus distinguishes *what* is intended in the object and *the object intended* or, as he also puts the distinction, the intentional and the extra-intentional content of the object. Husserl does not discuss the problems such distinctions raise: Is the intentional content of the object real or ideal or does it have some third sort of ontological status? How are the various intentional contents related to each other and to the extra-intentional content? Finally, how shall we conceptualize the fact that the "object as it is intended" is intended as intendable in other ways? All these questions will arise and be dealt with in *Ideas* where the intentional content of the object and even the extra-intentional content is absorbed in the intentional correlate or Noema.

For the moment, our problem is how to save the intentionalist thesis. If the intentional object is identical with the real object then an act may fail to have an intentional object in this sense. In compensation we must find a sense in which the *Sinn* is, if not the intentional object, at least some sort of inevitable objective correlate of the intentional act.

We must distinguish two orientations of the subject who performs the intentional act. We have said that in our ordinary everyday attitude what we have before our minds is the reference, not the *Sinn*, of our acts. We can make the *Sinn* an object, however, if we turn from a natural to a reflective attitude.

> Instead of being absorbed in our manifold compounded acts and thereby naively positing as existing or determinable, or hypothetical, the objects meant through the sense of these acts, we must rather 'reflect,' that is, we must make these acts and their immanent sense into our objects. [Husserl, LU 9]

This method of reflection practiced by the phenomenologist, whereby he turns the objective correlate of his act into an object, is not a method invented by the phenomenologist. Although it is an unnatural (*wider-natürlich*) orientation for the active involved individual, it is perfectly natural for the reflective thinker, and has from the beginning been practiced by logicians.

> If we perform an act and at the same live in it then we naturally intend its reference and not its sense. If, for example, we make an assertion, then we judge about the state of affairs, not about the meaning of the assertion, the judgment in the logical sense. The *Bedeutung* first becomes an object by means of a reflective act in which we not only look around at the consummated assertion, but also perform the necessary abstraction (or better,

ideation). This logical reflection is not an act which only takes place under artificial (*künstlich*) conditions and in exceptional cases; rather it is a normal ingredient of *logical* thinking. [Husserl, LU 103]

This is important to note lest this act of logical reflection be confused with the phenomenological reduction which Husserl felt was his original contribution and which he did not discover in its final form until after his lectures on phenomenology of 1907.

In this logical reflection we became aware of what we do not ordinarily notice, viz., that, when we are thinking of, wishing for, or passing judgment on objects or states of affairs, there is a thought, a wish or a judgment involved. Between our thinking and the object or reference of our thinking lies the sense, which, as Frege puts it, "is indeed no longer subjective like the idea, but is not quite the object either." Frege uses a suggestive analogy to show the role of these objective meanings in conception.

> Somebody observes the Moon through a telescope. I compare the Moon itself to the reference; it is the object of the observation, mediated by the real image projected by the object glass in the interior of the telescope, and by the retinal image of the observer. The former I compare to the sense, the latter is like the idea or experience. The optical image in the telescope is indeed one-sided and dependent upon the standpoint of observation; but it is still objective, inasmuch as it can be used by several observers. [Frege, BG 60]

The real image in the telescope is not normally what is observed. If it could be observed by the observer changing his position and looking at it through some instrument which itself involved a real image, the situation would be analogous to what the phenomenologist or logician is doing. The phenomenologist can at will, through an act of reflection, change the intentional correlate of his act into an intentional object of a second order act. He can think of the thought rather than of the object he is thinking about and he then becomes aware that the thought was present all along. On reflection we can thus discover something thought in all thinking, something wished in all wishing, something judged in all judging, etc. whether the objects of these thoughts, wishes and judgments exist or not. Even though we are not ordinarily reflectively aware of this fact it is nonetheless reflected in our grammar which treats the objects thought of, wished for, judged about, etc. as *indirect* objects, suggesting thereby that the direct object is the thought, the judgment, the wish. The signifying act can thus be said to have its own intermediary object, the sense, whether it is correlated with a filling act or not, i.e., whether or not it corresponds to any real object or state of affairs.

Thus the intentionalist thesis is saved, at least for the signifying acts such as thinking, judging, etc. But what about the other sorts of acts mentioned by Brentano? Brentano claims that: "In perception something is [always] perceived, in love something is [always] loved, . . . etc." Leaving aside the emotional acts such as love which are intermediate between the signifying acts and the filling acts and which present special problems, we must determine whether the filling acts such as perception lend themselves to the Fregean threefold analysis.

We should expect to encounter some difficulty since the filling acts, unlike the signifying acts, seem to establish a direct relation between consciousness and its object. This contrast between the signifying and the filling acts is built into our language and can be brought out in the following ways.

(1) WITH RESPECT TO REFERENTIAL OPACITY

Since, as Frege and Husserl noted, the same object can be meant by means of several different meanings, the act contexts of signifying acts must sometimes be construed as *referentially opaque*. (It is convenient here to adopt the terminology of *Principia Mathematica*.) For example, although the morning star and the evening star are the same physical object, I can take a certain star to be the morning star, or think about the morning star, without taking that star to be the evening star or thinking about the evening star. On the other hand, once I have seen the morning star, I have seen the evening star—although I may not be aware of it at the time. Once I accept that the morning star is the same object as the evening star I must agree that I have been seeing the evening star all along, although in the parallel case of thinking, there is a sense in which I have never before thought of the evening star. Thus filling acts can never be construed as referentially opaque in ordinary discourse, while signifying acts *may* be construed as opaque [cf. Chisholm, *Perceiving*, Ch. V]

There may indeed be cases where it seems that the filling acts may themselves be construed as opaque, e.g. cases in which I can perceive the same object in various ways, as in Wittgenstein's example of the duck-rabbit. It may seem that when I see the duck I do not see the rabbit, just as when I think of the evening star I do not think of the morning star. But in such cases as the duck-rabbit the transparency of perception is manifest in a more subtle, but for that very reason, more convincing form, for we say that we *see the figure as* a duck or *as* a rabbit, and thus assert that we *see the figure* in either case.

We shall see later that the phenomenological reduction can be viewed as a technique for revealing the opacity of filling acts, but it requires a special way of experiencing the filling acts and a special technical terminology which Husserl had not yet developed at the time of writing *Logische Untersuchungen*.

Filling acts are unique in this respect and can be contrasted with emotional as well as signifying acts. Emotional acts exhibit the opacity characteristic of signifying acts. A man may hate the murderer of his wife but love his neighbor. When he finds out that his neighbor is the murderer he may hate him from then on, but it would be strange to say that he hated him all along, although if he had been seeing his neighbor each day it would be natural to say that he had been seeing the murderer all along (although he didn't know it). In fact, if in court, in order to protect his neighbor (let us say from Christian motives), he testified that he had not seen the murderer until the day the crime was revealed, there would be no way of construing this statement except as outright perjury.

(2) AS REFLECTED IN OUR GRAMMAR

a) Grammatically, perception verbs, as contrasted with the verbs for expressing signifying acts, take a direct rather than an indirect object. (On this point, the emotional acts must be classed *with* perception.)

b) In the language of perception we have no substantives which can be distinguished from the object of the acts-verbs in the way that "the wish," "the thought," "the judgment," etc. can be distinguished from "the wished for," "the thought about," and "the judged." The 'look" of an object might seem to perform such a function but in ordinary English the "look" of an object means the way the *object* appears, what Husserl would call the intentional object exactly as intended. The look does not continue to be seen whether there is any objective reference or not, whereas in the case of signifying acts, "what is given is essentially the same whether the represented object exists, whether it is imagined, or even if it is contradictory." [Husserl, LU 373]

There are two traditional moves which Husserl might have made at this point in order to save the generalization of the intentionalist thesis to filling acts, i.e., in order to argue that acts such as perceiving always have an object. One could argue that perceiving is by definition veridical and that if there is no object there is no act of perceiving; or one could argue, with the sense data theorists, that there is always something perceived, namely sense data, whether perception is veridical or not. Husserl rejects both these ways out. He does not give his reasons for rejecting the former, but an argument in conformity with his phenomenological orientation would be as follows. In the case of illusion, when we are under the illusion our act of awareness, *as far as the experiencing subject is concerned,* exactly resembles perceiving—it must, or we would not be fooled by illusions—

and therefore *phenomenologically* such acts of awareness must be treated as acts of perception even if they turn out not to have objects. "The illusion was, as long as it was not known as deception, simply perception." [Husserl, LU 442] But if we assume that we were perceiving, the problem returns: Here is an act of perceiving whose object turns out not to exist. How can we claim that every act of perception is a perception of something?

In *Logische Untersuchungen* Husserl does not seek to hide this paradoxical fact, that perception claims to go directly to the object without intermediary, and yet does not do so, so that in fact it may have no object:

> . . . . Perception, since it claims to give the object 'itself,' claims thereby in no way to be a mere intention, but rather an act which may solicit further filling, but which does not need any further filling. [Husserl, LU II 26]

> But mostly, for example in the case of 'outer' perception, this remains merely a claim. The object is not really given, that is, it is not fully and completely given as that which it is. [Husserl, LU II 56]

Brentano takes the other way out to save his intentionalist thesis, holding that we can see sense data. Husserl, too, argues for the role of sense data in perception, but, as we shall see, he is too careful a phenomenologist to accept the view that sense data are the objects or even the implicit objects of our ordinary perceptual acts.

Having rejected these two dodges there is only one alternative remaining to Husserl if he is to preserve his conviction that the intentionalist thesis as stated by Brentano applies to all acts. He must generalize his Fregean threefold analysis of signifying acts to perception, or more generally, to filling acts. He must exhibit a perceptual sense as correlate of the perceptual act, to correspond to the conceptual sense we have been discussing thus far.

In *Logische Untersuchungen* Husserl simply announces

without preparation that when a sense-filling act has an object, "object" can mean one of two things: on the one hand, it can mean the reference or, "in a more genuine sense," it can mean "the ideal correlate of the reference in the sense-filling act . . . namely, the *fulfilling* sense (*erfüllende Sinn*)." [Husserl, LU II 50] We are not told how we know there is such a *Sinn* or in what sense it is an object. On the basis of this assertion Husserl then proceeds to distinguish two senses of the content of the filling act: the object (*Gegenstand*), and the fulfilling sense. Following this artificial analogy with conception, Husserl proposes to use the term "content" to refer specifically to the fulfilling sense. In perception, for example,

> we must distinguish between the content, that which is so to speak significant (*bedeutungsmässig*) in perception, and the perceived object. [Husserl, LU 51]

At this point Husserl does not justify the introduction of the *erfüllende Sinn* by phenomenological analysis; he seems to expect us to accept it on the basis of the implied parallel with his analysis of sense-conferring acts.

> Just as the ideal conception of the intentional essence of a sense-conferring act yields the intending meaning as· an idea, so the ideal conception of the correlative essence of the sense-filling act yields the fulfilling-sense as an idea. In perception this [fulfilling sense] is the identical content, which belongs to the totality of possible perceptual acts which mean the same object. . . . This content is thus the ideal correlate of an object, which moreover can quite well be fictive. [Husserl, LU II 51–52]

What is this identical content which belongs to all perceptual acts which intend the same object regardless of whether that object exists? So far this is by no means clear. Husserl is aware that the "application of the terms *Bedeutung* and *Sinn,* not just to the content of meaning-intentions, but also to the content of meaning-fulfillments results in an unpleasant equivocation for . . . the acts in which the intending and the fulfilling meanings are constituted, are in no way the same." [Husserl, LU II 52] He tries to justify the use of *Sinn* in both cases by pointing to the "peculiar nature of the unity of fulfillment in both cases, as a unity of identification or coincidence *(Deckung),*" but he does not at this point explain what a unity of coincidence is. When he does explain it, we shall see that there is a crucial difference in the two notions of *Sinn* involved, which is more important than their similarity. In any case, the assertion of a similarity of fulfillment in conception and perception leaves unjustified the underlying assumption that there is in perception a content or intermediate object which corresponds to the intermediate object in conception.

In the fifth investigation Husserl does try to show in what way each filling act is correlated with a fulfilling-sense. But before we turn to the fifth investigation it will be helpful to summarize what we have found in the first investigation, and to point ahead to our general view of Husserl's development. This can be done by considering what characteristics the fulfilling-sense must have in order to support the intentionalist thesis as Husserl, combining the work of Brentano and Frege, understands it. The brilliant success of this combination in the realm of signifying acts has shown that the *Sinn* can be both the thought as such of Brentano, i.e., that which we think whenever we think of something—whether that something exists or not, and Frege's ideal correlate of a plurality of subjective acts.

Generalizing to perception we can characterize the perceptual entity we are seeking as follows: (1) To satisfy Brentano, as what is perceived whenever there is an act of perception it must (a) not itself be an object of perception in the ordinary sense, because we know that perception may sometimes be illusory and have no object in the ordinary sense; (b) it must nonetheless be present in perception, whether we perceive a material object or not. (2) To satisfy Frege, as the ideal basis of objectivity it must be the identical correlate of all perceptual acts which intend the same perceptual object in the same way.

Husserl's development in the theory of perception can be viewed as a search for this entity which the success of the theory of intentionality in the field of conception made him feel must exist. I will contend that, because of the nature of perception, Husserl never found what he was looking for, not in *Logische Untersuchungen* nor in any of his subsequent works. He comes closest in *Ideen,* where he satisfies the Brentanian demands with his notion of Noesis and the Fregean condition with his notion of the perceptual Noema, but even this synthesis breaks down upon further investigation. In the course of his search, however, he found something far more significant: the distinction between pre-objective and objective perception. What this distinction means and how it emerges from this search will only be clear when we have followed the tortuous movement by which Husserl arrived at it.

Anticipating the detailed argument, we can suggest that this way of regarding Husserl's development confirms the impression many critics have had, that Husserl constantly changed his mind while refusing to give up the positions he rejected. It also shows how Husserl could nonetheless claim to have been constantly and consistently elaborating one insight throughout his work, ever since his rejection of psychologism. At each stage of his development Husserl tried a new way of combining Frege and Brentano, of paralleling conception and perception, and each time he failed. In spite of these setbacks, however, he incorporated into his next work the phenomenological insights he had gained, and throughout his efforts he continued to hold that there was an object for each perceptual act and that this object was in some sense a *Sinn.* It is this developing sense of *Sinn* throughout Husserl's work which we propose to follow, and to show that even Husserl's broadened sense of *Sinn* in *Ideen* must be broadened still further in *Erfahrung und Urteil* in order to take account of Husserl's own insights.

LETTER to HUSSERL

FRANZ BRENTANO

Florence, 9 January, 1905

Dear Friend,

I thank you for your cordial letter and good wishes which I warmly return. I have read with great interest what you say about your endeavours, over the long years that have separated us, and about your present point of view.

If I understand correctly, you distinguish a twofold logic. One is an art, the other a theoretical discipline. The latter is supposed to comprise all pure mathematics (geometry apparently being a discipline which is applied only to space). What is its subject-matter? Apparently objects of reason and their combinations. It is supposed to be a part of philosophy and not to be based upon our knowledge of psychology. And this latter seems to you to be the point of greatest importance, for otherwise the validity of logic could be restricted to beings who happen to have the same make-up as we do. This theoretical logic is concerned, not with evidence for us, but with an evidence of truths in themselves, so to speak. You praise Bolzano as your teacher and guide.

.   .   .

I think you may be justified in holding that the task of pure mathematics falls within the sphere of logic. But what seems unclear to me is whether this logic is anything other than the *art* of logic.

.   .   .

Reprinted from *The True and the Evident*, translated by Roderick Chisholm (New York: Humanities Press, 1968), pp. 135–138, by permission of the publisher and Routledge & Kegan Paul.

211

You are certainly right in emphatically rejecting any theory which would thus demolish the concept of knowledge and truth. But you are mistaken if you think that, in giving psychology this position in relation to logic, one has no way of avoiding such an error.

Whoever really makes an evident judgment really *knows* the truth and is certain of it; whoever really knows something with *direct* evidence is *directly* certain of the truth. This is unaffected by the fact that the knower, as a person judging, came into being, is subject to causation, and is dependent upon the particular cerebral organization which he happens to have. To the one who judges with evidence, the truth is secured *in itself*, and *not* by reflection on any such preconditions.

. . .

There is no need at all to postulate any such thing as a truth-in-itself or a judgment-in-itself. There are only particular individuals who judge and only particular individuals who judge with evidence; what there is, no matter what area we are talking about, can consist only of things that are individually determined.

What you call "psychologism" is essentially the παντων των οντων μετρον ανθρωπος of Protagoras. This is anathema to me, as it is to you. But this does not mean that we should countenance a realm of entities of reason. It is unfortunate that a mind such as that of the highly respected Bolzano should have soared too high and lost its way at this point. For the supposition of such a realm can be shown to be absurd.

But I do wish you good fortune in your intellectual contact with this noble and sincere thinker. Even the errors of such a person are more instructive than are the truths which may occasionally be found in the glib talk of others.

In sincere friendship,
F.B.

PHENOMENOLOGY

GILBERT RYLE

I want to distinguish the question what Phenomenology is from certain special questions about certain special claims that are made for it.

I. What Phenomenology Is

Phenomenology is not specially concerned with phenomena in the sense of sense-data. Nor is it, unless *per accidens,* any sort of Phenomenalism.

The title (which is a misleading one) derives from the following historical source. Brentano, following Herbart, repudiated the psychologies which treated mental faculties as the ultimate terms of psychological analysis, and insisted instead that the ultimate date of psychology are the particular manifestations of consciousness. These he called "psychic phenomena," not as being appearances as opposed to noumena or things in themselves, but as being directly discernible manifestations of mental functioning as opposed to being inferred or constructed mental "powers." So "Phenomenology" only means, as it stands, the science of the manifestations of consciousness and might have been used—though it is not—as another name for psychology.

Brentano next distinguished between two radically different sorts of enquiry into mental functioning. One is empirical—or what he calls, oddly, "genetic"—psychology, which is inductive, experimental and statistical, and the conclusions of which are only probable generalizations. The other is the enquiry into the concepts or presuppositions of any such empirical psychology, namely, such enquiry as "What is it to be a case of remembering, judging, inferring, wishing, choosing, regretting, etc.?" It asks, what ultimate forms of mental functioning there are to be exemplified in particular instances, and so is not concerned, *e.g.*, with what it is that makes this or that man remember something, but with what it is for a mental act to be a case of remembering.

He got to this position, I gather, in this way. Convinced that the physiological and the associationist psychologies were radically false, he had to examine and reject their presuppositions—in particular, the presuppositions (1) that mental life is a mere avalanche of atomic "ideas" and (2) that these "ideas" are in no sense *of* anything. Instead, he argued, we can know *a priori* (1) that any case of consciousness of any form must be a case of consciousness *of* something and (2) that there are irreducibly different sorts of mental functioning, so that while "ideas" may be necessary ingredients in judging and wanting, judging and wanting cannot be analysed without residue into "ideas" or complexes of them.

Whatever his line of approach may have been, he and his pupils were always perfectly clear that the analysis of the root types of mental functioning is one thing and the experimental or statistical search for the natural laws governing the occurrence of mental acts and states was quite another. And I think that they were right.

Husserl uses the term "Phenomenology" to denote the analysis of the root types of mental functioning. And he tries to show (1) that Phenomenology is anyhow a part of philosophy; (2) that it is an enquiry which can become a rigorous *science;* (3) that it is *a priori.* (1) and (3) seem to me to be true; (2) seems to me to be either false or an awkward terminological innovation. For I don't think that philosophy or any part of philosophy is properly called a "science." Philosophical methods are neither scientific nor unscientific. But this is not a question which I want to deal directly with here.

It is not a new discovery or a new theory that at least a part and an important part of philosophy consists in the analytical investigation of types of mental functioning. Theories of knowledge, belief, opinion, perception, error, imagination, memory, inference, and abstraction, which can all be classed together as epistemology, have ever since Plato constituted at least an important part of philosophy. And anyhow a large part of Ethics has, since Plato and Aristotle, consisted in the analysis of the concepts of motive, impulse, desire, purpose, intention, choice, regret, shame, blame, approbation, and the like. And while parts of the treatments given by historical philosophers to these subjects have been not analytical, but speculative or hypothetical or dogmatic, other parts have always been strictly analytical and critical and have therefore been proper cases of what Husserl describes as the phenomenological method. So nothing much save a rather misleading title would have been secured by Husserl had he merely asserted that these and such like enquiries are all phenomenological enquiries, in that all are enquiries into the nature of more or less radical types of mental functioning.

He does, of course, go a good deal further than this. First of all he argues, in opposition, I take it, to special schools of positivists and experimental psychologists as well as to the whole associationist theory of psychology, that the way in which types of mental functioning are analysed by philosophers or phenomenologists when they know their business is quite different from the way in which empirical psychology enquires into the causal laws governing the occurrence of mental states, acts and dispositions in the life-history of actual persons in the world. For (1) the method of philosophy proper is *a priori*, whereas that of the others is inductive; and (2) the very questions raised by empirical psychology embody the concepts the analysis of which belongs to phenomenology. So that in two connected ways phenomenology is independent of empirical psychology: (1) that being *a priori* phenomenology cannot employ as its premises either the particular observations or the inductive generalizations of empirical psychology and (2) that being analytical or critical it enquires what any psychological proposition of this or that sort really means (whether it is true or false), and so throws light on and cannot derive light from the particular psychological propositions which psychologists put forward as true or probable.

This seems to me to be true and generalizable. Not only psychology, but all sciences and all sorts of search for knowledge or probable opinion aim at establishing particular or general propositions. But whether in any particular case such a proposition is true or false, the analysis of what it means, or of what would be the case if it were true, is different from and in principle prior to the discovery of what proves it or makes it probable. Thus, the philosophy of physics is indifferent to the answers that physicists give to the questions of physics, the philosophy of mathematics does not wait for the solution of all possible equations, and in ethics we must have some notion of desert, and one which we are already in principle ready to analyse, whether or not we are able to decide that a given defendant deserves a certain punishment.

No philosophical propositions are empirical either in the sense of being about this as distinct from that particular subject of attributes, or in the sense of implying as premises propositions which are so.

This does not, of course, involve that philosophical arguments should not contain references to particular cases as instances or examples. On the contrary, a good illustrative example is often of great utility. But an *exempli gratia* is not an *ergo*—as is shown by the fact that imaginary examples are often just as useful as actual ones, which would not be the case in a genuine inductive argument.

Husserl's apriorism is, perhaps, nothing very alarming. But, at the time of the last century, naturalism and empiricism were so fashionable that Husserl had to prosecute very difficult and painstaking logical enquiries in order to justify it. And we should first notice three cardinal points in his account of the *a priori* nature of philosophical propositions.

1. He does not hold that philosophers should or can construct deductive systems. Demonstration *ordine geometrico* belongs to mathematics and not to philosophy. For Husserl Spinoza's notion of philosophy as a sort of metaphysical geometry is a completely mistaken sort of apriorism. And I think Husserl is right.

2. Further, Husserl refuses to admit into phenomenology or,

by implication, into philosophy in general, any sort of metaphysical system-building or speculative construction. Dogmatic metaphysics is put out of court by Husserl just as much as by Kant. (It is, however, arguable that some of Husserl's conclusions are of the nature of metaphysical constructions. His half solipsist and half monadological account of the experienced world is not at all what one would expect to find deriving from a purely analytical inquiry into the *summa genera* of the manifestations of mind.) But with his official view that the business of philosophy is not to give new information about the world, but to analyse the most general forms of what experience finds to be exemplified in the world I completely agree.

3. On the other hand Husserl's special account of the nature of *a priori* thinking seems to me to be wrong. Rather like Meinong he holds, or used to hold, that universals or essences as well as propositions, are objects of a higher order. And of these we can have a knowledge by acquaintance analogous to (though of a higher order than) our perceptual acquaintanceship with particulars like this tree and that man. We can, he holds, perceive or intuit essences in the same sort of way as we can perceive or intuit particulars, except that the direct intuition of an essence requires to be founded in the direct intuition of a particular instance of it (which may be real or imaginary). Philosophy is, accordingly, a sort of observational science (like geography); only the objects which it inspects are not spatiotemporal entities but semi-Platonic objects which are out of space and time. These are correlates to acts of conception and judgment, though whether it is essential to them to be so correlative or whether it is accidental, is left rather obscure in Husserl's writings. I fancy that Husserl used to think of them as independently subsisting and now regards them as intrinsically contents of possible acts of thinking.

I do not myself believe that phrases such as "being a so and so," "being such and such" and "that so and so is such and such" do denote objects or subjects of attributes. For I don't think that they are denoting expressions at all. Consequently, though I can know what it is for something to be a so and so, I think that this knowledge is wrongly described as an "intuition of an essence." For intuition, which I take to be a synonym for knowledge by acquaintance or perception, does seem to be or to involve a relation between two subjects of attributes, the perceiver and the thing perceived. And I do not think that what Husserl calls "essences" are subjects of attributes at all. However, I do not think that the whole notion of phenomenology hinges on this special theory, so I do not think that it need be discussed here. But we shall have to discuss later a more general question, which is connected with this one, concerning the theory of intentional objects.

So much for the general plan of phenomenology. It is that part, or those parts of philosophy in which the root types of mental functioning are distinguished and analysed. And most philosophers have talked phenomenology, as M. Jourdain talked prose. What Husserl has done so far is (*a*) to distinguish, as his predecessors had largely failed to do, between the philosophical and the psychological methods of investigating consciousness; (*b*) to make clear that anyhow this part of philosophy is analytical and not speculative or hypothetical; and (*c*) to name it with a rather unfortunate name.

II. Now for His Main Doctrines in Phenomenology

It is an "essential intuition," that is, it can be known *a priori* that all consciousness is consciousness of something. To wish is to wish for something, to regret is to regret something, to remember, expect, decide and choose are to remember something, expect something, decide something and choose something. To every piece of mental functioning there is intrinsically correlative something which is the "accusative" of that functioning. But though all consciousness is "intentional"[1] or "transitive," it

---

[1] "Intentionality" has nothing special to do with intending in our sense of purposing. It is a revival of a scholastic term and is used only as a name for the fact that mental acts are *of* objects. I use the term "accusative" to render "gegenstand." "Object" is damagingly equivocal since it may mean "entity" or "subject of attributes" as well as meaning "object of . . . ."

is not all intentional or transitive in the same way. The act of remembering may have the same object as one of regretting, but they are different sorts of facts and "have" their object in different manners. Moreover, some sorts of "consciousness of" demand others as their platform. I cannot regret without remembering, though I can remember without regretting. And again, I cannot remember without having once directly perceived, but I can perceive without having to remember. And so on.

Next, all intentional experiences, whatever their "accusatives," must belong to an experiencing ego. *Cogito ergo sum* is a cardinal proposition in Husserl's phenomenology. "What is it to be an 'I'?" is perhaps, the most general way of formulating the question of phenomenology—indeed Husserl coins the unattractive alternative title for phenomenology of "descriptive transcendental egology."

These two marks of intentional experiences—namely, that in all of them there is a subject-pole and in all of them there is an object-pole—are not independent. They are intrinsically correlative. But the correlation can take as many different forms as there are different types of intentionality. For a type of intentionality is simply a not further analysable way in which an I may be about something.

On the other hand, the subject-pole is, for Husserl as for Descartes, something the reality of which is philosophically unimpugnable and presuppositionless, whereas any of its objects upon which it may from time to time be directed may have no other reality than that with which it is endowed by being what the self is dreaming, say, or expecting or believing in.

As we shall see, Husserl does, in fact, terminate in a subjectivist or egocentric philosophy, though he is at pains to argue that it is not a form of solipsism.

THE PHENOMENOLOGICAL REDUCTION

In our everyday frames of mind, and particularly in our scientific frame of mind, we treat the world and the things and happenings in it as independently existing. That is, we focus on their relationships to one another and ignore the fact that they all alike stand to us as pegs upon which we are hooking *our* interests, attentions, queries, emotions, decisions and volitions. They are—but we habitually fail to remember that they are—constituents of our variegated cognitive-*cum*-volitional-*cum*-emotional experiences. We think about things, but do not ordinarily notice that they are at least, whatever else they are, what we are thinking about.

Now, Husserl argues, of our experiences we can have direct and self-evident perception. Reflective inspection of our own *actus* of consciousness can give us knowledge in the strict sense of the term. I can know both that I am enacting an act of a certain description and what that description is. And he rather assumes than argues, following Descartes, that there is no other sort of self-evident (or knowing) inspection of particulars.

Let us, then, by a sort of Method of Doubt bracket out or shelve all that we accept in our everyday scientific frames of mind over and above what reflective inspection can warrant. This will leave as one of our most important sets of data to be studied, such facts as that we accept the proposition that the sun is bigger than the moon, but will bracket out the fact (if it is one) that the sun *is* bigger than the moon. We are left with Erlebnisse, and that means that we are left with the whole experienced world. But what (if anything) exists or happens or is the case without being a constituent of experiences is not the theme of any phenomenological proposition.

What an "object" is now is nothing save what sort of an "accusative" it is to what sorts of intentional experiences. It is just that which constitutes particular mental functionings as the particular mental functions that they are. In a word, it is just the special character of an act or set of acts, or, to employ a misleading expression of which Husserl is fond, the object of an intentional experience, treated as such, is just the intrinsic meaning or sense of the experience.

We can now say that whatever may be the special objects of such studies and interests as physics, biology, astronomy, psychology, and the other natural sciences—history, sociology, economics and law, business, politics, and, in a word, of all intellectual, practical and emotional occupation, all alike have and have essentially the character of being constituents of experiences. They are the ways in which I or we function.

Consequently, Husserl argues, both the scientific search for the laws governing the existence of such things and the special philosophical analyses of the essences of them presuppose the philosophical analysis of the types of mental functioning in the several instances of which these objects present themselves as the specifying or individuating constituents.

So phenomenology is the first philosophy, or the science of sciences. It and it alone has for its topic the *summum genus* of the objects of all the other sciences and interests. It even has priority over logic.

It is therefore, for Husserl, part of the nature of all possible subjects of attributes to be constitutents in the intentional experiences of an "I." But as persons in the ordinary sense of the term are only empirically discovered things in the world of objects, it is not empirical selves, but a pure or transcendental self whose "intentions" are the home of the being of objects. And Husserl accordingly develops a Kantian or neo-Kantian doctrine of a pure or absolute subject which is other than you or I for the reason that you and I are merely items in the list of the possible accusatives of intentional experiences.

I think myself that Husserl is (with Kant) confusing "I-ness" with a new I. Propositions about "Bewüsstsein überhaupt" are really about what it is to be an I having experiences, and not about an I that has them. But I doubt if it would be profitable to let our discussion turn upon this question.

Husserl now seems to have reached the position that nothing exists—indeed, that it is nonsense to speak of anything existing—save, on the one hand, a pure subject of experiences, or several such subjects which exist in their own right, and, on the other hand, the entire realm of intentional objects, the being of which is their being "intended."

This conclusion seems to me to be false, and with it the

consequential doctrine that phenomenology is logically prior to all other philosophical or scientific enquiries. Phenomenology seems to have turned in Husserl's hands into an egocentric metaphysic. But this seems to be the result of one or two false theories which need never and should never have trespassed into the analysis of types of mental functioning.

(a) The Doctrine of Intentional Objects

It was an assumption rooted in the Cartesian and Lockean theories of mental life that what I am aware of when I am aware of something must always be an "idea." We need not bother our heads about the definition of "idea" (for nonentities are not necessarily definable), but at least it was held that an idea is a mental something and something existing or occurring inside the mind that is aware of it. The theory of intentionality is an attempt not to repudiate, but to modify, elaborate and reform the "idea" epistemology. The first modification was the distinction between the act and its object, the *ideatio* and the *ideatum, e.g.,* in the idea of a circle, the circle is something with a centre but the ideating of it is not. But it was still supposed that the circle was really existing or occurring in the mind together with the act of which it was the "content." Similarly, the proposition which I judge and the desideratum which I desire, through distinguishable from the acts of judging and desiring, were still supposed to be actually resident where these resided.

Husserl, however, like Meinong in this respect, denies that what an act is "of" is essentially contained in or adjoined to the act. "Contents" are not real parts of mental functioning. Introspection cannot find them. (This is proved by the fact that two acts of different dates can have the same object.)

Nor can all possible "contents" be lodged in the actual world of space and time. For what fancies, false beliefs, wishes, expectations and conceptions are of, are nowhere to be found there. And as Husserl seems, anyhow latterly, to reject Platonic or Meinongian subsistence theories, it becomes very hard to see in what sense he holds that "intentional objects" really are genuine objects or subjects of attributes at all. He *should* hold (I believe) that what we miscall "the object or content of an act of consciousness" is really the specific character or nature of that act, so that the intentionality of an act is not a relation between it and something else, but merely a property of it so specific as to be a *differentia* or in some cases an individualizing description of it. He does in fact, however, continue to speak as if every intentional act is related, though related by an internal relation, to a genuine subject of attributes.

I would urge against this view (1) that it is erroneous in itself and (2) that it originates from an erroneous assumption that "consciousnes of . . ." is a true *summum genus* of which the several forms of mental functioning (including knowing) are true homogeneous species.

1. It is certainly a convenient and popular idiom to speak of "the objects of" imagination, desire, belief, knowledge, etc., when we wish to refer to what some one imagines, desires, believes or knows. And as we often use "object" as a synonym for "thing," as when we call a Chippendale chair "a handsome" or "expensive object," we have anyhow this motive for supposing that some subject of attributes is being referred to when we speak of what Jones imagines or wants or believes or knows. But the supposition seems to be a mistake. For the phrase "the object of Jones' desire or fancy," *e.g.,* is not necessarily a referentially used "the"-phrase, any more than the "the"-phrase in "Poincaré is not the King of France." It is almost certainly a systematically misleading expression. For there is nothing of which we can say truly or even falsely *"that* is the object of Jones' desire or fancy." We can indeed state which attributes Jones is imagining something to be characterized by or what are the features of his situation, the absence or alteration of which Jones desiderates. But these statements will not require us to employ descriptive phrases referring to queer non-actual objects. Such references could not be made for they would be self-contradictory.

If, then, the doctrine of intentionality implies that to every case of mental functioning of whatever sort there must be correlative, a special something describable as an "intentional object," then this doctrine seems to be false.

2. Husserl assumes that all forms of mental functioning are species or sub-species of a *summum genus called* "consciousness of . . ." And by "consciousness of . . ." he means to denote not *knowing,* but something of which knowing is, with believing, guessing, dreaming, craving, etc., only a species. From this, of course it has to follow that often I am "conscious of" something which is not a known reality and so is not real at all. (It is not possible to state this sort of view in an unobjectionable way.)

Now in my opinion Cook Wilson has shown in a strictly phenomenological manner that this whole assumption is vicious. Knowing is not one definable species of "consciousness of . . ." among others, it is something anyhow partly in terms of which believing, fancying, guessing, wanting and the rest have to be defined. Belief, *e.g.,* is a state of mind involving *ignorance* of such and such a *knowledge* of so and so: it involves more than that, but at least it involves this double reference to knowledge.

Consequently the "intentionality" of mental acts must be defined in terms not of "consciousness of . . ." but of "knowledge of . . ." And as it is, if not self-evident, anyhow plausible to say that what I know to be the case is so whether I know it or not, a phenomenology operating with this modified notion of intentionality would not be obviously bound to terminate in an egocentric metaphysic, or to claim a priority over all other branches of philosophy, such as logic or the philosophy of physics. For it would no longer be essential to any subject of attributes to be "accusative" to a mental act. Intentionality will not now be an internal relation.

(b) Immanent versus Transcendent Perception

An important premiss in Husserl's argument which helps to involve him in his quasi-solipsistic conclusions is his theory of the self-evidence of immanent perception and the fallibility of transcendent perception.

By "immanent perception" he refers to the direct recognition or inspection that I can have of my own mental states and acts, when these are concurrent with the inspection of them. I take it that he is referring to what we call introspection. When, which is fairly infrequent, I introspect upon my present Erlebnis, I can *know* in the strict sense that I am enjoying this Erlebnis and what sort of an Erlebnis it is. Introspection tells the truth, the whole truth and nothing but the truth.

By "transcendent perception" he refers to the perception of physical things and events, the mental acts and states of others, and those mental acts and states of my own which are not contemporary with the inspection of them. This, Husserl maintains, can never be or give *knowledge*. It is never self-evident, and the possibility of delusion is always present. It follows that sciences of "the external world" cannot be or give knowledge, but that the science of the self can: and all that I can *know* about the world is what I can know about my fallible cognizings of the world and my resultant practical and emotional attitudes towards it. And if this were true, Husserl would, I think, have established some sort of primacy for phenomenology.

But (1), while I see no reason to doubt that we *can* inspect and recognize states and acts of our own minds, I think that this introspection is not really perception (save in an enlarged sense). I believe that introspection is merely remembrance controlled by a special interest. But whatever it is, it seems clear that we often make mistakes about our mental condition. Very likely these should not be attributed to "mistaken introspection," but are mistakes due to an unnoticed omission to introspect. But then the same indulgence should be allowed to what is very likely miscalled "mistaken perception" in the sphere of what Husserl calls "transcendent perception."

(2) I can see no *a priori* grounds for supposing that perception can only be knowledge where the object perceived and the perceiving of it are conjoined parts of one stream of experience. It seems to me just the old prejudice that the thing known should be in some way very near to the knowing of it.

So I see no grounds for denying universally that we can have knowledge by perception of physical things and events. Husserl's arguments on this point, which I have not expounded, seem to me only to show that particular perceptions don't tell the whole truth about their objects. But if they can tell us the

truth and nothing but the truth, no conclusions damaging to the
world seem to arise from the comparison of this sort of perception with introspection.

My conclusion is, then, this:—(1) There is an important
part of philosophy describable as the philosophy of psychology.
It is, like any other part of philosophy, *a priori* in the sense that
its methods are not inductive and that its objects are not this
as distinct from that particular matter of fact. It is an inquiry
into the forms of certain classes of facts, or, to put it in another
way, it inquires what is really meant by such propositions as,
"Jones knows or believes such and such," "Jones wanted this
but chose that," "Jones took what he saw to be a so and so," "I
am a such and such." And we can, if we like, call this part of
philosophy "phenomenology."

(2) The fact that Husserl concludes that the world consists
of nothing but bi-polar mental experiences, and consequently that
phenomenology is "first philosophy" is the result of his acceptance of one or two theories which are not true and are not arrived at by genuine phenomenological analysis.

MEANING
AND
CONSTITUTION

Unities of meaning presuppose . . . a sense-giving conscious-ness, which, on its side, is absolute and not dependent in its turn on senses bestowed on it from another source.

—Edmund Husserl IDEAS (I)

Yet the greatest problems of all are the functional problems, or those of the 'constituting of the objective field of con-sciousness.'

—Edmund Husserl IDEAS

INTRODUCTION

According to Husserl, the object of an intentional act of consciousness gives the *meaning* of that act. Moreover, it is the intentional act that *constitutes* the object. From his book *Ideas* on, Husserl comes to refer to the constituting act as the *noesis*, and what is constituted as the object (the meaning) as the *noema*. But what is the object? What is the relation of object to *noema?* What is constitution, the *production* of the object or a structured but passive *seeing* it? In the first two selections, Husserl attempts to answer these questions. Then Aron Gurwitsch, a distinguished student of Husserl, gives his rather idealist defense of this dual conception of *noesis–noema*. Merleau-Ponty offers a less idealist and more "existential" account of constitution. Dagfin Føllesdal, a Norwegian philosopher who divides his work between Quinean-style formal semantics and Husserl, argues a more Fregean and more formal notion of *noema*.

NOEMA AND NOESIS

EDMUND HUSSERL

Corresponding at all points to the manifold data of the real (*reellen*) noetic content, there is a variety of data displayable in really pure (*wirklich reiner*) intuition, and in a correlative "*noematic content*," or briefly "*noema*"—terms which we shall henceforth be continually using.

Perception, for instance, has its noema, and at the base of this its perceptual meaning, that is, the *perceived as such*. Similarly, the recollection, when it occurs has as its own its *remembered as such* precisely as it is "meant" and "consciously known" in it; so again judging has as its own the *judged as such*, pleasure the pleasing as such, and so forth. We must everywhere take the noematic correlate, which (in a very extended meaning of the term) is here referred to as "meaning" (*Sinn*) *precisely as it lies* "immanent" in the experience of perception, of judgment, of liking, and so forth, i.e., *if we question in pure form this experience itself*, as we find it there presented to us. . . .

From our phenomenological standpoint we can and must put the question of essence: *What is the "perceived as such"? What essential phases does it harbour in itself in its capacity as noema?* We win the reply to our question as we wait, in pure surrender, on what is essentially *given*. . . .

Like perception, *every* intentional experience—and this is indeed the fundamental mark of all intentionality—has its "intentional object," i.e., its objective meaning. Or to repeat the same in other words: To have a meaning, or to have something "in mind," is the cardinal feature of all consciousness, that on ac-

Reprinted with permission of the Macmillan Company from *Ideas*, by Edmund Husserl, trans. W. R. Boyce-Gibson, pp. 238, 240–241, 250, First Collier Books Edition, 1962. Copyright 1931 by Crowell Collier and Macmillan, Inc., New York.

count of which it is not only experience generally but meaningful, "noetic." . . . the law of the essence universally attested runs
to this effect: *No noetic phase without a noematic phase that
belongs specifically to it.*

CONSTITUTION, "REASON" AND "UNREASON"

EDMUND HUSSERL

Phenomenological constitution has been for us, up to now,
constitution of any intentional object whatever. It has embraced
the full breadth of the topic, cogito—cogitatum. We shall now
proceed to differentiate this breadth structurally, and to prepare
for a *more pregnant concept of constitution.* It has not mattered
up to now, whether the objects in question were truly existent or
non-existent, or whether they were possible or impossible. These
differences are not perchance excluded from the field of inquiry
by abstaining from decision about the being or non-being of the
world (and, consequently, of other already-given objectivities).
On the contrary, under the broadly understood titles, *reason and
unreason,* as correlative titles for being and non-being, they are
an all-embracing theme for phenomenology. By epoché we effect
a reduction to our pure meaning (cogito) and to the meant,
purely as meant. The predicates *being and non-being,* and their
modal variants, relate to the latter—accordingly, not to objects
simpliciter but to the *objective sense.* The predicates *truth (correctness) and falsity,* albeit in a most extremely broad sense,
relate to the former, to the particular *meaning or intending.*
These predicates are not given ipso facto as phenomenological
data, when the subjective meaning processes, or correlatively the
meant objects as meant, are given; yet they have their "phenom-

Reprinted from *Cartesian Meditations,* trans. D. Cairns (The Hague,
Netherlands: M. Nijhoff, 1960), section 23, pp. 56–57, by permission of the
publisher.

enological origin". As we have said, the multiplicities of modes
of consciousness that belong together synthetically and pertain
to any meant object, of no matter what category, can be explored
as to their phenomenological types. Among such multiplicities
are included those syntheses that, with regard to the initial intending, have the typical style of verifying and, in particular,
evidently verifying syntheses—or else, on the contrary, that of
nullifying and evidently nullifying syntheses. When such a synthesis takes place, the meant object has, correlatively, the evident characteristic *existing*, or else the evident characteristic
non-existing (the characteristic of annulled, of "cancelled"
being). These synthetic occurences are intentionalities of a
higher level, which, as acts and correlates of "reason", essentially
producible by the transcendental ego, pertain (in exclusive disjunction) to all objective senses. *Reason is not an accidental de
facto ability*, not a title for possible accidental matters of fact,
but rather a title for an *all-embracing essentially necessary structural form belonging to all transcendental subjectivity*.

Reason refers to possibilities of verification; and verification refers ultimately to making evident and having as evident.
About evidence we had to speak even at the beginning of our
meditations—when, with our initial naïveté, we were still seeking
the guiding lines for a method and had not yet set foot within
the realm of phenomenology. It now becomes our phenomenological theme.

HUSSERL'S NOESIS-NOEMA DOCTRINE

ARON GURWITSCH

The preceding discussion leaves us with the problem of how
identical and identifiable objects may exist for, and stand before,

Reprinted from "On The Intentionality of Consciousness," in *Studies
in Phenomenology and Psychology* (Evanston, Ill.: Northwestern University
Press, 1966), pp. 131–134, 138–140 by permission of the publisher.

a consciousness whose acts perpetually succeed one another; every one of these acts, in addition to their succeeding one another, is incessantly undergoing temporal variations. For what is meant by James's "stream of thought" and by Bergson's *durée* does express an experienced reality, of which we may become conscious at any moment, if we are attentive to what happens in our conscious lives.

A solution has been given to this problem by Husserl by means of his theory of intentionality; and as far as I know, it is the only one that exists. Lack of space prevents me from studying the growth of this theory throughout Husserl's writings. When in the *Logische Untersuchungen* he tackled intentionality for the first time, Husserl was not yet dealing with the problem we have emphasized. His theory of intentionality gradually got a reference to this problem, and though this reference did not become manifest until the *Formale und transzendentale Logik,* it seems to us that the form in which intentionality is advanced in the *Ideen,* chiefly in the *noesis-noema doctrine,* already constitutes an answer to our problem. Taking the noesis-noema doctrine into consideration from this point of view, we shall proceed beyond what was explicitly formulated by Husserl himself.

When an object is perceived, there is, on the one hand, the act with its elements, whatever they may be: the act as a real event in psychical life, happening at a certain moment of phenomenal time, appearing, lasting, disappearing, and, when it has disappeared, never returning. On the other hand, there is what, in this concrete act, stands before the perceiving subject's mind. [Husserl, *Ideen* 88] Let the thing perceived be a tree. This tree, at any rate, presents itself in a well-determined manner: it shows itself from this side rather than from that; it stands straight before the observer or occupies a rather lateral position; it is near the perceiving subject or removed from him at a considerable distance, and so on. [Husserl, *CMP.* 39ff.] Finally, it offers itself with a certain prospect, e.g., as giving shade, or, when the subject perceiving the tree recalls to his mind his past life, the tree perceived appears in the light of this or that scene of his youth. What has been described by these allusions is the *noema of perception*—namely, the object just (exactly so and only so) as the perceiving subject is aware of it, as he intends it in this concrete experienced mental state. It is with respect to the noema that the given perception is not only a perception of this determined object but is also that awareness of the object rather than another: that is to say, the subject experiencing the act in question, the *noesis*, finds himself confronted with a certain object appearing from such a side, in the orientation it has, in a certain aspect, and so on. Hence the noema may also be designated as the perceptual sense.

The noema is to be distinguished from the real object. [Husserl, *Ideen* 89–90] The latter, the tree for instance, as a real thing appears now in this determined manner; but it may offer itself from a different side, at another distance, in a different orientation and aspect; and it does so in fact when the subject goes around it. It shows itself in a multiplicity of perceptions, through all of which the same real tree presents itself; but the "perceived tree as such" varies according to the standpoint, the orientation, the attitude, etc., of the perceiving subject, as when for instance he looks at the tree from above or at another time perceives it while in the garden. Indeed, a real thing may not present itself as such except by means of a series of perceptions succeeding one another. [*Ibid.* 42, 44, 143] These perceptions enter into a synthesis of identification with one another, and it is by, and in, this synthesis and the parallel synthesis among the corresponding noemata that what appears successively constitutes itself, for consciousness, into this real thing which it is, one and identical as opposed to the multiple perceptions and also to the multiple noemata. [*Ibid.* 41, 86, 135, 145, 150; *CM* 17–18] Hence problems arise as to the relation of the act and its noema to the real thing perceived through the act and, further, as to what relations the noemata uniting themselves by the synthesis of identification bear to one another. [*Ideen* 98, 128–131] At any rate, it is obvious that the real object ought not to be confounded with a single noema.

On the other hand, the noema is distinct from the act in the sense that it does not constitute a part, an element, a factor of the act and does not really exist within consciousness, as the act does. [*Ibid.*, 97] When, looking at a thing, we alternately shut and open our eyes again, without any change in the position of our body or in the direction of the glance, we experience a number of perceptual acts, all different from one another. Through every one of these acts, however, not only does the same object offer itself, but it appears also in the same aspect and orientation, from the same side, at the same distance, and so on. The tree presents itself now in exactly the same manner as it did a moment ago, as it did yesterday, as it is expected to do tomorrow. The "perceived tree as such" is identically the same, notwithstanding the variety of the acts to which it corresponds. *In the noema,* then, *we have something identical* which, for this very reason, ought not to be mistaken for an element of the corresponding act. Were it such an element, it would appear and disappear with the act, and it would be tied up, as the act is, to the place the latter occupies in phenomenal time.

The noema, as distinct from the real object as well as from the act, turns out to be an irreal or ideal entity which belongs to the same sphere as meanings or significations. This is the sphere of sense (*Sinn*). [*Ibid.,* 133] The irreality of entities belonging to this sphere lies, first of all, in their atemporality, i.e., in a certain independence of the concrete act by which they are actualized, in the sense that every one of them may correspond, as identically the same, to another act, and even to an indefinite number of acts. Noemata are not to be found in perceptual life alone. There is a noema corresponding to every act of memory, expectation, representation, imagination, thinking, judging, volition, and so on. In all these cases, the object, matter of fact, etc., in itself, towards which the subject directs himself through the act, it to be distinguished from the object just, exactly just, as the subject has it in view, as, through the act, the object stands before the subject's mind. With regard to judging, the difference is between *objects about which* and *that which is judged as such.* It is worth noting that somehow James anticipated Husserl's notion of the noema of thinking and judging.

Husserl's noesis-noema doctrine, which we must content ourselves with summarizing briefly, far from being a constructive or explanatory theory, is simply a descriptive statement of an objectivating mental state, i.e., of a mental state through which the experiencing subject is confronted with an object. Every mental state of this kind must then be accounted for in terms of identity as well as of temporality. The traditional conception of consciousness, in which emphasis is placed upon temporality, the succession of acts and the variations each act undergoes by its duration, is certainly not false, since the fact emphasized is a real fact of consciousness. But this conception is incomplete and unilateral. No mental state is to be conceived only and exclusively as a real and temporal event in the stream of consciousness, without any reference to a sense. This reference is overlooked in the traditional conception. *Identity is to be acknowledged as a fact irreducible to any other; it turns out to be a fact of consciousness, no less authentic and no less fundamental than temporality is.* Thus we are led to a duality. And it must be stressed that this duality holds good even for the most elementary level of consciousness, where the question concerns the repeated appearance of an object in the same manner of presentation, without there being a need for going on to consider the appearance of an object one time in perception, another time in memory, representation, etc., and, still more, to take into consideration the successive presentations of an object, appearing as identically the same, from various sides and in the most different aspects.

THE CORRELATION CONCEPTION
OF CONSCIOUSNESS

To each act there corresponds a noema—namely, an object just, exactly and only just, as the subject is aware of it and has it in view, when he is experiencing the act in question. *Consciousness* is not to be mistaken for a mere unidimensional sphere composed of acts, as real psychical events, which co-exist with and succeed one another. Rather, it ought to be considered as a *correlation, or correspondence, or parallelism between the plane of acts, psychical events, noeses, and a second plane which is that of sense (noemata)*. This correlation is such that corresponding to each act is its noema, but the same noema may correspond to an indefinite number of acts. It is then not a one-to-one correspondence.

The noetico-noematic correlation is what the term intentionality must signify. In this light the formula consciousness *of* something is to be understood: a conscious act is an act of awareness, presenting to the subject who experiences it a sense, an ideal atemporal unity, identical, i.e., identifiable. [Husserl, CM p. 33] It is not by virtue of favorable circumstances calling for an explanation and for a reduction to more elementary facts but by virtue of what constitutes the nature of consciousness itself that an experienced act bears a reference to a sense. Consciousness is to be defined by its bearing reference to a sphere of sense, so that *to experience an act is the same thing as to actualize a sense.* Hence every fact of consciousness must be treated in terms of the relation *cogito-cogitatum qua cogitatum,* and no mental state may be accounted for except with regard to the objective sense (*gegenständlicher Sinn*), of which the experiencing subject becomes aware through this act. [*Ibid.,* p. 36, Husserl, FTL, p. 120]

Intentionality means the objective function of consciousness. In its most elementary form, this function consists in confronting the subject with senses, ideal unities, to which, as identical ones, he is free to revert an indefinite number of times. No sooner than this elementary structure of the objectivating function has been established, problems may be tackled as to higher structures of intentionality, concerning, for instance, syntheses by means of which particular perceptual senses are united into systems which are the real perceptual things, concerning categorial forms bestowed upon the perceptual data in thinking, concerning syntactical operations by which, in apophantics, more and more complicated meanings and significations are constructed from simpler ones, and so on. [Husserl, LU II, VI; FTL, 13] All structures of intentionality rest upon the noetico-noematic correlation, which, for this reason, is the most elementary structure. But it is, at the same time, also the most fundamental and the most universal one, since every sense entity, of whatever kind and of whatever degree of complication, is an identical and identifiable unity, to which the subject may come back again and again. Thus the noetico-noematic parallelism enters into all forms of mental activity; and it is to it that one is led by the basic problems of logic. [Husserl, FTL, 73]

The objectivating function belongs to an act, but not as taken in itself and as isolated from other mental states. On the contrary, this function is possessed by an act even when the latter has the distinctive character of evidence or self-presentation, on account of its being inserted into the whole of the experiencing life and only with regard to this whole. [*Ibid.*, pp. 142–143] Objectivity is identifiableness, i.e., the possibility of reverting again and again to what, through the present experienced act, is offered to consciousness and the possibility of so doing whether in the same or in any other mode of awareness. [*Ibid.*, p. 139] This holds good for real as well as ideal objects. [*Ibid.*, 61–62] It holds good also for "inner perception." When a present experienced mental state is grasped by an act of reflection and is thus made the object of this act of inner perception, the latter possesses the character of evidence, since the apprehended act is offered directly, immediately, and bodily, not by memory or in any symbolic manner. Nevertheless, it is not on this account that the act of inner perception is objectivating; it is so only because what appears through it, although its self-presentation never can be actualized again, may yet be recalled later and may be so an indefinite number of times. [*Ibid.*, pp. 140–141, 170] Objectivity and identity, then, have sense with regard to a multiplicity of acts—that is to say, with reference to the temporality of conscious life. These analyses of Husserl concerning objectivity, by which he has cleared up the ultimate meaning of his struggle against psychologism, [*Ibid.*, 56–57, 65, 67] throw a new light upon the correlation conception of consciousnes advanced here.

Though never formulated by Husserl in quite explicit terms, this conception seems to be at the root of a large part of his theories, and, when his work is considered in its growth, this conception reveals itself, I submit, to be one of the teleological goals towards which phenomenology is tending.

EXPERIENCE AND OBJECTIVE THOUGHT

MAURICE MERLEAU-PONTY

Our perception ends in objects, and the object once constituted, appears as the reason for all the experiences of it which
we have had or could have. For example, I see the next-door
house from a certain angle, but it would be seen differently from
the right bank of the Seine, or from the inside, or again from
an aeroplane: the house *itself* is none of these appearances; it is,
as Leibnitz said, the flat projection of these perspectives and of
all possible perspectives, that is, the perspectiveless position
from which all can be derived, the house seen from nowhere.
But what do these words mean? Is not to see always to see from
somewhere? To say that the house itself is seen from nowhere is
surely to say that it is invisible! Yet when I say that I see the
house with my own eyes, I am saying something that cannot be
challenged: I do not mean that my retina and crystalline lens,
my eyes as material organs, go into action and cause me to see
it: with only myself to consult, I can know nothing about this.
I am trying to express in this way a certain manner of approaching the object, the 'gaze' in short, which is as indubitable as my
own thought, as directly known by me. We must try to understand how vision can be brought into being from somewhere
without being enclosed in its perspective.

To see an object is either to have it on the fringe of the
visual field and be able to concentrate on it, or else respond to
this summons by actually concentrating upon it. When I do
concentrate my eyes on it, I become anchored in it, but this
coming to rest of the gaze is merely a modality of its movement:
I continue inside one object the exploration which earlier
hovered over them all, and in one movement I close up the landscape and open the object. The two operations do not fortuitously

Reprinted from *The Phenomenology of Perception*, translated by C.
Smith (New York: Humanities Press, 1962), pp. 67–69 by permission of
the publisher and Routledge & Kegan Paul.

coincide: it is not the contingent aspects of my bodily make-up, for example the retinal structure, which force me to see my surroundings vaguely if I want to see the object clearly. Even if I knew nothing of rods and cones, I should realize that it is necessary to put the surroundings in abeyance the better to see the object, and to lose in background what one gains in focal figure, because to look at the object is to plunge oneself into it, and because objects form a system in which one cannot show itself without concealing others. More precisely, the inner horizon of an object cannot become an object without the surrounding objects' becoming a horizon, and so vision is an act with two facets. For I do not identify the detailed object which I now have with that over which my gaze ran a few minutes ago by expressly comparing these details with a memory of my first general view. When, in a film, the camera is trained on an object and moves nearer to it to give a close-up view, we can *remember* that we are being shown the ash tray or an actor's hand, we do not actually identify it. This is because the screen has no horizons. In normal vision, on the other hand, I direct my gaze upon a sector of the landscape, which comes to life and is disclosed, while the other objects recede into the periphery and become dormant, while, however, not ceasing to be there. Now with them I have at my disposal their horizons, in which there is implied, as a marginal view, the object on which my eyes at present fall. The horizon, then, is what guarantees the identity of the object throughout the exploration; it is the correlative of the impending power which my gaze retains over the objects which it has just surveyed, and which it already has over the fresh details which it is about to discover. No distinct memory and no explicit conjecture could fill this rôle: they would give only a probable synthesis, whereas my perception presents itself as actual. The object-horizon structure, or the perspective, is no obstacle to me when I want to see the object: for just as it is the means whereby objects are distinguished from each other, it is also the means whereby they are disclosed. To see is to enter a universe of beings which *display themselves*, and they would not do this if they could not be hidden behind each other or behind me. In other words: to look at an object is to inhabit it, and from this habitation to grasp all things in terms of the aspect which they present to it. But in so far as I see those things too, they remain abodes open to my gaze, and, being potentially lodged in them, I already perceive from various angles the central object of my present vision. Thus every object is the mirror of all others. When I look at the lamp on my table, I attribute to it not only the qualities visible from where I am, but also those which the chimney, the walls, the table can 'see'; the back of my lamp is nothing but the face which it 'shows' to the chimney. I can therefore see an object in so far as objects form a system or a world, and in so far as each one treats the others round it as spectators of its hidden aspects which guarantee the permanence of those aspects by their presence. Any seeing of an object by me is instantaneously repeated between all those objects in the world which are apprehended as co-existent, because each of them is all that the others 'see' of it. Our previous formula must therefore be modified; the house itself is not the house seen from nowhere, but the house seen from everywhere. The completed object is translucent, being shot through from all sides by an infinite number of present scrutinies which intersect in its depths leaving nothing hidden.

What we have just said about the spatial perspective could equally be said about the temporal. If I contemplate the house attentively and with no thought in my mind, it has something eternal about it, and an atmosphere of torpor seems to be generated by it. It is true that I see it from a certain point in my 'duration', but it is the same house that I saw yesterday when it was a day younger; it is the same house that either an old man or a child might behold. It is true, moreover, that age and change affect it, but even if it should collapse tomorrow, it will remain forever true that it existed today: each moment of time calls all the others to witness; it shows by its advent 'how things were meant to turn out' and 'how it will all finish'; each present permanently underpins a point of time which calls for recognition from all the others, so that the object is seen at all times as it is seen from all directions and by the same means, namely the structure imposed by a horizon.

HUSSERL'S NOTION OF NOEMA

DAGFINN FØLLESDAL

The general theme of phenomenology, according to Husserl, is intentionality, that is, the peculiarity of consciousness to be consciousness *of* something. [*Ideen,* p. 203]

This concern with intentionality Husserl had taken over from his teacher, Brentano. According to Brentano,

> Every mental phenomenon is characterized by what the scholastics in the Middle Ages called the intentional (and also mental) inexistence of an object, and what we could call, although in not entirely unambiguous terms, the reference to a content, a direction upon an object.[1]

This may sound commonplace, but it leads to difficulties, e.g., when we try to apply the principle to a person who has hallucinations or to a person who thinks of a centaur. Brentano held that, even in these cases, our mental activity, our thinking or our sensing, is directed toward some object. The directedness has nothing to do with the object's being real, Brentano held; the object is itself contained in our mental activity, "intentionally" contained in it.

However, whereas the view that the objects of acts are real leads to difficulties in the case of centaurs and hallucinations, the view that the objects are unreal, whatever that may mean, leads

---

[1] Franz Brentano, *Psychologie vom empirischen Standpunkt,* vol. 1, book 2, chap. 1. Here quoted from D. B. Terrell's English translation of this chapter in Roderick M. Chisholm, ed., *Realism and the Background of Phenomenology* (Glencoe, Ill.: Free Press, 1960), p. 50.

Reprinted from the *Journal of Philosophy,* 66 (1969), pp. 680–687, by permission of the *Journal of Philosophy* and the author. Presented at a symposium on phenomenology, sponsored by the American Philosophical Association with H. L. Dreyfus and R. C. Solomon.

to difficulties in the case of many other acts, e.g., acts of normal perception: it seems that, on that view, what we see when we see a tree is not the real tree in front of us, but something else, which we would also have seen if we were hallucinating.

So we are faced with a dilemma.

Husserl resolved this dilemma by holding that, although every act is directed, this does not mean that there always is some object toward which it is directed. According to Husserl, there is associated with each act a *noema*, in virtue of which the act is directed toward its object, if it has any. When we think of a centaur, our act of thinking has a noema, but it has no object; there exists no object of which we think. Because of its noema, however, even such an act is directed. To be *directed* simply is to have a noema.

Husserl's notion of noema, therefore, is a key notion in his theory of intentionality and, thereby, in his phenomenology. According to Husserl, a proper understanding and grasp of the distinctions connected with the noema "is of the greatest importance for phenomenology, and decisive for giving it a right foundation" [Husserl, *Ideen* 239.35].

In this paper, I shall present a number of theses concerning the noema and support them by systematic arguments and textual evidence from Husserl's writings. I shall try to make the picture of the noema that thereby emerges, as accurate and complete as is permitted by the evidence that is available in Husserl's various published and unpublished works.

My main thesis is the following:

1. The noema is an intensional entity, a generalization of the notion of meaning (Sinn, Bedeutung).

This thesis and its consequences go against the usual interpretations of Husserl, but they accord well with Husserl's own writings. Thus, in the third volume of *Ideen*, page 89, Husserl says: "The noema is nothing but a generalization of the idea of meaning (Sinn) to the field of all acts."

Also in many of his other works, Husserl expresses similar views. Thus, in *Ideen*, volume I, he says, "Originally, these words ['Bedeuten' and 'Bedeutung'] related only to the linguistic sphere, that of 'expressing'. It is, however, almost unavoidable and at the same time an important advance, to widen the meaning of these words and modify them appropriately, so that they in a certain way are applicable to the whole noetic-noematic sphere: that is to all acts, whether these are intertwined with expressing acts or not" (304.7–14). And in *Ideen*, I, page 233.35–37, Husserl characterizes the full noema as a " 'Sinn' (in the widest sense)." Compare also 219.1 and 223.4.

One should be aware of an ambiguity in Husserl's use of the word 'Sinn' as applied to the noema. Sometimes he means the full noema, other times just a part of it, a part which may be the same in acts of many different kinds, e.g., acts of perception, remembering, imagining, etc. Our second thesis is therefore the following:

> 2. A noema has two components: (1) one which is common to all acts that have the same object, with exactly the same properties, oriented in the same way, etc., regardless of the "thetic" character of the act, i.e., whether it be perception, remembering, imagining, etc. and (2) one which is different in acts with different thetic character.

The first of these components Husserl calls "noematischer Sinn" (321.38) and also, alternatively, "der Gegenstand im wie seiner Bestimmtheiten" (321.37) and "gegenständlicher Sinn" (250.4). Compare also 249.11 and 322.4. The second component he calls the noematic correlate of the "Gegebenheitsweise" of the object (323.18, 250.16) or of the "Weise, wie der Gegenstand bewusst ist."[2] An important part of the "Gegebenheitsweise" is the "thetic character," the "Setzungscharacter" of the act (323.18; cf. also NuS 6). Another part that enters into the "Gegebenheitsweise" is the "filling," the "Anschauungssinn." As we should expect, Husserl says that the second component, like

---

[2] From the unpublished manuscript *Noema und Sinn*, (NuS) p. 6.

the first, can be regarded as a component of the act's "Sinn" in an extended sense (223.17–18). In the *Logical Investigations* (5. Unters., §§ 20–21), Husserl calls the first component "Materie," the second "Qualität" and the two together "Sinn." In *Ideen*, Husserl normally uses 'Sinn' for the first component, 'Noema' for the two together.

A third thesis is the following:

> 3. The noematic Sinn is that in virtue of which consciousness relates to the object.

This thesis, too, is well supported by the Husserlian text. Thus, in *Ideen*, I, 316.15: "Consciousness relates in and through this Sinn to its object." And "each intentional experience has a noema and in it a Sinn, through which it relates to the object" (329.9). Compare also 316.18 and 318.18.

A key point in Husserl's phenomenology is the following:

> 4. The noema of an act is not the object of the act (i.e., the object toward which the act is directed).

This is a crucial difference between Husserl and Brentano: Brentano's dilemma, mentioned at the beginning of this paper, arose because he held that the object that gives the act its directedness is the object toward which the act is directed. Brentano struggled throughout his life to make clear the relation of the act to its object, but he never succeeded in making this salutary distinction.

The object of an act is a function of the act's noematic Sinn in the sense that

> 5. To one and the same Noema, there corresponds only one object.

In fact, Husserl even asserts that: "Sameness of Sinn occurs only where the object besides being identically the same, is meant in 'the same Sinn' that is, from the same side, with the same properties etc." (NuS 4). See also *Logische Untersuchungen*, II (1928), § 28, page 416.

The converse, however, is not the case:

6. To one and the same object there may correspond several different noemata.

This is trivially true in view of thesis 2, since two noemata that have the same noematic Sinn and hence (as just observed) the same object, can nevertheless have different thetic characters and hence be different noemata. Thus, for example, acts of perception, memory, etc., can have the same object. However, thesis 6 may be strengthened to:

6. To one and the same object there may correspond several different noematic Sinne.

This follows, in fact, from the quotation from Husserl's *Noema und Sinn* that we just gave in order to support our thesis 5: The object being identically the same is not sufficient to guarantee sameness of Sinn; we also have to require that the object be given from the same side, with the same properties etc. Compare also *Ideen*, I 321.8 and *Logische Untersuchungen*, II, page 416.

The noemata help to individualize the acts, in that

7. Each act has one and only one noema.

Compare, e.g., NuS, page 2: "Each [act has] *its* noema as its individual characteristic."

It should be noted that the converse does not hold: to one and the same noema there may correspond several distinct acts. These acts will be similar; they will be directed toward the same object, with exactly the same properties and oriented in the same way; and they will have the same thetic character. Yet they may be distinct acts; they may, for example, have different temporal coordinates.

As could be expected, the noemata are like linguistic Sinne in most respects. Thus, the following important consequence of thesis 1 should be noted:

8. Noemata are abstract entities.

As textual support of thesis 8 we note the following: Husserl says in *Ideen*, I (222.3) : "The tree, the thing in nature, is by no means the perceived tree as such, which belongs inseparably to the perceiving as the perceptual Sinn. The tree can burn, may be dissolved in its chemical elements, etc. The Sinn, however—the Sinn of *this* perception, which belongs by necessity to its essence —cannot burn, it has no chemical elements, no forces, no real properties." In the manuscript *Noema und Sinn,* Husserl says: "Sinne are nonreal objects, they are not objects that exist in time" (NuS 109). And further out in the same manuscript: "A Sinn does not have reality, it is related to a temporal interval through the act in which it occurs, but it does not itself have reality [Dasein], an individual connection with time and duration" (NuS 114).

Here Husserl is talking about the noematic Sinn, but, since the other components of the noema are also "Sinn" components (223.17–18), the same presumably applies to them and, thereby, to the whole noema. Husserl says in *Ideen*, 314.23–25 that all noematic Sinne and complete noemata belong to one and the same species. That the noema is not a spatial object is clear from *Ideen*, page 97.23–24, where Husserl observes that spatial objects can be experienced only through perspectives (Abschattungen). Since in principle noemata are not experienced through perspectives, they are not spatial objects.

Closely connected with this is the following point, which is contrary to most currently accepted views on what the noemata are:

9. Noemata are not perceived through our senses.

This view is not clearly expressed in any of Husserl's published writings. However, it is an immediate consequence of thesis 8, and, if it should turn to be false, thesis 8 and several of our other theses would fall with it. It is therefore important to find and evaluate whatever evidence there is for or against thesis 9 in Husserl's writings. The closest Husserl comes to expressing his view on it in his published writings is on page 97 in *Ideen*, I, where he observes that all visible objects can be expe-

rienced only through perspectives. Since noemata, as just mentioned, are not experienced through perspectives, they are hence
not visible. Presumably, they are not perceived by the other
senses either.

In the unpublished manuscript *Noema und Sinn,* however,
to which I referred earlier, Husserl is more explicit on this
point. He there says, in a long passage which I will quote in full:

> The perception is perception "of" ("von") this Sinn, but not
> in the way in which the perception is perception of this house.
> The perception "has" the Sinn, but the Sinn is not perceived.
> Now I judge with respect to the perception that it has this
> Sinn, and that it accordingly (according to its Sinn) is char-
> acterized as perception of a renaissance building, whose facade
> has sandstone columns etc. If I close my eyes and have the
> house correspondingly given to me in memory, then I say again
> of the memory that it is memory of the same Sinn, in it the
> same thing is presented through memory which was formerly
> perceived. And if I am describing a mere fantasy, then I say
> again that according to its Sinn, it is a fantasy of . . . and there
> is the possibility that a fantasy has exactly the same Sinn as a
> perception (NuS 4).

Again, Husserl is here talking about the noematic Sinn, but, as
noted above, the remark presumably applies to all components
of the noema.

One might wonder how, then, one gets to know anything
about the noemata. Husserl's answer is

10. Noemata are known through a special reflection, the phenomenological reflection.

Our earlier theses on the noema now help us to see what this
reflection is and what it is not. It is a grasping of a Sinn. To
quote Husserl: "Toward this Sinn . . . one may always direct a
peculiar reflection, and *only* what is grasped in it is the basis of
the phenomenological judgment" (222.36). Also in *Noema und
Sinn* Husserl stresses that "the reflecting judgment of phenomenology and logic is directed toward the Sinn, and hence not

toward that which is the object of the nonreflecting judgment itself" (NuS 99–100). That the whole noema and not just the noematic Sinn is reflected upon, is made clear several places, for example, in *Ideen,* page 369.

Phenomenological reflection is, hence, not a special way of looking or using our senses; the objects grasped in phenomenological reflection are, as we already have observed in the preceding two theses, abstract and nonperceivable.

According to Husserl,

11. The phenomenological reflection can be iterated.

That is, to quote *Noema und Sinn,* "The Sinn corresponding to an object is in its turn an object . . . it can be made the object of a judgment. . . . As such it has a Sinn of the second level: the Sinn of a Sinn . . . hence we come to an infinite regress, insofar as the Sinn of the Sinn may in its turn be made an object and then again has a Sinn and so on" (NuS 107–108). As Husserl points out, this again has a consequence that "the Sinn cannot be a real component of the object" (NuS 108).

This is one of many striking similarities between Husserl's notion of noema and Frege's notion of Sinn. There are also important differences, however. Thus, for example, whereas Frege held that, in contexts like 'believes that . . .', terms refer not to their ordinary reference but to their ordinary Sinn, Husserl held, as we have seen (thesis 4), that acts normally are directed toward ordinary objects and not toward Sinne or noemata of such objects. This leads to major differences in their analyses of act contexts.

We might like to know much more in detail what noemata are. Like Frege, Husserl is not very helpful. One of the few hints Frege gave concerning his Sinne, was that they serve to illuminate aspects of the reference.[3] This fits the noemata to some extent, in that acts with a common object but with different noemata can be said to focus on different aspects of their object,

[3] Über Sinn und Bedeutung," *Zeitschrift für Philosophie und philosophische Kritik,* c (1892) : 27.

grasp it from different points of view. Also, Husserl, like Frege, held that a physical object has an infinity of noemata and Sinne corresponding to it and can never be exhausted by any of them. Physical objects are "transcendent," to use Husserl's term. [Husserl, *Ideen*, p. 100, 238 ff.: Cf, Frege, BG.]

Husserl also gives some more help. According to thesis 3 above, the noema, or, more precisely, the noematic Sinn, is that in virtue of which consciousness relates to an object. Take seeing as an example. That seeing is intentional, object-directed, means that the near side of the thing we have in front of us is regarded only as a side of a thing, and that the thing we are seeing has other sides and determinations which are co-intended to the extent that the full thing is regarded as something more than the one side. These determinations are not perceptually filled; they are more or less vaguely represented, and lead us on to further perceptual processes, which make the invisible visible. [Merleau-Ponty, *Phen. Psych*]

The noema is a complex system of such determinations (*Ideen*, I 93) which make a multitude of visual, tactile and other data be appearances of one object (*op. cit.*, 173–174). To quote Husserl: "The pure perceptual data . . . are not themselves perspectives, but they become perspectives through that which we also call apprehension (Auffassung), just that which gives them the subjective function of being appearances of the objective" (*op. cit.*, 163.11–17).

It is in this way, through perspectives, that we perceive objects. As long as the further course of our experience fits into the more or less vaguely predelineated pattern, we continue to perceive the same object and get an ever more "many-sided" experience of it, without ever exhausting the pattern, which develops with our experience of the object to include ever new, still unexperienced determinations. Sometimes our experiences do not fit into the predelineated pattern. We get an "explosion" of the noema, and a new noema of a new and different object. We were subject to misperception, to illusion or hallucination, as the case may be, and we say that the old act did not have the object that it seemed to have.

12. This pattern of determinations, together with the "Gegebenheitsweise," is the noema.

My twelve theses concerning the noema by no means exhaust the
subject; they barely put us in a position to ask questions like:
If phenomenology is a study of meaning, in an extended sense,
then what light does it throw upon the questions concerning
meaning that have played a major role in philosophy since its
beginnings and which are a major concern of so many contemporary philosophers? Does phenomenology overcome the
difficulties that are besetting so many ancient and recent theories
of meaning? A close study of Husserl's work can, I think, give
partial answers to these questions. And, even if the answers
should be negative, I trust that such a study will help to bring
out more clearly what these difficulties consist in.

ESSENCES AND NECESSARY TRUTH

Pure or transcendental phenomenology will be established not as a science of facts, but as a science of essential being (as 'Eidetic' science) ; a science which aims exclusively at establishing 'knowledge of essences' and absolutely no 'facts'.

—Edmund Husserl IDEAS (1)

INTRODUCTION

Phenomenology, Husserl insists, is concerned not with the *facts* of consciousness, but with *essences*—the essence of consciousness and the essences of its objects. An essence gives rise to a necessary, as opposed to merely factual, truth. Husserl's search for essence is parallel to Kant's demand for "synthetic a priori" truths. An essential truth is neither trivially ("analytically") true nor is it merely factually true. In the following selection from *Ideas*, Husserl argues for the fact-essence distinction. The second selection compares Husserl, Frege, and contemporary analysts on the question of essential truth. Finally, Moritz Schlick, a logical positivist and one of the key members of the "Vienna Circle", attacks the very idea of such truth.

FACT AND ESSENCE

EDMUND HUSSERL

(2) Individual Being of every kind is, to speak quite generally, *"accidental."* It is so-and-so, but essentially it could be other than it is. Even if definite laws of nature obtain according to which such and such definite consequences must in fact follow when such and such real conditions are in fact present, such laws express only orderings that do in fact obtain, which might run quite differently, and already presuppose, as pertaining *ab initio* to the *essence* of objects of possible experience, that the objects thus ordered by them, when considered in themselves, are accidental.

But the import of this contingency, which is there called matter-of-factness (*Tatsächlichkeit*), is limited in this respect that the contingency is correlative to a *necessity* which does not carry the mere actuality-status of a valid rule of connexion obtaining between temporo-spatial facts, but has the character of *essential necessity*, and therewith a relation to *essential universality*. Now when we stated that every fact could be "essentially" other than it is, we were already expressing thereby *that it belongs to the meaning of everything contingent that it should have essential being and therewith an Eidos to be apprehended in all its purity;* and this Eidos comes under *essential truths of varying degrees of universality.* An individual object is not simply and quite generally an individual, a "this-there" something unique; but being constituted thus and thus *"in itself"* it has *its own proper mode of being,* its own supply of *essential* predicables which must qualify it (*qua* "Being as it is in itself"), if other secondary relative determinations are to qualify it also.

Reprinted with permission of the Macmillan Company from *Ideas,* translated by W. R. Boyce-Gibson, pp. 47–55. First Collier Books Edition, 1962. Copyright 1931 by Crowell Collier and Macmillan, Inc. New York.

Thus, for example, every tone in and for itself has an essential nature, and at the limit the universal meaning-essence "tone in general," or rather the acoustic in general—understood in the pure sense of a phase or aspect intuitively derivable from the individual tone (either in its singleness, or through comparison with others as a "common element"). So too every material thing has its own essential derivatives, and at the limit the universal derivative "material thing in general," with time-determination-in-general, duration-, figure-, materiality-in-general. *Whatever belongs to the essence of the individual can also belong to another individual* and the *broadest* generalities of essential being, of the kind we have been indicating through the help of examples, delimit *"regions"* or *"categories" of individuals.*

3. ESSENTIAL INSIGHT AND INDIVIDUAL INTUITION

At first "essence" indicated that which in the intimate self-being of an individual discloses to us *"what"* it is. But every such What can be "set out as Ideas." *Empirical or individual intuition* can be transformed into *essential insight* (ideation)—a possibility which is itself not to be understood as empirical but as essential possibility. The object of such insight is then the corresponding *pure* essence or eidos, whether it be the highest category or one of its specializations, right down to the fully "concrete."

Of whatever kind the individual intuition may be, whether adequate or not, it can pass off into essential intuition, and the latter, whether correspondingly adequate or not, has the character of a dator act. And this means that—

The essence (Eidos) is an object of a new type. Just as the datum of individual or empirical intuition is an individual object, so the datum of essential intuition is a pure essence.

Here we have not a mere superficial analogy, but a radical community of nature. *Essential insight is still intuition,* just as the eidetic object is still an object. . . . If it is insight in the pregnant sense of the term, and not a mere, and possibly a vague, representation, it is a *primordial* dator Intuition, grasping the essence in its "bodily" selfhood.[1] But, on the other hand, it is an intuition of a fundamentally *unique* and *novel* kind, namely in contrast to the types of intuition which belong as correlatives to the object-matters of other categories, and more specifically to intuition in the ordinary narrow sense, that is, individual intuition.

It lies undoubtedly in the intrinsic nature of essential intuition that it should rest on what is a chief factor of individual intuition, namely the striving for this, the visible presence of individual fact, though it does not, to be sure, presuppose any apprehension of the individual or any recognition of its reality. Consequently it is certain that no essential intuition is possible without the free possibility of directing one's glance to an individual *counterpart* and of shaping an illustration; just as contrariwise no individual intuition is possible without the free possibility of carrying out an act of ideation and therein directing one's glance upon the corresponding essence which exemplifies itself in something individually visible; but that does not alter the fact that *the two kinds of intuition differ in principle,* and in assertions of the kind we have just been making it is only the essential relations between them that declare themselves. Thus, to the essential differences of the intuitions correspond the essential relations between "existence" (here clearly in the sense of individual concrete being) and "essence," between *fact* and *eidos.*

4. ESSENTIAL INSIGHT AND THE PLAY OF FANCY. KNOWLEDGE OF ESSENCES INDEPENDENT OF ALL KNOWLEDGE OF FACTS

The Eidos, the *pure essence,* can be exemplified intuitively in the data of experience, data of perception, memory, and so forth, but just as readily *also in the mere data of fancy (Phan-*

---

[1] In my *Logical Studies* I used to employ the word *Ideation* to represent the primordial dator insight into essential being . . .

tasie). Hence, with the aim of grasping an essence itself in its *primordial* form, we can set out from corresponding empirical intuitions, *but we can also set out just as well from non-empirical intuitions, intuitions that do not apprehend sensory existence, intiutions rather "of a merely imaginative order."*

It follows essentially from all this that *the positing of the essence,* with the intuitive apprehension that immediately accompanies it, *does not imply any positing of individual existence whatsoever; pure essential truths do not make the slightest assertion concerning facts;* hence from them *alone* we are not able to infer even the pettiest truth concerning the fact-world. Just as to think a fact or to express it needs the grounding of experience (so far as the *essential relevancy* of such thinking *necessarily* demands it), so thought concerning pure essence—the unmixed thought, not that which connects essence and facts together— needs for its *grounding* and support and insight into the essences of things.

One should not confuse the *unrestricted generality of natural laws* with *essential generality.* The proposition "all bodies are heavy" does not indeed take any determinate potential thing within the universe to be a concrete existent. And yet it has not the unconditional generality of eidetically general propositions in so far, in accordance with its meaning as a natural law, it continues to carry with it a reference to concrete existence (*Daseinssetzung*), to that, namely, of Nature itself, of temporo-spatial reality: all bodies—*in Nature,* all "real" bodies are heavy. On the other hand, the proposition "all material things are extended" has eidetic validity and can be taken as *purely* eidetic if the reference to concrete existence conveyed by the subject is excluded as irrelevant. It states that which has its pure ground in the essence of a material thing, and in the essence of extension, that which we can bring home to insight, as "unconditioned" generality. This is done by bringing the essence of a material thing (any fictitious image of a thing of this type will here serve as a basis) to primordial givenness, and then in this object-giving consciousness completing the mental steps required for the "insight," for the primordial givenness, that is, of the essential content which the foregoing proposition openly expressed.

.   .   .

7. SCIENCES OF FACTS AND SCIENCES OF ESSENCE

The connexion (itself eidetic) which holds between individual object and essence, and which is such that to each individual object a state of essential being belongs as *its* essence, just as conversely to each essence there corresponds a series of possible individuals as its factual instancings (*Vereinzelungen*), is the ground for a corresponding reciprocal relationship between sciences of fact and sciences of the essence. There are *pure sciences of essential being* such as pure logic, pure mathematics, pure time-theory, space-theory, theory of movement, etc.

These, in all their thought-constructions, are free throughout from any positings of actual fact; or, what comes to the same thing, *in them no experience qua experience*, i.e., *qua* consciousness that apprehends or sets up reality or concrete being, *can take over the function of supplying a logical ground.* Where experience functions in them, it is not *as* experience. The *geometer* who draws his figures on the blackboard produces in so doing strokes that are actually there on a board that is actually there. But his experience of what he thus produces, *qua* experience, affords just as little *ground* for his sight and thought of the geometrical essence as does the physical act of production itself. Whether or no he thereby suffers hallucination, and whether instead of actually drawing the lines he draws his lines and figures in a world of fancy, does not really matter. The *student of nature* behaves quite differently. He observes and experiments, i.e., he fixes *what is concretely there* just as he experiences it; *experience for him is an act that supplies grounds*, and for which mere imagining could never be a substitute. For this very reason science of *fact* and science of experience (*Erfahrung*) are equivalent concepts. But for the geometer, who studies not actualities, but "ideal possibilities," not actual but essential relationships, *essential insight* and not experience is *the act that supplies the ultimate grounds.*

SENSE AND ESSENCE: FREGE AND HUSSERL

ROBERT C. SOLOMON

Pure or transcendental phenomenology will be established not as as a science of facts, but as a science of essential being (as 'Eidetic' science; a science which aims exclusively at establishing "knowledge of essences" and absolutely no "facts."

(*Ideen*, p. 40, Introduction)[1]

It is singularly unfortunate that Husserl, who conscientiously avoided use of terminology with long and varied philosophical histories, should choose the notion "essence" as a central concept in his philosophy. In the Introduction to *Ideen*, he comments that "its equivocations are harmless." But this is far from true regarding the disastrous effects of his own use of the notion. His talk of "essential Being" and "essences as objects of knowledge" has generated such antagonism among American philosophers that the formulation of an acceptable interpretation of Husserl's philosophy has become an almost thankless task. While most of his supporters remain content to give their endorsement to the insistence that philosophy must concern itself only with *essences*

[1] All references to *Ideen* are to the Gibson translation, *Ideas* (New York: Collier-Macmillan, 1962). Page numbers are included in parentheses in the texts or immediately following quotations, and followed by chapter number, section number.

Reprinted from the *International Philosophical Quarterly*, 10, 3 (1970), by permission of the *International Philosophical Quarterly*.

and the *Being of essences,* Husserl's detractors have not found it difficult to dismiss all talk of "essences" as an unwelcome remnant of a paradigm of philosophy long out-moded.

We find Husserl's philosophy thus dismissed in the dress of any number of doctrines not his own: the doctrine of essential Being is dismissed as a regression to Platonic "realism"; the notion that essences "inhere in" facts is rejected as a hangover from scholasticism; the notion of "intuition of essences" is suspected to be an attempt to block all criticism; or, what is worse, it is thought to be a new variety of mysticism. This same notion of "intuition of essences," coupled with Husserl's own characterization of his philosophy as a "radical empiricism," has given critics cause to claim that Husserl attempted to give an empirical analysis of essences and essential truths. Other critics, focusing rather on Husserl's sharp separation of fact and essence, complain that Husserl is altogether opposed to factual science and causal explanations. All of these criticisms are misguided, but, to show this, we shall require an overall reevaluation of Husserl's doctrine of *essence* in much clearer analysis than Husserl ever affords us.

In this essay, I shall attempt to dislodge Husserl's notion of "essence" from "Platonic Ideas" and "Scholastic essences" as well as from the speculative metaphysics, the mysticism, and the too-radical empiricism with which it has been confused, and display it in the philosophical context in which it rightfully belongs. This context, I shall suggest, is one best defined by Husserl's contemporary and critic, Gottlob Frege. It has always appeared curious to me that Husserl and Frege are so often considered so very far apart, when the two men were, in fact, so similar in background, in interests, in the specific problems they encountered, and, I shall argue, in some of the solutions they offered to these problems. Of course, the two very different movements these two thinkers set in motion explains our tendency to think of them as so markedly different. But if, as I shall argue, the differences between them is largely a matter of terminology and emphasis, there may be real hope for a sympathetic meeting between "analytic" and "phenomenological" philosophies as well.

Why should Husserl want to talk about "essences" at all, much less make such a problematic notion the central concern of his philosophy? Of course, Husserl might easily have coined a new term in place of "essence" (*Wesen*), but some such term is indispensable, we will argue, in just the same way that similar concepts are vital in the philosophy of Frege.

In the 1880's both Husserl and Frege were probing the foundations of mathematics, attempting to discover the source of validity of the basic principles of arithmetic. Frege's *Grundlagen der Arithmetik* (1884), [*GA*] did not receive the attention it deserved, largely because it deviated so markedly from the then fashionable "psychologistic" approach to this and other philosophical questions. Husserl's dissertation at Halle (1887) and his first book, *Philosophie der Arithmetik* (1891), [*PA*] which did accept this approach, were much better received. Husserl had studied with Franz Brentano, and worked with Carl Stumpf, the leading proponents of Psychologism, a theory in which all necesary truths, including the basic principles of arithmetic, were reduced to empirical laws of psychology. Thus Husserl, in these early works, argued that the laws of arithmetic are nothing more than causal laws governing our experiences of *counting* and "collective association." Frege, at first ineffectively, argued against the psychologists that such treatment neglected the *necessity* of mathematical truths, and that psychologism was a confusion of two very different disciplines, a "building of dangerous inroads of psychology into logic." [*GA*, xiv]

Frege published his more important *Grundgesetz der Arithmetik* in 1893, which began with a renewed attack on psychologism, and, in 1894, he attacked Husserl's *Philosophie der Arithmetik* specifically (in a review of the book in *Zeitschrift für Philosophie*). Again, Frege argued that there was a decisive difference between numbers and whatever ideas people might have about numbers. Arithmetic, he argued, gives us precise and necessary principles, while psychology can give us only imprecise and at best probable generalizations. Psychology is incapable of clarifying the most important notion of *necessity* which is so characteristic of mathematical truths, and so there can be no reduction of necessary principles of arithmetic to psychological principles governing our experiences of numbers.

Husserl's reaction to this onslaught was admirable. He cancelled the projected second volume of *Philosophie der Arithmetik*, and, seeing the validity of Frege's claims, utterly rejected his psychologistic approach to the philosophy of mathematics. In doing so, however, Husserl saw a general deficiency in the empirical methods he had learned from Brentano; they could not provide an analysis of necessary truth, and philosophy in general is concerned only with necessary truths. In his next work, the *Logische Untersuchungen* (1901), [*LU*] Husserl joins with Frege in a relentless attack on psychologistic methods. He begins by quoting Goethe, "One is opposed to nothing more severely than to errors recently laid aside."

After the traumatic encounter with Frege, Husserl's interest in philosophy turned to this newly discovered (very Kantian) problem—how is necessary truth possible? The introduction of the notion of "essence" is designed to solve this problem: ". . . and here is the place for the phenomenological analysis of *essence*, which however strange and unsympathetic it may sound to the naturalistic psychologist, can in no way be an empirical analysis." [Husserl, PRS]

Husserl, like Frege, came to see that the account of necessary truth must reject any appeal to experience. In particular, such an account must reject any thesis which maintains that necessary truths are derivable by abstraction from particular experiences, using as its foundation some such notion as John Locke's "abstract ideas." In *PA* Husserl had employed just such a notion, and Frege had since convinced him that this consisted in a

> . . . blurring of the distinction between image and concept, between imagination and thought. . . . The constituents of the thought, and *a fortiori* things themselves, must be distinguished from the images that accompany in some mind the act of grasping the thought-images that each man forms of things. [Frege, BG 79]

Frege accuses Husserl of ignoring the distinction, which Husserl was later to adopt (and be given credit for), between empirical and essential generality: "It is surely clear that when anyone uses the sentence 'all men are mortal,' he does not want to assert something about some Chief Akpanya, of whom perhaps he has never heard." [Frege, BG 83]

In the *LU*, Husserl turns to the notion of "meaning" (*Sinn*) to account for necessary truth. In *LU*, we are introduced to "meaning-structures" and "meaning-designation" and "constitution of meanings." "Meanings," we are told, "come from consciousness" and are "conferred on facts by consciousness." In the same context, we are introduced to "essences," which are also 'in consciousness' and are given in a "categorical intuition." It is quite evident, both in *LU* and *Ideen*, that "meaning" and "essence" are intimately related. (In *Ideen*, Husserl even employs the two jointly in a hyphenated expression, "meaning-essence.") Essences or meanings exist in a manner very different from the existence of *facts:* the "Being" and the Knowledge of essences or meanings and the assertion of necessary truths are distinct from the "Being," or experiencing, of *facts* or "individuals":

> The positing of the essence . . . does not imply any positing of individual existence whatsoever: pure essential truths do not make the slightest assertion concerning facts. [Husserl, *Ideas* 4]
> Knowledge of essences: independent of all knowledge of Facts. [Husserl, *Ideas* 4]
> It is a matter of indifference [with regard to the essence] whether such things have ever been given in actual experience. [Husserl, *Ideas* 4]

This independence of essences from actual existence or from facts illuminates a most important point about "essences": the intuiting or the knowledge of essences is completely independent of any ontological commitment concerning the actual existence or actual experience of "individuals" who "have" that essence. Necessary truths are not "about" the world and are true independently of there being any individuals about which they are true. "All perfect circles are round," as a necessary truth, remains true although there might be no perfect circles. The fact that there are no perfect circles has nothing to do with the necessary truth.

The independence of "essence" and "fact" allows us to understand another thesis of central importance to Husserl's thought. In his earlier writings (*LU*), we intuit essences by concentrating on particular experiences of individuals: by *Ideen*, it is the role of *imagination* or *fancy* which occupies a central role in "grasping" essences. "The element which makes up the life of phenomenology as of all eidetic science is 'fiction,' that fiction is the source whence the knowledge of 'eternal truths' draws its sustenance." [Husserl, *Ideas* 70]

A geometer, who gives us necessary truths, and a physicist, who gives us empirical truths, can thus be distinguished by the role of "fancy" in their studies. A geometer, Husserl tells us, can prove his theorems on any figure he should like to employ: any triangle he imagines will suffice for a proof as well as any other. The physicist, however, must take into account only the results of actual experiments, not the possible results of any imaginable experiences. With geometric figures Husserl tells us, we "through direct analysis determine their immanent meaning." [*Ideas* 25] For a physicist, "experiments conducted in imagination would be imagined experiments." [*Ideas* 25]

The consideration of the role of imagination in "intuiting essences" allows us to understand yet another important Husserlian doctrine and shows us the way to a simple parallel in current analytic philosophy. Husserl tells us that, ". . . no essential intuition is possible without the free possibility of directing one's glance to an individual counterpart and of shaping an illustration." [Husserl, *Ideas* 3]

In other words, one intuits an essence (or, I suggest, 'understands a meaning') by considering all possible *examples* and *counter-examples*. One does not intuit an essence if he cannot think of a single example of an instance of that essence: again, one does not intuit an essence if he cannot distinguish a case that is not an instance of that essence from one that is. [Certain qualifications have to be made here if we are talking about "formal" essences; to grasp the "essence" of the law of contradiction, we should not require that someone can imagine a case in which the law would not apply.] We can now begin to understand the significance of Husserl's characterization of "essence" in terms of "what a thing is": "At first 'essence' indicated that which in the intimate self-being of an individual discloses to us *'what'* it is." [Husserl, *Ideas* 3]

Husserl sometimes relates "essence" to the concept of a "concept" (e.g. *Ideen,* 1:10, 2:22) and tells us that an essence is a "body of essential predicables." This should afford us an easy interpretation of some of Husserl's more obscure comments on "essence." He claims that "essences are repeatable," and that,

> . . . whatever belongs to the essence of the individual can also belong to another individual, (47, 1:2).
> Essential intuition is the consciousness of something, of an "object" . . . but which then can be "presented" in other acts . . . (49, 1:3).

An essence or meaning applies to indefinitely many particular instances. The word "dog" *means* not just this dog or that dog, but *means,* or is the essence of all possible dogs. As we shall see in a moment, Husserl's notion of *meaning (Sinn)* or essence is at least in this respect identical to Frege's notion of *Sinn.* In Frege's language, the *Sinn* of "dog" is such that "dog" can *refer* to any or every actual or possible dog.

We are told that *essences* are "non-spatio-temporal" but yet not "Platonically independent." By the first, we understand that there is a difference between the sense in which an essence exists and the sense in which "real" individuals which instantiate that essence exist: only the latter have spatial location or can be said to occur in or endure through time. However, Husserl is forced (for obvious reasons) to continually defend himself against charges of "Platonism," a postulation of the existence of essences "somewhere" other than the "real" (spatio-temporal) world. It is thus necessary for him to persistently deny that essences are independent of all *possible* facts. Husserl insists that essences always demand the *possibility* of individual "counterparts," and that essences, like these individual counterparts, are given in intuition.

For a fuller understanding of this notion of "essence," I suggest we turn to the comparatively enviably clear writings of Gottlob Frege. Frege introduces a distinction between *"sense"* (*Sinn*) and *"reference"* (*Bedeutung*) of a *name* or a *sign*. A name or a sign is to be construed as a linguistic expression, a word, phrase, sentence, or set of sentences, whether written or spoken, or simply thought. We have already employed the distinction in our discussion of Husserl, and indicated the more-than-notational similarity between Husserl's notion of *"Sinn"* and Frege's notion of *"Sinn."* *"Bedeutung,"* however, is an expression used very differently by the two authors. For Husserl, *"Bedeutung"* will refer to a special kind of *meaning*, very close, in fact, to Frege's notion of *"Sinn."* *"Bedeutung"* for Frege means *reference*, and the reference of a sign is an *object*. A sign "stands for" or "designates" or "denotes" (or, of course, "refers to") its referent. This object, however, need not be a material object, an "individual," but may be, for example, a number. Numbers are referred to by numerals (i.e., "1," "2," "3," . . .) and numbers are therefore objects in the appropriate sense. Similarly, *concepts* or meanings can be the referent objects of a sign, as when we speak of "the meaning of the word . . ." or "the concept of man. . . ."

The sense or meaning (*Sinn*) of a sign must be distinguished from the reference of the sign. Frege allows that signs are often used simply to *refer*, but there are cases in which they clearly do not. We can speak, for example, of unicorns, where "unicorn" has a sense but no reference. We can assert, "unicorns do not exist," and what we say can only be intelligible if we suppose that "unicorn" in this sentence has a sense independent of any referents. We usually *learn* the sense of signs through our familiarity with their referents, but our learning the sense through reference is irrelevant to this distinction. Because of their mutual opposition to psychologism, this separation of

learning a sense and the sense itself is vital to both Frege and
Husserl.

"A sign *expresses* its sense" (*BG* 61). Each and every
[grammatically well-formed] sign in language has a sense,
whether or not it has reference. However, each sense may have
indefinitely many signs: "It is raining" and "it rains" are two
different signs with the same sense, as are "it is raining" and
"*Es regnet.*" There are as many signs for a single sense as there
are intertranslatable expressions within any language and among
all *possible* languages.

Because it is Frege's notion of "*Sinn*" which we intend to
utilize in our analysis of Husserl's notion of "essence," we must
further inquire into the nature of this. One might think that the
Sinn of a sign can be distinguished from both the sign itself and
from the reference of the sign by taking the *Sinn* to be an
"image" that one associates with the sign (e.g. Locke's theory
or Husserl in *PA*), or a "picture" (e.g. Wittgenstein, *Tractatus*,
2.1). [I shall certainly not attempt to examine the very close
connection between such "pictures" and sentences (*Satz*) in
Wittgenstein. I simply work on the supposition that the "image-
theory" which Wittgenstein later sets out to refute is not wholly
distinct from the "picture-sentence" theory in the *Tractatus*.]
Frege categorizes all such 'associated images' as "Ideas."

> If the reference of the sign is an object perceivable by the
> senses, my idea of it is an internal image, arising from memories
> of sense impressions which I have had and acts, both internal
> and external, which I have performed. (BG 59)

Husserl's early analysis of "number" in terms of counting
and ideas of "collective association" would neatly fit this notion
of "Idea." However, Frege, as evidenced by his rejection of
Husserl's *PA*, will have no part of this as an analysis of *Sinn*;

> The reference and sense of a sign are to be distinguished
> from the associated idea. (*BG* 59)
> The same sense is not always connected even in the same

man, with the same idea. The idea is subjective, one man's idea
is not that of another. There results, as a matter of course, a
variety of differences in the ideas associated with the same
sense. A painter, a horseman, and a zoologist will probably
connect different ideas with the name "Bucephalus." This constitutes an essential distinction between the idea and the sign's
sense, which may be the common property of many and therefore is not a part of a mode of the individual mind. (*BG* 59)

For our comparison of Husserl and Frege, it is vitally important that we take special note of two very different employ-
ments of the English term "Idea." For Frege, the "idea" (*Vorstellung*) is the associated image: for Husserl, "Idea" (*Idee*) is
closely allied with "essence." We shall therefore avoid use of this
term as much as possible, and simply restrict ourselves to a discussion of "images" and "essences."

"Image" for Frege, is contrasted with "thought" (*Gedanke*),
and it is thoughts, not images, which constitute sense. Thoughts,
unlike images, are *public*, not *private*. Images are "had" by one
and by only one consciousness ("your images are 'yours' and
my images are 'mine' "). In this sense of "image," it is logically
impossible that you and I should "think the same thing." An
image is not a property of a sign, it is a 'property' of individual
men. However,

It is quite otherwise for thoughts; one and the same thought
can be grasped by many men. [Frege, BG 79]
For one can hardly deny that mankind has a common store
of thoughts which is transmitted from one generation to another. [Frege, BG 59]

With "thought," therefore, we can say that many men
"think" the same "thought," or that you mean by "P" just what
I mean by "P." [E.g. we both learn *the* pythagorean theorem; I
do not learn *my* pythagorean theorem: Frege, "The Thought,"
trans. Quinton, *Journal of Philosophy*, 65 (1956), 302.]
This is clearly necessary for the sense of a sign—that it
remain one and the same sense which is "expressed" by who-

ever employs that sign. A thought, therefore, is neither the object referred to by a sign, nor any image associated with the sign or arising from my perceptions or memories of the object, nor is it the sign itself, which only *expresses* the thought. The thought is the sense of a sign, and is independent of the particular employer of that sign, independent of any objects referred to in the employment of that sign, and independent of the sign itself (any thought can be expressed by any number of signs).

The analysis of Frege's "sense" (*Sinn*) thus reduces to an analysis of the notion of "thought," or "The Thought." I hope that it is now becoming evident just how Frege's "sense (thought)" is remarkably similar to Husserl's "essence." Both clearly refer to "meaning" in some sense, and both philosophers are utilizing these notions of "meaning" as an approach to the analysis of necessary truth. We are now in a position to begin to bring these two authors together, and, in doing so, clarify some most puzzling passages in Husserl. "Essence" is to be distinguished from all objects that are instances of it, and from all signs which might "express" that essence (Husserl also utilizes this notion of "expression") ; and, most importantly, an essence is to be distinguished from all 'psychological' ideas which we might have associated with it, i.e. all (sensory) experience and individual (factual) intuitions.

We can now begin to see how essences can yield necessary truths. Insofar as essences are senses or meanings, a statement about essences will be a statement which is non-empirical. To utilize one of Husserl's few examples, a statement about the essence of *sound* and the essence of *colour* to the effect that "The essence . . . Colour is other than the essence . . . Sound, [Husserl, *Ideas* 5] or, differently, "A colour in general is different from a sound in general" [Husserl, *Ideas* 5] will be essentially true, a statement of "essential generality." The latter is implicitly, as the former is explicitly, not a judgment about colour and sound but a judgment about the *essences* of colour and sound. In a different vernacular, these judgments are not "about the world" but "about the meanings of words," "the senses of signs." This would explain the necessity of truths which are about essences, and would explain the non-empirical nature and "independence of facts" of our "knowledge of essences."

Our suggested equation between Husserl's notion of "essence" and Frege's notions of "*Sinn*" and "thought" thus begins to show us some reward. However, there are important differences between the two sets of concepts. We must ask ourselves, quite critically, to what extent this equivalence can be maintained, and to what degree "essence" and "sense" are markedly different. It is equally important to ask ourselves to what extent the differences between the two authors are not so much differences in the concepts of "essence," "sense-thought," but differences in their theories *about* essences and sense-thoughts. I shall argue that these concepts are equivalent, but that Husserl makes important claims about essences that Frege does not make about thoughts. Notably, Husserl claims that essences are to be "grasped" through *intuition:* Frege claims that thoughts are to be "grasped" through an examination of language.

It would certainly seem that the most important difference between Frege and Husserl, a difference more than sufficient to destroy our equivalence between Husserl's "essence" and Frege's "sense," lies in their very different attitudes towards language in their treatment of these two concepts. Frege is clearly a philosopher of language, and his analysis of "sense" is an analysis of the *sense of a sign.* Husserl, quite to the contrary, is dealing with essences *simpliciter,* not essences *of* verbal expressions. It would appear, therefore, that our attempted reduction of both "*Sinn*" and "*Wesen*" to the same notion of "meaning" is most implausible.

The standard picture of Frege as a strictly "linguistic" philosopher and Husserl as an anti-linguistic philosopher is, however, an oversimplification in both directions. Frege is concerned with language, and his interest in *Sinn* is an interest in analyzing language, but the notion of "*Sinn*," as I shall attempt to argue, is not itself a purely "linguistic" notion. Moreover, Husserl is not so antagonistic to a philosophy of language as we are often led to suppose. Although Husserl has little to say about language, there is some reason to suppose that he would not have been willing to make any claim as harsh as the denial that essences were relevant to and even, in an important but puzzling way, dependent upon language. Thus, I shall argue that the alleged difference between the two philosophers *vis-à-vis* the importance of language for philosophy does not reflect a difference between their respective notions of *"Sinn"* and *"Wesen."*

We have already stressed Frege's insistence that the *sense* of a sign (the thought) must not be confused with the reference of that sign, any image associated with that sign, or most importantly, with the sign itself. The distinction between sense and sign can be demonstrated in many ways: a given sense can be "expressed" by many different signs—the sense of the word "cat" can be expressed by this inscription, or by my pronouncing a corresponding sequence of phonemes, or by appropriate inscriptions or pronouncements in any other language. Moreover, we can refer to a sense without expressing it with a sign at all; e.g. "Whatever that word means must be obscene in that context," and we can refer to a sense that could never be expressed at all; e.g. "There are inexpressible thoughts." Therefore, a sense of a sign is not the sign itself, nor is it equivalent to any combinations or sets of signs.

From Frege's characterization of the sense as the *thought*, it becomes clear that the sense-thought is something quite apart from language and language users. But here we encounter a fascinating problem: what is this entity which Frege clearly claims is necessary for any adequate analysis of language (a necessity reclaimed by Russell, and more recently by Church[2]). But does the interpretation of the thought as an abstract entity necessary to do justice to an account of language give us the only possible approach to thoughts? Or, can one recognize and identify thoughts independently of their expressions in language? Unfortunately, we can say little more about Frege's own analysis of sense or thought, for he nowhere attempts to give us such a pre-linguistic analysis. His informal introduction in "On Sense

2 "The Need for Abstract Entities in Semantics" in *Structure of Language*, Katz and Fodor (Prentice-Hall, 1964).

and Reference," and his essay, "The Thought," are attempts to make clear several things a thought is *not* (e.g. "Thoughts are neither things of the outer world nor ideas," [Frege, "The Thought," p. 302] but Frege then leaves us, much as Husserl leaves us, with a statement to the effect that *thoughts* have their own "mode of Being."

It might be helpful at this point if we were to digress slightly and note that this tendency to introduce non-worldly, non-"mental," non-linguistic entities was not in the least peculiar to Husserl and Frege. Although German philosophy-psychology was well served by philosophers who simply treated all entities as either "physical" or "psychical" (e.g. Brentano and Stumpf), at least two very prominent philosophers of the nineteenth century shared this concern for peculiar entities. In the early part of the century, Bolzano had introduced the notion of "proposition-in-itself" (*Salz-an-sich*) and like notions of "truth-in-itself" and "idea-in-itself" to refer to those entities which were asserted, questioned, believed to be true but which were themselves neither assertions (sentences or statements) questions, or beliefs. In the later part of the century, Alexius von Meinong, whose reputation in Anglo-American philosophy has largely been administered in the not-always-reliable historical criticism of Bertrand Russell, introduced a new "objective" "world" of entities to suit the same purpose. In his "Theory of Objects," Meinong presents us with a world of "objects" which have *Being*, but not *existence*, in order to explain how it is the case that we can talk about *non-existent* objects; e.g. in "Unicorns do not exist." Of special interest to us, however, is a special sort of non-worldly (i.e. non-existent) entity which Meinong refers to as an "objective." An "objective," like Bolzano's "proposition-in-itself," is that which is expressed in assertions, is believed, is doubted, and so on. The peculiar ontological status of Frege's *sense* and Husserl's *essence* is a common problem in 1890; what is it that is *expressed* by assertions?

Of particular importance in our discussion of Husserl is our understanding that Bolzano and Meinong, as well as Husserl, were not exclusively concerned with language and its uses but with the nature of *mental acts*. Asserting is a verbal expression of a *Satz-an-sich* or an "objective," but it is also an *act* of asserting. This is not to say that it is an act which is clearly different from the act of assertively expressing the same *Satz-an-sich* or "objective" in language, nor is it even to say that it is possible to assert without asserting through language. Rather, asserting through language is but one very special instance of a huge number of mental acts, only some of which have any connection with linguistic expression. Husserl, we must emphasize, did not *deny* any role to language in mental acts; he simply did not concern himself *primarily* with linguistic acts.

Frege, however, also distinguished between mental acts and linguistic acts. We have insisted that the *thought* is not itself a linguistic entity, but rather, "itself immaterial, [it] clothes itself in the material garment of a sentence and thereby becomes comprehensible to us." [Frege, "The Thought," p. 292]

Frege distinguishes:

1. the apprehension of a thought—(thinking)
2. the recognition of the truth of a thought—(judgment)[3]
3. the manifestation of this thought—(assertion)

Thus, for Frege, assertion (while it is a necessarily linguistic act), is already two steps removed from the apprehension of a thought. The difference between Frege and Husserl would thus not seem to be Frege's employing a strictly linguistic notion of *Sinn* as opposed to Husserl's non-linguistic notion of "essence." The difference is rather one of emphasis; Frege concentrates his philosophical genius on the analysis of *assertion*, an essentially linguistic activity, and on an analysis of *judgments*, in which the truth-value of sentences (more properly of senses which sentences express) is recognized. Frege has little interest in the analysis of thinking itself, the prelinguistic mental act in which one has not yet attempted to evaluate the truth of a thought or

---

[3] This use of "judgment" is at odds with a usage in "On Concept and Object." "Language presents the thought as a judgment" (*BG* 49).

its possible expression in language. Yet this is just what interests Husserl, who is not interested particularly in either judgments or assertions. Husserl and Frege differ not in their analysis of *thought*, but in their interest in it. Husserl is interested in the nature of thought *before* it gets captured in language. He is also interested in thoughts before they are recognized as true or false; this latter form of judgments "reduced" to unevaluated thoughts is the significance of Husserl's famous *epoche*, or "bracketing of existence." In phenomenology, he is interested only in the thoughts, i.e. the essences, themselves, barring any possible questions concerning the value of that thought or essence, as a model of the "real" world.

I do not wish to leave an impression that Husserl maintained, much less argued, that the grasping of essences can dispense with any consideration of language in which thoughts are expressed. Rather, his position on this matter seems to be ambivalent (not to say confused) concerning the role of language in the essences to be examined. In his early essay, "Philosophy as a Rigorous Science," he tells us: "The phenomenologist . . . derives no judgments at all from word concepts, but rather looks into the phenomena *that language occasions by means of the words in question*." [Husserl, PRS, p. 95, my italic]

In *Ideas*, Husserl tells us again that "essences are distinguished from their verbal expression," but that verbal expressions, "relate to the essence and the essential connections which they *once fixated* and now express." [Husserl, *Ideas*, p. 67, my italics]

This would seem to indicate that language has a role in "fixing" essences (i.e. "we can learn to think [employ concepts] only by learning a language"); but Husserl pays no heed to the *origins* of our knowledge of essences, and so this claim is never investigated.

Husserl's views on language become yet more complex when we attempt to investigate further our reduction of both Frege's "sense-thought" and Husserl's "essence" to a notion of "meaning," as we did in the beginning of this essay. Husserl gives us three distinct notions of "meaning." Husserl notes that these different notions are used as equivalents in ordinary speech, but must, for purposes of philosophy be distinguished. They are:

(a) *Sinn,* "Sense of Meaning *simpliciter,*" or Sense in its most general meaning.
(b) *Bedeutung,* "meaning at the conceptual level," "logical," or "expressing meaning."
(c) *Meinen,* "meaning as a functional act," or simply "intentionality."

It is only (b) in which we are interested. The sense of "sense" (*Sinn*) (a) encompasses Frege's "reference" as well as "sense." (c) *Meinung* is a very general term of intentionality and would go far beyond the "sense" of a sign to whatever a person might *mean* (intend) in any act of consciousness. In this sense, every act of perception, imagination, becoming angry, falling in love, being hungry, or trying to insult someone would have a *meaning.* Again, this sense of meaning is much broader than the concept of "essence."

What Husserl says about (b) is perplexing. He says, ". . . originally these words (*Bedeutung, bedeuten*) relate only to the sphere of speech, that of 'expression,' " [Husserl, *Ideas,* p. 319] but then he immediately suggests we extend their meanings to all acts, "whether these are interwoven with expression acts or not." [*Ibid.*] But later in the same section, he tells us that when we "grasp a meaning,"

> This process makes no call whatsoever on "expression," neither on expression in the sense of verbal sound nor on the like as verbal meaning, and here the latter can also be present independently of the verbal sound.

and then,

> Every meaning (*Meinung*) of any act can be expressed conceptually (*durch Bedeutungen*) . . . Logical meaning is an expression.

and then,

> The verbal sound can be referred to as expression only be-
> cause the meaning which belongs to it expresses: it is in it
> that the expressing originally lies. [*Ibid.*, p. 320]

These passages indicate that Husserl clearly takes "expressing," including "conceptual expression" to be prelinguistic ("preverbal") notions. The expression of "meaning" (*Bedeutung*) is
an act of consciousness which is distinct from and precedes
"verbal expression" (Frege's "assertion"). We can express the
meaning (*Meinung*) of every act of consciousness as conceptual
meaning (*Bedeutung*) and can, in turn, express every such
conceptual meaning in some linguistic expression. Husserl would
thus make a claim for language that is more ambitious than many
"linguistic" philosophers would assent to: there is nothing that
can be thought that cannot be expressed in language.

What I have argued thus far in this essay is what I believe
to be a most important correspondence between the philosophies
of two supposedly very different philosophers. Granted that Husserl benefits far more from this statement of resemblance than
Frege, I should not like to leave the merits of Husserl's doctrine
of *essence* wholly dependent on his similarity to Frege. To a
certain extent, Husserl does repeat more obscurely and less
systematically, some of Frege's central positions. However, the
difference in emphasis we have discussed is of considerably more
than historical interest, for it holds a key, not only to the major
breach between analysis and phenomenology, but also to some
important disputes in contemporary analytic philosophy of
language.

Neither the notion of "essence" nor the notions of "sense"
and "thought" play as large a role in contemporary philosophy
as they once did. However, current philosophy is quite occupied
with notions derivative of these: "concept" is such a notion, and
the ontological status of *concepts* remains as large a question
for contemporary philosophers of the analytic tradition as the

status of *essence* continued to be for Husserl. Of equal importance in current discussions is the problematic notion of a "proposition." Frege occasionally used *"Satz"* to refer to that entity which was not a physical sentence (also *"Satz"*; which meaning is determinable in context), but which was expressed by a sentence. Thus, in Frege, we can suggest a third concept like "sense" and "thought," and we can draw a further equivalence between Husserl's "essence" and "proposition." However, we must understand that this use of "proposition" is foreign to Husserl (for whom "proposition" and "judgment" are equivalent), and rare in Frege. This modern use is due to Russell and Wittgenstein, not Frege and Husserl. Of importance to us in the remarkable similarity between the functions of propositions, senses, thoughts, and essences in these various philosophies. Today, "proposition" is the most acceptable name for that peculiar entity which "has meaning," is "expressed" by a sentence, is true or false, but which is distinct from worldly objects, expressing sentences, and any "mental" occurrences (intentions, images) of persons who "hold" that proposition. In other words, "proposition" is the new name for Husserl's "essence," Frege's "sense" or "thought": "It is clear that by "thought" expressed by a declarative, he [Frege] means what other philosophers call a "proposition."[4]

The status of propositions is not an isolated problem in the philosophy of language, however; it has rather become the (often-unrecognized) fulcrum of a wide-spread debate between what F. P. Ramsey called several *paradigms of philosophy.* The acceptance or rejection of these special entities, under whatever name, determines an entire philosophical outlook. I take the attitude toward the ontological status of *propositions (thoughts, essences)* to be the key point of departure of Husserl's phenomenology from analytic philosophy, as I take it to be the key factor in what at present is probably the largest single split among analytic philosophers.

The rejection of Russell's theory of descriptions by Strawson

---

[4] L. Linsky, *Referring* (London: Routledge, Kegan Paul, 1967), p. 25.

has often been interpreted, notably by Strawson himself, as a rejection of a single theory concerning referring expressions within a mutually accepted philosophical framework. In fact, however, the problem of referring is only a focal point˙ for a most general problem in philosophy, namely, the subject matter of philosophical investigation. According to Bertrand Russell (and the "early" Wittgenstein, and most practitioners of "philosophical analysis") the subject matter of philosophy was the structure of *propositions,* an examination of which would show us the structure of "the world." Russell's philosophical analysis is an analysis of "propositions and their constituents"; the problem of philosophy must be the clarification of these. What are these? In his famous article "On Denoting," Russell sometimes indicates that the constitutents of propositions are *words,* but that cannot be right, since the proposition and its parts are clearly to be distinguished from the language that expressed them. Elsewhere he mentions "single propositions of which the thing itself (i.e. the referent) is a constituent,"[5] but that cannot be right either, for the proposition is to be distinguished from the things referred to. But the status of propositions and their constituents remains a problem unilluminated by Russell. Wittgenstein gave the problem its due attention, and his attitude, most representative of that to which Husserl is a viable alternative, is that "I don't know *what* the constitutents of a thought are, but I know that it must have such constituents which correspond to the words of language."[6]

In this view, confusedly indicated by Russell, and expressly argued by Church (*op. cit.*), propositions (thoughts, essences) are entities which are expressed in language, which we can get to know *through* an analysis of language, but whose nature ultimately must remain a mystery. Wittgenstein, for example, adopts the same ploy used by Frege, and takes "thought" to be a logical

[5] E.g. in Feigl and Sellars' reprint of "On Denoting," in *Readings in Philosophical Analysis* (New York: Appleton-Century-Crofts, 1949), p. 115.

[6] Wittgenstein, *Notebooks,* 1914, 1916, trans. Anscombe (Oxford: Blackwell, 1961), p. 129.

"primitive," inexplicable apart from its necessary functions in language.

The alternatives to this mystical concept of *proposition* (*essence, thought*) lie in two very different directions. First, there is the rejection of the notion of *propositions* and a simple appeal to the *use* of language. Thus, for Strawson, J. L. Austin, and the "later" Wittgenstein, philosophy studies not propositions but *sentences* and the *uses of sentences*. Through this examination, we discover the "structures of the world," presumably the same world explored earlier by Russell and the "early" Wittgenstein. Strawson's own attack seemed to be quite unaware of the nature of the disagreement between the two philosophers. Strawson attacks Russell's analysis on the basis of its failure as an analysis of our everyday uses of statements, while Russell's analysis was of a very different nature—an analysis of the propositions which are expressed by (but exist independently of) our ordinary uses of language. Strawson's conclusion to his article "On Referring" is symptomatic of the misdirection of the entire attack on Russell: "Ordinary language has no exact logic." But Russell's concern was with propositions, which are true or false, while Strawson's concern was with our use of statements in ordinary language "to make true or false assertions." Russell's criterion for the success of his analysis was to capture the structure of those entities which were expressed in language; Strawson's criterion for success was to satisfy the "purposes for which we ordinarily use language." In short, the dispute between Russell and Strawson was not over an analysis of certain referring expressions; it was "whether in our everyday discourse we speak in statements or in propositions?" [Linsky, *op. cit.*, p. 99]

But this, according to Husserl, Frege, and Russell, is not the problem of philosophy, which is concerned with truth, meaning, reference, and so on, but a matter which may be described as *empirical*. (If we all learned language from Russell's philosophy, we should speak in propositions.) The problem of philosophy, as characterized by Frege and Husserl at least, are not the empirical problems of how people do *in fact* use their language, but matters of *essence* (*thought and logic*). The problems raised by Russell's theory about propositions are no more vulnerable to ordinary language criticism than our proofs of geometry are vulnerable to empirical refutation.

But despite the misplaced battle between Russell and Strawson, the underlying dispute is of momentous importance. The rejection of the role of propositions (thought, essences) in discussions of philosophy has been best expressed by the unique philosopher who was prominent as a defender of both views. In his later writings, Wittgenstein looked back at his almost mystical analysis of propositions, and complained that, "We don't get free of the idea that the sense of a sentence accompanies the sentence, is there along side it."[7]

The "innocent" claim that the *thought* is "primitive" and has no extra-linguistic characterization is, Wittgenstein now argues, "the decisive movement in the conjuring trick,"[8] a "myth of our symbolism." Philosophy must forget about this "occult sphere" of propositions and thoughts (and essences) and restrict itself to looking at "the given," which is, for Wittgenstein, our uses of language to *do* things.

But when one gives up the notion of propositions, all sorts of old taboos are broken, and with troublesome results. Once again, philosophy seems to become an *empirical* study of how persons (we) use language. But this leaves open an old Fregean-Husserlian wound, what justification can this seemingly *empirical* search provide us for the sorts of philosophical, i.e. *necessary* truths that we seek?

Why should we accept or not accept the existence of propositions? One reason for not accepting them, from what we have seen above, is the sort of serious problems we encounter in attempting to say what these entities are. Furthermore, as evidenced (but not made fully explicit) in the Russell-Strawson dispute, the introduction of propositions can generate problems

[7] Wittgenstein, *Zettel*, No. 139, trans., ed., Anscombe and Von Wright (Oxford: Blackwell, 1967), p. 56 (e).

[8] *Philosophical Investigations*, No. 308, trans. Anscombe and Von Wright (Oxford: Blackwell, 1967), p. 56 (e).

of its own. But most important is the question of whether these entities are *necessary* for adequate explanation of the behavior of language, and, in particular an account of truth, meaning and necessary truth, in order to compensate for the disadvantages of adding mysterious entities to our ontology and generating new problems. Church has recently argued that such entities *are* necessary for the purpose of explanation of language. [Linsky, *Op. cit.*] All of those who reject propositions, or all of those who accept the procedures of ordinary language analysis (whether or not they have questioned the existence of propositions), do not accept this necessity.

However, the standard dispute covered in the preceding paragraph bases itself on a supposition about the nature of propositions (thoughts, essences) which has not been questioned sufficiently in analytic circles (just as the analytic suppositions here involved have not been sufficiently examined by phenomenologists). All of these considerations assume that the only way to approach these peculiar entities is through an analysis of language, and the dispute between the two analytic camps thus rests upon a common ground—the assumption that, if propositions are anything at all, they must be entities which can *only* be expressed in language but not independently characterized in any way:

> There is, I think, a discoverable relation between the structure of sentences and the structure of the occurrences to which the sentences refer. I do not think the structure of non-verbal facts wholly unknowable, and I believe that, with sufficient caution, the properties of language may help us to understand the structure of the world.[9]

Husserl and phenomenology make an important claim: they maintain that the peculiar entities we have been discussing do **allow** themselves to be expressed in language by sentences, but **that** they can be characterized without such appeal to their

[9] Russell, *Inquiry into Meaning and Truth* (London: Allen and Unwin, 1940), p. 341.

expression in language through a direct reflection upon "intuition." Because we can investigate essences (propositions, thoughts) without appeal to language, it is therefore possible to reestablish the role of propositions in the examination of language, but on a different basis than their necessity for an adequate accounting for language. If we could show that intuition itself provides us with the data which make necessary truths necessarily true, which give us the prelinguistic structures of languages and the structure of thought, then philosophy would have to accept a very different paradigm indeed.

One turns to "use"-theory in philosophy precisely because of the seeming impossibility of getting an adequate grasp on propositions (essences, thoughts). Husserl and Frege would both find this approach abhorrent to their vision of philosophy; the alternative would be to turn to the direct examination of the "things themselves" or the "given"—in other words, the propositions, thoughts, or essences rather than what expresses these propositions, thoughts, or essences. The business of philosophy is to provide and practice a technique for "reducing" our intuitions to those "eidetic" elements about which philosophers have been talking in so many ways. It is the function of Husserl's "eidetic reduction" to display for us these "pure essences" (or propositions). If Husserl is correct, then philosophers need not grapple with inaccessible "abstract" linguistic-related entities, nor need they look at how people *in fact* use language. Rather, philosophy would consist of a *theory of intuition* and a method for extracting *essential structures* from intuition.

The problem with all this, of course, is that it has not clearly been done. Husserl's own stylistic paraplegia makes his doctrine most unwelcome reading, and, for those who do master his exposition of his method in *Ideen*, there is the disappointment, I believe, of discovering that the endless distinctions there are based upon an obscure foundation, if not an insecure one. But phenomenology has had few articulate spokesmen in this country, and very few who have allowed themselves to become sympathetic to the goals of analytic philosophers. In this essay, I have attempted to make some sense out of one of Husserl's most

obscure and most central concepts. As a result, I hope that I
have indicated the direction which philosophers on both sides
of the analysis-phenomenology breach must follow if there is to
be a serious meeting of philosophical cultures. I suggest that the
problems confronting analytic and phenomenological philosophers are identical: what has yet to be proved, even to those
of us who are hopeful about the possible fruits of Husserl's
method, is that the phenomenological approach is a fruitful one.

IS THERE A FACTUAL A PRIORI?

MORITZ SCHLICK

The future historian of the philosophy of the nineteenth and
twentieth centuries will find himself forced to the conclusion that
in the systems which followed Kant, very little remained of the
spirit of the Critical Philosophy even among those who either
appealed directly to Kant, or believed themselves to be giving a
further development to his ideas. That this is true of the *metaphysical* systems which followed Kant up to the time of Schopen-
hauer and after, is reasonably clear. It is equally true, however,
of those admirers of Kantian methods who believed themselves
able to transfer his theory of knowledge, oriented as it was to
Newtonian physics, to the sciences of mind and culture; and,
finally, it is true of those critics of Kant who use his terminology,
but who would like to give it a new meaning.

The signal merit which must be allowed Kant, of having
most clearly delimited and applied his concept of the *a priori*,
has come to be neglected and misunderstood today, particularly
by the phenomenologists, in that they employ the term "*a priori*"

Reprinted from: *Readings in Philosophical Analysis*, edited by Herbert
Feigl and Wilfrid Sellars. Copyright 1949. Reprinted by permission of
Appleton-Century-Crofts, Meredith Corporation. First published in "*Wis-
senschaftlicher Jahresbericht der Philosophischen Gesellschaft and der
Universitaet zu Wien fuer das Vereinsjahr* 1930/31". Translated by W.
Sellars and reprinted by kind permission of Mrs. Schlick.

in a completely unKantian way, and invent new definitions for it.
Thus Scheler writes,[1] in explicit agreement with the position of
Husserl, "We characterize as '*a priori*' all those ideal meaning-
wholes and propositions which, irrespective of any mode in
which they are considered by the subject which thinks them and
of the nature of that subject, as well as irrespective of any mode
in which an object is posited to which they might be applicable,
are bodily given through the content of an immediate intuition."
Such a usage of the term "*a priori*" would naturally be quite
inadmissible if that which is set down by the definition had
nothing in common with the meaning established by Kant—and
it is certainly the opinion of the phenomenologists themselves
that such a common element exists. Indeed, it clearly consists in
the fact that they as well as Kant intend this term to refer to the
source of propositions of absolutely universal validity. To be
sure, Scheler and others of like mind speak of a phenomenological "experience" as the source of such propositions, but this
signifies nothing more than confusion confounded, since they
also give a new meaning to the term "experience". To what
extent this so differently defined "*a priori*" shares further significant characteristics with that of Kant, is a matter on which there
is room for difference of opinion. The phenomenologists, in any
case, believe themselves justified in blaming Kant for making
the *a priori* co-extensive with the formal. Scheler puts it as
follows: "The identification of the '*a priori*' with the 'formal' is
a fundamental mistake of the Kantian doctrine." [*Ibid.*, p. 49] It
is clearly implied by this assertion that propositions whose universal validity is absolute need not be of a purely formal character. As a matter of fact the decisive difference between the
"*Wesensschau*" (intuition of essences) of Husserl and the pure
intuition of Kant is that the former leads to propositions of absolute validity which nevertheless have something to say concerning the stuff or material of experience.

Husserl himself writes: "Finally all the basic confusions of

[1] *Der Formalismus in der Ethik und die Materiale Wertethik*, 2nd ed.,
p. 43.

the Kantian critique of reason hang together . . . in that he lacked the phenomenologically correct concept of the *a priori*." [Husserl, LU II, 2, p. 203] We get an inkling as to how clear, in Husserl's opinion, the philosophy of Kant might have turned out to be after phenomenological correction, when we go on to read: "It was disastrous that Kant held the domain of the purely logical in the narrowest sense to be adequately taken care of by the remark that it falls under the principle of contradiction. Not only did he never see how little the laws of logic have the character of analytic propositions in the sense which he laid down as a matter of definition; he didn't even see how little is gained in the way of a clarification of the function of analytic thought, by a reference to a self-evident principle of analytic propositions."

The truth of the matter is that analytic judgments, that is, tautological propositions, actually need no clarification, the theoretical task with respect to them consisting at most in coming to see that this is indeed the case (which, of course, is not a matter of a psychological investigation of thought). Kant's insight was quite correct, and his opinion that logic as a whole is to be understood in terms of the principle of contradiction can accordingly be interpreted as a recognition of its purely tautological character. This conclusion is not weakened by the fact that the verbal form in which Kant clothed his definition of analytic propositions no longer satisfies us. Moreover, Husserl's conception of the principle of contradiction, which he characterizes as a "self-evident principle," is far more psychologistic than that of Kant.

An analytic proposition is one which is true by virtue of its form alone. Whoever has grasped the meaning of a tautology, has in doing so seen it to be true. It is because of this that it is *a priori*. In the case of a synthetic proposition, on the other hand, one must first understand its meaning, and afterwards determine whether it is true of this that it is *a posteriori*.

Let us next ask by what way Kant arrived at an inseparable connection between the *a priori* and the formal. His point of departure was, of course, an amazement over the presence of synthetic and yet universally valid judgments in the exact sciences; and the entire labor of the *Critique of Pure Reason* was dedicated to the task of solving the problem of how this was possible. He concluded that it was entirely impossible, if these judgments claimed to assert anything concerning the stuff of experience, and the only solution for this problem that came to him after unspeakable toil was this, that the *a priori* validity of these judgments can only be understood on the condition that they express nothing but the *form* of experience which consciousness gives to all knowledge.

The identification of the *a priori* with the formal was for Kant neither presupposition nor prejudice, but rather a conclusion to which he was led by sheer force of argument, and, so to speak, against his rationalistic instinct. If in this process he made an error, then the problem of synthetic *a priori* judgments remains unsolved. Whoever stands by the existence of such judgments and yet rejects Kant's solution, must take the finding of another solution to be his most important task. Now the phenomenologists not only believe in these judgments so astounding in their implications for knowledge, they even fix their boundaries astonishingly wider than Kant. Thus, they would certainly seem to be under an obligation to explain their possibility. This they have in no way attempted to do. They are clearly undisturbed by the problems to which the *Critique of Pure Reason* owes its origin. They have either forgotten the issue, or seem to make a detour whenever they get in its neighborhood. Thus Scheler writes in connection with a critique of Kant's proposal to equate the "material" (that is, the non-formal) with "sensuous" content: "It is, it seems to me, the πρωτον ψευδος of this identification that instead of asking the simple question, 'What *is* given?', one asks, 'What *can* be given?'" [Husserl, *Op. cit.*, p. 50] In Phenomenology we do not meet with the question as to the "can", the question of "possibility" in the Kantian sense. Is this not, however, a genuine problem? May one not go on to ask how the *"Wesensschau"* goes about the business of delivering synthetic, universally valid knowledge to us, or must we accept this as a simple matter of fact? Even in Husserl himself we find on this point only obscure passages concerning "self-evidence" which are of highly dubious propriety, coming as they do, from the great warrior against psychologism.

The defenders of the factual *a priori*, the ranks of which include others beside the phenomenologists, have, I repeat, far more reason than Kant to ask the question: "How are synthetic *a priori* judgments possible?" In the first place, because according to them the domain of such judgments is much more inclusive, and in the second place, because they explicitly reject the answer given by Kant. We have every cause to raise in the presence of this philosophy the still more penetrating question, which forced our empiricism to take a stand in opposition to the Kantian system, and which it had to answer in the negative, "Are the judgments actually synthetic and *a priori* which you take to be so?" And if the answer should be in the affirmative with respect to the judgments arising from *"Wesensschau"* (intuition of essences), we ought not to rest until we had clarified their puzzling existence, their possibility. Indeed, as long as we had not succeeded in doing this, we should be in a state of constantly recurring doubt lest we had been deceived in the very assertion of their existence, and should reckon with the possibility that further insight would lead us to a more adequate account, just as an improved insight into the nature of mathematics and the natural sciences has shown the Kantian thesis that they contain synthetic *a priori* judgments, to be untenable. For we are today of the opinion that the propositions of pure mathematics are not synthetic, while those of the science of nature (to which geometry belongs, in so far as it is conceived to be the science of Space) are not *a priori*. Our empiricism makes the assertion that there are no other *a priori* judgments than the analytic, or rather, as we prefer to say today, that only tautological propositions are *a priori*. It willingly admits, however, that the propositions which the phenomenologist traces to *"Wesensschau"* and characterizes as constituting a factual *a priori* are worthy of the most exacting test, and appear to be a more serious threat to its position than those with which the *Critique of Pure Reason* is concerned. It is ready to revise its standpoint, if the result of the test should not be in its favor.

(A philosopher who believes in a factual *a priori,* and would like to clarify its possibility, would have, as far as I can see, no other way out than to carry over the Kantian theory from the form to the content of experience. He would have to assume that not only the form of our cognitions, but also their matter springs from the knowing consciousness—for only thus could *a priori* propositions relating to them be made intelligible. This would amount to a subjective Idealism of the Fichtean variety; one would find oneself entangled in a weird metaphysics.)

.   .   .

What, then, are the propositions which the phenomenologist brings forward to substantiate his contention, and which he believes, as Husserl put it, to found a science which "achieves an abundance of knowledge of the most rigorous type decisive in its import for all philosophy to come"? It is common knowledge that they are such judgments as these, that every tone has an intensity and a pitch, that one and the same surface cannot be simultaneously red and green, that (according to Scheler) "spiritual values have a higher place in the scale of values than vital values, and the values of the Holy a higher place than the spiritual" [*Ibid.,* p. 109], and so on. In the analysis which follows, we shall limit ourselves to propositions of the type represented by the first two examples, since the ethical proposition, because of its lack of clarity, offers no foothold for an exact analysis. We ask first whether these propositions are genuinely *a priori,* or are *a posteriori* in the same way as the proposition: "This organ pipe emits the note A" or "This cloth is red".

.   .   .

Should I assert that the height of a certain person is 160 cm., no one would take a statement to the effect that the individual in question isn't 180 cm. tall to give new insight or information. For everyone knows that the second piece of information is already included in the first by virtue of the meaning of the number symbols. He knows this as well as he knows that by the use of the above number nothing is said as to whether the person is a Frenchman or a Spaniard, whether polite or rude. Just as it belongs to the meaning of a statement giving someone's age that a person has only one age at a given time, and cannot be, for example, both 30 and 40 years old, so it belongs to the meaning of the word "tone" that one and only one determinate pitch characterizes a tone, and so it belongs to the logical grammar of color words that a word of this kind designates a specific property only on condition that I cannot designate this same property by means of a different color word. Should I permit this, the color words I use would have an entirely different meaning from that which we give them in everyday usage. In that case, the sentences which are the showpieces of the phenomenological philosophy would no longer be correct. Thus, they say nothing about existence, or about the nature of anything, but rather only exhibit the content of our concepts, that is, the mode and manner in which we employ the words of our language. Given the meanings of the words, they are *a priori,* but purely formal tautological, as indeed are all other *a priori* propositions. As expressions which have nothing to say, they bring no knowledge, and cannot serve as the foundation of a special science. Such a science as the phenomenologists have promised us just does not exist.

PART TWO

EXISTENTIAL PHENOMENOLOGY

INTRODUCTION

The existentialists shift the focus of phenomenological investigation away from Husserl's demand for a "rigorous science" and towards the question "What is it to be a person?" They place a new emphasis on "lived experience" rather than knowledge. They reject Husserl's *epoché;* they move from pure phenomenology back to traditional ontology; they reject the Husserlian transcendental ego and its transcendental realm; and they take "freedom" as their central concern. Among the existential phenomenologists, Jean-Paul Sartre is the best known, and needs no introduction here. Martin Heidegger, in his early work *Being and Time,* influenced not only Sartre but most European philosophers writing since 1930. Although Heidegger has abandoned the directions he initiated there, his book is one of the most important works in German philosophy since Husserl's *Ideas.*

In the selections here, we find characterizations of existential phenomenology by Paul Ricoeur, Maurice Merleau-Ponty, Gabriel Marcel, and Hubert Dreyfus. Paul Ricoeur is today France's most prominent active phenomenologist and has sympathy for both Husserl's transcendental phenomenology and existential phenomenology. Merleau-Ponty was, before his untimely death, the most promising voice of French existentialism and phenomenology. He was for years a friend and colleague of Sartre, and only recently have the glaring differences between them begun to be fully appreciated. Gabriel Marcel is an early Christian existentialist who became a major influence on French philosophy. He did not study Husserl, but developed a variation of the phenomenological method independently. His original thinking about the self, the body, relations with Others, and faith, had an important influence on Sartre, Merleau-Ponty, and particularly Ricoeur.

EXISTENTIAL PHENOMENOLOGY

PAUL RICOEUR

It is now possible to distinguish the main themes of contemporary existential phenomenology deriving from the conjunction of Husserlian phenomenology and the philosophy of existence. But these descriptive themes cannot be torn out of their philosophical context without injury. Even when they are elaborated by the same method and at times in the same terms by different philosophers, they are each traversed by a different intention which profoundly alters the sense. Existential phenomenology never describes merely for the pleasure of describing. The examples of Hegel, Kierkegaard, and Nietzsche are sufficient indication that description is effective only in the service of a great plan: to denounce an alienation, to rediscover the place of man in the world, or, on the other hand, to recover his metaphysical dimension, and so on. For each of these senses given to man's existence, there are so many descriptive styles in existential phenomenology. Let us take as examples three themes which are like the three melodic lines of existential phenomenology:

(1) First, the example of the "owned body." In Gabriel Marcel this theme has a function of break and recovery: on the one hand, break with the idolatry of the anonymous epistemological subject which is without situation, unmenaced, inaccessible to drama and to personal death, and, on the other hand, recovery of the concrete, restoration of an experience at once personal and integral which extends between the two poles of the carnal and the mysterious. This dual path, both critical and restorative, orients the patient, subtle, and sometimes evasive descriptions of

Reprinted from *Husserl, An Examination of His Philosophy*, translated by E. Ballard and L. Embree (Evanston, Ill.: Northwestern University Press, 1967), pp. 208–212, by permission of the publisher.

the "owned body." It oscillates between being and having (I am it, and I have it), between the organ and the instrument, between the same and the different. Thought, misled by the object, works to restore the complete sense of "I exist." But at the very moment when this existential phenomenology seems to be identified with a philosophy of incarnation, it escapes this philosophy and repays it with an investigation of experiences which can be called ontological because they reveal the insertion of my being into being: fidelity, hope, etc. Existential phenomenology then signifies the "positing and concentrated approach to the ontological mystery." In other words, the phenomenology of the "owned body" plays the equivocal role of a rerooting in the concrete and of a counterpole to the ontological mystery.

In Merleau-Ponty, on the other hand, the description of the owned body is entirely in the service of a philosophy of finitude or of an exorcism of standpointless thinking; ultimately it is in the service of a philosophy without an absolute. The *Phenomenology of Perception* should be followed from one end to the other without reference to the true object, seen from nowhere, which would justify the possibility of perception, even without ever denying the inherence of consciousness in a point of view. To be sure, this program assumes that the other operations of consciousness—principally science and also all that is amenable to speech and to the λογος—bear the same fundamental structures, "the same syntheses of transition, the same sort of horizon" as perceptual experience; in short, it assumes that "every consciousness is perceptual, even the consciousness of ourselves." Thus, the first pact concluded between cognition and finitude orients the whole phenomenology of perception. The description of the "owned body" is its touchstone. This description, just as in both Husserl and Gabriel Marcel, goes hand in hand with a critique of sensation as reconstructed by psycho-physiology, i.e., as the simple effect of a physical stimulus. Phenomenology calls description from the sensation, from that late developed object of scientific consciousness, to perception, just as it is given. This perception is given as at once significational, in contrast to the pretended sensation of sensualism, but not intelligible, in contrast to the judgment of experience according to the intellectualist tradition which runs from Lachelier and Lagneau to Alain and Brunschvicg.

The theory of the "owned body" is then the critical point where the breakdown of objective thinking is consummated and where the perspectivist doctrine of perception is established. Neither the psychic, according to reflective philosophy, nor the "physiological," according to scientific thinking, accounts for the owned body. For it is the movement of being-in-the-world (*être au monde*), indivisibly voluntary and involuntary, as projected and as given. Beginning at this point, every analysis of behavior is conducted in such a way as to avoid the alternatives of automatism and abstract intelligence. The "owned body" is the locus of all ambiguities between the nascent sense and facticity, between the enacted and the reflected. Merleau-Ponty's existential phenomenology thus represents the strictest disagreement with the Platonic conversion of the here-below to the beyond. Placed in the service of a reconversion from reflection to the pre-reflective, existential phenomenology becomes identified with the justification of being-in-the-world. One can only wonder, though, how the moment of reflection on the unreflected, how the devotion to universality and to truth, and finally how the philosophical act itself are possible if man is so completely identified with his insertion into his field of perception, action, and life.

(2) The theme of freedom gives rise to contrasts even greater than those of the "owned body" and confirms the subordination of the descriptive method to the existential intention in this sector of phenomenology. The reason is clear: in the case of freedom the ontological status of man is in question. Heidegger had already placed phenomenology in the service of a fundamental ontology where the explication of the being of man was to open the horizon to a theory of being qua being. Thereafter, it is not surprising that a phenomenology of freedom, such as is at the center of Jean-Paul Sartre's work, should carry an ontological title—*Being and Nothingness*—and a subtitle which combines phenomenology and ontology. Even so, we have scarcely left the field of existential phenomenology, for with

freedom, the existential and the ontological become synonymous. The being of man consists in existing, in the emphatic sense which Kierkegaard has conferred on this word.

The overthrow which Sartre introduced into the problem-set of freedom consists precisely in having inverted the ontological index of freedom. Did we just say that the being of man consists in existing? Let us rather say that existing consists in being its own nothingness. Here is where phenomenology comes into play, for it has the function of collecting the experiences where I discover my freedom in the negative style of absence, of rapture, of distance, of failure to cohere, and of constancy, of anguish, of rejection, in short, where freedom is revealed as the nihilation of the past, of the completed, in a word, of being. Evidently it is presupposed that being was previously reduced to the being of a thing, to thinghood. It is then clear that the abandonment of the great metaphysical tradition, whereby being is act par excellence, is what directs this phenomenology of nihilating acts. Moreover, this phenomenology manifests an abundance, a perspicacity, and a force rarely equaled. The "sense of the negative" of which Hegel took possession on behalf of philosophy (and to which, as we have seen, Husserl lost the key), re-emerges in contemporary philosophy with Sartre. This dialectical sense is enriched along the way with the Kierkegaardian and Marxian themes of anxiety and conflict. In addition, Sartre uses an agile imagination of concrete situations which as philosopher he takes over from the playwright. Finally, Husserl's concept of intentionality takes on a new look after this bath in negativity. It becomes the original distance, the stepping away of the self from itself, the nothing which separates existence from its having-been. But the step which carries this phenomenology of nihilating acts to the level of an ontology of nothingness is made by the philosopher, not by the phenomenologist.

Yet the same patience, the same descriptive strictness can serve an entirely different purpose, for one can describe, with Gabriel Marcel, another level of freedom, which consists less in tearing oneself away from oneself, in annulling every datum in-itself and beyond oneself, than in letting oneself be opened up by a liberating presence. A phenomenology of liberation, which describes the passage of unavailability to availability (*disponi-bilité*), from avarice to generosity, here becomes the harbinger of a quite different ontology, one where the main accent is on participation in being rather than on the nihilation of being. But this descriptive spirit is not what makes for the difference between the two phenomenologies. The difference lies rather in the sense of the word "being," which for one signifies act, the giving of existence, and for the other signifies the brute datum or dead thing.

In Merleau-Ponty the phenomenology of freedom can also take form within the phenomenology of the "owned body" which, as we have seen, joins the ego to the world instead of completing the break between the "for-itself" an the "in-itself." If in fact the body is the movement of my being-in-the-world, if it is a spontaneity which offers itself to a situation in order to form it, then the decisive experience of freedom is to be sought not in the dramatic moment of breaking away but rather in the moment of engagement which includes the whole involvement in situation. To project our past, our future, our human milieu around ourselves is precisely to situate ourselves. Henceforth, concrete freedom is not to be sought elsewhere than in this general power to place oneself in situation. And the all or nothing of Sartrean freedom appears to have no measure in common with actual experience, which does not know the sovereign "in-itself" and never encounters anything but a relative freedom which incessantly "busies itself in taking up some proposition about the world." The phenomenology of freedom follows up the metaphysics of finitude which the theory of the owned body began.

(3) The theme of the Other supports our analysis of the relations between the phenomenological method and the ontological intention in existential phenomenology. Jean-Paul Sartre initiates his analysis of the existence of the Other with the experience of being seen, of being caught by a gaze which freezes me in my tracks, reduces me to the condition of an object, steals my world from me, and takes away my freedom along with my subject position. The existence of the Other thus constitutes my

"original fall," that is to say, the movement by which I fall into the world and am condemned to parry and thrust, i.e., to the struggle which is pursued in incipient or indirect ways even in sexual activity. But the choice of this glance that encroaches, fixes, determines, this glance which menaces because it is menaced, this freezing gaze—this choice comes to phenomenology from far away. If the Other appears to me by primordial right as power of encroachment (*d'empiètement*) and of theft, is this not because freedom itself has been described without the experience of generosity or of giving? Is it not only in a foregone project of unavailability, as Emmanuel Mounier says somewhere, that the Other's gaze is a gaze that petrifies and not instead a gaze that overthrows?

However such things stand, when it is a question of the Other, just as when it is a question of freedom or of the owned body, the field of existential phenomenology is an oriented field. One does not describe just anything simply for the pleasure of making brilliant analyses. The privilege accorded to misunderstanding, to conflict, to encounter, to reciprocity, to the collaboration of a teammate or of a galley slave betrays a different ontological style, according to whether being renders the constitution of a *we* possible or not, wherein the difference and the distance between me and the Other would somehow be overcome.

Thus, existential phenomenology makes the transition between transcendental phenomenology, born of the reduction of every thing to its appearing to me, and ontology, which restores the question of the sense of being for all that is said to "exist."

THE BATTLE OVER EXISTENTIALISM

MAURICE MERLEAU-PONTY

Reprinted from *Sense and Non-Sense*, translated by H. and P. Dreyfus (Evanston, Ill.: Northwestern University Press, 1964), pp. 71–73, by permission of the publisher.

It has been two years since the publication of Jean-Paul Sartre's *L'Être et le néant*. At first a profound silence settled over this 700-page book: were the critics holding back their ink? Does their respect for the united front extend even to philosophy? Were they waiting until a free discussion would again be possible? In any case, the silence has now been broken. On the Left, weeklies and reviews are bombarded with critical articles which they do or do not publish. On the Right the anathemas are piling up. High-school girls are warned against existentialism as if it were the sin of the century. The June 3d edition of *La Croix* speaks of a danger "graver than 18th-century rationalism and 19th-century positivism." It is remarkable how a thoroughgoing discussion is almost always put off until later, while criticism takes the form of a warning to the faithful. Sartre's book is labeled a poison of which we must beware instead of a philosophy which we might discuss; it is condemned for its horrible consequences instead of for its intrinsic falsity. It is a matter of first things first, and the first thing to do is to enforce a quarantine. For the established doctrines to refuse discussion is no indication of strength. If it is true that many young people are welcoming the new philosophy with open arms, it will take more than these peevish criticisms, which deliberately avoid the question raised by Sartre's work, to convince them to reject it.

The question is that of man's relationship to his natural or social surroundings. There are two classical views: one treats man as the result of the physical, physiological, and sociological influences which shape him from the outside and make him one thing among many; the other consists of recognizing an a-cosmic freedom in him, insofar as he is spirit and represents to himself the very causes which supposedly act upon him. On the one hand, man is a part of the world; on the other, he is the constituting consciousness of the world. Neither view is satisfactory. After Descartes one can object to the first on the grounds that, if man were indeed one thing among many, he could not know any of them because he would be locked in his own limits like this chair or that table, *present* at a certain location in space and therefore incapable of *representing* to himself all the others. We must grant man a very special way of being—intentional being—which consists of being oriented towards all things but of not residing in any. But if we tried to conclude from this that our fundamental nature makes us absolute spirit, our corporal and social ties with the world and our insertion in it would become incomprehensible, and we would give up thinking about the human condition. The merit of the new philosophy is precisely that it tries, in the notion of existence, to find a way of thinking about our condition. In the modern sense of the word, "existence" is the movement through which man is in the world and involves himself in a physical and social situation which then becomes his point of view on the world. All involvement is ambiguous because it both affirms and restricts a freedom: my undertaking to do a certain thing means both that it would be possible for me not to do it and that I exclude this possibility. My involvement in nature and history is likewise a limitation of my view on the world and yet the only way for me to approach the world, know it, and do something in it. The relationship between subject and object is no longer that *relationship of knowing* postulated by classical idealism, wherein the object always seems the construction of the subject, but a *relationship of being* in which, paradoxically, the subject *is* his body, his world, and his situation, by a sort of exchange.

We are not saying that *l'Être et le néant* makes this paradox of consciousness and action entirely clear. In our opinion the book remains too exclusively antithetic: the antithesis of my view of myself and another's view of me and the antithesis of the *for itself* and the *in itself* often seem to be alternatives instead of being described as the living bond and communication between one term and the other. It is obvious that the author's primary concern in dealing with the subject and freedom is to present them as uninvolved in any compromise with things and that he is putting off the study of the "realization" of nothingness in being —which is action and which makes morality possible—until some other time. *L'Être et le néant* is first of all a demonstration that the subject is freedom, absence, and negativity and that, in this sense, there is nothingness. But that also means that the subject is *only* nothingness, that he needs being to sustain himself, that he can only be thought of against a background of the world, and, finally, that he feeds on being like the shadows in Homer feed on the blood of the living. We can therefore expect all manner of clarification and completion after *l'Être et le néant*. But it cannot be denied that Sartre's descriptions pose the central problem of philosophy, as it appears after the acquisitions of the last centuries, pointedly and with new profundity. After Descartes, it was impossible to deny that existence as consciousness is radically different from existence as thing and that the relationship of the two is that of emptiness to plentitude. After the 19th century and all it taught us about the historicity of the spirit, it was impossible to deny that consciousness always exists in a situation. It is up to us to understand both things at once. Simply reaffirming one classical position or the other is not a solution for either Catholics or Marxists. This is impossible in itself and even impossible according to the internal logic of Christianity and Marxism.

from THE MYSTERY OF BEING

GABRIEL MARCEL

Interpreting it in the most general way, we can say that this idea of resolution, of the resolving of discords or contradictions, is that of the passage from a situation in which we are ill at ease to one in which we feel ourselves almost melting away with relief. The general notion of a *situation* is one which is destined to play a great part in my lectures, and I have my reasons for first bringing it to your notice at this point. It will be only much later on that we shall grasp its full significance. For the moment, let us be content to say that a situation is something in which I find myself involved; but that however we interpret the notion

Reprinted from *The Mystery of Being*, vol. 1 (Chicago, Henry Regnery, 1951), pp. 8–10, by permission of the publisher.

of the involved self, the situation is not something which presses on the self merely from the outside, but something which colours its interior states; or rather we shall have to ask ourselves whether, at this level or discourse, the usual antithesis between inner and outer is not beginning to lose a good deal of its point. The only point that I want, however, to emphasize at this moment is that a philosophical investigation, of the sort in which we are now engaged, can be considered as a gathering together˙ of the processes by which I can pass from a situation which is experienced as basically discordant, a situation in which I can go so far as to say that I am at war with myself, to a different situation in which some kind of expectation is satisfied.

This is still all pretty vague, but already, I am afraid, it begins to raise awkward questions, all centering round this indeterminate notion of the involved self, of my involved self, which I have been forced to take as my reference-point. The really important question that is raised may be framed in the following terms: is there not a risk of the investigation that is being undertaken here reducing itself to an account of the succession of stages by which I, I as this particular person, Gabriel Marcel, attempt, starting off from some state of being which implies a certain suffering, to reach another state of being which not only does not imply suffering but may be accompanied by a certain joy? But what guarantee can I have that this personal progress of mine has anything more than a subjective value? Nevertheless, in the end is it not the case that something more than subjective value is needed to confer on any chain of thoughts what I may describe as a proper philosophic dignity? In other words, are there any means at all of assuring ourselves whether this indeterminate involved self, which I have been forced to take as my reference-point, is or is not, for instance, immortal?

In this connection, some remarks which I have previously made might be of a kind to arouse a certain uneasiness. Have I not seemed to reserve the privilege of universality in thinking to scientists or technicians whose method is that of a series of operations which can be carried out by anybody else in the world who is placed in the same setting and can make use of similar tools?

The answer to this very important question will only clarify itself very gradually, as our thoughts about it work back upon themselves. I think it necesary, nevertheless, to indicate even at this moment—partly to allay a very understandable nervousness—in what direction the answer ought to be sought for.

Let us say, to put it very roughly, that the dilemma in which this question leaves us—that of choice between the actual individual man, delivered over to his own states of being and incapable of transcending them, and a kind of generalized thinking as such, what the Germans call *Denken überhaupt*, which would be operative in a sort of Absolute and so claim universal validity for its operations—let us say that this dilemma is a false one, and must be rejected. Between these two antithetic terms, we must intercalate an intermediary type of thinking, which is precisely the type of thinking that the lecture following this will illustrate. The point should at once be made here that, even outside the limits of philosophy properly so called, there are incontestable examples of this type of thinking. We have only to think, for instance, of what we describe, rather vaguely indeed, as the understanding of works of art; it would be better no doubt, in this connection, to talk of their appreciation—so long as we eliminate from that word its root reference to a *pretium*, a market price. It would be an illusion and even an absurdity to suppose that the *Missa Solemnis* or some great work of pictorial art is meant for just anybody who comes along; on the contrary, we must in honest sincerity accept the fact that there are plenty of people whose attention is not arrested, and who have nothing communicated to them, by such works. It is none the less certain that when a genuine emotion is felt at the impact of a work of art it infinitely transcends the limits of what we call the individual consciousness. Let us try to clarify this in more detail.

When I look at or listen to a masterpiece, I have an experience which can be strictly called a revelation. That experience will just not allow itself to be analysed away as a mere state of simple strongly felt satisfaction. . . . On the other hand, it is just as incontestably a fact that, for reasons that remain impenetrable to us—if it is right to talk at all about reasons in this connection—such revelations appear not to be granted to other people, people with whom, nevertheless, I have no difficulty at all in communicating on other topics. There would be no point in bringing into play my stores of learning, let me even say my gifts as a teacher! I would never succeed in exciting, in the other person, the thrill of admiration that the great work of art had excited in me. It is just as if the other person were, in the root sense of the word, refractory—one who repels the particles of light—or as if a kind of grace that is operative for me were not operative for him.

PHENOMENOLOGY
AND
ONTOLOGY

The compound expression 'Being-in-the-world' indicates in the very way we have coined it, that it stands for a *unitary* phenomenon. This primary datum must be seen as a whole. . . . Of course Being-in-the-world is a state of Dasein which is necessary *a priori*, but it is far from sufficient for completely determining Dasein's Being.

—Martin Heidegger BEING AND TIME

Being is. Being is in-itself. Being is what it is.

Jean Paul Sartre BEING AND NOTHINGNESS

INTRODUCTION

In rejecting Husserl's *epoché* or phenomenological reduction, the existentialists are forced to raise anew the traditional skeptical questions about the "external world." But rather than reply to those questions, Heidegger, Sartre, and Merleau-Ponty reject the questions themselves as illegitimate. Having given up the *epoché*, they have rejected the basis of skepticism as well. For the existentialists, the world exists beyond a Cartesian doubt.

The central question of Heidegger's philosophy is the "Question of Being." Heidegger distinguishes the questions, "What is it for something to be an X?" and "What is it for something to be?" Since the Greeks, Heidegger argues, philosophers including Husserl have asked only the first question. In the following selections, Heidegger, Sartre, and Merleau-Ponty attempt to ask the second.

THE QUESTION OF BEING

MARTIN HEIDEGGER

"For manifestly you have long been aware of what you mean when you use the expression *"being"*. We, however, who used to think we understood it, have now become perplexed." [Plato]

Do we in our time have an answer to the question of what we really mean by the word 'being' [*seiend*]? Not at all. So it is fitting that we should raise anew *the question of the meaning of Being*. . . . This question has today been forgotten. Even though in our time we deem it progressive to give our approval to 'metaphysics' again, it is held that we have been exempted from the exertions of a newly rekindled γιγαντομαχια περι της ουσιας. Yet the question we are touching upon is not just any question. It is one which provided a stimulus for the researches of Plato and Aristotle, only to subside from then on *as a theme for actual investigation*. What these two men achieved was to persist through many alterations and 'retouchings' down to the 'logic' of Hegel. And what they wrested with the utmost intellectual effort from the phenomena, fragmentary and incipient though it was, has long since become trivialized.

Not only that. On the basis of the Greeks' initial contributions towards an Interpretation of Being, a dogma has been developed which not only declares the question about the meaning of Being to be superfluous, but sanctions its complete neglect. It is said that 'Being' is the most universal and the emptiest of concepts. As such it resists every attempt at definition. Nor does

From *Being and Time* by Martin Heidegger. Translated by John Macquarrie and Edward Robinson. Copyright © 1962 by SCM Press Ltd. Reprinted by permission of Harper & Row, Publishers, Inc. Pp. 19, 21, 25–26, 32–33, 49–50, 61, 67–69.

this most universal and hence indefinable concept require any definition, for everyone uses it constantly and already understands what he means by it. In this way, that which the ancient philosophers found continually disturbing as something obscure and hidden has taken on a clarity and self-evidence such that if anyone continues to ask about it he is charged with an error of method. . . .

In the question which we are to work out, *what is asked about is* Being—that which determines entities as entities, that on the basis of which [woraufhin] entities are already understood, however we may discuss them in detail. The Being of entities 'is' not itself an entity. If we are to understand the problem of Being, our first philosophical step consists in not μυθον τινα διηγεισθαι, in not 'telling a story'—that is to say, in not defining entities as entities by tracing them back in their origin to some other entities, as if Being had the character of some possible entity. Hence Being, as that which is asked about, must be exhibited in a way of its own, essentially different from the way in which entities are discovered. Accordingly, *what is to be found out by the asking*—the meaning of Being—also demands that it be conceived in a way of its own, essentially contrasting with the concepts in which entities acquire their determinate signification.

In so far as Being constitutes what is asked about, and "Being" means the Being of entities, then entities themselves turn out to be *what is interrogated*. These are, so to speak, questioned as regards their Being. But if the characteristics of their Being can be yielded without falsification, then these entities must, on their part, have become accessible as they are in themselves. When we come to what is to be interrogated, the question of Being requires that the right way of access to entities shall have been obtained and secured in advance. But there are many things which we designate as 'being' ["seiend"], and we do so in various senses. Everything we talk about, everything we have in view, everything towards which we comport ourselves in any way, is being; what we are is being, and so is how we are. Being lies in the fact that something is, and in its Being as it is; in Reality; in presence-at-hand; in subsistence; in validity; in Dasein; in the 'there is'. In *which* entities is the meaning of Being to be discerned? From which entities is the disclosure of Being to take its departure? Is the starting-point optional, or does some particular entity have priority when we come to work out the question of Being? Which entity shall we take for our example, and in what sense does it have priority?

THE THEME OF THE ANALYTIC OF DASEIN

We are ourselves the entities to be analysed. The Being of any such entity is *in each case mine*. These entities, in their Being, comport themselves towards their Being. As entities with such Being, they are delivered over to their own Being. *Being* is that which is an issue for every such entity. This way of characterizing Dasein has a double consequence:

1. The 'essence' ["Wesen"] of this entity lies in its "to be" [Zu-sein]. Its Being-what-it-is [Was-sein] (*essentia*) must, so far as we can speak of it at all, be conceived in terms of its Being (*existentia*). But here our ontological task is to show that when we choose to designate the Being of this entity as "existence" [Existenz], this term does not and cannot have the ontological signification of the traditional term "*existentia*"; ontologically, *existentia* is tantamount to *Being-present-at-hand*, a kind of Being which is essentially inappropriate to entities of Dasein's character. To avoid getting bewildered, we shall always use the Interpretative expression "*presence-at-hand*" for the term "*existentia*" while the term "existence", is a designation of Being, will be allotted solely to Dasein.

The 'essence' of Dasein lies in its existence. Accordingly those characteristics which can be exhibited in this entity are not 'properties' present-at-hand of some entity which 'looks' so and so and is itself present-at-hand; they are in each case possible ways for it to be, and no more than that. All the Being-as-it-is [So-sein] which this entity possesses is primarily Being. So when we designate this entity with the term 'Dasein', we are expressing not its "what" (as if it were a table, house or tree) but its Being.

2. That Being which is an *issue* for this entity in its very Being, is in each case mine. . . .

In determining itself as an entity, Dasein always does so in the light of a possibility which it *is* itself and which, in its very Being, it somehow understands. This is the formal meaning of Dasein's existential constitution. But this tells us that if we are to Interpret this entity *ontologically*, the problematic of its Being must be developed from the existentiality of its existence. This cannot mean, however, that "Dasein" is to be construed in terms of some concrete possible idea of existence. At the outset of our analysis it is particularly important that Dasein should not be Interpreted with the differentiated character [Differenz] of some definite way of existing, but that it should be uncovered [aufgedeckt] in the undifferentiated character which it has proximally and for the most part. This undifferentiated character of Dasein's everydayness is *not nothing*, but a positive phenomenal characteristic of this entity. Out of this kind of Being—and back into it again—is all existing, such as it is. We call this everyday undifferentiated character of Dasein *"averageness"* [*Durchschnittlichkeit*].

And because this average everydayness makes up what is ontically proximal for this entity, it has again and again been *passed over* in explicating Dasein. That which is ontically closest and well known, is ontologically the farthest and not known at all; and its ontological signification is constantly overlooked. When Augustine asks: *"Quid autem propinquius meipso mihi?"* and must answer: *"ego certe laboro hic et laboro in meipso: factus sum mihi terra difficultatis et sudoris nimii"*, this applies not only to the ontical and pre-ontological opaqueness of Dasein but even more to the ontological task which lies ahead; for not only must this entity not be missed in that kind of Being in which it is phenomenally closest, but it must be made accessible by a positive characterization.

Dasein's average everydayness, however, is not to be taken as a mere 'aspect'. Here too, and even in the mode of inauthenticity, the structure of existentiality lies *a priori*. And here too Dasein's Being is an issue for it in a definite way; and Dasein comports itself towards it in the mode of average everydayness, even if this is only the mode of fleeing *in the face of it* and forgetfulness *thereof*. . . .

It is peculiar to this entity that with and through its Being, this Being is disclosed to it. *Understanding of Being is itself a definite characteristic of Dasein's Being.* Dasein is ontically distinctive in that it *is* ontological. . . .

That kind of Being towards which Dasein can comport itself in one way or another, and always does comport itself somehow, we call *"existence"* [*Existenz*]. And because we cannot define Dasein's essence by citing a "what" of the kind that pertains to a subject-matter [eines sachhaltigen Was], and because its essence lies rather in the fact that in each case it has its Being to be, and has it as its own, we have chosen to designate this entity as "Dasein", a term which is purely an expression of its Being. . . .

Dasein always understands itself in terms of its existence—in terms of a possibility of itself: to be itself or not itself. Dasein has either chosen these possibilities itself, or got itself into them, or grown up in them already. Only the particular Dasein decides its existence, whether it does so by taking hold or by neglecting. The question of existence never gets straightened out except through existing itself. The understanding of oneself which leads *along this way* we call *"existentiell"*. The question of existence is one of Dasein's ontical 'affairs'. This does not require that the ontological structure of existence should be theoretically transparent. The question about that structure aims at the analysis [Auseinanderlegung] of what constitutes existence. The context [Zusammenhang] of such structures we call *"existentiality"*. Its analytic has the character of an understanding which is not existentiell, but rather *existential*. The task of an existential analytic of Dasein has been delineated in advance, as regards both its possibility and its necessity, in Dasein's ontical constitution.

So far as existence is the determining character of Dasein,

the ontological analytic of this entity always requires that existentiality be considered beforehand. By "existentiality" we understand the state of Being that is constitutive for those entities that exist. But in the idea of such a constitutive state of Being, the idea of Being is already included. And thus even the possibility of carrying through the analytic of Dasein depends on working out beforehand the question about the meaning of Being in general.

Sciences are ways of Being in which Dasein comports itself towards entities which it need not be itself. But to Dasein, Being in a world is something that belongs essentially. Thus Dasein's understanding of Being pertains with equal primordiality both to an understanding of something like a 'world', and to the understanding of the Being of those entities which become accessible within the world. So whenever an ontology takes for its theme entities whose character of Being is other than that of Dasein, it has its own foundation and motivation in Dasein's own ontical structure, in which a pre-ontological understanding of Being is comprised as a definite characteristic. . . .

THE PHENOMENOLOGICAL METHOD
OF INVESTIGATION

In provisionally characterizing the object which serves as the theme of our investigation (the Being of entities, or the meaning of Being in general), it seems that we have also delineated the method to be employed. The task of ontology is to explain Being itself and to make the Being of entities stand out in full relief. And the method of ontology remains questionable in the highest degree as long as we merely consult those ontologies which have come down to us historically, or other essays of that character. Since the term "ontology" is used in this investigation in a sense which is formally broad, any attempt to clarify the method of ontology by tracing its history is automatically ruled out.

When, moreover, we use the term "ontology", we are not talking about some definite philosophical discipline standing in interconnection with the others. Here one does not have to measure up to the tasks of some discipline that has been presented beforehand; on the contrary, only in terms of the objective necessities of definite questions and the kind of treatment which the 'things themselves' require, can one develop such a discipline.

With the question of the meaning of Being, our investigation comes up against the fundamental question of philosophy. This is one that must be treated *phenomenologically*. Thus our treatise does not subscribe to a 'stand-point' or represent any special 'direction'; for phenomenology is nothing of either sort, nor can it become so as long as it understands itself. The expression 'phenomenology' signifies primarily a *methodological conception*. This expression does not characterize the what of the objects of philosophical research as subject-matter, but rather the *how* of that research. The more genuinely a methodological concept is worked out and the more comprehensively it determines the principles on which a science is to be conducted, all the more primordially is it rooted in the way we come to terms with the things themselves, and the farther is it removed from what we call "technical devices", though there are many such devices even in the theoretical disciplines.

Thus the term 'phenomenology' expresses a maxim which can be formulated as 'To the things themselves!' It is opposed to all free-floating constructions and accidental findings; it is opposed to taking over any conceptions which only seem to have been demonstrated; it is opposed to those pseudo-questions which parade themselves as 'problems', often for generations at a time. . . .

The way in which Being and its structures are encountered in the mode of phenomenon is one which must first of all be *wrested* from the objects of phenomenology. Thus the very *point of departure* [*Ausgang*] for our analysis requires that it be secured by the proper method, just as much as does our *access* [*Zugang*] to the phenomenon, or our *passage* [*Durchgang*] through whatever is prevalently covering it up. The idea of grasping and explicating phenomena in a way which is 'original' and

'intuitive' ["originären" und "intuitiven"] is directly opposed
to the *naïveté* of a haphazard, 'immediate', and unreflective
'beholding'. ["Schauen"].

With regard to its subject-matter, phenomenology is the
science of the Being of entities—ontology.

THE ONTOLOGICAL PROOF

JEAN-PAUL SARTRE

Being has not been given its due. We believed we had dis-
pensed with granting transphenomenality to the being of the
phenomenon because we had discovered the transphenomenality
of the being of consciousness. We are going to see, on the contrary, that this very transphenomenality requires that of the
being of the phenomenon. There is an "ontological proof" to be
derived not from the reflective *cogito* but from the *pre-reflective*
being of the *percipiens*. This we shall now try to demonstrate.

All consciousness is consciousness *of* something. This definition of consciousness can be taken in two very distinct senses:
either we understand by this that consciousness is constitutive of
the being of its object, or it means that consciousness in its
inmost nature is a relation to a transcendent being. But the first
interpretation of the formula destroys itself: to be conscious *of*
something is to be confronted with a concrete and full presence
which *is not* consciousness. Of course one can be conscious of an
absence. But this absence appears necessarily as a pre-condition
of presence. As we have seen, consciousness is a real subjectivity
and the impression is a subjective plenitude. But this subjectivity can not go out of itself to posit a transcendent object in such

a way as to endow it with a plenitude of impressions. If then we wish at any price to make the being of the phenomenon depend on consciousness, the object must be distinguished from consciousness not by its *presence* but by its *absence*, not by its plentitude, but by its nothingness. If being belongs to consciousness, the object is not consciousness, not to the extent that it is another being, but that it is non-being. This is the appeal to the infinite of which we spoke in the first section of his work. For Husserl, for example, the animation of the hyletic nucleus by the only intentions which can find their fulfillment (*Erfüllung*) in this *hyle* is not enough to bring us outside of subjectivity. The truly objectifying intentions are empty intentions, those which aim beyond the present subjective appearance at the infinite totality of the series of appearances.

We must further understand that the intentions aim at appearances which are never to be given at one time. It is an impossibility on principle for the terms of an infinite series to exist all at the same time before consciousness, along with the real absence of all these terms except for the one which is the foundation of objectivity. If present these impressions—even in infinite number—would dissolve in the subjective; it is their absence which gives them objective being. Thus the being of the object is pure non-being. It is defined as a *lack*. It is that which escapes, that which by definition will never be given, that which offers itself only in fleeting and successive profiles.

But how can non-being be the foundation of being. How can the absent, *expected* subjective become thereby the objective? A great joy which I hope for, a grief which I dread, acquire from that fact a certain transcendence. This I admit. But that transcendence in immanence does not bring us out of the subjective. It is true that things give themselves in profile; that is, simply by appearances. And it is true that each appearance refers to other appearances. But each of them is already in itself alone a *transcendent being*, not a subjective material of impressions—a *plenitude of being*, not a lack—a *presence*, not an absence. It is futile by a sleight of hand to attempt to found the *reality* of the object on the subjective plenitude of impressions and its *objectivity* on non-being; the objective will never come out of the subjective nor the transcendent from immanence, nor being from non-being. But, we are told, Husserl defines consciousness precisely as a transcendence. In truth he does. This is what he posits. This is his essential discovery. But from the moment that he makes of the *noema* an *unreal*, a correlate *of* the *noesis*, a noema whose *esse* is *percipi*, he is totally unfaithful to his principle.

Consciousness is consciousness *of* something. This means that transcendence is the constitutive structure of consciousness; that is, that consciousness is born *supported by* a being which is not itself. This is what we call the ontological proof. No doubt someone will reply that the existence of the demand of consciousness does not prove that this demand ought to be satisfied. But this objection cannot hold up against an analysis of what Husserl calls intentionality, though, to be sure, he misunderstood its essential character. To say that consciousness is consciousness of something means that for consciousness there is no being outside of that precise obligation to be a revealing intuition of something—*i.e.*, of a transcendent being. Not only does pure subjectivity, if initially given, fail to transcend itself to posit the objective; a "pure" subjectivity disappears. What can properly be called subjectivity is consciousness (of) consciousness. But this consciousness (of being) consciousness must be qualified in some way, and it can be qualified only as revealing intuition or it is nothing. Now a revealing intuition implies something revealed. Absolute subjectivity can be established only in the face of something revealed; immanence can be defined only within the apprehension of a transcendent. It might appear that there is an echo here of Kant's refutation of problematical idealism. But we ought rather to think of Descartes. We are here on the ground of being, not of knowledge. It is not a question of showing that the phenomena of inner sense imply the existence of objective spatial phenomena, but that consciousness implies in its being a non-conscious and transphenomenal being. In particular there is no point in replying that in fact subjectivity implies objectivity and that it constitutes itself in constituting the objective; we have seen that subjectivity is powerless to constitute the objective. To say that consciousness is consciousness of something is to say that it must produce itself as a revealed-revelation of a being which is not it and which gives itself as already existing when consciousness reveals it.

Thus we have left pure appearance and have arrived at full being. Consciousness is a being whose existence posits its essence, and inversely it is consciousness of a being, whose essence implies its existence; that is, in which appearance lays claim to *being*. Being is everywhere. Certainly we could apply to consciousness the definition which Heidegger reserves for *Dasein* and say that it is a being such that in its being, its being is in question. But it would be necessary to complete the definition and formulate it more like this: *consciousness is a being such that in its being, its being is in question in so far as this being implies a being other than itself.*

We must understand that this being is no other than the transphenomenal being of phenomena and not a noumenal being which is hidden behind them. It is the being of his table, of this package of tobacco, of the lamp, more generally the being of the world which is implied by consciousness. It requires simply that the being of that which *appears* does not exist *only* in so far as it appears. The transphenomenal being of what exists *for consciousness* is itself in itself (*lui-même en soi*). . . .

THE QUESTION

Our inquiry has led us to the heart of being. But we have been brought to an impasse since we have not been able to establish the connection between the two regions of being which we have discovered. No doubt this is because we have chosen an unfortunate approach. Descartes found himself faced with an analogous problem when he had to deal with the relation between soul and body. He planned then to look for the solution on that level where the union of thinking substance and extended substance was actually effected—that is, in the imagination. His advice is valuable. To be sure, our concern is not that of Descartes and we do not conceive of imagination as he did. But what we can retain is the reminder that it is not profitable first to separate the two terms of a relation in order to try to join them together again later. The relation is a synthesis. Consequently the *results* of analysis can not be covered over again by the *moments* of this synthesis.

M. Laporte says that an abstraction is made when something not capable of existing in isolation is thought of as in an isolated state. The concrete by contrast is a totality which can exist by itself alone. Husserl is of the same opinion; for him *red* is an abstraction because color can not exist without form. On the other hand, a spatial-temporal *thing*, with all its determinations, is an example of the concrete. From this point of view, consciousness is an abstraction since it conceals within itself an ontological source in the region of the in-itself, and conversely the phenomenon is likewise an abstraction since it must "appear" to consciousness. The concrete can be only the synthetic totality of which consciousness, like the phenomenon, constitutes only moments. The concrete is man within the world in that specific union of man with the world which Heidegger, for example, calls "being-in-the-world." We deliberately begin with the abstract if we question "experience" as Kant does, inquiring into the conditions of its possibility—or if we effect a phenomenological reduction like Husserl, who would reduce the world to the state of the noema-correlate of consciousness. But we will no more succeed in restoring the concrete by the summation or organization of the elements which we have abstracted from it than Spinoza can reach substance by the infinite summation of its modes.

PREFACE TO THE PHENOMENOLOGY
OF PERCEPTION

MAURICE MERLEAU-PONTY

What is phenomenology? It may seem strange that this question has still to be asked half a century after the first works of Husserl. The fact remains that it has by no means been answered. Phenomenology is the study of essences; and according to it, all problems amount to finding definitions of essences: the essence of perception, or the essence of consciousness, for example. But phenomenology is also a philosophy which puts essences back into existence, and does not expect to arrive at an understanding of man and the world from any starting point other than that of their 'facticity'. It is a transcendental philosophy which places in abeyance the assertions arising out of the natural attitude, the better to understand them; but it is also a philosophy for which the world is always 'already there' before reflection begins—as an inalienable presence; and all its efforts are concentrated upon re-achieving a direct and primitive contact with the world, and endowing that contact with a philosophical status. It is the search for a philosophy which shall be a 'rigorous science', but it also offers an account of space, time and the world as we 'live' them. It tries to give a direct description of our experience as it is, without taking account of its psychological origin and the causal explanations which the scientist, the historian or the sociologist may be able to provide. Yet Husserl in his last works mentions a 'genetic phenomenology', [Husserl, *CM* pp. 120 ff.] and even a 'constructive phenomenology'. [Husserl, CM, unpublished 6th med.] One may try to do away with these contradictions by making a distinction between Husserl's

Reprinted from *The Phenomenology of Perception*, translated by C. Smith (New York: Humanities Press, 1962), pp. vii–xxi by permission of the publisher and Routledge & Kegan Paul.

and Heidegger's phenomenologies; yet the whole of *Sein und Zeit* springs from an indication given by Husserl and amounts to no more than an explicit account of the 'natürlicher Weltbegriff' or the 'Lebenswelt' which Husserl, towards the end of his life, identified as the central theme of phenomenology, with the result that the contradiction reappears in Husserl's own philosophy. The reader pressed for time will be inclined to give up the idea of covering a doctrine which says everything, and will wonder whether a philosophy which cannot define its scope deserves all the discussion which has gone on around it, and whether he is not faced rather by a myth or a fashion.

Even if this were the case, there would still be a need to understand the prestige of the myth and the origin of the fashion, and the opinion of the responsible philosopher must be that *phenomenology can be practised and identified as a manner or style of thinking, that it existed as a movement before arriving at complete awareness of itself as a philosophy.* It has been long on the way, and its adherents have discovered it in every quarter, certainly in Hegel and Kierkegaard, but equally in Marx, Nietzsche and Freud. A purely linguistic examination of the texts in question would yield no proof; we find in texts only what we put into them, and if ever any kind of history has suggested the interpretations which should be put on it, it is the history of philosophy. We shall find in ourselves, and nowhere else, the unity and true meaning of phenomenology. It is less a question of counting up quotations than of determining and expressing in concrete form this *phenomenology for ourselves* which has given a number of present-day readers the impression, on reading Husserl or Heidegger, not so much of encountering a new philosophy as of recognizing what they had been waiting for. Phenomenology is accessible only through a phenomenological method. Let us, therefore, try systematically to bring together the celebrated phenomenological themes as they have grown spontaneously together in life. Perhaps we shall then understand why phenomenology has for so long remained at an initial stage, as a problem to be solved and a hope to be realized.

It is a matter of describing, not of explaining or analysing. Husserl's first directive to phenomenology, in its early stages, to be a 'descriptive psychology', or to return to the 'things themselves', is from the start a rejection of science. I am not the outcome or the meeting-point of numerous causal agencies which determine my bodily or psychological make-up. I cannot conceive myself as nothing but a bit of the world, a mere object of biological, psychological or sociological investigation. I cannot shut myself up within the realm of science. All my knowledge of the world, even my scientific knowledge, is gained from my own particular point of view, or from some experience of the world without which the symbols of science would be meaningless. The whole universe of science is built upon the world as directly experienced, and if we want to subject science itself to rigorous scrutiny and arrive at a precise assessment of its meaning and scope, we must begin by reawakening the basic experience of the world of which science is the second-order expression. Science has not and never will have, by its nature, the same significance *qua* form of being as the world which we perceive, for the simple reason that it is a rationale or explanation of that world. I am, not a 'living creature' nor even a 'man', nor again even 'a consciousness' endowed with all the characteristics which zoology, social anatomy or inductive psychology recognize in these various products of the natural or historical process—I am the absolute source, my existence does not stem from my antecedents, from my physical and social environment; instead it moves out towards them and sustains them, for I alone bring into being for myself (and therefore into being in the only sense that the word can have for me) the tradition which I elect to carry on, or the horizon whose distance from me would be abolished—since that distance is not one of its properties—if I were not there to scan it with my gaze. Scientific points of view, according to which my existence is a moment of the world's are always both naïve and at the same time dishonest, because they take for granted, without explicitly mentioning it, the other point of view, namely that of consciousness, through which from the outset a

world forms itself round me and begins to exist for me. To return
to things themselves is to return to that world which precedes
knowledge, of which knowledge always *speaks,* and in relation
to which every scientific schematization is an abstract and derivative sign-language, as is geography in relation to the countryside
in which we have learnt beforehand what a forest, a prairie or
a river is.

This move is absolutely distinct from the idealist return to
consciousness, and the demand for a pure description excludes
equally the procedure of analytical reflection on the one hand,
and that of scientific explanation on the other. Descartes and
particularly Kant *detached* the subject, or consciousness, by
showing that I could not possibly apprehend anything as existing
unless I first of all experienced myself as existing in the act of
apprehending it. They presented consciousness, the absolute
certainty of my existence for myself, as the condition of there
being anything at all; and the act of relating as the basis of
relatedness. It is true that the act of relating is nothing if
divorced from the spectacle of the world in which relations are
found; the unity of consciousness in Kant is achieved simultaneously with that of the world. And in Descartes methodical doubt
does not deprive us of anything, since the whole world, at least
in so far as we experience it, is reinstated in the *Cogito,* enjoying
equal certainty, and simply labelled 'thought about . . .'. But the
relations between subject and world are not strictly bilateral: if
they were, the certainty of the world would, in Descartes, be
immediately given with that of the *Cogito,* and Kant would not
have talked about his 'Copernican revolution'. Analytical reflection starts from our experience of the world and goes back to
the subject as to a condition of possibility distinct from that
experience, revealing the all-embracing synthesis as that without
which there would be no world. To this extent it ceases to remain
part of our experience and offers, in place of an account, a reconstruction. It is understandable, in view of this, that Husserl,
having accused Kant of adopting a 'faculty psychologism', [Hus-
serl, LU, p. 93] should have urged, in place of a noetic analysis
which bases the world on the synthesizing activity of the subject,

his own '*noematic reflection*' which remains within the object and, instead of begetting it, brings to light its fundamental unity.

The world is there before any possible analysis of mine, and it would be artificial to make it the outcome of a series of syntheses which link, in the first place sensations, then aspects of the object corresponding to different perspectives, when both are nothing but products of analysis, with no sort of prior reality. Analytical reflection believes that it can trace back the course followed by a prior constituting act and arrive, in the "inner man"—to use Saint Augustine's expression—at a constituting power which has always been identical with that inner self. Thus reflection itself is carried away and transplanted in an impregnable subjectivity, as yet untouched by being and time. But this is very ingenuous, or at least it is an incomplete form of reflection which loses sight of its own beginning. When I begin to reflect my reflection bears upon an unreflective experience; moreover my reflection cannot be unaware of itself as an event, and so it appears to itself in the light of a truly creative act, of a changed structure of consciousness, and yet it has to recognize, as having priority over its own operations, the world which is given to the subject, because the subject is given to himself. The real has to be described, not constructed or formed. Which means that I cannot put perception into the same category as the syntheses represented by judgments, acts or predications. My field of perception is constantly filled with a play of colours, noises and fleeting tactile sensations which I cannot relate precisely to the context of my clearly perceived world, yet which I nevertheless immediately 'place' in the world, without ever confusing them with my daydreams. Equally constantly I weave dreams round things. I imagine people and things whose presence is not incompatible with the context, yet who are not in fact involved in it: they are ahead of reality, in the realm of the imaginary. If the reality of my perception were based solely on the intrinsic coherence of 'representations', it ought to be forever hesitant and, being wrapped up in my conjectures on probabilities, I ought to be ceaselessly taking apart misleading syntheses, and reinstating in reality stray phenomena which I had excluded in the first place. But this does not happen. The real is a closely woven fabric. It does not await our judgment before incorporating the most surprising phenomena, or before rejecting the most plausible figments of our imagination. Perception is not a science of the world, it is not even an act, a deliberate taking up of a position; it is the background from which all acts stand out, and is presupposed by them. The world is not an object such that I have in my possession the law of its making; it is the natural setting of, and field for, all my thoughts and all my explicit perceptions. Truth does not 'inhabit' only 'the inner man', or more accurately, there is no inner man, man is in the world, and only in the world does he know himself. When I return to myself from an excursion into the realm of dogmatic common sense or of science, I find, not a source of intrinsic truth, but a subject destined to be in the world.

All of which reveals the true meaning of the famous phenomenological reduction. There is probably no question over which Husserl has spent more time—or to which he has more often returned, since the 'problematic of reduction' occupies an important place in his unpublished work. For a long time, and even in recent texts, the reduction is presented as the return to a transcendental consciousness before which the world is spread out and completely transparent, quickened through and through by a series of apperceptions which it is the philosopher's task to reconstitute on the basis of their outcome. Thus my sensation of redness is *perceived as* the manifestation of a certain redness experienced, this in turn as the manifestation of a red surface, which is the manifestation of a piece of red cardboard, and this finally is the manifestation or outline of a red thing, namely this book. We are to understand, then, that it is the apprehension of a certain *hylè*, as indicating a phenomenon of a higher degree, the *Sinngebung,* or active meaning-giving operation which may be said to define consciousness, so that the world is nothing but 'world-as-meaning', and the phenomenological reduction is idealistic, in the sense that there is here a transcendental idealism which treats the world as an indivisible unity of value shared by Peter and Paul, in which their perspectives blend. 'Peter's consciousness' and 'Paul's consciousness' are in communication, the perception of the world 'by Peter' is not Peter's doing any more than its perception 'by Paul' is Paul's doing; in each case it is the doing of pre-personal forms of consciousness, whose communication raises no problem, since it is demanded by the very definition of consciousness, meaning or truth. In so far as I am a consciousness, that is, in so far as something has meaning for me, I am neither here nor there, neither Peter nor Paul; I am in no way distinguishable from an 'other' consciousness, since we are immediately in touch with the world and since the world is, by definition, unique, being the system in which all truths cohere. A logically consistent transcendental idealism rids the world of its opacity and its transcendence. The world is precisely that thing of which we form a representation, not as men or as empirical subjects, but in so far as we are all one light and participate in the One without destroying its unity. Analytical reflection knows nothing of the problem of other minds, or of that of the world, because it insists that with the first glimmer of consciousness there appears in me theoretically the power of reaching some universal truth, and that the other person, being equally without thisness, location or body, the Alter and the Ego are one and the same in the true world which is the unifier of minds. There is no difficulty in understanding how *I* can conceive the Other, because the I and consequently the Other are not conceived as part of the woven stuff of phenomena; they have validity rather than existence. There is nothing hidden behind these faces and gestures, no domain to which I have no access, merely a little shadow which owes its very existence to the light. For Husserl, on the contrary, it is well known that there is a problem of other people, and the *alter ego* is a paradox. If the other is truly for himself alone, beyond his being for me, and if we are for each other and not both for God, we must necessarily have some appearance for each other. He must and I must have an outer appearance, and there must be, besides the perspective of the For Oneself—my view of myself and the other's of himself—a perspective of For Others—my view of

others and theirs of me. Of course, these two perspectives, in each
one of us, cannot be simply juxtaposed, *for in that case it is not
I that the other would see, nor he that I should see.* I must be the
exterior that I present to others, and the body of the other must
be the other himself. This paradox and the dialectic of the Ego
and the Alter are possible only provided that the Ego and the
Alter Ego are defined by their situation and are not freed from
all inherence; that is, provided that philosophy does not cul-
minate in a return to the self, and that I discover by reflection
not only my presence to myself, but also the possibility of an
'outside spectator'; that is, again, provided that at the very
moment when I experience my existence—at the ultimate extremity of reflection—I fall short of the ultimate density which
would place me outside time, and that I discover within myself
a kind of internal weakness standing in the way of my being
totally individualized: a weakness which exposes me to the gaze
of others as a man among men or at least as a consciousness
among consciousnesses. Hitherto the *Cogito* depreciated the perception of others, teaching me as it did that the I is accessible
only to itself, since it defined *me* as the thought which I have of
myself, and which clearly I am alone in having, at least in this
ultimate sense. For the 'other' to be more than an empty word,
it is necessary that my existence should never be reduced to my
bare awareness of existing, but that it should take in also the
awareness that *one* may have of it, and thus include my incarnation in some nature and the possibility, at least, of a historical
situation. The *Cogito* must reveal me in a situation, and it is on
this condition alone that the transcendental subjectivity can, as
Husserl puts it, [Husserl, *Krisis* III] be an intersubjectivity. As
a meditating Ego, I can clearly distinguish from myself the
world and things, since I certainly do not exist in the way in
which things exist. I must even set aside from myself my body
understood as a thing among things, as a collection of physico-
chemical processes. But even if the *cogitatio,* which I thus discover, is without location in objective time and space, it is not
without place in the phenomenological world. The world, which I
distinguished from myself as the totality of things or of processes

linked by causal relationships, I rediscover 'in me' as the permanent horizon of all my *cogitationes* and as a dimension in relation to which I am constantly situating myself. The true *Cogito* does not define the subject's existence in terms of the thought he has of existing, and furthermore does not convert the indubitability of the world into the indubitability of thought about the world, nor finally does it replace the world itself by the world as meaning. On the contrary it recognizes my thought itself as an inalienable fact, and does away with any kind of idealism in revealing me as 'being-in-the-world'.

It is because we are through and through compounded of relationships with the world that for us the only way to become aware of the fact is to suspend the resultant activity, to refuse it our complicity (to look at it *ohne mitzumachen*, as Husserl often says), or yet again, to put it 'out of play'. Not because we reject the certainties of common sense and a natural attitude to things—they are, on the contrary, the constant theme of philosophy—but because, being the presupposed basis of any thought, they are taken for granted, and go unnoticed, and because in order to arouse them and bring them to view, we have to suspend for a moment our recognition of them. The best formulation of the reduction is probably that given by Eugen Fink, Husserl's assistant, when he spoke of 'wonder' in the face of the world. Reflection does not withdraw from the world towards the unity of consciousness as the world's basis; it steps back to watch the forms of transcendence fly up like sparks from a fire; it slackens the intentional threads which attach us to the world and thus brings them to our notice; it alone is consciousness of the world because it reveals that world as strange and paradoxical. Husserl's transcendental is not Kant's and Husserl accuses Kant's philosophy of being 'worldly', because it *makes use* of our relation to the world, which is the motive force of the transcendental deduction, and makes the world immanent in the subject, instead of *being filled with wonder* at it and conceiving the subject as a process of transcendence towards the world. All the misunderstandings with his interpreters, with the existentialist "dissidents' and finally with himself, have arisen from the fact that in order

to see the world and grasp it as paradoxical, we must break with
our familiar acceptance of it and, also, from the fact that from
this break we can learn nothing but the unmotivated upsurge of
the world. The most important lesson which the reduction teaches
us is the impossibility of a complete reduction. This is why
Husserl is constantly re-examining the possibility of the reduction. If we were absolute mind, the reduction would present no
problem. But since, on the contrary, we are in the world, since
indeed our reflections are carried out in the temporal flux on
to which we are trying to seize (since they *sich einströmen,* as
Husserl says), there is no thought which embraces all our
thought. The philosopher, as the unpublished works declare, is
a perpetual beginner, which means that he takes for granted
nothing that men, learned or otherwise, believe they know. It
means also that philosophy itself must not take itself for granted,
in so far as it may have managed to say something true; that it
is an ever-renewed experiment in making its own beginning;
that it consists wholly in the description of this beginning, and
finally, that radical reflection amounts to a consciousness of its
own dependence on an unreflective life which is its initial situation, unchanging, given once and for all. Far from being, as has
been thought, a procedure of idealistic philosophy, phenomenological reduction belongs to existential philosophy: Heidegger's
'being-in-the-world' appears only against the background of the
phenomenological reduction.

A misunderstanding of a similar kind confuses the notion
of the 'essences' in Husserl. Every reduction, says Husserl, as
well as being transcendental is necessarily eidetic. That means
that we cannot subject our perception of the world to philosophical scrutiny without ceasing to be identified with that act
of positing the world, with that interest in it which delimits us,
without drawing back from our commitment which is itself thus
made to appear as a spectacle, without passing from the *fact* of
our existence to its *nature,* from the Dasein to the Wesen. But it
is clear that the essence is here not the end, but a means, that
our effective involvement in the world is precisely what has to
be understood and made amenable to conceptualization, for it

is what polarizes all our conceptual particularizations. The need to proceed by way of essences does not mean that philosophy takes them as its object, but, on the contrary, that our existence is too tightly held in the world to be able to know itself as such at the moment of its involvement, and that it requires the field of ideality in order to become acquainted with and to prevail over its facticity. The Vienna Circle, as is well known, lays it down categorically that we can enter into relations only with meanings. For example, 'consciousness' is not for the Vienna Circle identifiable with what we are. It is a complex meaning which has developed late in time, which should be handled with care, and only after the many meanings which have contributed, throughout the world's semantic development, to the formation of its present one have been made explicit. Logical positivism of this kind is the antithesis of Husserl's thought. Whatever the subtle changes of meaning which have ultimately brought us, as a linguistic acquisition, the word and concept of consciousness, we enjoy direct access to what it designates. For we have the experience of ourselves, of that consciousness which we are, and it is on the basis of this experience that all linguistic connotations are assessed, and precisely through it that language comes to have any meaning at all for us. 'It is that as yet dumb experience . . . which we are concerned to lead to the pure expression of its own meaning.' (Husserl, CM, p. 33) Husserl's essences are destined to bring back all the living relationships of experience, as the fisherman's net draws up from the depths of the ocean quivering fish and seaweed. Jean Wahl is therefore wrong in saying that 'Husserl separates essences from existence.' The separated essences are those of language. It is the office of language to cause essences to exist in a state of separation which is in fact merely apparent, since through language they still rest upon the ante-predicative life of consciousness. In the silence of primary consciousness can be seen appearing not only what words mean, but also what things mean: the core of primary meaning round which the acts of naming and expression take shape.

Seeking the essence of consciousness will therefore not consist in developing the *Wortbedeutung* of consciousness and escaping from existence into the universe of things said; it will consist in rediscovering my actual presence to myself, the fact of my consciousness which is in the last resort what the word and the concept of consciousness mean. Looking for the world's essence is not looking for what it is as an idea once it has been reduced to a theme of discourse; it is looking for what it is as a fact for us, before any thematization. Sensationalism 'reduces' the world by noticing that after all we never experience anything but states of ourselves. Transcendental idealism too 'reduces' the world since, in so far as it guarantees the world, it does so by regarding it as thought or consciousness of the world, and as the mere correlative of our knowledge, with the result that it becomes immanent in consciousness and the aseity of things is thereby done away with. The eidetic reduction is, on the other hand, the determination to bring the world to light as it is before any falling back on ourselves has occurred, it is the ambition to make reflection emulate the unreflective life of consciousness. I am at and perceive a world. If I said, as do the sensationalists, that we have here only 'states of consciousness', and if I tried to distinguish my perceptions from my dreams with the aid of 'criteria', I should overlook the phenomenon of the world. For if I am able to talk about 'dreams' and 'reality', to bother my head about the distinction between imaginary and real, and cast doubt upon the 'real', it is because this distinction is already made by me before any analysis; it is because I have an experience of the real as of the imaginary, and the problem then becomes one not of asking how critical thought can provide for itself secondary equivalents of this distinction, but of making explicit our primordial knowledge of the 'real', of describing our perception of the world as that upon which our idea of truth is for ever based. We must not, therefore, wonder whether we really perceive a world, we must instead say: the world is what we perceive. In more general terms we must not wonder whether our self-evident truths are real truths, or whether through some perversity inherent in our minds, that which is self-evident for us might not be illusory in relation to some truth in itself. For in so far as we talk about illusion, it is because we have identified illusions, and done so solely in the light of some perception which at the same time gave assurance of its own truth. It follows that doubt, or the fear of being mistaken, testifies as soon as it arises to our power of unmasking error, and that it could never finally tear us away from truth. We are in the realm of truth and it is 'the experience of truth' which is self-evident. To seek the essence of perception is to declare that perception is, not presumed true, but defined as access to truth. So, if I now wanted, according to idealistic principles, to base this *de facto* self-evident truth, this irresistible belief, on some absolute self-evident truth, that is, on the absolute clarity which my thoughts have for me; if I tried to find in myself a creative thought which bodied forth the framework of the world or illumined it through and through, I should once more prove unfaithful to my experience of the world, and should be looking for what makes that experience possible instead of looking for what it is. The self-evidence of perception is not adequate thought or apodictic self-evidence. [There is no apodicitic self-evidence, Husserl, FTL, p. 142 says in effect.] The world is not what I think, but what I live through. I am open to the world, I have no doubt that I am in communication with it, but I do not possess it; it is inexhaustible. 'There is a world', or rather: 'There is the world'; I can never completely account for this ever-reiterated assertion in my life. This facticity of the world is what constitutes the *Weltlichkeit der Welt,* what causes the world to be the world; just as the facticity of the *cogito* is not an imperfection in itself, but rather what assures me of my existence. The eidetic method is the method of a phenomenological positivism which bases the possible on the real.

We can now consider the notion of intentionality, too often cited as the main discovery of phenomenology, whereas it is understandable only through the reduction. "All consciousness is consciousness of something'; there is nothing new in that. Kant showed, in the *Refutation of Idealism*, that inner perception is impossible without outer perception, that the world, as a collection of connected phenomena, is anticipated in the consciousness of my unity, and is the means whereby I come into being as a consciousness. What distinguishes intentionality from the Kantian relation to a possible object is that the unity of the world, before being posited by knowledge in a specific act of identification, is 'lived' as ready-made or already there. Kant himself shows in the *Critique of Judgement* that there exists a unity of the imagination and the understanding and a unity of subjects *before the object,* and that, in experiencing the beautiful, for example, I am aware of a harmony between sensation and concept, between myself and others, which is itself without any concept. Here the subject is no longer the universal thinker of a system of objects rigorously interrelated, the positing power who subjects the manifold to the law of the understanding, in so far as he is to be able to put together a world—he discovers and enjoys his own nature as spontaneously in harmony with the law of the understanding. But if the subject has a nature, then the hidden art of the imagination must condition the categorial activity. It is no longer merely the aesthetic judgement, but knowledge too which rests upon this art, an art which forms the basis of the unity of consciousness and of consciousnesses.

Husserl takes up again the *Critique of Judgement* when he talks about a teleology of consciousness. It is not a matter of duplicating human consciousness with some absolute thought which, from outside, is imagined as assigning to it its aims. It is a question of recognizing consciousness itself as a project of the world, meant for a world which it neither embraces nor possesses, but towards which it is perpetually directed—and the world as this pre-objective individual whose imperious unity decrees what knowledge shall take as its goal. This is why Husserl distinguishes between intentionality of act, which is that of our judgements and of those occasions when we voluntarily take up a position—the only intentionality discussed in the *Critique of Pure Reason*—and operative intentionality (*fungierende Intentionalität*), or that which produces the natural and antepredicative unity of the world and of our life, being apparent in our desires, our evaluations and in the landscape we see, more clearly than in objective knowledge, and furnishing the text which our knowledge tries to translate into precise language. Our relationship to the world, as it is untiringly enunciated within us, is not a thing which can be any further clarified by analysis; philosophy can only place it once more before our eyes and present it for our ratification.

Through this broadened notion of intentionality, phenomenological 'comprehension' is distinguished from traditional 'intellection', which is confined to 'true and immutable natures', and so phenomenology can become a phenomenology of origins. Whether we are concerned with a thing perceived, a historical event or a doctrine, to 'understand' is to take in the total intention—not only what these things are for representation (the 'properties' of the thing perceived, the mass of 'historical facts', the 'ideas' introduced by the doctrine)—but the unique mode of existing expressed in the properties of the pebble, the glass or the piece of wax, in all events of a revolution, in all the thoughts of a philosopher. It is a matter, in the case of each civilization, of finding the Idea in the Hegelian sense, that is, not a law of the physico-mathematical type, discoverable by objective thought, but that formula which sums up some unique manner of behaviour towards others, towards Nature, time and death: a certain way of patterning the world which the historian should be capable of seizing upon and making his own. These are the *dimensions* of history. In this context there is not a human word, not a gesture, even one which is the outcome of habit or absent-mindedness, which has not some meaning. For example, I may have been under the impression that I lapsed into silence through weariness, or some minister may have thought he had uttered merely an appropriate platitude, yet my silence or his words immediately take on a significance, because my fatigue or his falling back upon a ready-made formula are not accidental, for they express a certain lack of interest, and hence some degree of adoption of a definite position in relation to the situation.

When an event is considered at close quarters, at the moment when it is lived through, everything seems subject to chance: one man's ambition, some lucky encounter, some local circumstance or other appears to have been decisive. But chance happenings offset each other, and facts in their multiplicity coalesce and show up a certain way of taking a stand in relation to the human situation, reveal in fact an *event* which has its definite outline and about which we can talk. Should the starting-point for the understanding of history be ideology, or politics, or religion, or economics? Should we try to understand a doctrine from its overt content, or from the psychological make-up and the biography of its author? We must seek an understanding from all these angles simultaneously, everything has meaning, and we shall find this same structure of being underlying all relationships. All these views are true provided that they are not isolated, that we delve deeply into history and reach the unique core of existential meaning which emerges in each perspective. It is true, as Marx says, that history does not walk on its head, but it is also true that it does not think with its feet. Or one should say rather that it is neither its 'head' nor its 'feet' that we have to worry about, but its body. All economic and psychological explanations of a doctrine are true, since the thinker never thinks from any starting-point but the one constituted by what he is. Reflection even on a doctrine will be complete only if it succeeds in linking up with the doctrine's history and the extraneous explanations of it, and in putting back the causes and meaning of the doctrine in an existential structure. There is, as Husserl says, a 'genesis of meaning' (*Sinngenesis*) [Husserl, *FTL*, pp. 184 ff.] which alone, in the last resort, teaches us what the doctrine 'means.' Like understanding, criticism must be pursued at all levels, and naturally, it will be insufficient, for the refutation of a doctrine, to relate it to some accidental event in the author's life: its significance goes beyond, and there is no pure accident in existence or in coexistence, since both absorb random events and transmute them into the rational.

Finally, as it is indivisible in the present, history is equally so in its sequences. Considered in the light of its fundamental dimensions, all periods of history appear as manifestations of a single existence, or as episodes in a single drama—without our knowing whether it has an ending. Because we are in the world, we are *condemned to meaning*, and we cannot do or say anything without its acquiring a name in history.

Probably the chief gain from phenomenology is to have united extreme subjectivism and extreme objectivism in its notion of the world or of rationality. Rationality is precisely measured by the experiences in which it is disclosed. To say that there exists rationality is to say that perspectives blend, perceptions confirm each other, a meaning emerges. But it should not be set in a realm apart, transposed into absolute Spirit, or into a world in the realist sense. The phenomenological world is not pure being, but the sense which is revealed where the paths of my various experiences intersect, and also where my own and other people's intersect and engage each other like gears. It is thus inseparable from subjectivity and intersubjectivity, which find their unity when I either take up my past experiences in those of the present, or other people's in my own. For the first time the philosopher's thinking is sufficiently conscious not to anticipate itself and endow its own results with reified form in the world. The philosopher tries to conceive the world, others and himself and their interrelations. But the meditating Ego, the 'impartial spectator' (*uninteressierter Zuschauer*) [Husserl, CM, 6th med.] do not rediscover an already given rationality, they 'establish themselves', [*Ibid.*] and establish it, by an act of initiative which has no guarantee in being, its justification resting entirely on the effective power which it confers on us of taking our own history upon ourselves.

The phenomenological world is not the bringing to explicit expression of a pre-existing being, but the laying down of being. Philosophy is not the reflection of a pre-existing truth, but, like art, the act of bringing truth into being. One may well ask how this creation is *possible,* and if it does not recapture in things a pre-existing Reason. The answer is that the only pre-existent Logos is the world itself, and that the philosophy which brings it into visible existence does not begin by being *possible;* it is actual or real like the world of which it is a part, and no explanatory hypothesis is clearer than the act whereby we take up this unfinished world in an effort to complete and conceive it. Rationality is not a *problem.* There is behind it no unknown quantity which has to be determined by deduction, or, beginning with it, demonstrated inductively. We witness every minute the miracle of related experiences, and yet nobody knows better than we do how this miracle is worked, for we are ourselves this network of relationships. The world and reason are not problematical. We may say, if we wish, that they are mysterious, but their mystery defines them: there can be no question of dispelling it by some 'solution', it is on the hither side of all solutions. True philosophy consists in relearning to look at the world, and in this sense a historical account can give meaning to the world quite as 'deeply' as a philosophical treatise. We take our fate in our hands, we become responsible for our history through reflection, but equally by a decision on which we stake our life, and in both cases what is involved is a violent act which is validated by being performed.

Phenomenology, as a disclosure of the world, rests on itself, or rather provides its own foundation. All knowledge is sustained by a 'ground' of postulates and finally by our communication with the world as primary embodiment of rationality. Philosophy, as radical reflection, dispenses in principle with this resource. As, however, it too is in history, it too exploits the world and constituted reason. It must therefore put to itself the question which it puts to all branches of knowledge, and so duplicate itself infinitely, being, as Husserl says, a dialogue or infinite meditation, and, in so far as it remains faithful to its intention, never knowing where it is going. The unfinished nature of phenomenology and the inchoative atmosphere which has surrounded it are not to be taken as a sign of failure, they were inevitable because phenomenology's task was to reveal the mystery of the world and of reason. If phenomenology was a movement before becoming a doctrine or a philosophical system, this was attributable neither to accident, nor to fraudulent intent. It is as painstaking as the works of Balzac, Proust, Valéry or Cézanne—by reason of the same kind of attentiveness and wonder, the same demand for awareness, the same will to seize the meaning of the world or of history as that meaning comes into being. In this way it merges into the general effort of modern thought.

EXISTENCE

What [Existentialists] have in common is simply the fact that they believe that *existence* comes before *essence*—or, if you will, that we must begin from the subjective.
—Jean-Paul Sartre EXISTENTIALISM IS A HUMANISM

Yet that which, above all, 'is', is Being. Thought brings to fulfillment the relation of Being to the essence of man, it does not make or produce this relation.
—Martin Heidegger LETTER ON HUMANISM

INTRODUCTION

We have seen that in Heidegger's philosophy, the central problem becomes—and remains—the "Question of Being." But in Heidegger's early ("Existential") writings, the concept of "Being" is inseparably tied to *"human* being", and so the first question, which dominates *Being and Time,* is an analysis of the concept of "human being" (the ontology of *Dasein*). Jean-Paul Sartre shares this concern with human being, and he distinguishes (using terms borrowed from Hegel) "being-for-itself" (human consciousness) and "being-in-itself" (objects in general). Human being is marked by the dialectic amalgam of both species of being, giving man both facticity (a determinate factual nature) and *transcendence* (open possibilities for the future). In Heidegger's later works (e.g. "A Letter on Humanism," parts of which are included here), he turns against the French existentialists whom he inspired, and rejects their "humanism" in general and Sartre's existentialism in particular.

BEING-FOR-ITSELF

JEAN-PAUL SARTRE

Now the *cogito* never gives out anything other than what we ask of it. Descartes questioned it concerning its functional aspect—"*I doubt, I think*." And because he wished to pass without a conducting thread from this functional aspect to existential dialectic, he fell into the error of substance. Husserl, warned by this error, remained timidly on the plane of functional description. Due to this fact he never passed beyond the pure description of the appearance as such; he has shut himself up inside the *cogito* and deserves—in spite of his denial—to be called a phenomenalist rather than a phenomenologist. His phenomenalism at every moment borders on Kantian idealism. Heidegger, . . . begins with the existential analytic without going through the *cogito*. But since the *Dasein* has from the start been deprived of the dimension of consciousness, it can never regain this dimension. Heidegger endows human reality with a self-understanding which he defines as an "ekstatic pro-ject" of its own possibilities. It is certainly not my intention to deny the existence of this project. But how could there be an understanding which would not in itself be the consciousness (of) being understanding? This ekstatic character of human reality will lapse into a thing-like, blind in-itself unless it arises from the consciousness of ekstasis. In truth the *cogito* must be our point of departure, but we can say of it, parodying a famous saying, that it leads us only on condition that we get out of it. . . .

I think, therefore I am. What am I? A being which is not its own foundation, which qua being, could be other than it is to the extent that it does not account for its being. This is that first intuition of our own contingency which Heidegger gives as the first motivation for the passage from the un-authentic to the authentic. There is restlessness, an appeal to the conscience (*Ruf des Gewissens*), a feeling of guilt. In truth Heidegger's description shows all too clearly his anxiety to establish an ontological foundation for an Ethics with which he claims not to be concerned, as also to reconcile his humanism with the religious sense of the transcendent. The intuition of our contingency is not identical with a feeling of guilt. Nevertheless it is true that in our own apprehension of ourselves, we appear to ourselves as having the character of an unjustifiable fact. . . .

We indicated earlier that we can be nothing without playing at being. "If I am a café waiter," we said, "this can be only in the mode of *not being* one." And that is true. If I could *be* a café waiter, I should suddenly constitute myself as a contingent block of identity. And that I am not. This contingent being in-itself always escapes me. But in order that I may freely give a meaning to the obligations which my state involves, then in one sense at the heart of the for-itself, as a perpetually evanescent totality, being-in-itself must be given as the evanescent contingency of my *situation*. This is the result of the fact that while I must *play at being* a café waiter in order to be one, still it would be in vain for me to play at being a diplomat or a sailor, for I would not be one. This inapprehensible *fact* of my condition, this impalpable difference which distinguishes this drama of realization from drama pure and simple is what causes the for-itself, while choosing the *meaning* of its situation and while constituting itself as the foundation of itself in situation, *not to choose* its position. This part of my condition is what causes me to apprehend myself simultaneously as totally responsible for my being—inasmuch as I am its foundation— and yet as totally unjustifiable. Without facticity consciousness could choose its attachments to the world in the same way as the souls in Plato's *Republic* choose their condition. I could determine myself to "be born a worker" or to "be born a bourgeois." But on the other hand facticity can not constitute me as *being* a bourgeois or *being* a worker. It is not even strictly speaking a *resistance* of fact since it is only by recovering it in the substructure of the *pre-reflective cogito* that I confer on it its meaning and its resistance. Facticity is only one indication which I give myself of the being to which I must reunite myself in order to be what I am.

It is impossible to grasp facticity in its brute nudity, since all that we will find of it is already recovered and freely constructed. The simple fact "of being there," at that table, in that chair is already the pure object of a limiting-concept and as such can not be grasped. Yet it contained in my "consciousness of being-there," as its full contingency, as the nihilated in-itself on the basis of which the for-itself produces itself as consciousness of being there. The for-itself looking deep into itself as the consciousnes of being there will never discover anything in itself but *motivations;* that is, it will be perpetually referred to itself and to its constant freedom. (I am there in order to . . . *etc.*) But the contingency which paralyzes these motivations to the same degree as they totally found themselves is the facticity of the for-itself. The relation of the for-itself, which is its own foundation qua for-itself, to facticity can be correctly termed a factual necessity. It is indeed this factual necessity which Descartes and Husserl seized upon as constituting the evidence of the *cogito.* The for-itself is necessary in so far as it provides its own foundation. And this is why it is the object reflected by an apodictic intuition. I can not doubt that I am. But in so far as this for-itself as such could also not be, it has all the contingency of fact. Just as my nihilating freedom is apprehended in anguish, so the for-itself is conscious of its facticity. It has the feeling of its complete gratuity; it apprehends itself as being there *for nothing,* as being *de trop.*

* * *

This *self* with its *a priori* and historical content is the *essence* of man. Anguish as the manifestation of freedom in the face of self means that man is always separated by a nothingness from his essence. We should refer here to Hegel's statement: *"Wesen ist was gewesen ist."* Essence is what has been. Essence is everything in the human being which we can indicate by the words—that *is*. Due to this fact it is the totality of characteristics which *explain* the act. But the act is always beyond that essence; it is a human act only in so far as it surpasses every explanation which we can give of it, precisely because the very application of the formula "that is" to man causes all that is designated, *to have-been*. Man continually carries with him a pre-judicative comprehension of his essence, but due to this very fact he is separated from it by a nothingness. Essence is all that human reality apprehends in itself as *having been*.

· · ·

I emerge alone and in anguish confronting the unique and original project which constitutes my being; all the barriers, all the guard rails collapse nihilated by the consciousness of my freedom. I do not have nor can I have recourse to any value against the fact that it is I who sustain values in being. Nothing can ensure me against myself, cut off from the world and from my essence by this nothingness which I *am*. I have to realize the meaning of the world and of my essence; I make my decision concerning them—without justification and without excuse.

A LETTER ON HUMANISM.

MARTIN HEIDEGGER

If man, . . . is once again to find himself in the nearness of Being, he must first learn to exist in the nameless. He must recognize the seduction of the public, as well as the impotence of the

Reprinted from "A Letter on Humanism," translated by Edgar Lohner in Henry Aiken and William Barrett, eds. *Philosophy in the Twentieth Century*, Vol. 2 (New York: Random House, 1962), pp. 274–281. Reprinted with the permission of William Barrett, H. D. Aiken, and Harper & Row, Inc.

private. Man must, before he speaks, let himself first be claimed again by Being at the risk of having under this claim little or almost nothing to say. Only in this way will the preciousness of its essence be returned to the word, and to man the dwelling where he can live in the truth of Being.

But is there not now in this claim upon man, is there not in the attempt to make man ready for this claim, an effort in behalf of man? Where else does "Care" (*Sorge*) go, if not in the direction of bringing man back to his essence again? What else does this mean, but that man (*homo*) should become human (*humanus*)? Thus *humanitas* remains the concern of such thought; for this is humanism: to reflect and to care that man be human and not un-human, "inhuman", i.e. outside of his essence. Yet, of what does the humanity of man consist? It rests in his essence. . . .

But whence and how is the essence of man determined? Marx demands that the "human man" be known and acknowledged. He finds this man in society. The "social" man is for him the "natural" man. In "society" the "nature" of man, which means all of his "natural needs" (food, clothing, reproduction, economic sufficiency), is equally secured. The Christian sees the humanity of man, the *humanitas* of the *homo*, as the delimitation of *deitas*. He is, in the history of Grace, man as the "child of God," who hears in Christ the claim of the Father and accepts it. Man is not of this world, insofar as the "world," theoretically and Platonically understood, is nothing but a transitory passage into the other world.

Every humanism is either founded in a metaphysics or is converted into the basis for a metaphysics. Every determination of the essence of man that presupposes the interpretation of beings without asking the question of the truth of Being, be it wittingly or not, is metaphysical. Therefore, and precisely in view of the way in which the essence of man is determined, the characteristic of all metaphysics shows itself in the fact that it is "humanistic." For this reason every humanism remains metaphysical. Humanism not only does not ask, in determining the humanity of man, for the relation of Being to the essence of man, but humanism even impedes this question, since, by virtue of its derivation from metaphysics it neither knows nor understands it. Inversely, the necessary and the proper way of asking the question of the truth of Being, in metaphysics but forgotten by it, can only come to light, if amidst the domination of metaphysics the question is asked: "What is metaphysics?" First of all each question of "Being," even that of the truth of Being, must be presented as a "metaphysical" question.

The first humanism, the Roman, and all the humanisms that have since appeared, presupposes as self-evident the most general "essence" of man. Man is considered as the *animal rationale*. This determination is not only the Latin translation of the Greek ξωον λογον εχον but a metaphysical interpretation. This essential determination of man is not wrong, but it is conditioned by metaphysics. Its essential extraction and not merely its limit has, however, become questionable in *Sein und Zeit*. This questionableness is first of all given to thought as what has to be thought, but not in such a way as to be devoured by an empty skepticism.

Certainly metaphysics posits beings in their Being and so thinks of the Being of beings. But it does not discriminate between the two. Metaphysics does not ask for the truth of Being itself. Nor does it ever ask, therefore, in what way the essence of man belongs to the truth of Being. This question metaphysics has not only not asked up to now, but this question cannot be treated by metaphysics as metaphysics. Being still waits for Itself to become memorable to man. . . .

Metaphysics shuts itself off from the simple essential certitude that man is essentially only in his essence, in which he is claimed by Being. Only from this claim "has" he found wherein his essence dwells. Only from this dwelling "has" he "language" as the home which preserves the ecstatic for his essence. The standing in the clearing of Being I call the ex-sistence of man. Only man has this way to be. Ex-sistence, so understood, is not only the basis of the possibility of reason, *ratio*, but ex-sistence is that, wherein the essence of man preserves the source that determines him.

Ex-sistence can only be said of the essence of man, i.e. only of the human way "to be"; for only man, as far as we know, is admitted into the destiny of ex-sistence. Thus ex-sistence can never be thought of as a specific way, amongst other ways, of a living being, so long as man is destined to think of the essence of his Being and not merely to report theories of nature and history about his composition and activity. Thus all that we attribute to man as *animalitas* in comparing him to the "animal" is grounded in the essence of ex-sistence. The body of man is something essentially different from the animal organism. The error of biologism has not yet been overcome by the fact that one affixes the soul to corporeal man and the mind to the soul and the existential to the mind, and more strongly than ever before preaches the appreciation of the mind, in order that everything may then fall back into the experience of life, with the admonitory assurance that thought will destroy by its rigid concepts the stream of life and the thought of Being will deform existence. That physiology and physiological chemistry can scientifically examine man as an organism, does not prove that in this "organic" disposition, i.e. in the body scientifically explained, the essence of man rests. This has as little value as the opinion that the essence of nature is contained in atomic energy. It may very well be that nature hides its essence in that aspect of which human technology has taken possession. As little as the essence of man consists of being an animal organism, so little can this insufficient determination of the essence of man be eliminated and compensated for by the fact that man is equipped with an immortal soul or with the capability of reason or with the character of a person. Each time the essence is overlooked and, no doubt, on the basis of the same metaphysical design.

All that man is, i.e. in the traditional language of metaphysics the "essence" of man, rests in his ex-sistence. But ex-sistence, so thought of, is not identical with the traditional concept of *existentia*, which signifies actuality in contrast to essentia as possibility. In *Sein und Zeit* (p. 42) is the sentence, italicized: "The "essence" of being-there (*Dasein*) lies in its existence." Here, however, this is not a matter of opposing *existentia* and *essentia*,

because these two metaphysical determinations of Being have not
yet been placed in question, let alone their relationship. The
sentence contains even less a general statement about "being-
there," insofar as this term (brought into usage in the eighteenth
century for the word "object") is to express the metaphysical
concept of the actuality of the actual. The sentence says rather:
man is essentially such that he is "Here" (*Da*), i.e. within the
clearing of Being. This "Being" of the Here, and only this, has
the basic trait of ex-sistence: i.e. it stands outside itself within
the truth of Being. The ecstatic essence of man rests in the ex-
sistence that remains different from the metaphysically conceived
existentia. Medieval philosophy conceived this *existentia* as *actualitas*. Kant presents *existentia* as actuality in the sense of the
objectivity of experience. Hegel determines *existentia* as the self-
knowing idea of the absolute subjectivity. Nietzsche understands
existentia as the eternal return of the same. Whether, however,
through *existentia*, in its various interpretations as actuality,
different only at first glance, the Being of the stone, or even life
as the Being of plants and animals, has been sufficiently thought
about, remains an open question here. In each case animals are
as they are, without their standing—from their Being as such—
in the truth of Being and preserving in such standing what is
essentially their Being. Presumably, animals are the most difficult
of all entities for us to think of, because we are, on the one hand,
most akin to them and, on the other hand, they are, at the same
time separated from our ex-sistential essence by an abyss. And
against this it might seem that the essence of the divine is much
nearer us than the strangeness of animals, nearer in an essential
distance, which as distance is much more familiar to our existential essence than the barely conceivable abysmal corporeal
kinship to the animal. Such reflections cast a strange light on the
current and therefore still premature designation of man as an
animal rationale. Because plants and animals, although bound to
their environment, are never freely placed in the clearing of
Being—and only this clearing is "world"—they have no language. But it is not because they are without language that they
find themselves hanging worldless in their environment. Yet in

the word "environment" is concentrated all the enigma of the animal. Language is in its essence not utterance of an organism nor is it expression of an animal. Thus it is never thought of with exactness in its symbolical or semantic character. Language is the clearing-and-concealing advent of Being itself.

Ex-sistence, ecstatically thought of, does not coincide with *existentia* either in regard to content or form. Ex-sistence means substantially the emerging into the truth of Being. *Existentia* (existence) means, however, *actualitas,* actuality in contrast to mere possibility as idea. Ex-sistence states the characteristic of man as he is in the destiny of truth. *Existentia* remains the name for the actualization of something-that-is, is an instance of its idea. The phrase, "man exists," does not answer the question of whether there are actually men or not; it answers the question of the "essence" of man. We usually put this question in an equally unsuitable way, whether we ask what man is or who he is. For, in the Who or What we are already on the lookout for something like a person or an object. Yet the personal, no less than the objective, misses and obstructs at the same time all that is essentially ex-sistence in its historical Being. Therefore, the quoted phrase in *Sein und Zeit* (p. 52) deliberately puts the word "essence" in quotation marks. This indicates that the "essence" is not now determined either from the *esse essentiae* or from the *esse existentiae,* but from the ec-static nature of "being-there." Insofar as he ex-sists, man endures the "being-there" by taking the There as the clearing of Being within his "care." The *Dasein* itself, however, is essentially the "thrown" (*geworfene*). It is essentially in the cast (*Wurf*) of Being, a destiny that destines, projects a destiny.

Sartre formulates, on the other hand, the basic principle of existentialism as this: existence precedes essence, whereby he understands *existentia* and *essentia* in the sense of metaphysics, which since Plato has said *essentia* precedes *existentia.* Sartre reverses this phrasing. But the reversal of a metaphysical phrase remains a metaphysical phrase. As such it remains with metaphysics in the oblivion of the truth of Being. For though philosophy may determine the relationship between *essentia* and *existentia* in the sense of the controversy of the Middle Ages or in the sense of Leibniz or others, one must first of all ask, through what destiny of Being this difference in Being as *esse essentiae* and *esse existentiae* precedes thought. It remains to be considered why this question about the destiny of Being has never been asked and why it could never be thought. Or isn't this a sign of the oblivion of Being that there is this difference between *essentia* and *existentia?* We may suppose that this destiny does not lie in a mere neglect by human thought, let alone in an inferior capacity of earlier western thought. The difference— hidden in its essential source—between *essentia* (essentiality) and *existentia* (actuality) dominates the destiny of Western history and of all the history determined by Europe.

Sartre's key phrase on the superiority of *existentia* over *essentia* undoubtedly justifies the name "existentialism" as a suitable title for this philosophy. But the key phrase of "existentialism" has not the least thing in common with the same phrase in *Sein und Zeit;* apart from the fact that in *Sein und Zeit* a phrase about the relationship between *essentia* and *existentia* cannot yet be expressed, for there we are concerned with settling something preliminary. This, as can be seen from what has been said, is done there rather clumsily. What is yet to be said today might, perhaps, become an impulse to guide the essence of man to attend in thought to the dimension of the truth of Being, which pervades it. Yet even this can only happen for the dignity of Being and for the benefit of *Dasein* which man endures in existing; not for the sake of man, but that through his works civilization and culture may be vindicated. . . .

The unique thought that *Sein und Zeit* attempts to express, wants to achieve, is something simple. As such, Being remains mysterious, the plain closeness of an unobtrusive rule. This closeness is essentially language itself. Yet the language is not merely language, insofar as we imagine it at the most as the unity of sound-form (script), melody and rhythm and meaning. We think of sound-form and script as the body of the word; of melody and rhythm as the soul and of meaning as the mind of language. We generally think of language as corresponding to the essence of man, insofar as this essence is represented as *animal rationale*, i.e. as the unity of body-soul-mind. But as in the *humanitas* of the *homo animalis* ex-sistence remains concealed and through this the relation of the truth of Being to man, so does the metaphysical-animal interpretation of language conceal its essence from the point of view of the history of Being. According to this, language is the house of Being, owned and pervaded by Being. Therefore, the point is to think of the essence of language in its correspondence to Being and, what is more, as this very correspondence, i.e., the dwelling of man's essence.

Man, however, is not only a living being, who besides other faculties possesses language. Language is rather the house of Being, wherein living, man ex-sists, while he, guarding it, belongs to the truth of Being. . . .

THE LIFE WORLD

Consciousness is in the first place not a matter of 'I think that' but of 'I can'.

—Maurice Merleau-Ponty
THE PHENOMENOLOGY OF PERCEPTION

INTRODUCTION

In his last works, Husserl placed increasing emphasis on what he calls the *Lebenswelt,* the world of lived experience. There is some debate as to the extent of this conversion in Husserl, but it is clear that this theme is central to the work of Heidegger, Sartre, and Merleau-Ponty. Here Aron Gurwitsch outlines Husserl's conception of the *Lebenswelt.* Heidegger replaces the philosophical notion of the "thing" with the prior and more primitive idea of the "tool" which is not known but employed. Richard Schmitt provides us with an analysis of Heidegger's argument. Merleau-Ponty argues that our lived experience begins with our experience of our body and that the Husserlian notion of "intentionality" (primarily a cognitive notion) must be replaced by the more primitive notion of "motility." Consciousness is *essentially* bodily movement as well as awareness of things.

THE LAST WORK OF EDMUND HUSSERL:
THE *LEBENSWELT*

ARON GURWITSCH

Under the impact of modern science as inaugurated by
Galileo, the *Lebenswelt*—i.e., the world of common experience—
has been superseded by the objectively true and valid universe of
science which, in the thinking of modern Western man, passes
for reality. Whereas no "objective" entity—objective in the
sense of science—is, in principle, accessible to direct and immediate experience in the proper sense of the term, the *Lebenswelt*
does present itself, actually or virtually, in such experience,
perceptual experience as well as its derivative forms like memory,
representation, imagination, etc. Since the universe of science
proves to be a tissue of ideal constructs, or, as Husserl puts it,
a theoretico-logical superstructure, its conception and apprehension is of the same nature as that of any infinite ideas, e.g., geometrical ones. The construction of the universe of science involves, as a mental accomplishment, certain specific operations,
especially that of idealization. Obviously, idealization presupposes materials to be idealized. By virtue of its intrinsic sense as
a superstructure, the universe of science requires a foundation
upon which it rests and upon which it is constructed. This foundation is no other than the *Lebenswelt* and the evidence of common experience—the term "evidence" denoting, as always with
Husserl, bodily presence or self-presentation of the object
in question. All theoretical truth—logical, mathematical, scientific—finds its ultimate validation and justification in evidences
which concern occurrences in the *Lebenswelt*. If Husserl assigns
to the evidences of the *Lebenswelt* a privileged status with respect

Reprinted from *Studies in Phenomenology and Psychology* (Evanston,
Ill.: Northwestern University Press, 1966), pp. 418–421, by permission of
the publisher.

to those of objective and scientific theory, it is in the sense of the latter being founded upon the former. That is to say, the mental operations, whose products and constituted correlates objective theory and the objective universe of science are, presuppose those acts of consciousnes through which the *Lebenswelt* appears as ever-present and pre-given, i.e., as existing independently of, and prior to, all scientific activity. For an ultimate clarification of the universe of science, one has, therefore, to turn to the *Lebenswelt* and to bring out the role which it plays, in several respects, in the construction and constitution of science.

Radical philosophical reflection must begin by rendering explicit the universal "presupposition" which underlies all our life and all our activities. This "presupposition" is the unquestioned and even unformulated acceptance of the world in which we find ourselves and with which we always have a certain familiarity. At every moment of our life, we concern ourselves in some mode or other, with things, animals, fellow-men, etc., which present themselves as mundane existents, and we conceive of ourselves as also belonging to the world. None of those existents is ever given in isolation. Every one of them refers to a context into which it is inserted; it appears within an all-encompassing and indefinitely extended horizon: the *world-horizon.* Unlike particular mundane existents which may occasionally appear and disappear, the world is continually present to our mind as the universal field of all our actual and possible activities of any nature whatever. If the world is always there as pre-given, if living means living in the world, it is because the world announces itself along with the appearance of every particular mundane existent with which we might be dealing. The explicit and inarticulate awareness of the world pervades all our activities and enters into them as their most general, though unformulated, "premise" or "presupposition." Correspondingly, the world, silently accepted as a matter of course, proves to be the ground upon which we pursue all our activities, whatever their orientation.

To be sure, the world includes nature. The nature here in

question is obviously nature as given in direct and immediate experience and not the idealized nature of physics. However, the world comprises more than mere nature. Among the existents by which we find ourselves surrounded, there are not only natural things—i.e., objects which may exhaustively be described by indicating their color, shape, size, weight, etc.—but also instruments, books, objects of art, and so on: in short, objects which have human significance, serve human ends and purposes, satisfy human desires and needs. Because the world contains objects of this kind and, therefore, proves to be the frame within which we lead our human existence, we speak of it as our *Lebenswelt*.

Within the *Lebenswelt*, we encounter our fellow-men and take it for granted that they not only exist in the world but are also aware of it, that they are confronted with the same things and objects as we are, though to each one of us, depending upon his point of view, the objects and the world at large may and do appear under varying aspects and perspectives. It is one of the unquestioned and even unformulated certainties of common experience that the world is one and the same for all of us, a common intersubjective world.

Encountering our fellow-men in the common world, we may adopt with regard to them, and they with regard to us, the attitude of detached and disinterested observers, or else we may become involved with one another and enter into the manifold relationships of cooperation and collaboration. We then not only live in the same world but live, function, and operate in it together and corporately; we interlock and interlink our intentions, designs, and activities with theirs in thoroughgoing mutuality and interplay. If on account of its reference to human life and existence the world assumes the character of a *Lebenswelt*, the reference is not only to individuals but also, and even primarily, to a historical community whose societal life consists in the interrelatedness and interplay of thought and action in various forms. *The term* Lebenswelt *has essentially a historico-social connotation*: a *Lebenswelt* is relative to a certain society at a given moment of its history; it must be taken as it is conceived by the historical community whose world it is—e.g., in mythico-magical interpretation, as in the case of societies and civilizations which had not yet been influenced by the Greek idea of philosophy and θεωρια. Whether we happen to act alone or, cooperate with others, engage in common pursuits, the things and objects with which we are confronted as well as our own plans and designs, finally the world as a whole, appear to us in the light of beliefs, opinions, conceptions, certainties, etc. that prevail in the community to which we belong. Community may here be understood in the largest and most encompassing sense so as to denote the whole historical civilization to which we belong or in the more restricted sense of a special group within a given society, e.g., the group of contemporary scientists, doctors, scholars, artists, philosophers, etc. The *Lebenswelt* proves to be the ground of our existence, a ground which is accepted as a matter of course, as pre-given and existing independently of, and previous to, all our activities, individual as well as collective, and which these activities presuppose for their pursuit. Upon this ground, common to all of us, we meet one another as mundane existents among mundane existents. Besides being *objects in the Lebenswelt*, we are at the same time *subjects with respect to the Lebenswelt*, so far as it derives its meaning and the sense of its existence from our collective mental life, from our acts (concatenated and interlocked with those of our fellow-men) of perceiving, experiencing, reasoning, purposefully acting, etc. Collective accomplishments become part and parcel of the *Lebenswelt* which not only is as it is conceived of by the respective community but also comprises all communal creations, both material and mental. In and through the life of a community, the interplay of the activities of its members, its *Lebenswelt* undergoes transformation, change, reinterpretation, etc. Reflecting upon this, we become aware of the *Lebenswelt* as a mental acquisition (*geistiger Erwerb*), as having grown and continuing to grow: i.e., we come to disclose its historical character and its relativity to a living community.

THE BEING OF ENTITIES ENCOUNTERED IN THE ENVIRONMENT

MARTIN HEIDEGGER

The Being of those entities which we encounter as closest to us can be exhibited phenomenologically if we take as our clue our everyday Being-in-the-world, which we also call our *"dealings" in* the world and *with* entities within-the-world. Such dealings have already dispersed themselves into manifold ways of concern. The kind of dealing which is closest to us is as we have shown, not a bare perceptual cognition, but rather that kind of concern which manipulates things and puts them to use; and this has its own kind of 'knowledge'. The phenomenological question applies in the first instance to the Being of those entities which we encounter in such concern. To assure the kind of seeing which is here required, we must first make a remark about method.

In the disclosure and explication of Being, entities are in every case our preliminary and our accompanying theme [das Vor-und-Mitthematische]; but our real theme is Being. In the domain of the present analysis, the entities we shall take as our preliminary theme are those which show themselves in our concern with the environment. Such critics are not thereby objects for knowing the 'world' theoretically; they are simply what gets used, what gets produced, and so forth. As entities so encountered, they become the preliminary theme for the purview of a 'knowing' which, as phenomenological, looks primarily towards Being, and which, in thus taking Being as its theme, takes these entities as its accompanying theme. This phenomenological interpretation is accordingly not a way of knowing those characteristics of entities which themselves are [seiender Beschaffenheiten des Seienden]; it is rather a determination of the structure of the Being which entities possess. But as an investigation of Being, it brings to completion, autonomously and explicitly, that understanding of Being which belongs already to Dasein and which 'comes alive' in any of its dealings with entities. Those entities which serve phenomenologically as our preliminary theme—in this case, those which are used or which are to be found in the course of production—become accessible when we put ourselves into the position of concerning ourselves with them in some such way. Taken strictly, this talk about "putting ourselves into such a position" [Sichversetzen] is misleading; for the kind of Being which belongs to such concernful dealings is not one into which we need to put ourselves first. This is the way in which everyday Dasein always *is:* when I open the door, for instance, I use the latch. The achieving of phenomenological access to the entities which we encounter, consists rather in thrusting aside our interpretative tendencies, which keep thrusting themselves upon us and running along with us, and which conceal not only the phenomenon of such 'concern', but even more those entities themselves *as* encountered of their own accord *in* our concern with them. These entangling errors become plain if in the course of our investigation we now ask which entities shall be taken as our preliminary theme and established as the pre-phenomenal basis for our study.

One may answer: "Things." But with this obvious answer we have perhaps already missed the pre-phenomenal basis we are seeking. For in addressing these entities as 'Things' (*res*), we have tacitly anticipated their ontological character. When analysis starts with such entities and goes on to inquire about Being, what it meets is Thinghood and Reality. Ontological explication discovers, as it proceeds, such characteristics of Being as substantiality, materiality, extendedness, side-by-side-ness, and so forth. But even pre-ontologically, in such Being as this, the entities which we encounter in concern are proximally hidden. When one designates Things as the entities that are 'proximally given', one goes ontologically astray, even though ontically one has something else in mind. What one really has in mind remains undetermined. But suppose one characterizes these 'Things' as Things 'invested with value'? What does "value" mean ontologically? How are we to categorize this 'investing' and Being-invested? Disregarding the obscurity of this structure of investiture with value, have we thus met that phenomenal characteristic of Being which belong to what we encounter in our concernful dealings?

The Greeks had an appropriate term for 'Things': πραγματα —that is to say, that which one has to do with in one's concernful dealings (πραξις). But ontologically, the specifically 'pragmatic' character of the πραγματα is just what the Greeks left in obscurity; they thought of these 'proximally' as 'mere Things'. We shall call those entities which we encounter in concern *"equipment"*. In our dealings we come across equipment for writing, sewing, working, transportation, measurement. The kind of Being which equipment possesses must be exhibited. The clue for doing this lies in our first defining what makes an item of equipment—namely, its equipmentality.

Taken strictly, there 'is' no such thing as *an* equipment. To the Being of any equipment there always belongs a totality of equipment, in which it can be this equipment that it is. Equipment is essentially 'something in-order-to . . .' ["etwas um-zu . . ."]. A totality of equipment is constituted by various ways of the 'in-order-to', such as serviceability, conduciveness, usability, manipulability.

In the 'in-order-to' as a structure there lies an *assignment* or *reference* of something to something. Only in the analyses which are to follow can the phenomenon which this term "assignment" indicates be made visible in its ontological genesis. Provisionally, it is enough to take a look phenomenally at a manifold of such assignments. Equipment—in accordance with its equipmentality —always is *in terms of* [*aus*] its belonging to other equipment: ink-stand, pen, ink, paper, blotting pad, table, lamp, furniture, windows, doors, room. These 'Things' never show themselves proximally as they are for themselves, so as to add up to a sum of *realia* and fill up a room. What we encounter as closest to us (though not as something taken as a theme) is the room; and we encounter it not as something 'between four walls' in a geometrical spatial sense, but as equipment for residing. Out of this the 'arrangement' emerges, and it is in this that any 'individual' item of equipment shows itself. *Before* it does so, a totality of equipment has already been discovered.

Equipment can genuinely show itself only in dealings cut to its own measure (hammering with a hammer, for example) ; but in such dealings an entity of this kind is not *grasped* thematically as an occurring Thing, nor is the equipment-structure known as such even in the using. The hammering does not simply have knowledge about [um] the hammer's character as equipment, but it has appropriated this equipment in a way which could not possibly be more suitable. In dealings such as this, where something is put to use, our concern subordinates itself to the 'in-order-to" which is constitutive for the equipment we are employing at the time; the less we just stare at the hammer-Thing, and the more we seize hold of it and use it, the more primordial does our relationship to it become, and the more unveiledly is it encountered at that which it is—as equipment. The hammering itself uncovers the specific 'manipulability' ["Handlichkeit"] of the hammer. The kind of Being which equipment possesses—in which it manifests itself in its own right—we call *"readiness-to-hand"* [*Zuhandenheit*]. Only because equipment has *this* 'Being-in-itself' and does not merely occur, it is manipulable in the broadest sense and at our disposal. No matter how sharply we just *look* [Nur-noch-*hinsehen*] at the 'outward appearance' ["Aussehen]" of Things in whatever form this takes, we cannot discover anything ready-to-hand. If we look at Things just 'theoretically', we can get along without understanding readiness-to-hand. But when we deal with them by using them and manipulating them, this activity is not a blind one; it has its own kind of sight, by which our manipulation is guided and from which it acquires its specific Thingly character. Dealings with equipment subordinate themselves to the manifold assignments of the 'in-order-to'. And the sight with which they thus accommodate themselves is *circumspection*.

'Practical' behaviour is not 'atheoretical' in the sense of

"sightlessness". The way it differs from theoretical behaviour does not lie simply in the fact that in theoretical behaviour one observes, while in practical behaviour one *acts* [*gehandelt* wird], and that action must employ theoretical cognition if it is not to remain blind; for the fact that observation is a kind of concern is just as primordial as the fact that action has *its own* kind of sight. Theoretical behaviour is just looking, without circumspection. But the fact that this looking is non-circumspective does not mean that it follows no rules: it constructs a canon for itself in the form of *method*.

The ready-to-hand is not grasped theoretically at all, nor is it itself the sort of thing that circumspection takes proximally as a circumspective theme. The peculiarity of what is proximally ready-to-hand is that, in its readiness-to-hand, it must, as it were, withdraw [zurückzuziehen] in order to be ready-to-hand quite authentically. That with which our everyday dealings proximally dwell is not the tools themselves [die Werkzeuge selbst]. On the contrary, that which we concern ourselves primarily is the work —that which is to be produced at the time; and this is accordingly ready-to-hand too. The work bears with it that referential totality within which the equipment is encountered.

·   ·   ·

The kind of Being which belongs to these entities is readiness-to-hand. But this characteristic is not to be understood as merely a way of taking them, as if we were talking such 'aspects' into the 'entities' which we proximally encounter, or as if some world-stuff which is proximally present-at-hand in itself were 'given subjective colouring' in this way. Such an Interpretation would overlook the fact that in this case these entities would have to be understood and discovered beforehand as something purely present-at-hand, and must have priority and take the lead in the sequence of those dealings with the 'world' in which something is discovered and made one's own. But this already runs counter to the ontological meaning of cognition, which we have exhibited as a *founded* mode of Being-in-the-world. To lay bare what is just present-at-hand and no more, cognition must first penetrate *beyond* what is ready-to-hand in our concern. *Readiness-to-hand is the way in which entities as they are 'in themselves' are defined ontologico-categorially.* Yet only by reason of something present-at-hand, 'is there' anything ready-to-hand. Does it follow, however, granting this thesis for the nonce, that readiness-to-hand is ontologically founded upon presence-at-hand?

To the everydayness of Being-in-the-world there belong certain modes of concern. These permit the entities with which we concern ourselves to be encountered in such a way that the worldly character of what is within-the-world comes to the fore. When we concern ourselves with something, the entities which are most closely ready-to-hand may be met as something unusable, not properly adapted for the use we have decided upon. The tool turns out to be damaged, or the material unsuitable. In each of these cases *equipment* is here, ready-to-hand. We discover its unusability, however, not by looking at it and establishign its properties, but rather by the circumspection of the dealings in which we use it. When its unusability is thus discovered, equipment becomes conspicuous. This *conspicuousness* presents the ready-to-hand equipment as in a certain un-readiness-to-hand. But this implies that what cannot be used just lies there; it shows itself as an equipmental Thing which looks so and so, and which, in its readiness-to-hand as looking that way, has constantly been present-at-hand too. Pure presence-at-hand announces itself in such equipment, but only to withdraw to the readiness-to-hand of something with which one concerns oneself—that is to say, of the sort of thing we find when we put it back into repair. This presence-at-hand of something that cannot be used is still not devoid of all readiness-to-hand whatsoever; equipment which is present-at-hand *in this way* is still not just a Thing which occurs somewhere. The damage to the equipment is still not a mere alteration of a Thing—not a change of properties which just occurs in something present-at-hand.

In our concernful dealings, however, we not only come up against unusable things *within* what is ready-to-hand already: we also find things which are missing—which not only are not 'handy' ["handlich"] but are not to 'hand' ["zur Hand"] at all. . . .

In our dealings with the world of our concern, the un-ready-to-hand can be encountered not only in the sense of that which is unusable or simply missing, but as something un-ready-to-hand which is *not* missing at all and *not* unusable, but which 'stands in the way' of our concern.

• • •

The structure of the Being of what is ready-to-hand as equipment is determined by references or assignments. In a peculiar and obvious manner, the 'Things' which are closest to us are 'in themselves' ["Ansich"]; and they are encountered as 'in themselves' in the concern which makes use of them without noticing them explicitly—the concern which can come up against something unusable. When equipment cannot be used, this implies that the constitutive assignment of the "in-order-to" to a "towards-this" has been disturbed. The assignments themselves are not observed; they are rather 'there' when we concernfully submit ourselves to them [Sichstellen unter sie]. But *when an assignment has been disturbed*—when something is unusable for some purpose—then the assignment becomes explicit. Even now, of course, it has not become explicit as an ontological structure; but it has become explicit ontically for the circumspection which comes up against the damaging of the tool. When an assignment to some particular "towards-this" has been thus circumspectively aroused, we catch sight of the "towards-this" itself, and along with it everything connected with the work—the whole 'workshop'—as that wherein concern always dwells. The context of equipment is lit up, not as something never seen before, but as a totality constantly sighted beforehand in circumspection. With this totality, however, the world announces itself.

• • •

Being-in-the-world, according to our Interpretation hitherto, amounts to a non-thematic circumspective absorption in references or assignments constitutive for the readiness-to-hand of a totality of equipment. Any concern is already as it is, because of some familiarity with the world. In this familiarity Dasein can lose itself in what it encounters within-the-world and be fascinated with it. What is it that Dasein is familiar with? Why can the worldly character of what is within-the-world be lit up? The presence-at-hand of entities is thrust to the fore by the possible breaks in that referential totality in which circumspection 'operates'; how are we to get a closer understanding of this totality?

HEIDEGGER'S ANALYSIS OF "TOOL"

RICHARD SCHMITT

Unlike many contemporary philosophers, Heidegger does not believe that he is ready to proceed with concrete explications or analyses of 'person' before having reflected about the concept of 'thing' (in the sense in which persons are not things). He has several reasons for choosing this starting point for his analyses. He believes that there are two different senses of 'thing'. Moreover, a good deal of philosophical discussion in the past has approached the question of what persons are via questions about human knowers. Persons were discussed in relations to things. What we say about persons, therefore, depends (or may depend) on what kinds of relations we claim to find between persons and things, and that, in turn, depends (or may depend) on whether there are things in more than one sense of 'thing'. If all things are things in the sense of 'material object' then all relations between persons and things are either causal or spatio-temporal relations—for those are the only real relations which material objects can sustain—or they are intentional relations—relations which are independent of the existence of the material object.

Reprinted from *The Monist,* Vol. 49, No. 1 (1965), La Salle, Illinois, with the permission of the author and publisher and their approval of editing.

This implies that all human intercourse with things as, e.g., using, making, knowing, can be analysed into causal-plus-intentional relations. As I shall have occasion to show below, this engenders many of the familiar epistemological puzzles. At the same time it commits one to a specific analysis of person, one in which using a tool (for instance) is to know certain rules (the intentional relation to the tool) plus performing certain bodily movements (the causal relation to the tool). This sort of analysis, as we shall see, commits one to Cartesian dualism. We must therefore consider whether the relations sustained by persons are not much more varied. This requires that we consider the relata of these varied relations, specifically, whether there are things in more than one sense of that term. Heidegger believes that there are things in two different senses.

I

Heidegger marks the distinction which he wants to draw by introducing two technical expressions, 'being on hand' (*vorhanden*) and 'being at hand' (*zuhanden*). The former applies to what philosophers have, traditionally, called 'material objects'. It is true, for instance, of something that it is a stone if it has certain properties—and is located somewhere in geometrical space. A list of its properties together with a statement of its location describes the stone. [Heidegger, BT, pp. 67–68] If someone asks 'what is it for?' we may reject the question as inapplicable by saying "it isn't for anything; it's just a stone." That kind of things are called 'at hand' about which the question 'what is it for?' cannot be refused in the same way. ["assignment or reference" in Macquarrie and Robinson translation] Suppose I describe a hammer to you. I cannot say, if you ask me what the hammer is for, that it isn't for anything because "it's just a hammer." Hammers are tools, and tools and all kinds of 'gear' are examples of the second sense of 'thing' which Heidegger sets off by means of the expression 'being at hand'.

Heidegger's term 'gear' (*Zeug*) ["Equipment" in Macquarrie and Robinson translation] is extended beyond its ordinary use for technical purposes. It is supposed to embrace all things of which we can say that they are 'for' something. This does not only include tools, implements, utensils, instruments, equipment, etc. It also includes materials, stuff, ingredients, raw-materials, media, etc. This vagueness is not, I think, fatal here. The central point, that things which can be said to be for something are things in a different sense of 'thing' from those of which this cannot be said, can still be brought out and argued. It is important, however, to insist that not everything that we may be inclined to call a 'thing' can be said either truly or falsely to be for something. A distinction must be drawn, in other words, between, say, tools which are not 'good for' anything at the moment because they are broken or "in the way" and a glacial boulder on a mountain pass to which the question 'what is it for?' is not applicable. Only the boulder and things like it are 'on hand'. The tool for which we have no use at this moment is still 'at hand', it is still a thing in the sense of 'gear'.

The different sorts of things which are collected under the term 'gear' are for something in different ways. Since there is no space for discussing each of these different sorts of gear individually, I shall limit this discussion to tools. Heidegger's claim, however, is that whatever is true of 'thing' in the sense in which tools are things is also true of all the other sorts of gear.

If we are going to make the applicability of the question 'what is it for?' the mark of that sense of 'thing' which is alleged to be different from the sense in which material objects are things, we must make clearer under what conditions that question applies. It is easy to see that possession of the kinds of properties possessed by material objects—color, shape, size, tactile qualities, location—is not a sufficient condition for making the question 'what is it for?' applicable. Stones, or clouds, or streaks of dirt on the window pane possess those properties but cannot be said to be for anything. Nor does the possession of a *particular* set of properties constitute a sufficient condition for being for anything in particular. To say that 'this hammer is for hammering' is to say more than that the hammer has certain observable properties. For suppose that a hammer survives a nuclear holocaust and finds its way into a museum 50,000 years from now. Suppose that no one knows what sort of thing it is. The hammer may still

have all the observable properties it has now, but it isn't for anything anymore because no one knows what to do with it. Suppose,
alternatively, that some manuals of carpentry have survived
together with the hammer. The archeologists know that this
object was called 'a hammer'. They even know what it was used
for. They might then say "hammers were used for hammering."
But to the question 'what is it for?' they would have to answer
"It isn't for anything. It is part of our collection of American
artifacts."

This brings up the possibility that for anything to 'be for'
something, in the sense of having 'a use' or 'a function' is to be
related to persons who use that thing. Hammers are for hammering because that is what we use them for. But it is false that it is
a sufficient condition for hammers being for hammering that
they are *actually* used for that. A hammer is a hammer even if
it is not, in fact, being used. Nor is it a hammer only if it has,
at some time, been used for hammering. The makers of hammers
are not misusing the word 'hammer' when they sell their products
as hammers, although these things have never been used for hammering. We can at best make a more modest claim and say that
hammers are for hammering, if and only if, hammers, when used
at all, are used for that.

But even that claim is false. Hammers are used for all kinds
of things. They are used as weapons. Their handles are used to
poke things. They are used to prop up things. These are uses for
something which hammers are not for. Tools may be, and often
are, misused in this way. In fact, to say that hammers are for
hammering would be pointless if it were impossible to use them
for anything else. Hence to say that a given tool is for . . . is not
the same thing as to say that it is used for . . . and vice versa. The
function of a tool often differs from what it is used for.

The next suggestion is that hammers are said to be for
hammering because that is what they are *most often* used for.
But it is obvious that we want to and do make statements like

'Swords are for fighting but nowadays they are only used for
saluting visiting dignitaries'.

In this statement we are saying that swords are used but that only very few, if any, are used for what they are said to be for. We might express this by saying that tools are said to be for what they *are meant for* and that they are not necessarily used for what they are meant for. But this locution 'meant for' would only serve to confuse us, if it suggested that the hammer's being for hammering depends on any mental concomitants in the user. What a hammer is for does not depend on the beliefs or intentions or purpose of the user. His beliefs may be mistaken. His intention may be to misuse it. Nor are the intentions of the maker of hammers relevant. The manufacturer of hammers intends them to be used in as many different ways as possible so that he can sell more hammers. What the intentions or purposes were of the first man who made a hammer is utterly unknown to us and hence his intentions cannot be a condition for the hammers being for hammering.

Although its being used for x more frequently than for y, is not a sufficient condition for some tool being 'for x' rather than 'for y', there seems to be a close connection, nevertheless, between what a tool is for and what it is used for. Tools go out of use and then are not tools at all any more. The most that we can say is that they *were* tools. What, for instance, are pikestaffs for? Clearly, for nothing whatsoever. But they were used as the long sticks to which a weapon called a 'pike' was attached. Pikes and, hence, pikestaffs have gone out of use and now are not for anything anymore. What we must note here, however, is that pikes and pikestaffs did not go out of use singly or in isolation. They went out with a whole arsenal of similar weapons and with a particular way of waging war together with the corresponding military formations and strategies. Tools are not for something in isolation but only as elements in a *'Zeugganzes'*, ["totality of equipment" in Macquarrie and Robinson translation] a context of tools and gear and objects of use. Hammers are for hammering nails, which are for holding boards together. Boards form walls which are, for instance, for keeping wind and rain and cold out of a house which is for providing shelter and privacy. Hammers are for hammering as long as nails are for . . . and saws are for . . . and lumber is for . . . , etc. When the day comes that furniture and houses are moulded from plastic, hammers may well go out of use. They will then go out of use not merely because they are not used any more but because the sort of context in which they were used no longer exists. This context consists of other tools, materials and persons who use them for set purposes.

The concept of a person enters into that of a tool-context in several ways. All the tools and materials in a given tool-context subserve a set of common ends and these are ends pursued by persons. [Heidegger, BT p. 84] The tools in the carpenter's workshop serve to build shelter, furniture to equip that shelter, etc. At the same time the tools are to be used by persons. That determines some of their properties. [*Ibid.*, p. 70] Furthermore, the tool-context contains, as essential constituents, some users—persons who know how to use these tools and who know, thereby, what each component member of the tool-context is for. It is a necessary condition for something being a tool that there be someone who knows what it is for in the specific context to which it belongs. This was already suggested earlier by the case of the hammer that turns up in the museum 50,000 years from now. [*Ibid.*, p. 71]

There is no denying that there are many different ways in which a tool may belong to a tool-context. There is also no denying that things may be used outside a specific tool-context, as, e.g., when one improvises a stretcher from ice axes in an emergency ('improvises' and 'emergency' are the key terms here). There is, finally, no denying that there are tools, which are correctly said to be for . . . , which do not belong to any tool-context anymore. This is the case where a tool-context is becoming obsolete. Often this does not happen overnight. A particular form of combat becomes obsolete with the invention and perfection of rifles. More and more, swords and related weapons are used only for ceremonial occasions. We still say, and say so truly, that swords are for fighting but they are actually used less and less for that as a new kind of warfare replaces older forms. If the tool, as swords did, finds a use in a different tool-context, that of dress-parades, we mark this change by changing the tool's name. We now call them 'ceremonial swords' although they still have sharp points and edges.

But unless something was at one time, not too far in the past, or is now a member of a tool-context, it is not a tool and cannot be said to be for anything. ["Strictly speaking a tool never exists (by itself) . . ." Heidegger, BT, p. 68] If it is now a member of a tool-context, we may say with equal plausibility that it is for . . . because it is used most often for . . . and that it is used most often for . . . because it is for. . . .

II

The preceding discussion has exhibited the differences between the sense of 'things' in which tools and the sense in which material objects are things. A material object, for instance a boulder, has a certain shape, color, certain tactile qualities, and it has a definite location. If we want to say that, besides these properties, it also has certain relations we must say that its properties are like the properties of some other material object and that it is at a certain distance from some other thing. We would furthermore ascribe certain causal properties to the object, e.g., that it was formed from cooling lava in early Devonian times. No other properties and/or relations need be considered if anyone is to say truly (or falsely) that this is a boulder. But when we say that something is a hammer we are not merely ascribing properties, like being round, hard or yellow, to it. This was shown above. Quite clearly we are also ascribing certain relations to it. But these relations are different from those we ascribe to material objects. It is clear that these are not relations of resemblance or of spatio-temporal distance, but are relations, for instance, of being known to be for. . . , to be used with for the sake of . . . or of being used clumsily or skillfully. All these are relations to persons.

But could we not say that the relations to persons are causal relations or causal relations accompanied by intentional ones? It seems clear that being known to be for . . . is not merely a causal relation—the burden of proof rests for the time being still on the materialist who wants to claim that intentional relations are 'really' causal relations. It is important, therefore, to see clearly that this account of 'being a tool' which analyses it into a set of causal-plus-intentional-relations completely misses the points Heidegger wants to make. If we adapt this analysis we shall engender just those misunderstandings which the distinction between two senses of things was designed to forestall.

Suppose we adopt this analysis. We may then describe using a tool as a set of causal episodes involving my body and the material object which we call a hammer together with certain mental episodes in the user, e.g., his belief that this is a hammer, that hammers are for hammering, etc. In that case a hammer is a material object about which people have certain beliefs, e.g., that it is correctly used in such and such ways. About material objects we may ask what they are 'in themselves', i.e., independently of being known, or of any true beliefs that anyone may have about them. If hammers are material objects, we may ask the same question about them. The answer will consist of listing their material object properties like shape and color as well as their location and causal properties. What will not be mentioned is that hammers are for hammering, because that requires, as we saw, certain beliefs on the part of the users of hammers and hence is not one of the properties that material objects possess 'in themselves'. If we adopt the causal-plus-intentional-relation analysis of tools we find that being for something is 'in the mind of the user' as beauty is said to be 'in the eye of the beholder'. For, given the classification of relations and properties implicit in the causal-plus-intentional analysis of 'being for', an intentional relation, e.g., someone's belief that hammers are for hammering, is a necessary condition for the hammer's actually being a tool. But this raises all the difficulties that are familiar to us from the 'subjectivism'-'objectivism' controversies in ethics and aesthetics. Shall we say that our belief about the hammer must be true? In that case, we are unable to specify the truth-conditions. The properties possessed by the hammer 'in itself' are not sufficient as truth conditions for 'the hammer is for hammering'. The only other properties possessed by the tool are its intentional ones, whose truth conditions are in question. We therefore seem constrained to say that any belief, whether true or false, is the necessary condition for the hammer's being a tool; this view is even less plausible when applied to tools than it is in ethics or aesthetics.

This is, however, not the only reason for rejecting the view that tools are things in the same sense as material objects. If we adopt this view then we must describe the relations of persons to tools as causal-plus-intentional relations. This means that using a hammer consists of certain causal relations between *my body* and the tool, plus certain *mental* concomitants which we call beliefs. This analysis would not merely commit us to some kind of dualism—Heidegger would not object to that—but it commits us to a specifically Cartesian dualism and like many other contemporary philosophies, Heidegger does reject that form of dualism. As Descartes saw very clearly, adoption of such a dualism leads inevitably to the demand that the existence of a world 'outside' the mind be demonstrated. For mind is here exhaustively characterized by its intentional relations. Intentional relations are such that a true description of such a relation implies the existence of a mind but not of its object. Evidence is required to show that the object does in fact exist. This is true even if the object under discussion is my own body. Like many contemporary analytic philosophers, Heidegger thinks that it is not only a mistake to try to prove the existence of the external world. It is a mistake even to ask for a proof. [Heidegger, BT, p. 205] Yet if we adopt the causal-plus-intentional analysis of tools, we must ask that question, sooner or later. Hence we would do much better if we construed tools as things in a sense different from material things. If we do this we recognize that 'being for' is *sui generis,* it cannot be treated as being a causal-plus-intentional relation. We reject the classification of relations into either causal or intentional ones. In that case it becomes possible to escape Cartesian dualism together with the epistemological quandaries which it has presented to philosophers.

The theses defended here are not intended as refutations of materialism. The material objects discussed are the material objects encountered in everyday life, stones, clouds, etc., which are 'in themselves' describable in sensory terms. What the relation is between these everyday material objects and the atoms, molecules and smaller particles of science, is a separate question. Whatever Heidegger has to say in *Sein und Zeit* is intended to be consistent with any scientific results, even those that show that statements about persons can be restated in the language of physics exclusively. That is, in part, what is meant by Heidegger's insistence on the distinction between 'ontic' (i.e., roughly, 'scientific') and 'ontological' (roughly, 'conceptual') questions. However, his views are not necessarily compatible with any possible philosophical interpretation of such scientific results.

III

So far I have argued that to be a tool is to be for something and that 'being for . . .' cannot be analysed into causal-plus-intentional relations. To be a tool is not to be a material object about which certain people have certain beliefs. This does not suffice to show, however, that tools are not at all material objects, albeit material objects which differ from, say, boulders by sustaining a relation to human beings which is *sui generis,* e.g., the relation of "being used for . . . in tool-context. . . ." Yet Heidegger does want to claim that to be a tool is not to be a material object at all. This claim must be supported by arguing that the sorts of predicates which we use in speaking of material objects are not applied to tools (except by mistake) and vice versa. This claim may appear outrageous, but can be given considerable plausibility.

We might agree that there are properties which are only possessed by tools and not by material objects. We may say that a hammer is 'clumsy' if it is too heavy for the job, badly balanced or does not give one a good grip. Boulders are neither 'clumsy' nor 'not clumsy', they are not 'well balanced'. Some adjectives are applicable only to tools because they have to do with the tools' use. Similarly tools might be said to be 'suitable', 'convenient', etc., with respect to what they are for and these adjectives do not apply to material objects for the same reasons. [Heidegger, BT, p. 69]

But granting that some adjectives can only be used with names of tools is not also granting that there are not some adjectives which are applicable both to material object names and the names of tools. Hammers have a certain shape, they have color; they are hard or soft, their surfaces have tactile qualities, they are light or heavy. All these seem to have properties which they share with material objects.

Here, however, language will mislead us unless we pay close attention to it. To be sure we may say that a hammer is light or heavy as we would of a stone. But to say that a stone is heavy means that it takes a good deal of exertion to lift it. A heavy hammer may be heavy in the same sense, i.e., heavy to lift or it may be heavy 'for a hammer', in the same way as a boulder may be heavy 'for a boulder'. But a hammer may also be 'heavy for . . .' where the dots are replaced by the name of some particular activity for which hammers are used. 'This hammer is heavy for nailing together a picture frame' or perhaps 'this hammer is too heavy for . . .' Being heavy or light in this sense is logically independent from being heavy or light in the material object senses. A hammer may be heavy for a particular job but be light as hammers go and light to lift. A hammer may be heavy as hammers go and heavy to lift but light for the job. 'Heavy' and 'light' are used under very different conditions if applied to tools from when they are applied to material objects.

Corresponding arguments may be given for the other phenomenal predicates of hammers. 'Hard' and 'soft' behave in the same way as 'heavy' and 'light'. The head of the hammer may be hard (if it is made of iron) or soft (if it is made of rubber). It is one thing to say that the head of the hammer is 'hard for a hammer' and to say that a certain job needs a hammer with a hard head. A hammer may be hard in one of these senses and not in the other, and vice versa.

In the case of tactile qualities we do not use the same word in different senses for the material object and for the tool, but have different words for each. The handles of hammers are smooth or sticky, they are 'hot' or 'cool'—where this does not ascribe any measurable temperature to them—they give one a good grip or they don't. The predicates for the surface of material objects, on the other hand, are words like 'rough' and 'smooth'.

It is difficult to see however how we can argue either that the names of colors have different senses if applied to hammers and material objects or that there are some color names which are only applied to hammers and others which only apply to material objects. Heidegger's view on this would seem to have to be that color adjectives are not at all applicable to hammers as tools precisely because the color of the handle or of the head makes no difference to what it is for or what it is used for or to its actual employment. I could send someone to the hardware store to buy a light tackhammer or a sledgehammer with a good grip, but if I ask someone to buy me a yellow hammer this would require some explanation. The explanation would most likely consist of some reason for buying the hammer which has nothing to do with what hammers are for. E.g., I need a yellow hammer as a prop in a play or as part of a store window decoration.

These arguments show that there are predicates which are only applicable to tools and not to material objects. In order to complete Heidegger's argument corresponding arguments must be provided for relational predicates, particularly those describing location and causal relations. Heidegger devotes part of *Sein und Zeit* to an analysis of the concept of space in which he attempts to show that tools are located in a very different sense from material objects. [Heidegger, BT pp. 102 ff.] This argument deserves separate discussion. Heidegger has nothing to say about causal concepts as applied to material objects and to tools respectively.

The preceding arguments have shown that there are phenomenal predicates that apply to tools only and not to material objects. But it still seems true that the material object predicates apply to tools. We must note however that when they are applied to the hammer, for instance, they signalize either a linguistic confusion or the fact that we are talking about the hammer not as a tool but as a material object. It is true, of course, that it is a necessary condition for the hammer's being a tool that it also be a material object. But this fact does not invalidate the distinction between the two senses of things. Objects or events are known to us under more than one description. In some circumstances these descriptions are extensionally equivalent. Only if I move my facial muscles in certain ways may I be said to smile and vice versa. Only if I move a hammer in a certain way may I be said to be hammering and vice versa. This does not take away that the two descriptions are not synonymous and that, therefore, if one and the same word applies to the object under two different descriptions, this word is used in two senses.

THE EXISTENTIAL CONSTITUTION OF THE "THERE"

MARTIN HEIDEGGER

BEING THERE AS STATE-OF-MIND

What we indicate *ontologically* by the term "state-of-mind" is *ontically* the most familiar and everyday sort of thing; our mood, our Being-attuned. Prior to all psychology of moods, a field which in any case still lies fallow, it is necessary to see this phenomenon as a fundamental *existentiale*, and to outline its structure.

Both the undisturbed equanimity and the inhibited ill-humour of our everyday concern, the way we slip over from one to the other, or slip off into bad moods, are by no means

From *Being and Time* by Martin Heidegger. Translated by John Macquarrie and Edward Robinson. Copyright © 1962 by SCM Press Ltd. Reprinted by permission of Harper & Row, Publishers, Inc. Pp. 172–173, 235–237.

nothing ontologically, even if these phenomena are left unheeded as supposedly the most indifferent and fleeting in Dasein. The fact that moods can deteriorate [verdorben werden] and change over means simply that in every case Dasein always has some mood [gestimmtist]. The pallid, evenly balanced lack of mood [Ungestimmtheit], which is often persistent and which is not to be mistaken for a bad mood, is far from nothing at all. Rather, it is in this that Dasein becomes satiated with itself. Being has become manifest as a burden. Why that should be, one does not *know*. And Dasein cannot know anything of the sort because the possibilities of disclosure which belong to cognition reach far too short a way compared with the primordial disclosure belonging to moods, in which Dasein is brought before its Being as "there". Furthermore, a mood of elation can alleviate the manifest burden of Being; that such a mood is possible also discloses the burdensome character of Dasein, even while it alleviates the burden. A mood makes manifest 'how one is, and how one is faring' ["wie einem ist und wird"]. In this 'how one is', having a mood brings Being to its "there".

•   •   •

DASEIN'S BEING AS CARE

Since our aim is to grasp the totality of this structural whole ontologically, we must first ask whether the phenomenon of anxiety and that which is disclosed in it, can give us the whole of Dasein in a way which is phenomenally equiprimordial, and whether they can do so in such a manner that if we look searchingly at this totality, our view of it will be filled in by what has thus been given us. The entire stock of what lies therein may be counted up formally and recorded: anxiousness as a state-of-mind is a way of Being-in-the-world; that in the face of which we have anxiety is thrown Being-in-the-world; that which we have anxiety about is our potentiality-for-Being-in-the-world. Thus the entire phenomenon of anxiety shows Dasein as factically existing Being-in-the-world. The fundamental ontological characteristics of this entity are existentiality, facticity, and Being-fallen. These existential characteristics are not pieces belonging to something composite, one of which might sometimes be missing; but there is woven together in them a primordial context which makes up that totality of the structural whole which we are seeking. In the unity of those characteristics of Dasein's Being which we have mentioned, this Being becomes something which it is possible for us to grasp as such ontologically. How is this unity itself to be characterized?

Dasein is an entity for which, in its Being, that Being is an issue. The phrase 'is an issue' has been made plain in the state-of-Being of understanding—of understanding as self-projective Being towards its ownmost potentiality-for-Being. This potentiality is that for the sake of which any Dasein is as it is. In each case Dasein has already compared itself, in its Being, with a possibility of itself. Being-free *for* one's ownmost potentiality-for-Being, and therewith for the possibility of authenticity and inauthenticity, is shown, with a primordial, elemental concreteness, in anxiety. But ontologically, Being towards one's ownmost potentiality-for-Being means that in each case Dasein is already *ahead* of itself [ihm selbst . . . *vorweg*] in its Being. Dasein is always 'beyond itself' ["über sich hinaus"], not as a way of behaving towards other entities which it is *not*, but as Being towards the potentiality-for-Being which it is itself. This structure of Being, which belongs to the essential 'is an issue', we shall denote as Dasein's *"Being-ahead-of-itself"*.

But this structure pertains to the whole of Dasein's constitution. "Being-ahead-of-itself" does not signify anything like an isolated tendency in a worldless 'subject', but characterizes Being-in-the-world. To Being-in-the-world, however, belongs the fact that it has been delivered over to itself—that it has in each case, already been thrown *into a world*. The abandonment of Dasein to itself is shown with primordial concreteness in anxiety. "Being-ahead-of-itself" means, if we grasp it more fully, *"ahead-of-itself-in-already-being-in-a-world"*. As soon as this essentially unitary structure is seen as a phenomenon, what we have set forth earlier in our analysis of worldhood also becomes plain.

The upshot of that analysis was that the referential totality of significance (which as such is constitutive for worldhood) has been "tied up" with a "for-the-sake-of-which". The fact that this referential totality of the manifold relations of the 'in-order-to' has been bound up with that which is an issue for Dasein, does not signify that a 'world' of Objects which is present-at-hand has been welded together with a subject. It is rather the phenomenal expression of the fact that the constitution of Dasein, whose totality is now brought out explicitly as ahead-of-itself-in-Being-already-in . . . , is primordially a whole. To put it otherwise, existing is always factical. Existentiality is essentially determined by facticity. . . . In this falling Being-alongside . . . , fleeing in the face of uncanniness (which for the most part remains concealed with latent anxiety, since the publicness of the "they" suppresses everything unfamiliar), announces itself, whether it does so explicitly or not, and whether it is understood or not. Ahead-of-itself-Being-already-in-a-world essentially includes one's falling and one's *Being alongside* those things ready-to-hand within-the-world with which one concerns itself.

The formally existential totality of Dasein's ontological structure whole must therefore be grasped in the following structure: the Being of Dasein means ahead-of-itself-Being-already-in-(the-world) as Being-alongside (entities encountered within-the-world). This Being fills in the signification of the term *"care"* [*Sorge*], which is used in a purely ontologico-existential manner. From this signification every tendency of Being which one might have in mind ontically, such as worry [Besorgnis] or carefreeness [Sorglosigkeit], is ruled out.

Because Being-in-the-world is essentially care, Being-alongside the ready-to-hand could be taken in our previous analyses as *concern*, and Being with the Dasein-with of Others as we encounter it within-the-world could be taken as *solicitude*.

THE BODY, MOTILITY AND SPATIALITY

MAURICE MERLEAU-PONTY

Starting from the spectacle of the world, which is that of a nature open to plurality of thinking subjects, it looks for the conditions which make possible this unique world presented to a number of empirical selves, and finds it in a transcendental ego in which they participate without dividing it up, because it is not a Being, but a Unity or a Value. This is why the problem of the knowledge of other people is never posed in Kantian philosophy: the transcendental ego which it discusses is just as much other people's as mine, analysis is from the start located outside me, and has nothing to do but to determine the general conditions which make possible a world for an ego—myself or others equally—and so it never comes up against the question: *who is thinking?* If on the other hand contemporary philosophy takes this as its main theme, and if other people become a problem for it, it is because it is trying to achieve a more radical self-discovery. Reflection cannot be thorough-going, or bring a complete elucidation of its object, if it does not arrive at awareness of itself as well as of its results. We must not only adopt a reflective attitude in an impregnable *Cogito,* but furthermore reflect on this reflection, understand the natural situation which it is conscious of succeeding and which is therefore part of its definition; not merely practise philosophy, but realize the transformation which it brings with it in the spectacle of the world and in our existence. Only on this condition can philosophical knowledge become absolute knowledge, and cease to be a specialty or a technique. So there will be no assertion of an absolute Unity, all the less doubtful for not having to come into Being. The core

Reprinted from *The Phenomenology of Perception,* translated by C. Smith (New York: Humanities Press, 1962), pp. 62, 121, 137–147 by permission fo the publisher and Routledge & Kegan Paul.

of philosophy is no longer an autonomous transcendental subjectivity, to be found everywhere and nowhere: it lies in the perpetual beginning of reflection, at the point where the individual life begins to reflect on itself. Reflection is truly reflection only if it is not carried outside itself, only if it knows itself as reflection-on-an-unreflective-experience, and consequently as a change in structure of our existence. We earlier attacked Bergsonian intuitionism and introspection for seeking to know by coinciding. But at the opposite extremity of philosophy, in the notion of a universal constituting consciousness, we encounter an exactly corresponding mistake. Bergson's mistake consists in believing that the thinking subject can become fused with the object thought about, and that knowledge can swell and be incorporated into being. The mistake of reflective philosophies is to believe that the thinking subject can absorb into its thinking or appropriate without remainder the object of its thought, that our being can be brought down to our knowledge. As thinking subject we are never the unreflective subject that we seek to know; but neither can we become wholly consciousness, or make ourselves into the transcendental consciousness.

As soon as there is consciousness, and in order that there may be consciousness, there must be something to be conscious of, an intentional object, and consciousness can move towards this object only to the extent that it "derealizes' itself and throws itself into it, only if it is wholly in this reference to . . . something, only if it is a pure meaning-giving act. If a being is consciousness, he must be nothing but a network of intentions. If he ceases to be definable in terms of the act of sense-giving, he relapses into the condition of a thing, the thing being precisely what does not know, what slumbers in absolute ignorance of itself and the world, what consequently is not a true 'self', i.e. a 'for-itself', and has only a spatio-temporal form of individuation, existence in itself. [Husserl has often been credited with this distinction. In fact, it is found in Descartes and Kant. In our opinion Husserl's originality lies beyond the notion of intentionality; it is to be found in the elaboration of this notion and in the discovery, beneath the intentionality of representations, of a deeper intentionality, which others have called existence.] Consciousness, therefore, does not admit of degree.

. . . .

These elucidations enable us clearly to understand motility as basic intentionality. Consciousness is in the first place not a matter of 'I think that' but of 'I can'. Schneider's motor trouble cannot, any more than his visual deficiency, be reduced to any failure of the general function of representation. Sight and movement are specific ways of entering into relationship with objects and if, through all these experiences, some unique function finds its expression, it is the momentum of existence, which does not cancel out the radical diversity of contents, because it links them to each other, not by placing them all under the control of an 'I think', but by guiding them towards the intersensory unity of a 'world'. Movement is not thought about movement, and bodily space is not space thought of or represented. 'Each voluntary movement takes place in a setting, against a background which is determined by the movement itself. . . . We perform our movements in a space which is not "empty" or unrelated to them, but which on the contrary, bears a highly determinate relation to them: movement and background are, in fact, only artificially separated stages of a unique totality.' In the action of the hand which is raised towards an object is contained a reference to the object, not as an object represented, but as that highly specific thing towards which we project ourselves, near which we are, in anticipation, and which we haunt. Consciousness is being towards the thing through the intermediary of the body. A movement is learned when the body had understood it, that is, when it has incorporated it into its 'world', and to move one's body is to aim at things through it; it is to allow oneself to respond to their call, which is made upon it independently of any representation. Motility, then, is not, as it were, a handmaid of consciousness, transporting the body to that point in space of which we have formed a representation beforehand. In order that we may be able to move our body towards an object, the object must first exist for it, our body must not belong to the realm of the 'in-itself'. Objects no longer exist for the arm of the apraxic, and this is what causes it to remain immobile. Cases of pure apraxia in which the perception of space remains unaffected, in which even the 'intellectual notion of the gesture to be made' does not appear to be obscured, and yet in which the patient cannot copy a triangle, cases of constructive apraxia, in which the subject shows no gnosic disturbance except as regards the localization of stimuli on his body, and yet is incapable of copying a cross, a *v* or an *o*, all prove that the body has its world and that objects or space may be present to our knowledge but not to our body.

We must therefore avoid saying that our body is *in* space, or *in* time. It *inhabits* space and time. If my hand traces a complicated path through the air, I do not need, in order to know its final position, to add together all movements made in the same direction and subtract those made in the opposite direction. 'Every identifiable change reaches consciousness already loaded with its relations to what has preceded it, as on a taximeter the distance is given already converted into shillings and pence. At every moment, previous attitudes and movements provide an ever ready standard of measurement. It is not a question of a visual or motor 'memory' of the starting position of the hand: cerebral lesions may leave visual memory intact while destroying awareness of movement. As for the 'motor memory', it is clear that it could hardly establish the present position of the hand, unless the perception which gave rise to it had not, stored up in it, an absolute awareness of 'here', for without this we should be thrown back from memory to memory and never have a present perception. Just as it is necessarily 'here', the body necesarily exists 'now'; it can never become 'past', and if we cannot retain in health the living memory of sickness, or, in adult life that of our body as a child, these 'gaps in memory' merely express the temporal structure of our body. At each successive instant of a movement, the preceding instant is not lost sight of. It is, as it were, dovetailed into the present, and present perception generally speaking consists in drawing together, on the basis of one's present position, the succession of previous positions, which envelop each other. But the impending position is also covered by the present, and through it all those which will occur throughout the movement. Each instant of the movement embraces its whole span, and particularly the first which, being the active initiative, institutes the link between a here and a yonder, a now and a future which the remainder of the instants will merely develop. In so far as I have a body through which I act in the world, space and time are not, for me, a collection of adjacent points nor are they a limitless number of relations synthesized by any consciousness, and into which it draws my body. I am not in space and time, nor do I conceive space and time; I belong to them, my body combines with them and includes them. The scope of this inclusion is the measure of that of my existence; but in any case it can never be all-embracing. The space and time which I inhabit are always in their different ways indeterminate horizons which contain other points of view. The synthesis of both time and space is a task that always has to be performed afresh. Our bodily experience of movement is not a particular case of knowledge; it provides us with a way of access to the world and the object, with a 'praktognosia', which has to be recognized as original and perhaps as primary. My body has its world, or understands its world, without having to make use of my 'symbolic' or 'objectifying function'.

As has often been said, it is the body which 'catches' (*kapiert*) and 'comprehends' movement. The cultivation of habit is indeed the grasping of a significance, but it is the motor grasping of a motor significance. Now what precisely does this mean? A woman may, without any calculation, keep a safe distance between the feather in her hat and things which might break it off. She feels where the feather is just as we feel where our hand is. If I am in the habit of driving a car, I enter a narrow opening and see that I can 'get through' without comparing the width of the opening with that of the wings, just as I go through a doorway without checking the width of the doorway against that of my body. The hat and the car have ceased to be objects with a size and volume which is established by comparison with other objects. They have become potentialities of volume, the demand for a certain amount of free space. In the same way the iron gate to the Underground platform, and the road, have become restrictive potentialities and immediately appear passable or impassable for my body with its adjuncts. The blind man's stick has ceased to be an object for him, and is no longer perceived for itself; its point has become an area of sensitivity, extending the scope and active radius of touch, and providing a parallel to sight. In the exploration of things, the length of the stick does not enter expressly as a middle term: the blind man is rather aware of it through the position of objects than of the position of objects through it. The position of things is immediately given through the extent of the reach which carries him to it, which comprises besides the arm's own reach the stick's range of action. If I want to get used to a stick, I try it by touching a few things with it, and eventually I have it 'well in hand', I can see what things are 'within reach' or our of reach of my stick. There is no question here of any quick estimate or any comparison between the objective length of the stick and the objective distance away of the goal to be reached. The points in space do not stand out as objective positions in relation to the objective position occupied by our body; they mark, in our vicinity, the varying range of our aims and our gestures. To get used to a hat, a car or a stick is to be transplanted into them, or conversely, to incorporate them into the bulk of our own body. Habit expresses our power of dilating our being in the world, or changing our existence by appropriating fresh instruments. It is possible to know how to type without being able to say where the letters which make the words are to be found on the banks of keys. To know how to type is not, then, to know the place of each letter among the keys, nor even to have acquired a conditioned reflex for each one, which is set in motion by the letter as it comes before our eye. If habit is neither a form of knowledge nor an involuntary action, what then is it? It is knowledge in the hands, which is forthcoming only when bodily effort is made, and cannot be formulated in detachment from that effort. The subject knows where the letters are on the typewriter as we know where one of our limbs is, through a knowledge bred of familiarity which does not give us a position in objective space. The movement of her fingers is not presented to the typist as a path through space which can be described, but merely as a certain adjustment of motility, physiognomically distinguishable from any other. The question is often framed as if the perception of a letter written on paper aroused the representation of the same letter which in turn aroused the representation of the movement needed to strike it on the machine. But this is mythological language. When I run my eyes over the text set before me, there do not occur perceptions which stir up representations, but patterns are formed as I look, and these are endowed with a typical or familiar physiognomy. When I sit at my typewriter, a motor space opens up beneath my hands, in which I am about to 'play' what I have read. The reading of the word is a modulation of visible space, the performance of the movement is a modulation of manual space, and the whole question is how a certain physiognomy of 'visual' patterns can evoke a certain type of motor response, how each 'visual' structure eventually provides itself with its mobile essence without there being any need to spell the word or specify the movement in detail in order to translate one into the other. But this power of habit is no different from the general one which we exercise over our body: if I am ordered to touch my ear or my knee, I move my hand to my ear or my knee by the shortest route, without having to think of the initial position of my hand, or that of my ear, or the path between them. We said earlier that it is the body which 'understands' in the cultivation of habit. This way of putting it will appear absurd, if understanding is subsuming a sense-datum under an idea, and if the body is an object. But the phenomenon of habit is just what prompts us to revise our notion of 'understand' and our notion of the body. To understand is to experience the harmony between what we aim at and what is given, between the intention and the performance—and the body is our anchorage in a world. When I put my hand to my knee, I experience at every stage of the movement the fulfilment of an intention which was not directed at my knee as an idea or even as an object, but as a present and real part of my living body, that is, finally, as a stage in my perpetual movement towards a world. When the typist performs the necessary movements on the typewriter, these movements are governed by an intention, but the intention does not posit the keys as objective locations. It is literally true that the subject who learns to type incorporates the key-bank space into his bodily space.

The example of instrumentalists shows even better how habit has its abode neither in thought nor in the objective body, but in the body as mediator of a world. It is known that an experienced organist is capable of playing an organ which he does not know, which has more or fewer manuals, and stops differently arranged, compared with those on the instrument he is used to playing. He needs only an hour's practice to be ready to perform his programme. Such a short preparation rules out the supposition that new conditioned reflxes have here been substituted for the existing sets, except where both form a system and the change is all-embracing, which takes us away from the mechanistic theory, since in that case the reactions are mediated by a comprehensive grasp of the instrument. Are we to maintain that the organist analyses the organ, that he conjures up and retains a representation of the stops, pedals and manuals and their relation to each other in space? But during the short rehearsal preceding the concert, he does not act like a person about to draw up a plan. He sits on the seat, works the pedals, pulls out the stops, gets the measure of the instrument with his body, incorporates within himself the relevant directions and dimensions, settles into the organ as one settles into a house. He does not learn objective spatial positions for each stop and pedal, nor does he commit them to 'memory'. During the rehearsal, as during the performance, the stops, pedals and manuals are given to him as nothing more than possibilities of achieving certain emotional or musical values, and their positions are simply the places through which this value appears in the world. Between the musical essence of the piece as it is shown in the score and the notes which actually sound round the organ, so direct a relation is established that the organist's body and his instrument are merely the medium of this relationship. Henceforth the music exists by itself and through it all the rest exists.[1] There is here no place for any 'memory' of the position of the stops, and it is not in objective space that the organist in fact is playing. In reality his movements during rehearsal are consecratory gestures: they draw affective vectors, discover emotional sources, and create a space of expressiveness as the movements of the augur delimit the *templum*.

The whole problem of habit here is one of knowing how the musical significance of an action can be concentrated in a certain place to the extent that, in giving himself entirely to the music, the organist reaches for precisely those stops and pedals which are to bring it into being. Now the body is essentially an expressive space. If I want to take hold of an object, already, at a point of space about which I have been quite unmindful, this power of grasping constituted by my hand moves upwards towards the thing. I move my legs not as things in space two and a half feet from my head, but as a power of locomotion which extends my motor intention downwards. The main areas of my body are devoted to actions, and participate in their value, and asking why common sense makes the head the seat of thought raises the same problem as asking how the organist distributes, through 'organ space', musical significances. But our body is not merely one expressive space among the rest, for that is simply the constituted body. It is the origin of the rest, expressive movement itself, that which causes them to begin to exist as things, under our hands and eyes. Although our body does not impose definite instincts upon us from birth, as it does upon animals, it does at least give to our life the form of generality, and develops our personal acts into stable dispositional tendencies. In this sense our nature is

---

[1] 'As though the musicians were not nearly so much playing the little phrase as performing the rites on which it insisted before it would consent to appear.' (Proust, *Swann's Way*, II, trans. C. K. Scott Moncrieff, Chatto & Windus, p. 180.) 'It's cries were so sudden that the violinist must snatch up his bow and race to catch them as they came.' (*Ibid.*, p. 186.)

not long-established custom, since custom presupposes the form of passivity derived from nature. The body is our general medium for having a world. Sometimes it is restricted to the actions necessary for the conservation of life, and accordingly it posits around us a biological world; at other times, elaborating upon these primary actions and moving from their literal to a figurative meaning, it manifests through them a core of new significance: this is true of motor habits such as dancing. Sometimes, finally, the meaning aimed at cannot be achieved by the body's natural means; it must then build itself an instrument, and it projects thereby around itself a cultural world. At all levels it performs the same function which is to endow the instantaneous expressions of spontaneity with 'a little renewable action and independent existence'. [Valéry] Habit is merely a form of this fundamental power. We say that the body has understood, and habit has been cultivated when it has absorbed a new meaning, and assimilated a fresh core of significance.

To sum up, what we have discovered through the study of motility, is a new meaning of the word 'meaning'. The great strength of intellectualist psychology and idealist philosophy comes from their having no difficulty in showing that perception and thought have an intrinsic significance and cannot be explained in terms of the external association of fortuitously agglomerated contents. The *Cogito* was the coming to self-awareness of this inner core. But all meaning was *ipso facto* conceived as an act of thought, as the work of a pure *I*, and although rationalism easily refuted empiricism, it was itself unable to account for the variety of experience, for the element of senselessness in it, for the contingency of contents. Bodily experience forces us to acknowledge an imposition of meaning which is not the work of a universal constituting consciousness, a meaning which clings to certain contents. My body is that meaningful core which behaves like a general function, and which nevertheless exists, and is susceptible to disease. In it we learn to know that union of essence and existence which we shall find again in perception generally, and which we shall then have to describe more fully.

PART THREE

SELF AND OTHERS

CONSCIOUSNESS AND THE EGO

I Think, therefore I am.
                    —Rene Descartes DISCOURSE ON METHOD

The *I Think* must accompany all my representations . . .
                    —Immanuel Kant CRITIQUE OF PURE REASON

INTRODUCTION

Husserl argues that one of the essential discoveries of phenomenological investigation is the transcendental ego. Jean-Paul Sartre, in an early work, argues that phenomenology "discovers" such an ego only by perverting its own aims and losing hold on its own methodological disciplines. Heidegger, in *Being and Time*, argues that our basic notion of "self" is not a personal or individual self but an anonymous impersonal *das Man* (the *they* in "they say that . . .").

THE TRANSCENDENTAL EGO

11. The Psychological and the Transcendental Ego. The Transcendency of the World

If I keep purely what comes into view—for me, the one who is meditating—by virtue of my free epoché with respect to the being of the experienced world, the momentous fact is that I, with my life, remain untouched in my existential status, regardless of whether or not the world exists and regardless of what my eventual decision concerning its being or non-being might be. This Ego, with his Ego-life, who necessarily remains for me, by virtue of such epoché, is not a piece of the world; and if he says, "I exist, *ego cogito*," that no longer signifies, "I, this man, exist.". . .

By phenomenological epoché I reduce my natural human Ego and my psychic life—the realm of my *psychological self-experience*—to my transcendental-phenomenological Ego, the realm of *transcendental-phenomenological self-experience*. The Objective world, the world that exists for me, that always has and always will exist for me, the only world that ever can exist for me—this world, with all its Objects, I said, derives its whole sense and its existential status, which it has for me, from me myself, *from me as the transcendental Ego*, the Ego who comes to the fore only with transcendental-phenomenological epoché.

Reprinted from *Cartesian Meditations*, translated by D. Cairns (The Hague, Netherlands: M. Nijhoff, 1960), sections 11, 30, 31, 33, pp. 25, 65–68 by permission of the publisher and the translator.

FOURTH MEDITATION

Development of the Constitutional Problems Pertaining to the Transcendental Ego Himself

30. The Transcendental Ego Inseparable from the Processes Making Up His Life

Objects exist for me, and are for me what they are, only as objects of actual and possible consciousness. If this is not to be an empty statement and a theme for empty speculations, it must be shown what makes up concretely this existence and being-thus for me, or what sort of actual and possible consciousness is concerned, what the structure of this consciousness is, what "possibility signifies here, and so forth. This can be done solely by constitutional investigation—first, in the broader sense introduced initially, and then in the narrower sense just now described. Moreover there is but one possible method, the one demanded by the essence of intentionality and of its horizons. Even from the preparatory analyses leading us upward to the sense of the problem, it becomes clear that the transcendental ego (in the psychological parallel, the psyche) is what it is solely in relation to intentional objectivities. Among these, however, are necessarily included for the ego existing objects and, for him as related to a world, not only objects within his (adequately verifiable) sphere of immanent time but also world Objects, which are shown to be existent only in his inadequate, merely presumptive, external experience—in the harmoniousness of its course. It is thus an essential property of the ego, constantly to have systems of intentionality—among them, harmonious ones —partly as going on within him [actually], partly as fixed potentialities, which, thanks to predelineating horizons, are available for uncovering. Each object that the ego ever means, thinks of, values, deals with, likewise each that he ever phantasies or can phantasy, indicates its correlative system and exists only as itself the correlate of its system.

31. The Ego As Identical Pole of the Subjective Processes

Now, however, we must call attention to a great gap in our exposition. The ego is himself *existent for himself* in continuous evidence; thus, in himself, he is *continuously constituting himself as existing.* Heretofore we have touched on only one side of this self-constitution, we have looked at only the *flowing cogito.* The ego grasps himself not only as a flowing life but also as *I*, who live this and that subjective process, who live through this and that cogito, *as the same I.* Since we were busied up to now with the intentional relation of consciousness to object, cogito to cogitatum, only that synthesis stood out for us which "polarizes" the multiplicities of actual and possible consciousness toward identical objects, accordingly in relation to *objects as poles,* synthetic unities. New we encounter a second polarization, a *second kind of synthesis,* which embraces all the particular multiplicities of *cogitationes* collectively and in its own manner, namely as belonging to the identical Ego, who, *as the active and affected subject of consciousness,* lives in all processes of consciousness and is related, *through* them, to all object-poles.

33. The Full Concretion of the Ego As Monad and the Problem of His Self-Constitution

From the Ego as identical pole, and as substrate of habitualities, we distinguish *the ego taken in full concreteness*—in that we take, in addition, that without which the Ego cannot after all be concrete. (The ego, taken in full concreteness, we propose to call by the Leibnizian name: monad.) The Ego can be concrete only in the flowing multiformity of his intentional life, along with the objects meant—and in some cases constituted as existent for him—in that life. Manifestly, in the case of an object so constituted, its abiding existence and being-thus are a correlate of the habituality constituted in the Ego-pole himself by virtue of his position-taking.

That is to be understood in the following manner. As ego, I have a surrounding world, which is continually "existing for

me"; and, in it, objects as "existing for me"—already with
the abiding distinction between those with which I am acquainted
and those only anticipated as objects with which I may become
acquainted. The former, the ones that are, in the first sense,
existent for me, are such by original acquisition—that is: by
my original taking cognizance of what I had never beheld previously, and my explication of it in particular intuitions of its
features. Thereby, in my synthetic activity, the object becomes
constituted originally, perceptively, in the explicit sense-form:
"something identical having its manifold properties", or "object
as identical with itself and undergoing determination in respect
of its manifold properties". This, my activity of positing and
explicating being, sets up a habituality of my Ego, by virtue of
which the object, as having its manifold determinations, is mine
abidingly. Such abiding acquisitions make up my surrounding
world, so far as I am acquainted with it at the time, with its
horizons of objects with which I am unacquainted—that is:
objects yet to be acquired but already anticipated with this
formal object-structure.

I exist for myself and am continually given to myself, by
experiential evidence, as "*I myself*". This is true of the transcendental ego and, correspondingly, of the psychologically pure
ego; it is true, moreover, with respect to any sense of the word
ego. Since the monadically concrete ego includes also the whole
of actual and potential conscious life, it is clear that the problem
of *explicating this monadic ego phenomenologically* (the problem
of his constitution for himself) must include *all constitutional
problems without exception.* Consequently the phenomenology of
this *self-constitution* coincides with *phenomenology as a whole.*

THE TRANSCENDENCE OF THE EGO

JEAN-PAUL SARTRE

Reprinted with the permission of Farrar, Straus & Giroux, Inc. and
Librairie A. Hatier from *The Transcendence of the Ego* by Jean-Paul
Sartre, translated by Forrest Williams and Robert Kirkpatrick, copyright
© 1957 by The Noonday Press, Inc. and Hatier. Pp. 31–42, 54–60, 104–106.

For most philosophers the ego is an "inhabitant" of consciousness. Some affirm its formal presence at the heart of *Erlebnisse*, as an empty principle of unification. Others—psychologists for the most part—claim to discover its material presence, as the center of desires and acts, in each moment of our psychic life. We should like to show here that the ego is neither formally nor materially *in* consciousness: it is outside, *in the world*. It is a being of the world, like the ego of another.

THE I AND THE ME

The Theory of the Formal Presence of the I

It must be conceded to Kant that "the I Think *must be able* to accompany all our representations." But need we then conclude that an *I in fact* inhabits all our states of consciousness and actually effects the supreme synthesis of our experience? This inference would appear to distort the Kantian view. The Critical problem being one of validity, Kant says nothing concerning the actual existence of the *I Think*. On the contrary, he seems to have seen perfectly well that there are moments of consciousness without the *I*, for he says "*must be able* to accompany." The problem, indeed, is to determine the conditions for the possibility of experience. One of these conditions is that I can always regard my perception or thought as *mine:* nothing more. But there is in contemporary philosophy a dangerous tendency—traces of which may be found in neo-Kantianism, empirico-Criticism, and an intellectualism like that of Brochard—which consists of making into a reality the conditions, determined by Criticism, for the possibility of experience. This is the tendency which leads certain writers to ask, for example, what "transcendental consciousness" can *be*. If one poses the problem in these terms, one is naturally constrained to conceive this consciousness—which is constitutive of our empirical consciousness—as an unconscious. But Boutroux, in his lectures on the philosophy of Kant, has already dealt sufficiently with these interpretations. The preoccupation of Kant was never with the way in which empirical consciousness is *in fact* constituted. He never deduced empirical consciousness, in the manner of a Neo-Platonic process, from a higher consciousness, from a constituting hyper-consciousness. For Kant, transcendental consciousness is nothing but the set of conditions which are necessary for the existence of an empirical consciousness. Consequently, *to make into a reality* the transcendental *I*, to make of it the inseparable companion of each of our "consciousness," is to pass on *fact*, not on validity, and to take a point of view radically different from that of Kant. And then to cite as justification Kantian considerations on the unity necessary to experience would be to commit the very error of those who make transcendental consciousness into a pre-empirical unconscious.

If we associate with Kant, therefore, the question of validity, the question of fact is still not broached. Consequently, it may be posed succinctly at this point: the *I think* must be able to accompany all our representations, but does it in fact accompany them? Supposing, moreover, that a certain representation, A, passes from some state unaccompanied by the *I Think* to a state in which the *I Think* does accompany it, will there follow a modification of the structure of A, or will the representation remain basically unchanged? This second question leads us to pose a third. The *I Think* must be able to accompany all our representations. But should we understand here that directly or indirectly the unity of our representations is effected by the *I Think*, or that the representations of a consciousness must be united and articulated in such a way that it is always possible in their regard to note an *I Think*? This third question seems to arise at the level of validity and, at this level, seems to renounce Kantian orthodoxy. But it is actually a question of fact, which may be formulated thus: is the *I* that we encounter in our consciousness made possible by the synthetic unity of our representations, or is it the *I* which in fact unites the representations to each other?

If we reject all the more or less forced interpretations of the *I Think* offered by the post-Kantians, and nevertheless wish to solve the problem of the existence *in fact* of the *I* in consciousness, we meet on our path the phenomenology of Husserl. Phenomenology is a scientific, not a Critical, study of consciousness.

Its essential way of proceeding is by intuition. Intuition, according to Husserl, puts us in the presence of *the thing*. We must recognize, therefore, that phenomenology is a science of *fact* and that the problems it poses are problems *of fact*, which can be seen, moreover, from Husserl's designation of phenomenology as a *descriptive* science. Problems concerning the relations of the *I* to consciousness are therefore existential problems. Husserl, too, discovers the transcendental consciousness of Kant, and grasps it by the ἐποχή. But this consciousness is no longer a set of logical conditions. It is a fact which is absolute. Nor is this transcendental consciousness a hypostatization of validity, an unconscious which floats between the real and the ideal. It is a real consciousness accessible to each of us as soon as the "reduction" is performed. And it is indeed this transcendental consciousness which constitutes our empirical consciousness, our consciousness "in the world," our consciousness with its psychic and psychophysical *me*.

For our part, we readily acknowledge the existence of a constituting consciousness. We find admirable all of Husserl's descriptions in which he shows transcendental consciousness constituting the world by imprisoning itself in empirical consciousness. Like Husserl, we are persuaded that our psychic and psycho-physical *me* is a transcendent object which must fall before the ἐποχή. But we raise the following question: is not this psychic and psycho-physical *me* enough? Need one double it with a transcendental *I*, a structure of absolute consciousness?

The consequences of a reply are obvious. If the reply is negative, the consequences are:

First, the transcendental field becomes impersonal; or, if you like, "pre-personal," *without an I.*

Second, the *I* appears only at the level of humanity and is only one aspect of the *me*, the active aspect.

Third, the *I Think* can accompany our representations because it appears on a foundation of unity which it did not help to create; rather, this prior unity makes the *I Think* possible.

Fourth, one may well ask if personality (even the abstract personality of an *I*) is a necessary accompaniment of a consciousness, and if one cannot conceive of absolutely impersonal consciousnesses.

To this question, Husserl has given his reply. After having determined (in *Logische Untersuchungen*) that the *me* is a synthetic and transcendent production of consciousness, he reverted in *Ideen Zu Einer Reinen Phänomenologie Und Phänomenologischen Philosophie* to the classic position of a transcendental *I*. This *I* would be, so to speak, behind each consciousness, a necessary structure of consciousnesses whose rays (*Ichstrahlen*) would light upon each phenomenon presenting itself in the field of attention. Thus transcendental consciousness becomes thoroughly personal. Was this notion necessary? Is it compatible with the definition of consciousness given by Husserl?

It is ordinarily thought that the existence of a transcendental *I* may be justified by the need that consciousness has for unity and individuality. It is because all my perceptions and all my thoughts refer themselves back to this permanent seat that my consciousness is unified. It is because I can say *my* consciousness, and because Peter and Paul can also speak of *their* consciousnesses, that these consciousnesses distinguish themselves from each other. The *I* is the producer of inwardness.

Now, it is certain that phenomenology does not need to appeal to any such unifying and individualizing *I*. Indeed, consciousness is defined by intentionality. By intentionality consciousness transcends itself. It unifies itself by escaping from itself. The unity of a thousand active consciousnesses by which I have added, do add, and shall add two and two to make four, is the transcendent object "two and two make four." Without the permanence of this eternal truth a real unity would be impossible to conceive, and there would be irreducible operations as often as there were operative consciousnesses. It is possible that those believing "two and two make four" to be the *content* of my representation may be obliged to appeal to a transcendental and subjective principle of unification, which will then be the *I*. But it is precisely Husserl who has no need of such a principle. The object is transcendent to the consciousnesses which grasp it, and it is in the object that the unity of the consciousnesses is found.

It will be said that a principle of unity *within duration* is nonetheless needed if the continual flux of consciousness is to be capable of positing transcendent objects outside the flux. Consciousnesses must be perpetual syntheses of past consciousnesses and present consciousness. This is correct. But it is characteristic that Husserl, who studied this subjective unification of consciousnesses in *Vorlesungen Zur Phänomenologie Des Inneren Zeitbewusstseins*, never had recourse to a synthetic power of the *I*. It is consciousness which unifies itself, concretely, by a play of "transversal" intentionalities which are concrete and real retentions of past consciousnesses. Thus consciousness refers perpetually to itself. Whoever says "a consciousness" says "the whole of consciousness," and this singular property belongs to consciousness itself, aside from whatever relations it may have to the *I*. In *Cartesianische Meditationen*, Husserl seems to have preserved intact this conception of consciousness unifying itself in time.

Furthermore, the individuality of consciousness evidently stems from the nature of consciousness. Consciousness (like Spinoza's substance) can be limited only by itself. Thus, it constitutes a synthetic and individual totality entirely isolated from other totalities of the same type, and the *I* can evidently be only an *expression* (rather than a condition) of this incommunicability and inwardness of consciousnesses. Consequently we may reply without hesitation: the phenomenological conception of consciousness renders the unifying and individualizing role of the *I* totally useless. It is consciousness, on the contrary, which makes possible the unity and the personality of my *I*. The transcendental *I*, therefore, has no *raison d'être*.

But, in addition, this superfluous *I* would be a hindrance. If it existed it would tear consciousness from itself; it would divide consciousness; it would slide into every consciousness like an opaque blade. The transcendental *I* is the death of consciousness. Indeed, the existence of consciousness is an absolute because consciousness is consciousness of itself. This is to say that the type of existence of consciousness is to be consciousness of itself. And consciousness is aware of itself *in so far as it is conscious-*

ness of a transcendent object. All is therefore clear and lucid in consciousness: the object with its characteristic opacity is before consciousness, but consciousness is purely and simply consciousness of being consciousness of that object. This is the law of its existence.

We should add that this consciousness of consciousness— except in the case of reflective consciousness which we shall dwell on later—is not *positional,* which is to say that consciousness is not for itself its own object. Its object is by nature outside of it, and that is why consciousness *posits* and *grasps* the object in the same act. Consciousness knows itself only as absolute inwardness. We shall call such a consciousness: consciousness in the first degree, or *unreflected* consciousness.

Now we ask: is there room for an *I* in such a consciousness? The reply is clear: evidently not. Indeed, such an *I* is not the object (since by hypothesis the *I* is inner); nor is it an *I of consciousness,* since it is something for consciousness. It is not a translucent quality of consciousness, but would be in some way an inhabitant. In fact, however formal, however abstract one may suppose it to be, the *I,* with its personality, would be a sort of center of opacity. It would be to the concrete and psycho-physical *me* what a point is to three dimensions: it would be an infinitely contracted *me.* Thus, if one introduces this opacity into consciousness, one thereby destroys the fruitful definition cited earlier. One congeals consciousness, one darkens it. Consciousness is then no longer a spontaneity; it bears within itself the germ of opaqueness. But in addition we would be forced to abandon that original and profound view which makes of consciousness a *non-substantial* absolute. A pure consciousness is an absolute quite simply because it is consciousness of itself. It remains therefore a "phenomenon" in the very special sense in which "to be" and "to appear" are one. It is all lightness, all translucence. This it is which differentiates the *Cogito* of Husserl from the Cartesian *Cogito.* But if the *I* were a necessary structure of consciousness, this opaque *I* would at once be raised to the rank of an absolute. We would then be in the presence of a monad. And this, indeed, is unfortunately the orientation of the new thought of Husserl (see *Cartesianische Meditationen*). Consciousness is loaded down; consciousness has lost that character which rendered it the absolute existent *by virtue of non-existence*. It is heavy and *ponderable*. All the results of phenomenology begin to crumble if the *I* is not, by the same title as the world, a relative existent: that is to say, an object *for* consciousness.

The Theory of the Material Presence of the Me

For Kant and for Husserl the *I* is a formal structure of consciousness. We have tried to show that an *I* is never purely formal, that it is always, even when conceived abstractly, an infinite contraction of the material *me*. But before going further we need to free ourselves of a purely psychological theory which for psychological reasons affirms the material presence of the *me* in all our consciousnesses. This is the theory of the "self-love" moralists. According to them, the love of self—and consequently the *me*—lies concealed within all emotions in a thousand different forms. In a very general way, the *me*, as a function of this love that it bears for itself, would desire *for itself* all the objects it desires. The essential structure of each of my acts would be a *reference to myself*. The "return to me" would be constitutive of all consciousnesses.

To object to this thesis that this return to myself is nowise present to consciousness—for example, to object that, when I am thirsty, it is a glass of water which I see and which appears to me as desirable—raises no issue. This point would willingly be granted. La Rochefoucauld was one of the first to have made use of the unconscious, without naming it. For him, self-love *conceals itself* under the most diverse forms. It must be ferreted out before it can be grasped. In a more general way, it has been admitted as a consequence that the *me*, if it is not present to consciousness, is hidden behind consciousness and is the magnetic pole of all our representations and all our desires. The *me* seeks, then, to procure the object in order to satisfy its desire. In other words, it is the desire (or, if one prefers, the desiring *me*) which is given as end, and the desired object is the means.

Now the interest of this thesis, it seems to us, is that it puts in bold relief a very frequent error among psychologists. The error consists in confusing the essential structure of reflective acts with the essential structure of unreflected acts. It is overlooked that two forms of existence are always possible for a consciousness. Then, each time the observed consciousnesses are given as unreflected, one superimposes on them a structure, belonging to reflection, which one doggedly alleges to be unconscious.

I pity Peter, and I go to his assistance. For my consciousness only one thing exists at that moment: Peter-having-to-be-helped. This quality of "having-to-be-helped" lies in Peter. It acts on me like a force. Aristotle said it: the desirable is that which moves the desiring. At this level, the desire is given to consciousness as centrifugal (it transcends itself; it is thetic consciousness of "having-to-be" and non-thetic consciousness of itself) and as impersonal (there is no *me:* I am in the presence of Peter's suffering just as I am in the presence of the color of this inkstand; there is an objective world of things and of actions, done or to be done, and the actions come to adhere as qualities to the things which call for them).

Now, this first moment of desire—supposing that it has not completely escaped the self-love theorists—is not considered a complete and autonomous moment. They have imagined another state behind it which remains in a half-light: for example, I help Peter in order to put an end to the disagreeable state into which the sight of his sufferings has put me. But this disagreeable state can be known as such, and one can try to suppress it only following an act of reflection. A distaste on the unreflected level, in fact, transcends itself in the same way that the unreflected consciousness of pity transcends itself. It is the intuitive apprehension of a disagreeable quality of an object. And to the extent that the distaste is accompanied by a desire, it does not desire to suppress *itself*, but to suppress the unpleasant object. It is therefore no use to place behind the unreflected pitying consciousness an unpleasant state which is to be made the underlying cause of the pitying act: for unless this consciousness of unpleasantness turns back on itself in order to posit itself as an unpleasant state, we will remain indefinitely in the impersonal and unreflected. Thus, without even realizing it, the self-love theorists suppose that the reflected is first, original, and concealed in the unconscious. There is scarcely need to bring to light the absurdity of such a hypothesis. Even if the unconscious exists, who could be led to believe that it contains spontaneities of a reflected sort? Is it not the definition of the reflected that it be posited by a consciousness? But, in addition, how can it be held that the reflected is first in relation to the unreflected? Undoubtedly, one can conceive that in certain cases a consciousness may appear immediately as reflected. But even then the unreflected has the ontological priority over the reflected because the unreflected consciousness does not need to be reflected in order to exist, and because reflection presupposes the intervention of a second-degree consciousness.

We arrive then at the following conclusion: unreflected consciousness must be considered autonomous. It is a totality which needs no completing at all, and we must acknowledge with no qualifications that the character of unreflected desire is to transcend itself by apprehending on the subject the quality of desirability. Everything happens as if we lived in a world whose objects, in addition to their qualities of warmth, odor, shape, etc., had the qualities of repulsive, attractive, delightful, useful, etc., and as if these qualities were forces having a certain power over us. In the case of reflection, and only in that case, affectivity is posited for itself, as desire, fear, etc. Only in the case of reflection can I think "*I* hate Peter," "*I* pity Paul," etc.

Contrary to what has been held, therefore, it is on the reflected level that the ego-life has its place, and on the unreflected level that the impersonal life has its place (which naturally does not mean that all reflected life is necessarily egoistic, or that all unreflected life is necessarily altruistic). Reflection "poisons" desire. On the unreflected level I bring Peter help because Peter is "having to be helped." But if my state is suddenly transformed into a reflected state, there I am watching myself act, in the sense in which one says of someone that he listens to himself talk.

It is no longer Peter who attracts me, it is *my* helpful consciousness which appears to me as having to be perpetuated. Even if I only think that I must pursue my action because "that is good," the good qualifies *my* conduct, *my* pity, etc. The psychology of La Rochefoucauld has its place. And yet this psychology is not *true:* it is not my fault if my reflective life poisons "by its very essence" my spontaneous life. Before being "poisoned" my desires were pure. It is the point of view that I have taken toward them which has poisoned them. The psychology of La Rochefoucauld is true only for particular emotions which have their origin in reflective life, that is to say, which are given first as *my emotions,* instead of first transcending themselves toward an object.

Thus a purely psychological examination of "intra-mundane" consciousness leads us to the same conclusions as our phenomenological study: the *me* must not be sought *in* the states of unreflected consciousness, nor *behind* them. The *me* appears only with the reflective act, and as a noematic correlate of a reflective intention. We begin to get a glimpse of the fact that the *I* and the *me* are only one. We are going to try to show that this ego, of which *I* and *me* are but two aspects, constitutes the ideal and indirect (noematic) unity of the infinite series of our reflected consciousnesses.

The *I* is the ego as the unity of actions. The *me* is the ego as the unity of states and of qualities. The distinction that one makes between these two aspects of one and the same reality seems to us simply functional, not to say grammatical.

The I and Consciousness in the *cogito*

One might ask why the *I* appears on the occasion of the *Cogito*, since the *Cogito*, correctly performed, is an apprehension of a pure consciousness, without any constitution of states or actions. To tell the truth, the *I* is not necessary here, since it is never a direct unity of consciousnesses. One can even suppose a consciousness performing a pure reflective act which delivers consciousness to itself as a non-personal spontaneity. Only we must realize that phenomenological reduction is never perfect. Here intervene a host of psychological motivations. When Descartes performs the *Cogito*, he performs it in conjunction with methodological doubt, with the ambition of "advancing science," etc., which are *actions* and *states*. Thus the Cartesian method, doubt, etc., are by nature given as undertakings of an *I*. It is quite natural that the *Cogito*, which appears at the end of these undertakings, and *which is given as logically bound to methodological doubt*, sees an *I* appear on its horizon. This *I* is a form of ideal connection, a way of affirming that the *Cogito* is indeed of the same form as doubt. In a word, the *Cogito* is impure. It is a spontaneous consciousness, no doubt, but it remains synthetically tied to consciousnesses of states and actions. The proof is that the *Cogito* is given at once as the logical result of doubt and as that which puts an end to doubt. A reflective apprehension of spontaneous consciousness as non-personal spontaneity would have to be accomplished *without any antecedent motivation*. This is always possible in principle, but remains very improbable or, at least, extremely rare in our human condition. At any rate, as we have said above, the *I* which appears on the horizon of the *I Think* is not given as the producer of conscious spontaneity. Consciousness produces itself facing the *I* and goes toward it, goes to rejoin it. That is all one can say.

My *I*, in effect, is *no more certain for consciousness than the I of other men*. It is only more intimate.

The theorists of the extreme Left have sometimes reproached phenomenology for being an idealism and for drowning reality in the stream of ideals. But if idealism is the philosophy without evil of Brunschvicg, if it is a philosophy in which the effort of spiritual assimilation never meets external resistances, in which suffering, hunger, and war are diluted in a slow process of the unification of ideas, nothing is more unjust than to call phenomenologists "idealists." On the contrary, for centuries we have not felt in philosophy so realistic a current. The phenomenologists have plunged man back into the world; they have given full measure to man's agonies and sufferings, and also to his rebellions. Unfortunately, as long as the *I* remains a structure of absolute consciousness, one will still be able to reproach phenomenology for being an escapist doctrine, for again pulling a part of man out of the world and, in that way, turning our attention from the real problems. It seems to us that this reproach no longer has any justification if one makes the *me* an existent, strictly contemporaneous with the world, whose existence has the same essential characteristics as the world. It has always seemed to me that a working hypothesis as fruitful as historical materialism never needed for a foundation the absurdity which is metaphysical materialism. In fact, it is not necessary that the object precede the subject for spiritual pseudo-values to vanish and for ethics to find its bases in reality. It is enough that the *me* be contemporaneous with the World, and that the subject-object duality, which is purely logical, definitively disappear from philosophical preoccupations. The World has not created the *me:* the *me* has not created the World. These are two objects for absolute, impersonal consciousness, and it is by virtue of this consciousness that they are connected. This absolute consciousness, when it is purified of the *I,* no longer has anything of the *subject.* It is no longer a collection of representations. It is quite simply a first condition and an absolute source of existence. And the relation of interdependence established by this absolute consciousness between the *me* and the World is sufficient for the *me* to appear as "endangered" before the World, for the *me* (indirectly and through the intermediary of states) to draw the whole of its content from the World. No more is needed in the way of a philosophical foundation for an ethics and a politics which are absolutely positive.

THE "WHO" OF DASEIN

MARTIN HEIDEGGER

From *Being and Time* by Martin Heidegger. Translated by John Macquarrie and Edward Robinson. Copyright © 1962 by SCM Press Ltd. Reprinted by permission of Harper & Row, Publishers, Inc. Pp. 150–153, 163–168.

Historiologically, the aim of the existential analytic can be made plainer by considering Descartes, who is credited with providing the point of departure for modern philosophical inquiry by his discovery of the *"cogito sum"*. He investigates the *"ego"*, at least within certain limits. On the other hand, he leaves the *"sum"* completely undiscussed, even though it is regarded as no less primordial than the *cogito*. Our analytic raises the ontological question of the Being of the *"sum"*. Not until the nature of this Being has been determined can we grasp the kind of Being which belongs to *cogitationes*.

At the same time it is of course misleading to exemplify the aim of our analytic historiologically in this way. One of our first tasks will be to prove that if we posit an "I" or subject as that which is proximally given, we shall completely miss the phenomenal content [Bestand] of Dasein. *Ontologically*, every idea of a 'subject'—unless refined by a previous ontological determination of its basic character—still posits the *subjectum* (ὑποκείμενον) along with it, no matter how vigorous one's ontical protestations against the 'soul substance' or the 'reification of consciousness'. The Thinghood itself which such reification implies must have its ontological origin demonstrated if we are to be in a position to ask what we are to understand *positively* when we think of the unreified *Being* of the subject, the soul, the consciousness, the spirit, the person. All these terms refer to definite phenomenal domains which can be 'given form' ["ausformbare"]: but they are never used without a notable failure to see the need for inquiring about the Being of the entities thus designated. So we are not being terminologically arbitrary when we avoid these terms—or such expressions as 'life' and 'man'—in designating those entities which we are ourselves.

AN APPROACH TO THE EXISTENTIAL QUESTION OF THE "WHO" OF DASEIN

The answer to the question of who Dasein is, is one that was seemingly given in Section 9, where we indicated formally the basic characteristics of Dasein. Dasein is an entity which is in each case I myself; its Being is in each case mine. This definition *indicates* an *ontologically* constitutive state, but it does no more than indicate it. At the same time this tells us *ontically* (though in a rough and ready fashion) that in each case an "I"—not Others—is this entity. The question of the "who" answers itself in terms of the "I" itself, the 'subject', the 'Self'. The "who" is what maintains itself as something identical throughout changes in its Experiences and ways of behaviour, and which relates itself to this changing multiplicity in so doing. Ontologically we understand it as something which is in each case already constantly present-at-hand, both in and for a closed realm, and which lies at the basis, in a very special sense, as the *subjectum*. As something selfsame in manifold otherness, it has the character of the *Self*. Even if one rejects the "soul substance" and the Thinghood of consciousness, or denies that a person is an object, ontologically one is still positing something whose Being retains the meaning of present-at-hand, whether it does so explicitly or not. Substantiality is the ontological clue for determining which entity is to provide the answer to the question of the "who". Dasein is tacitly conceived in advance as something present-at-hand. This meaning of Being is always implicated in any case where the Being of Dasein has been left indefinite. Yet presence-at-hand is the kind of Being which belongs to entities whose character is not that of Dasein.

The assertion that it is I who in each case Dasein is, is ontically obvious; but this must not mislead us into supposing that the route for an ontological Interpretation of what is 'given' in this way has thus been unmistakably prescribed. Indeed it remains questionable whether even the mere ontical content of the above assertion does proper justice to the stock of phenomena belonging to everyday Dasein. It could be that the "who" of everyday Dasein just is *not* the "I myself".

But is it not contrary to the rules of all sound method to approach a problematic without sticking to what is given as evident in the area of our theme? And what is more indubitable than the giveness of the "I"? And does not this givenness tell us that if we aim to work this out primordially, we must disregard everything else that is 'given'—not only a 'world' that is [einer

seienden "Welt"], but even the Being of other 'I's? The kind
of "giving" we have here is the mere, formal, reflective awareness
of the "I"; and perhaps what it gives is indeed evident. This
insight even affords access to a phenomenological problematic
in its own right, which has in principle the signification of
providing a framework as a 'formal phenomenology of consciousness'.

In this context of an existential analytic of factical Dasein,
the question arises whether giving the "I" in the way we have
mentioned discloses Dasein in its everydayness, if it discloses
Dasein at all. Is it then obvious *a priori* that access to Dasein
must be gained only by mere reflective awareness of the "I" of
actions? What if this kind of 'giving-itself' on the part of Dasein
should lead our existential analytic astray and do so, indeed, in
a manner grounded in the Being of Dasein itself? Perhaps when
Dasein addresses itself in the way which is closest to itself, it
always says "I am this entity", and in the long run says this
loudest when it is 'not' this entity. Dasein is in each case mine,
and this is its constitution; but what if this should be the very
reason why, proximally and for the most part, Dasein *is not
itself*? What if the aforementioned approach, starting with the
givenness of the "I" to Dasein itself, and with a rather patent
self-interpretation of Dasein, should lead the existential analytic,
as it were, into a pitfall? If that which is accessible by mere
"giving" can be determined, there is presumably an ontological
horizon for determining it; but what if this horizon should
remain in principle undetermined? It may well be that it is
always ontically correct to say of this entity that 'I' am it. Yet
the ontological analytic which makes use of such assertions must
make certain reservations about them in principle. The word 'I'
is to be understood only in the sense of a non-committal *formal
indicator*, indicating something which may perhaps reveal itself
as its 'opposite' in some particular phenomenal context of Being.
In that case, the 'not-I' is by no means tantamount to an entity
which essentially lacks 'I-hood' ["Ichheit"], but is rather a
definite kind of Being which the 'I' itself possesses, such as
having lost itself [Selbstverlorenheit].

Yet even the positive Interpretation of Dasein which we

have so far given, already forbids us to start with the formal givenness of the "I", if our purpose is to answer the question of the "who" in a way which is phenomenally adequate. In clarifying Being-in-the-world we have shown that a bare subject without a world never 'is' proximally, nor is it ever given. And so in the end an isolated 'I" without Others is just as far from being proximally given. If, however, 'the Others' already *are there with us* [*mit da sind*] in Being-in-the-world, and if this is ascertained phenomenally, even this should not mislead us into supposing that the *ontological* structure of what is thus 'given' is obvious, requiring no investigation. Our task is to make visible phenomenally the species to which this Dasein-with in closest everydayness belongs, and to Interpret it in a way which is ontologically appropriate.

Just as the ontical obviousness of the Being-in-itself of entities within-the-world misleads us into the conviction that the meaning of this Being is obvious ontologically, and makes us overlook the phenomenon of the world, the ontical obviousness of the fact that Dasein is in each case mine, also hides the possibility that the ontological problematic which belongs to it has been led astray. *Proximally* the "who" of Dasein is not only a problem *ontologically;* even *ontically* it remains concealed.

But does this mean that there are no clues whatever for answering the question of the "who" by way of existential analysis? Certainly not. Of the ways in which we formally indicated the constitution of Dasein's Being in Section 9 and 12 above, the one we have been discussing does not, of course, function so well as such a clue as does the one according to which Dasein's 'Essence' is grounded in its existence. *If the 'I' is an Essential characteristic of Dasein, then it is one which must be Interpreted existentially.* In that case the "Who?" is to be answered only by exhibiting phenomenally a definite kind of Being which Dasein possesses. If in each case Dasein is its Self only in *existing*, then the constancy of the Self no less than the possibility of its 'failure to stand by itself' requires that we formulate the question existentially and ontologically as the sole appropriate way of access to its problematic.

But if the Self is conceived 'only' as a way of Being of this entity, this seems tantamount to volatilizing the real 'core' of Dasein. Any apprehensiveness however which one may have about this gets its nourishment from the perverse assumption that the entity in question has at bottom the kind of Being which belongs to something present-at-hand, even if one is far from attributing to it the solidity of an occurrent corporeal Thing. Yet man's *'substance'* is not spirit as a synthesis of soul and body; it is rather *existence*.

EVERYDAY BEING-ONE'S-SELF AND THE "THEY"

The *ontologically* relevant result of our analysis of Being-with is the insight that the 'subject character' of one's own Dasein and that of Others is to be defined existentially—that is, in terms of certain ways in which one may be. In that with which we concern ourselves environmentally the Others are encountered as what they are; they *are* what they do [sie *sind* das, was sie betreiben].

In one's concern with what one has taken hold of, whether with, for, or against, the Others, there is constant care as to the way one differs from them, whether that difference is merely one that is to be evened out, whether one's own Dasein has lagged behind the Others and wants to catch up in relationship to them, or whether one's Dasein already has some priority over them and sets out to keep them suppressed. The care about this distance between them is disturbing to Being-with-one-another, though this disturbance is one that is hidden from it. If we may express this existentially, such Being-with-one-another has the character of *distantiality* [*Abständigkeit*]. The more inconspicuous this kind of Being is to everyday Dasein itself, all the more stubbornly and primordially does it work itself out.

But this distantiality which belongs to Being-with, is such that Dasein, as everyday Being-with-one-another, stands in *subjection* [*Botmässigkeit*] to Others. It itself *is* not; its Being has been taken away by the Others. Dasein's everyday possibilities of Being are for the Others to dispose of as they please. These

Others, moreover, are not *definite* Others. On the contrary, any
Other can represent them. What is decisive is just that inconspicuous domination by Others which has already been taken
over unawares from Dasein as Being-with. One belongs to the
Others oneself and enhances their power. 'The Others' whom one
thus designates in order to cover up the fact of one's belonging
to them essentially oneself, are those who proximally and for the
most part *'are there'* in everyday Being-with-one-another. The
"who" is not this one, not that one, not oneself [man selbst],
not some people [einige], and not the sum of them all. The 'who'
is the neuter, *the 'they"* [*das Man*].

We have shown earlier how in the environment which lies
closest to us, the public 'environment' already is ready-to-hand
and is also a matter of concern [mitbesorgt]. In utilizing public
means of transport and in making use of information services
such as the newspaper, every Other is like the next. This Being-
with-one-another dissolves one's own Dasein completely into the
kind of Being of 'the Others', in such a way, indeed, that the
Others, as distinguishable and explicit, vanish more and more.
In this inconspicuousness and unascertainability, the real dictatorship of the 'they" is unfolded. We take pleasure and enjoy
ourselves as *they* [*man*] take pleasure; we read, see, and judge
about literature and art as *they* see and judge; likewise we shrink
back from the 'great mass' as *they* shrink back; we find 'shocking' what *they* find shocking. The "they", which is nothing definite, and which all are, though not as the sum, prescribes the
kind of Being of everydayness.

The "they" has its own ways in which to be. That tendency
of Being-with which we have called "distantiality" is grounded
in the fact that Being-with-one-another concerns itself as such
with *averageness*, which is an existential characteristic of the
"they". The "they", in its Being, essentially makes an issue of
this. Thus the "they" maintains itself factically in the averageness of that which belongs to it, of that which it regards as valid
and that which it does not, and of that to which it grants success
and that to which it denies it. In this averageness with which it
prescribes what can and may be ventured, it keeps watch over

everything exceptional that thrusts itself to the fore. Every kind of priority gets noiselessly suppressed. Overnight, everything that is primordial gets glossed over as something that has long been well known. Everything gained by a struggle becomes just something to be manipulated. Every secret loses its force. This care of averageness reveals in turn an essential tendency of Dasein which we call the "levelling down" [*Einebnung*] of all possibilities of Being.

Distantiality, averageness, and levelling down, as ways of Being for the "they", constitute what we know as 'publicness' ["die Offentlichkeit"]. Publicness proximally controls every way in which the world and Dasein get interpreted, and it is always right—not because there is some distinctive and primary relationship-of-Being in which it is related to 'Things', or because it avails itself of some transparency on the part of Dasein which it has explicitly appropriated, but because it is insensitive to every difference of level and of genuineness and thus never gets to the 'heart of the matter' ["auf die Sachen"]. By publicness everything gets obscured, and what has thus been covered up gets passed off as something familiar and accessible to everyone.

The 'they" is there alongside everywhere [ist überall dabei], but in such a manner that it has always stolen away whenever Dasein presses for a decision. Yet because the "they" presents every judgment and decision as its own, it deprives the particular Dasein of its answerability. The "they" can, as it were, manage to have 'them' constantly invoking it. It can be answerable for everything most easily, because it is not someone who needs to vouch for anything. It 'was' always the "they" who did it, and yet it can be said that it has been 'no one'. In Dasein's everydayness the agency through which most things come about is one of which we must say that "it was no one".

Thus the particular Dasein in its everydayness is *disburdened* by the 'they". Not only that; by thus disburdening it of its Being, the 'they" accommodates Dasein [kommt . . . dem Dasein entgegen] if Dasein has any tendency to take things easily and make them easy. And because the "they" constantly accommodates the particular Dasein by disburdening it of its

Being, the "they" retains and enhances its stubborn dominion.

Everyone is the other, and no one is himself. The *"they"*, which supplies the answer to the question of the *"who"* of everyday Dasein, is the *"nobody"* to whom every Dasein has already surrendered itself in Being-among-one-other [Untereinandersein].

In these characters of Being which we have exhibited— everyday Being-among-one-another, distantiality, averageness, levelling down, publicness, the disburdening of one's Being, and accommodation—lies that 'constancy' of Dasein which is closest to us. This "constancy" pertains not to the enduring Being-present-at-hand of something, but rather to Dasein's kind of Being as Being-with. Neither the Self of one's own Dasein nor the Self of the Other has as yet found itself or lost itself as long as it is [seiend] in the modes we have mentioned. In these modes one's way of Being is that of inauthenticity and failure to stand by one's Self. To be in this way signifies no lessening of Dasein's facticity, just as the "they", as the "nobody", is by no means nothing at all. On the contrary, in this kind of Being. Dasein is an *ens realissimum*, if by 'Reality' we understand a Being that has the character of Dasein.

Of course, the "they" is as little present-at-hand as Dasein itself. The more openly the "they" behaves, the harder it is to grasp, and the slier it is, but the less is it nothing at all. If we 'see' it ontico-ontologically with an unprejudiced eye, it reveals itself as the 'Realest subject' of everydayness. And even if it is not accessible like a stone that is present-at-hand, this is not in the least decisive as to its kind of Being. One may neither decree prematurely that this "they" is 'really' nothing, nor profess the opinion that one can Interpret this phenomenon ontologically by somehow 'explaining' it as what results from taking the Being-present-at-hand-together of several subjects and then fitting them together. On the contrary, in working out concepts of Being one must direct one's course by these phenomena, which cannot be pushed aside.

Furthermore, the "they" is not something like a 'universal subject' which is a plurality of subjects have hovering above them. One can come to take it this way only if the Being of such 'subjects' is understood as having a character other than that of Dasein, and if these are regarded as cases of a genus of occurrents—cases which are factually present-at-hand. With this approach, the only possibility ontologically is that everything which is not a case of this sort is to be understood in the sense of genus and species. The "they" is not the genus to which the individual Dasein belongs, nor can we come across it in such entities as an abiding characteristic. That even the traditional logic fails us when confronted with these phenomena, is not surprising if we bear in mind that it has its foundation in an ontology of the present-at-hand—an ontology which, moreover, is still a rough one. So no matter in how many ways this logic may be improved and expanded, it cannot in principle be made any more flexible. Such reforms of logic, oriented towards the 'humane sciences', only increase the ontological confusion.

The "they" is an existentiale; and as a primordial phenomenon, it belongs to Dasein's positive constitution. It itself has, in turn, various possibilities of becoming concrete as something characteristic of Dasein [seiner daseinsmässigen Konkretion]. The extent to which its dominion becomes compelling and explicit may change in the course of history.

The Self of everyday Dasein is the *they-self*, which we distinguish from the *authentic Self*—that is, from the Self which has been taken hold of in its own way [eigens ergriffenen]. As they-self, the particular Dasein has been *dispersed* into the "they", and must first find itself. This dispersal characterizes the 'subject' of that kind of Being which we know as concernful absorption in the world we encounter as closest to us. If Dasein is familiar with itself as they-self, this means at the same time that the "they" itself prescribes that way of intepreting the world and Being-in-the-world which lies closest. Dasein is for the sake of the "they" in an everyday manner, and the "they" itself Articulates the referential context of significance. When entities are encountered, Dasein's world frees them for a totality of involvements with which the "they" is familiar, and within the limits which have been established with the "they's" averageness. *Proximally,* factical Dasein is in the with-world, which is discovered in an average way. *Proximally*, it is not 'I', in the sense of my own Self, that 'am', but rather the Others, whose way is that of the "they". In terms of the 'they", and as the 'they", I am 'given' proximally to 'myself' [mir "selbst"]. Proximally Dasein is "they", and for the most part it remains so. If Dasein discovers the world in its own way [eigens] and brings it close, if it discloses to itself its own authentic Being, then this discovery of the 'world' and this disclosure of Dasein are always accomplished as a clearing-away of concealments and obscurities, as a breaking up of the disguises with which Dasein bars its own way.

With this Interpretation of Being-with and Being-one's-Self in the 'they", the question of the "who" of the everydayness of Being-with-one-another is answered. These considerations have at the same time brought us a concrete understanding of the basic constitution of Dasein: Being-in-the-world, in its everydayness and its averageness, has become visible.

From the kind of Being which belongs to the "they"—the kind which is closest—everyday Dasein draws its pre-ontological way of interpreting its Being. In the first instance ontological Interpretation follows the tendency to interpret it this way: it understands Dasein in terms of the world and comes across it as an entity within-the-world. But that is not all: even that meaning of Being on the basis of which these 'subject' entities [diese seienden "Subjekte"] get understood, is one which that ontology of Dasein which is 'closest' to us lets itself present in term of the 'world'. But because the phenomenon of the world itself gets passed over in this absorption in the world, its place gets taken [tritt an seine Stelle] by what is present-at-hand within-the-world, namely, Things. The Being of those entities which *are there with us*, gets conceived as presence-at-hand. Thus by exhibiting the positive phenomenon of the closest eveyday Being-in-the-world, we have made it possible to get an insight into the reason why an ontological Interpretation of this state of Being has been missing. *This very state of Being, in its everyday kind of Being, is what proximally misses itself and covers itself up.*

If the Being of everyday Being-with-one-another is already different in principle from pure presence-at-hand—in spite of the fact that it is seemingly close to it ontologically—still less can the Being of the authentic Self be conceived as presence-at-hand. *Authentic Being-one's-Self* does not rest upon an exceptional condition of the subject, a condition that has been detached from the 'they"; *it is rather an existentiell modification of the "they" —of the "they" as an essential existentiale.*

But in that case there is ontologically a gap separating the selfsameness of the authentically existing Self from the identity of that "I" which maintains itself throughout its manifold Experiences.

INTERSUBJECTIVITY

The existence of other people is a difficulty and an outrage for objective thought . . .

With the *cogito* begins that struggle between consciousnesses, each of which, as Hegel says, seeks the death of the other.

—Maurice Merleau-Ponty THE PHENOMENOLOGY OF
PERCEPTION

Hell is other people.   —Jean-Paul Sartre NO EXIT

INTRODUCTION

How do we know that there are other people (rather than mere humanoids that appear to be people)? Husserl offers us a phenomenological analysis of "the Other" in the fifth of his *Cartesian Meditations*. The existentialists, however, reject the idea of *knowing* the Other and replace it with an analysis of *experiencing* the Other. Presented here are related arguments from Marcel, Heidegger, Sartre, and Merleau-Ponty.

FIFTH MEDITATION

EDMUND HUSSERL

42. Exposition of the Problem of Experiencing Someone Else, in Rejoinder to the Objection That Phenomenology Entails Solipsism

As the point of departure for our new meditations, let us take what may seem to be a grave objection. The objection concerns nothing less than the claim of transcendental phenomenology to be itself transcendental *philosophy* and therefore its claim that, in the form of a constitutional problematic and theory moving within the limits of the transcendentally reduced ego, it can solve the transcendental problems pertaining to the *Objective world*. When I, the meditating I, reduce myself to my absolute transcendental ego by phenomenological epoché do I not become *solus ipse;* and do I not remain that, as long as I carry on a consistent self-explication under the name phenomenology? Should not a phenomenology that proposed to solve the problems of Objective being, and to present itself actually as philosophy, be branded therefore as transcendental solipsism?

Let us consider the matter more closely. Transcendental reduction restricts me to the stream of my pure conscious processes and the unities constituted by their actualities and potentialities. And indeed it seems [is] obvious that such unities are inseparable from my ego and therefore belong to his concreteness itself.

But what about other egos, who surely are not a mere intending and intended *in me,* merely synthetic unities of possible verification *in me,* but, according to their sense, precisely *others?* Have we not therefore done transcendental realism an injustice?

Reprinted from *Cartesian Meditations,* translated by D. Cairns, Med. V, from sections 42, 43, 48, 49–51, 54, 55, 42–55 (The Hague, Netherlands: M. Nijhoff, 1960), by permission of the publisher.

The doctrine may lack a phenomenological foundation; but essentially it is right in the end, since it looks for a path from the immanency of the ego to the transcendency of the Other. Can we, as phenomenologists, do anything but agree with this and say: "The Nature and the whole world that are constituted 'immanently' in the ego are only my 'ideas' and have behind them the world that exists in itself. The way to this world must still be sought."? Accordingly can we avoid saying likewise: "The very question of the possibility of actually transcendent knowledge—above all, that of the possibility of my going outside my ego and reaching other egos (who, after all, as others, are not actually in me but only consciously intended in me)—this question cannot be asked purely phenomenologically"? It is not *self-understood* from the very beginning that my field of transcendental knowledge does not reach beyond my sphere of transcendental experience and what is synthetically comprised therein? Is it not self-understood that all of that is included without residue in my own transcendental ego?

But perhaps there is some mistake in thoughts like these. Before one decides in favor of them and the "self-understood" propositions they exploit, and then perchance embarks on dialectical argumentations and self-styled "metaphysical" hypotheses (whose supposed possibility may turn out to be complete absurdity), it might indeed be more fitting to undertake the *task of phenomenological explication* indicated in this connexion by the "alter ego" and carry it through in concrete work. We must, after all, obtain for ourselves insight into the explicit and implicit intentionality wherein the alter ego becomes evinced and verified in the realm of our transcendental ego; we must discover in what intentionalities, syntheses, motivations, the sense "other ego" becomes fashioned in me and, under the title, harmonious experience of someone else, becomes verified as existing and even as itself there in its own manner. These experiences and their works are facts belonging to my phenomenological sphere. How else than by examining them can I explicate the sense, existing others, in all its aspects?

43. The Noematic-Ontic Mode of Givenness of the Other, as Transcendental Clue for the Constitutional Theory of the Experience of Someone Else

First of all, my "transcendental clue" is the experienced Other, given to me in straightforward consciousness and as I immerse myself in examining the noematic-ontic content belonging to him (purely as correlate of my cogito, the particular structure of which is yet to be uncovered). By its remarkableness and multiplicity, that content already indicates the many-sidedness and difficulty of the phenomenological risk. For example: In changeable harmonious multiplicities of experience I experience others as actually existing and, on the one hand, as world Objects—not as mere physical things belonging to Nature, though indeed as such things in respect of one side of them. They are in fact experienced also as *governing psychically* in their respective natural organisms. Thus peculiarly involved with animate organisms, as "psychophysical" Objects, they are *"in" the world*. On the other hand, I experience them at the same time as *subjects for this world,* as experiencing it (this same world that I experience) and, in so doing, experiencing me too, even as I experience the world and others in it. Continuing along this line, I can explicate a variety of other moments noematically.

In any case then, within myself, within the limits of my transcendentally reduced pure conscious life, I *experience* the world (including others)—and, according to its experiential sense, *not* as (so to speak) my *private* synthetic formation but as other than mine alone [*mir fremde*], as an *intersubjective* world actually there for everyone, accessible in respect of its Objects to everyone. And yet each has his experiences, his appearances and appearance-unities, his world-phenomenon; whereas the experienced world exists in itself, over against all experiencing subjects and their world-phenomena.

•   •   •

Thus the problem is stated at first as a special one, namely that of the "thereness-for-me" of others, and accordingly as the theme of a *transcendental theory of experiencing someone else*, a transcendental theory of so-called "empathy". But it soon becomes evident that the range of such a theory is much greater than at first it seems, that it contributes to the founding of a *transcendental theory of the Objective world* and, indeed, to the founding of such a theory in every respect, notably as regards Objective Nature. The existence-sense [*Seinssinn*] of the world and of Nature in particular, as Objective Nature, includes after all, as we have already mentioned, thereness-for-everyone. This is always cointended whereever we speak of Objective actuality. In addition, Objects with "spiritual" predicates belong to the experienced world. These Objects, in respect of their origin and sense, refer us to subjects, usually other subjects, and their actively constituting intentionality. Thus it is in the case of all cultural Objects (books, tools, works of any kind, and so forth), which moreover carry with them at the same time the experiential sense of thereness-for-everyone (that is, everyone belonging to the corresponding cultural community, such as the European or perhaps, more narrowly, the French cultural community, and so forth).

 •   •   •

48. The Transcendency of the Objective World as Belonging to a Level Higher Than That of Primordial Transcendency

That my own essence can be at all contrasted for me with something else, or that I (who am I) can become aware of someone else (who is not I but someone other than I), presupposes that *not all my own modes of consciousness are modes of my self-consciousness*. Since actual being is constituted originally by harmoniousness of experience, my own self must contain, in contrast to self-experience and the system of its harmoniousness (the system, therefore, of self-explication into components of my ownness), yet other experiences united in harmonious systems. And now the *problem* is how we are to understand the fact that the ego has, and can always go on forming, in himself such intentionalities of a different kind, intentionalities with an existence-sense whereby *he wholly transcends his own being.* How can something actually existent for me—and, as that, not just somehow meant but undergoing harmonious verification in me —be anything else than, so to speak, a point of intersection belonging to my constitutive synthesis? As concretely inseparable from my synthesis, is it peculiarly my own? But even the possibility of a vaguest, emptiest intending of something alien is problematic, if it is true that, essentially, every such mode of consciousness involves its possibilities of an uncovering of what is intended, its possibilities of becoming converted into either fulfiling or disillusioning experiences of what is meant, and moreover, (as regards the genesis of the consciousness) points back to such experiences of the same intended object or a similar one.

The fact of experience of something alien (something that is not I), is present as experience of an Objective world and others in it (non-Ego in the form: other Ego); and an important result of the ownness-reduction performed on these experiences was that it brought out a substratum belonging to them, an intentional substratum in which a reduced "world" shows itself, as an "immanent transcendency". In the order pertaining to constitution of a world *alien to my Ego*—a world *"external"* to my *own concrete Ego* (but not at all in the natural spatial sense) —that reduced world is the intrinsically first, the *"primordial" transcendency* (or "world"); and, regardless of its *ideality* as a synthetic unity belonging to an infinite system of my potentialities, it is *still a determining part of my own concrete being,* the being that belongs to me as concrete ego.

It must now be made understandable *how,* at the founded higher level, the sense-bestowal pertaining to transcendency proper, to constitutionally secondary *Objective transcendency,* comes about—and does so as an experience. Here it is not a matter of uncovering a genesis going on in time, but a matter of *"static analysis".* The Objective world is constantly there before me as already finished, a datum of my livingly continuous Objective experience and, even in respect of what is no longer experienced, something I go on accepting habitually. It is a matter of examining this experience itself and uncovering intentionally the manner in which it bestows sense, the manner in which it can occur as experience and become verified as evidence relating to an actual existent with an explicatable essence of *its* own, which is not *my* own essence and has no place as a constituent part thereof, though it nevertheless can acquire sense and verification only in my essence.

49. Predelineation of the Course to Be Followed By Intentional Explication of Experiencing What Is Other

Constitution of the existence-sense, "Objective world", on the basis of my primordial "world", involves a number of levels. As the *first* of these, there is to be distinguished the constitutional level pertaining to the "other ego" or to any "other egos" whatever—that is: to egos *excluded* from my own concrete being (from me as the "primordial ego"). In connexion with that and, indeed, motivated by it, there occurs a *universal superaddition of sense to my primordial world*, whereby the latter becomes the *appearance "of"* a determinate "Objective" world, as the identical world for everyone, myself included. Accordingly *the intrinsically first other* (the first "non-Ego") *is the other Ego*. And the other Ego makes constitutionally possible a new infinite domain of what is "other"; an *Objective Nature* and a whole Objective world, to which all other Egos and I myself belong. This constitution, arising on the basis of the *"pure"* others (the other Egos who as yet have no worldly sense), is essentially such that the "others"-for-me do not remain isolated; on the contrary, an *Ego-community*, which includes me, becomes constituted (in my sphere of ownness, naturally) as a community of Egos existing with each other and for each other—*ultimately a community of monads*, which, moreover, (in its communalized intentionality) constitutes the *one identical world. In this world* all Egos again present themselves, but *in an Objectivating apperception* with the sense *"men"* or "psychophysical men as worldly Objects".

By virtue of the mentioned communalization [of constitutive intentionality], the transcendental intersubjectivity has an *inter-*

subjective sphere of ownness, in which it constitutes the Objective world; and thus, as the transcendental "We", it is a subjectivity for this world and also for the world of men, which is the form in which it has made itself Objectively actual. It, however, inter-subjective sphere of ownness and Objective world are to be distinguished here, nevertheless, when I as ego take my stand on the basis of the intersubjectivity constituted from sources within my own essence, I can recognize that the Objective world does not, in the proper sense, *transcend* that sphere or that sphere's own intersubjective essence, but rather inheres in it as an "immanent" transcendency. Stated more precisely: The Objective world as an *idea*—the ideal correlate of an intersubjective (intersubjectively communalized) experience, which ideally can be and is carried on as constantly harmonious—is essentially related to intersubjectivity (itself constituted as having the ideality of endless openness), whose component particular subjects are equiped with mutually corresponding and harmonious constitutive systems. Consequently *the constitution of the world essentially involves a "harmony" of the monads:* precisely this harmony among particular constitutions in the particular monads; and accordingly it involves also a harmonious generation that goes on in each particular monad. That is not meant, however, as a "metaphysical" hypothesizing of monadic harmony, any more than the monads themselves are metaphysical inventions or hypotheses. On the contrary, it is itself part of the explication of the intentional components implicit in the fact of the experiential world that exists for us. Here again it is to be noted that, as has been repeatedly emphasized, the ideas referred to are not phantasies or modes of the "as if", but arise constitutionally in integral connexion with all Objective experience and have their modes of legitimation and their development by scientific activity.

50. The Mediate Intentionality of Experiencing Someone Else, As Appresentation (Analogical Apperception)

After we have dealt with the prior stage, which is very important transcendentally—namely, definition and articulation of the primordial sphere—, the genuine difficulties (and in fact they are not inconsiderable) are occsasioned by the *first* of the above-indicated steps toward constitution of an Objective world: *the step taking us to the "other" ego.* They lie, accordingly, in the transcendental clarification of experiencing "someone else"—in the sense in which the other has not yet attained the sense "man".

Experience is original consciousness; and in fact we generally say, in the case of experiencing a man: the other is himself there before us "in person". On the other hand, this being there in person does not keeps us from admitting forthwith that, properly speaking, neither the other Ego himself, nor his subjective processes or his appearances themselves, nor anything else belonging to his own essence, becomes given in our experience originally. If it were, if what belongs to the other's own essence were directly accessible, it would be merely a moment of my own essence, and ultimately he himself and I myself would be the same. The situation would be similar as regards his animate organism, if the latter were nothing else but the "body" that is a unity constituted purely in my actual and possible experiences, a unity belonging—as a product of *my* "sensuousness" exclusively—in my primordial sphere. *A certain mediacy of intentionality* must be present here, going out from the substratum, "primordial world", (which in any case is the incessantly underlying basis) and making present to consciousness a "there too", which nevertheless is not itself there and can never become an "itself-there". We have here, accordingly, a kind of *making "co-present"*, a kind of *"appresentation."*

An appresentation occurs even in external experience, since the strictly seen front of a physical thing always and necessarily appresents a rear aspect and prescribes for it a more or less determinate content. On the other hand, experiencing someone else cannot be a matter of just this kind of appresentation, which already plays a role in the constitution of primordial Nature: Appresentation of this sort involves the possibility of verification by a corresponding fulfilling presentation (the back becomes the front); whereas, in the case of that appresentation which would lead over into the other original sphere, such verification must be excluded a priori. How can appresentation of another original sphere, and thereby the sense "someone else", be motivated in my original sphere and, in fact, motivated as experience —as the word "appresentation" (making intended as co-present) already indicates? Not every non-originary making-present can do that. A non-originary making-present can do it only in combination with an originary presentation, an itself-giving proper; and only as demanded by the originary presentation can it have the character of appresentation—somewhat as, in the case of experiencing a physical thing, what is there perceptually motivates [belief in] something else being there too.

Let us assume that another man enters our perceptual sphere. Primordially reduced, that signifies: In the perceptual sphere pertaining to my primordial Nature, a body is presented, which, as primordial, is of course only a determining part of myself: an "immanent transcendency". Since, in this Nature and this world, my animate organism is the only body that is or can be constituted originally as an animate organism (a functioning organ), the body over there, which is nevertheless apprehended as an animate organism, must have derived this sense by an *apperceptive transfer from my animate organism*, and done so in a manner that excludes an actually direct, and hence primordial, showing of the predicates belonging to an animate organism specifically, a showing of them in perception proper. It is clear from the very beginning that only a similarity connecting, within my primordial sphere, that body over there with my body can serve as the motivational basis for the "*analogizing*" *apprehension* of that body as another animate organism.

There would be, accordingly, a certain assimilative apperception; but it by no means follows that there would by an inference from analogy. Apperception is not inference, not a thinking act. *Every* apperception in which we apprehend at a glance, and noticingly grasp, objects given beforehand—for example, the already-given everyday world—every apperception in which we understand their sense and its horizons forthwith, points back to a "*primal instituting*", in which an object with a similar sense became constituted for the first time. Even the physical things of this world that are unknown to us are, to speak generally, known in respect of their type. We have already seen like things before, though not precisely this thing here. Thus *each everyday experience* involves an *analogizing transfer* of an originally instituted objective sense to a new case, with its anticipative apprehension of the object as having a similar sense. To the extent that there is givenness beforehand, there is such a transfer. At the same time, that sense-component in further experience which proves to be actually new may function in turn as institutive and found a pregivenness that has a richer sense. The child who already sees physical things understands, let us say, for the first time the final sense of scissors; and from now on he sees scissors at the first glance *as* scissors—but naturally not in an explicit reproducing, comparing, and inferring. Yet the manner in which apperceptions arise—and consequently in themselves, by their sense and sense-horizon, point back to their genesis— varies greatly. There are different levels of apperception, corresponding to different layers of objective sense. Ultimately we always get back to the *radical differentiation of apperceptions* into those that, according to their genesis, belong purely to the *primordial sphere* and those that present themselves *with the sense "alter ego"* and, *upon* this sense, have built a new one— thanks to a genesis at a higher level.

51. "Pairing" As an Associatively Constitutive Component of My Experience of Someone Else

If we attempt to indicate the peculiar nature of that analogizing apprehension whereby a body within my primordial sphere, being similar to my own animate body, becomes *apprehended as likewise an animate organism*, we encounter: first, the circumstance that here the *primally institutive original* is *always livingly present*, and the primal instituting itself is therefore always going on in a livingly effective manner; secondly, the peculiarity we already know to be necessary, namely that what is *appresented* by virtue of the aforesaid analogizing can never attain actual presence, never become an object of perception proper. Closely connected with the first peculiarity is the circumstance that *ego* and *alter ego* are always and necessarily given *in an original "pairing"*.

Pairing, occurence in configuration as a pair and then as a group, a plurality, is a *universal* phenomenon of the transcendental sphere (and of the parallel sphere of intentional psychology) ; and, we may add forthwith, as far as a pairing is actually present, so far extends that remarkable kind of primal instituting of an analogizing apprehension—its continuous primal institution in living actuality—which we have already stressed as the first peculiarity of experiencing someone else. Hence it is not exclusively peculiar to this experience.

First of all, let us elucidate the essential nature of any "pairing" (or any forming of a plurality). Pairing is a *primal form of that passive synthesis* which we designate as *"association"*, in contrast to passive synthesis of "identification". In a *pairing association* the characteristic feature is that, in the most primitive case, two data are given intuitionally, and with prominence, in the unity of a consciousness and that, on this basis—essentially, already in pure passivity (regardless therefore of whether they are noticed or unnoticed)—, as data appearing with mutual distinctness, they *found phenomenologically a unity of similarity* and thus are always constituted precisely as a pair. If there are more than two such data, then a phenomenally unitary group, a plurality, becomes constituted. On more precise analysis we find essentially present here an intentional overreaching, coming about genetically (and by essential necessity) as soon as the data that undergo pairing have become prominent and simultaneously intended; we find, more particularly, a living mutual awakening and an overlaying of each with the objective sense of the other. This overlaying can bring a total or a partial coincidence, which in any particular instance has its degree, the limiting case being that of complete "likeness". As the result of this overlaying, there takes place in the paired data a mutual transfer of sense—that is to say: an apperception of each according to the sense of the other, so far as moments of sense actualized in what is experienced do not annul this transfer, with the consciousness of "different".

from THE MYSTERY OF BEING

GABRIEL MARCEL

The time has come when we should attempt to draw out all
the implications of the notions of a situation, and of participation
as we have attempted to elucidate them in our three previous
chapters. It may be, however, that to reach our goal we may find
it convenient to go back, in the first instance, to the problem of
the relationships between myself and others, as that problem now
stands, in the light of our previous observations, and particularly
in the light of that criticism of the notion of a *state of consciousness* which I roughed out in chapter three. I think my best course
will be to present you with a condensed version of my analysis
in my essay, *Homo Viator,* an analysis which is a kind of nucleus
of the possible phenomenology of the relationships between myself and others.

We should notice, to start with, that the ego, as such, shows
up in an extraordinarily vivid and aggressive fashion in the
mental world of the child; and one might add that this vividness
and aggressiveness persist, in later years, to the degree to which
that mental world survives in the adult. The child, let us say,
runs up to his mother and offers her a flower. 'Look,' he says,
'that was me, *I* picked it.' His tone and his gestures are very
significant; he is pointing himself out as somebody who deserves
the admiration and gratitude of grown-ups. Look, it is I, I in person, I, all present and correct here, who have plucked this flower!
Above all, don't believe for a moment that it was Jim or Lucy
who picked it. The child's, '*I* did it', in fact, excludes in the most
definite fashion the deplorable misunderstanding by which *my*
exploit could be attributed to others. But we find adults standing
up in the same way for the ego's rights. Let us take the example

Reprinted from *The Mystery of Being,* vol. 1 (Chicago: Henry Regnery, 1951), pp. 175–178, by permission of the publisher.

of the amateur composer who has just been singing, in a throaty voice, a song for which he has written the tune. Some artless listener asks, was that by Debussy? 'Oh, no,' says the composer, bridling and smirking, 'that was a little thing of my own.' Here again the ego is trying to attract to itself the praise, the surprised and admiring comments, of a something *other* than itself, that it uses as a sounding-board. In every case of this sort one may say that the ego is present in the flesh, appealing or protesting, in various tones of voice, that nobody should infringe on its rights, or, if you like, tread on its toes. Notice, too, that in all such cases one essential factor is what I shall call, a little pedantically, *ecceity*: that is, a hereness and a nowness, or rather a here-and-nowness; we can think of the ego in this sense, in fact, as a sort of personified here-and-now that has to defend itself actively against other personified heres-and-nows, the latter appearing to it essentially as just so many threats to what I have called its rights. These rights, however, have essentially a pre-juridical character, they are from the beginning inseparably linked to the very fact of existing and thus are exposed continually to all sorts of more or less mortifying infringements. In so far as I feel myself in danger of being passively overlooked or actively slighted in a hundred different ways that all cut me to the quick, one might say, in fact, that I have no protective skin at all, that the quick is exposed already.

The obvious example to take at this point is, of course, that of the shy young man who is making his first appearance at some fashionable dance or cocktail party. Such a young man is, as you so admirably express it in English, to the highest degree *self-conscious*. He feels himself the cynosure, and the extremely vulnerable cynosure, of neighbouring eyes. It seems to him that all the other people at the party, none of whom he knows, are looking at him, and looking at him, too, with what meaning glances! Obviously they are making fun of him, perhaps of his new dinner jacket which does not fit him as well as it should, perhaps of his black bow tie, which was all right when he last looked in the mirror, but now, he feels quite sure, has gone lopsided. And then, of course, he cut himself when he was shaving.

And everybody must have noticed how clumsily he held his glass just a moment ago, so that some of the sherry slopped over. And so on, and so on . . . To such a young man it seems that he has been literally thrown (as Christians were thrown to the lions) to the malevolent lucidity of other people's glances. Thus he is at once preoccupied with himself to the highest possible degree and hypnotized at the same time to a quite supreme degree by others, by what he imagines other people may think of him. It is this paradoxical tension which your excellent word *self-consciousness* so compactly expresses.

But on the other hand this tension is quite at the opposite pole from what I have at various times called, and shall here call again, intersubjectivity. And the opposite nature of the two things cannot be too heavily underlined. Let us suppose that some unknown person comes up at our party to say a word or two to the shy young man and put him at his ease. The latter, to begin with, does not find himself entering into the direct relation with his new acquaintance that is expressed by the pronoun *you* but instead thinks of him as *him*. Why is *he* talking to me? What is *he* after? Is he trying to satisfy some sinister and mocking curiosity? Let us be on our guard anyway. Let us be extremely noncommittal in our answers to his questions. Thus, because he is on the defensive with this other guest, our young man has to the least possible degree what can be described as a genuine encounter or conversation *with* him. He is not really *with* the other any more than he can help being. But in a very general fashion, indeed, one might say that it is the relationship expressed by the preposition *with* that is eminently intersubjective. The relationship that *with* expresses, here, does not for instance really apply to the world of objects, which, taken as a whole, is a world merely of juxtaposition. A chair is *alongside* a table, or *beside* it, or we put the chair *by* the table, but the chair is never really *with* the table in this sense.

But let us get back to our example and let us suppose that the ice is after all broken, and that the conversation takes on a more intimate character. 'I am glad to meet you,' says the stranger, 'I once knew your parents', and all at once a bond is created and, what specially matters, there is a relaxation of tension. The attention of the young man ceases to be concentrated on himself, it is as if something gripped tight together inside him were able to loosen up. He is lifted out of that stifling here-and-nowness in which, if I may be allowed a homely comparison, his ego was sticking to him as an adhesive plaster sticks to a small cut. He is lifted right out of the here and now, and, what is very strange surely, this unknown person whom he has just met accompanies him on this sort of magic voyage. They are together in what we must call an elsewhere, an elsewhere, however, which has a mysteriously intimate character. Let us say, if you like, that they are linked to each other by a shared secret. I shall have to come back, no doubt, to the notion of the secret as a mainspring of intersubjectivity, but let us notice, before we leave our example, that ties of quite a different nature might have grown up between the stranger and the shy young man. A man whom I run into quite casually learns that I am very fond of coffee, coffee is desperately scarce in France at the time, so he gives me a hint about how to get some on the black market. One cannot say that this incident is enough in itself to create a bond between me and him; all we have in common is a *taste,* and that is not enough to draw us together at the ontological level, that is *qua* beings. And neither, on the other hand, is a taste for coffee, even combined with a certain broadmindedness about means of getting hold of coffee, enough in itself to create the sense of complicity and freemasonry in vice that might arise from the avowal, to somebody who shared it, of some much more dubious inclination. But such a sense of complicity is not really what we have in mind, either; rather it is in the sort of case where I discover that a stranger has recognized the deep, individual quality of somebody whom I myself have tenderly loved and who retains a place in my heart, that true intersubjectivity arises.

THE DASEIN-WITH OF OTHERS AND EVERYDAY BEING-WITH

MARTIN HEIDEGGER

The answer to the question of the "who" of everyday Dasein is to be obtained by analysing that kind of Being in which Dasein maintains itself proximally and for the most part. Our investigation takes its orientation from Being-in-the-world—that basic state of Dasein by which every mode of its Being gets co-determined. If we are correct in saying that by the foregoing explication of the world, the remaining structural items of Being-in-the-world have become visible, then this must also have prepared us, in a way, for answering the question of the "who".

In our 'description' of that environment which is closest to us—the work-world of the craftsman, for example,—the outcome was that along with the equipment to be found when one is at work [in Arbeit], those Others for whom the 'work' ["Werk"] is destined are 'encountered too'. If this is ready-to-hand, then there lies in the kind of Being which belongs to it (that is, in its involvement) an essential assignment or reference to possible wearers, for instance, for whom it should be 'cut to the figure'. Similarly, when material is put to use, we encounter its producer or 'supplier' as one who 'serves' well or badly. When, for example, we walk along the edge of a field but 'outside it', the field shows itself as belonging to such-and-such a person, and decently kept up by him; the book we have used was bought at So-and-so's shop and given by such-and-such a person, and so forth. The boat anchored at the shore is assigned in its Being-in-itself to an acquaintance who undertakes voyages with it; but even if it is a 'boat which is strange to us', it still is indicative of Others.

The Others who are thus 'encountered' in a ready-to-hand, environmental context of equipment, are not somehow added on in thought to some Thing which is proximally just present-at-hand; such 'Things' are encountered from out of the world in which they are ready-to-hand for Others—a world which is always mine too in advance. In our previous analysis, the range of what is encountered within-the-world was, in the first instance, narrowed down to equipment ready-to-hand or Nature present-at-hand, and thus to entities with a character other than that of Dasein. This restriction was necessary not only for the purpose of simplifying our explication but above all because the kind of Being which belongs to the Dasein of Others, as we encounter it within-the-world, differs from readiness-to-hand and presence-at-hand. Thus Dasein's world frees entities which not only are quite distinct from equipment and Things, but which also—in accordance with their kind of Being *as Dasein* themselves—are 'in' the world in which they are at the same time encountered within-the-world, and are 'in' it by way of Being-in-the-world. These entities are neither present-at-hand nor ready-to-hand; on the contrary, they are *like* the very Dasein which frees them, in that *they are there too, and there with it.* So if one should want to identify the world in general with entities within-the-world, one would have to say that Dasein too is 'world'.

Thus in characterizing the encountering of *Others,* one is again still oriented by that Dasein which is in each case one's *own.* But even in this characterization does one not start by marking out and isolating the 'I' so that one must then seek some way of getting over to the Others from this isolated subject? To avoid this misunderstanding we must notice in what sense we are talking about 'the Others'. By 'Others' we do not mean everyone else but me—those over against whom the "I" stands out. They are rather those from whom, for the most part, one does *not* distinguish oneself—those among whom one is too. This Being-there-too [Auch-dasein] with them does not have the ontological character of a Being-present-at-hand-along-'with' them within a world. This 'with' is something of the character of Dasein; the 'too' means a sameness of Being as circumspectively

concernful Being-in-the-world. 'With' and 'too' are to be understood *existentially*, not categorically. By reason of this *with-like*
[*mithaften*] Being-in-the-world, the world is always the one that
I share with Others. The world of Dasein is a *with-world* [*Mit-
welt*]. Being-in is *Being-with* Others. Their Being-in-themselves
within-the-world is *Dasein-with* [*Mitdasein*].

When Others are encountered, it is not the case that one's
own subject is *proximally* present-at-hand and that the rest of the
subjects, which are likewise occurrents, get discriminated beforehand and then apprehended; nor are they encountered by a
primary act of looking at oneself in such a way that the opposite
pole of a distinction first gets ascertained. They are encountered
from out of the *world*, in which concernfully circumspective
Dasein essentially dwells. Theoretically concocted 'explanations'
of the Being-present-at-hand of Others urge themselves upon us
all too easily; but over against such explanations we must hold
fast to the phenomenal facts of the case which we have pointed
out, namely, that Others are encountered *environmentally*. This
elemental worldly kind of encountering, which belongs to Dasein
and is closest to it, goes so far that even one's *own* Dasein becomes something that it can itself proximally 'come across' only
when it *looks away* from 'Experiences' and the 'centre of its
actions', or does not as yet 'see' them at all. Dasein finds 'itself'
proximally in *what* it does, uses, expects, avoids—in those things
environmentally ready-to-hand with which it is proximally *concerned*.

And even when Dasein explicitly addresses itself as "I here",
this locative personal designation must be understood in terms of
Dasein's existential spatiality. In Interpreting this we have already intimated that this "I-here" does not mean a certain privileged point—that of an I-Thing—but is to be understood as
Being-in in terms of the "yonder" of the world that is ready-to-
hand—the "yonder" which is the dwelling-place of Dasein as
concern.

W. von Humboldt has alluded to certain languages which
express the 'I' by 'here', the 'thou' by 'there', the 'he' by 'yonder',
thus rendering the personal pronouns by locative adverbs, to put

it grammatically. It is controversial whether indeed the primordial signification of locative expressions is adverbial or pronominal. But this dispute loses its basis if one notes that locative adverbs have a relationship to the "I" *qua* Dasein. The 'here' and the 'there' and the 'yonder' are primarily not mere ways of designating the location of entities present-at-hand within-the-world at positions in space; they are rather characteristics of Dasein's primordial spatiality. These supposedly locative adverbs are Dasein-designations; they have a signification which is primarily existential, not categorial. But they are not pronouns either; their signification is prior to the differentiation of locative adverbs and personal pronouns: these expressions have a Dasein-signification which is authentically spatial, and which serves as evidence that when we interpret Dasein without any theoretical distortions we can see it immediately as 'Being-alongside' the world with which it concerns itself, and as Being-alongside it spatially—that is to say, as deserving and giving directionality. In the 'here', the Dasein which is absorbed in its world speaks not towards itself but away from itself towards the 'yonder' of something circumspectively ready-to-hand; yet it still has *itself* in view in its existential spatiality.

Dasein understands itself proximally and for the most part in terms of its world; and the Dasein-with of Others is often encountered in terms of what is ready-to-hand within-the-world. But even if Others become themes for study, as it were, in their own Dasein, they are not encountered as person-Things present-at-hand: we meet them 'at work', that is, primarily in their Being-in-the-world. Even if we see the Other 'just standing around', he is never apprehended as a human-Thing present-at-hand, but his 'standing-around' is an existential mode of Being—an unconcerned, uncircumspective tarrying alongside everything and nothing [Verweilen bei Allem und Keinem]. The Other is encountered in his Dasein-with in the world.

The expression 'Dasein', however, shows plainly that 'in the first instance' this entity is unrelated to Others, and that of course it can still be 'with' Others afterwards. Yet one must not fail to notice that we use the term "Dasein-with" to designate that Being for which the Others who are [die seienden Anderen] are freed within-the-world. This Dasein-with of the Others is disclosed within-the-world for a Dasein, and so too for those who are Daseins with us [die Mitdaseienden], only because Dasein in itself is essentially Being-with. The phenomenological assertion that "Dasein is essentially Being-with" has an existential-ontological meaning. It does not seek to establish ontically that factically I am not present-at-hand alone, and that Others of my kind occur. If this were what is meant by the proposition that Dasein's Being-in-the-world is essentially constituted by Being-with, then Being-with would not be an existential attribute which Dasein, of its own accord, has coming to it from its own kind of Being. It would rather be something which turns up in every case by reason of the occurrence of Others. Being-with is an existential characteristic of Dasein even when factically no Other is present-at-hand or perceived. Even Dasein's Being-alone is Being-with in the world. The Other can *be missing* only *in* and *for* a Being-with. Being-alone is a deficient mode of Being-with; its very possibility is the proof of this. On the other hand, factical Being-alone is not obviated by the occurrence of a second example of a human being 'beside' me, or by ten such examples. Even if these and more are present-at-hand, Dasein can still be alone. So Being-with and the facticity of Being with one another are not based on the occurrence together of several 'subjects'. Yet Being-alone 'among' many does not mean that with regard to their Being they are merely present-at-hand there alongside us. Even in our Being 'among them' they are *there with* us; their Dasein-with is encountered in a mode in which they are indifferent and alien. Being missing and 'Being away' [Das Fehlen und "Fortsein"] are modes of Dasein-with, and are possible only because Dasein as Being-with lets the Dasein of Others be encountered in its world. Being-with is in every case a characteristic of one's own Dasein; Dasein-with characterizes the Dasein of Others to the extent that it is freed by its world for a Being-with. Only so far as one's own Dasein has the essential structure of Being-with, is it Dasein-with as encounterable for Others.

If Dasein-with remains existentially constitutive for Being-in-the-world, then, like our circumspective dealings with the ready-to-hand within-the-world (which, by way of anticipation, we have called 'concern'), it must be Interpreted in terms of the phenomenon of *care;* for as "care" the Being of Dasein in general is to be defined. Concern is a character-of-Being which Being-with cannot have as its own, even though Being-with, like concern, is a *Being towards* entities encountered within-the-world. But those entities towards which Dasein as Being-with comports itself do not have the kind of Being which belongs to equipment ready-to-hand; they are themselves Dasein. These entities are not objects of concern, but rather of *solicitude.*

Even 'concern' with food and clothing, and the nursing of the sick body, are forms of solicitude. But we understand the expression "solicitude" in a way which corresponds to our use of "concern" as a term for an *existentiale.* For example, 'welfare work' ["Fürsorge"], as a factical social arrangement, is grounded in Dasein's state of Being as Being-with. Its factical urgency gets its motivation in that Dasein maintains itself proximally and for the most part in the deficient modes of solicitude. Being for, against, or without one another, passing one another by, not "mattering" to one another—these are possible ways of solicitude. And it is precisely these last-named deficient and Indifferent modes that characterize everyday, average Being-with-one-another. These modes of Being show again the characteristics of inconspicuousness and obviousness which belong just as much to the everyday Dasein-with of Others within-the-world as to the readiness-to-hand of the equipment with which one is daily concerned. These Indifferent modes of Being-with-one-another may easily mislead ontological Interpretation into interpreting this kind of Being, in the first instance, as the mere Being-present-at-hand of several subjects. It seems as if only negligible variations of the same kind of Being lie before us; yet ontologically there is an essential distinction between the 'indifferent' way in which Things at random occur together and the way in which entities who are with one another do not "matter" to one another.

THE EXISTENCE OF OTHERS

JEAN-PAUL SARTRE

THE PROBLEM

We have described human reality from the standpoint of negating conduct and from the standpoint of the *cogito*. Following this lead we have discovered that human reality is-for-itself. Is this *all* that it is? Without going outside our attitude or reflective description, we can encounter modes of consciousness which seem, even while themselves remaining strictly in for-itself, to point to a radically different type of ontological structure. This ontological structure is *mine;* it is in relation to myself as subject that I am concerned about myself, and yet this concern (for-myself) reveals to me a being which is *my* being without being-for-me.

Consider for example shame. Here we are dealing with a mode of consciousness which has a structure identical with all those which we have previously described. It is a non-positional self-consciousness, conscious (of) itself as shame; as such, it is an example of what the Germans call *Erlebnis,* and it is accessible to reflection. In addition its structure is intentional; it is a shameful apprehension *of* something and this something is *me.* I am ashamed of what I *am.* Shame therefore realizes an intimate relation of myself to myself. Through shame I have discovered an aspect of *my* being. Yet although certain complex forms derived from shame can appear on the reflective plane, shame is not originally a phenomenon of reflection. In fact no matter what results one can obtain in solitude by the religious *practice* of shame, it is in its primary structure shame *before somebody.* I have just made an awkward or vulgar gesture. This gesture clings to me; I neither judge it nor blame it. I simply live it. I realize it in the mode of for-itself. But now suddenly I raise my head. Somebody was there and has seen me. Suddenly I realize the vulgarity of my gesture, and I am ashamed. It is certain that my shame is not reflective, for the presence of another in my consciousness, even as a catalyst, is incompatable with the reflective attitude; in the field of my reflection I can never meet with anything but the consciousness which is mine. But the Other is the indispensable mediator between myself and me. I am ashamed of myself *as I appear* to the Other.

By the mere appearance of the Other, I am put in the position of passing judgment on myself as on an object, for it is as an object that I appear to the Other. Yet this object which has appeared to the Other is not an empty image in the mind of another. Such an image in fact, would be imputable wholly to the Other and so could not "touch" me. I could feel irritation, or anger before it as before a bad portrait of myself which gives to my expression an ugliness or baseness which I do not have, but I could not be touched to the quick. Shame is by nature *recognition*. I recognize that I *am* as the Other sees me. There is however no question of a comparison between what I am for myself and what I am for the Other as if I found in myself, in the mode of being of the For-itself, an equivalent of what I am for the Other. In the first place this comparison is not encountered in us as the result of a concrete psychic operation. Shame is an immediate shudder which runs through me from head to foot without any discursive preparation. In addition the comparison is impossible; I am unable to bring about any relation between what I am in the intimacy of the For-Itself, without distance, without recoil, without perspective, and this unjustifiable being-in-itself which I am for the Other. There is no standard here, no table of correlation. Moreover the very notion of *vulgarity* implies an intermonad relation. Nobody can be vulgar all alone!

Thus the Other has not only revealed to me what I was; he has established me in a new type of being which can support new qualifications. This being was not in me potentially before the appearance of the Other, for it could not have found any place in the For-itself. Even if some power had been pleased to endow me with a body wholly constituted before it should be for-others, still my vulgarity and my awkwardness could not lodge there potentially; for they are meanings and as such they surpass the body and at the same time refer to a witness capable of understanding them and to the totality of my human reality. But this new being which appears *for* the other does not reside *in* the Other; I am responsible for it as is shown very well by the education system which consists in making children ashamed of what they are.

Thus shame is shame *of oneself before the Other;* these two structures are inseparable. But at the same time I need the Other in order to realize fully all the structures of my being. The For-itself refers to the For-others. Therefore if we wish to grasp in its totality the relation of man's being to being-in-itself, we can not be satisfied with the descriptions outlined in the earlier chapters of this work. We must answer two far more formidable questions: first that of the existence of the Other, then that of the relation of my *being* to the being of the Other.

• • • •

Human-reality remains alone because the Other's existence has the nature of a contingent and irreducible fact. We *encounter* the Other; we do not constitute him. And if this fact still appears to us in the form of a necessity, yet it does not belong with those "conditions of the possibility of our experience" or—if you prefer—with ontological necessity. If the Other's existence is a necessity, it is a "contingent necessity"; that is, it is of the same type as the factual necessity which is imposed on the *cogito.* If the Other is to be capable of being given to us, it is by means of a direct apprehension which leaves to the encounter its character as facticity, just as the *cogito* itself leaves all its facticity to my own thought, a facticity which nevertheless shares in the apodicity of the *cognito* itself—*i.e.,* in its indubitability.

This long exposition of doctrine will not therefore have been useless if it enables us to formulate the necessary and sufficient conditions under which a theory of the existence of others can be valid.

(1) Such a theory can not offer a new *proof* of the existence of others, or an argument better than any other against solipsism. Actually if solipsism is to be rejected, this can not be because it is impossible or, if you prefer, because nobody is truly solipsistic. The Other's existence will always be subject to doubt, at least if one doubts the Other only in words and abstractly, in the same way that without really being able to conceive of it, I can write, "I doubt my own existence." In short the Other's existence can not be a *probability*. Probability can concern only objects which appear in our experience and from which new effects can appear in our experience. There is probability only if a validation or invalidation of it is at every moment possible. Thus since the Other on principle and in its "For-itself" is outside my experience, the probability of his existence as *Another Self* can never be either validated or invalidated; it can be neither believed nor disbelieved, it can not even be measured; it loses therefore its very being as probability and becomes a pure fictional conjecture. In the same way M. Lalande has effectively shown that an hypothesis concerning the existence of living beings on the planet Mars will remain purely conjectural with no chance of being either true or false so long as we do not have at our disposal instruments or scientific theories enabling us to produce facts validating or invalidating this hypothesis. But the structure of the Other is on principle such that no new experiment will ever be able to be conceived, that no new theory will come to validate or invalidate the hypothesis of his existence, that no instrument will come to reveal new facts inspiring me to affirm or to reject this hypothesis. Therefore if the Other is not immediately present to me, and if his existence is not as sure as my own, all conjecture concerning him is entirely lacking in meaning. But if I do not conjecture about the Other, then, precisely, I affirm him. A theory of the Other's existence must therefore simply question me in my being, must make clear and precise the meaning of that affirmation; in particular, far from inventing a proof, it must make explicit the very foundation of that certainty. In

other words Descartes has not *proved* his existence. Actually I have always known that I existed, I have never ceased to practice the *cogito*. Similarly my resistance to solipsism—which is as lively as any I should offer to an attempt to doubt the *cogito*—proves that I have always known that the Other existed, that I have always had a total though implicit *comprehension* of his existence, that this "pre-ontological" comprehension comprises a surer and deeper understanding of the nature of the Other and the relation of his being to my being than all the theories which have been built around it. If the Other's existence is not a vain conjecture, a pure fiction, this is because there is a sort of *cogito* concerning it. It is this *cogito* which we must bring to light by specifying its structures and determining its scope and its laws.

(2) On the other hand, Hegel's failure has shown us that the only point of departure possible is the Cartesian *cogito*. Moreover the *cogito* alone establishes us on the ground of that factual necessity which is the necessity of the Other's existence. Thus what for lack of a better term we called the *cogito* of the Other's existence is merged with my own *cogito*. The *cogito* examined once again, must throw me outside it and onto the Other, just as it threw me outside upon the In-itself; and this must be done not by revealing to me an *a priori* structure of myself which would point toward an equally *a priori* Other but by disclosing to me the concrete, indubitable presence of a particular, concrete Other, just as it has already revealed to me my own imcomparable, contingent but necessary, and concrete existence. Thus we must ask the For-itself to deliver to us the For-others; we must ask absolute immanence to throw us into absolute transcendence. In my own inmost depths I must find not *reasons for believing* that the Other exists but the Other himself as not being me.

(3) What the *cogito* must reveal to us is not the-Other-as-object. For a long time now it must have been obvious that what is called an *object* is said to be *probable*. If the Other is an object for me, he refers me to probability. But probability is founded solely on the infinite congruity of our representations. Since the Other is neither a representation nor a system of representations nor a necessary unity of our representations, he can not be prob-

able: he can not *at* first be an object. Therefore if he is *for us*, this can be neither as a constitutive factor of our knowledge of the world nor as a constitutive factor of our knowledge of the self, but as one who 'interests" our being, and that not as he contributes *a priori* to constitute our being but as he interests it concretely and "ontically" in the empirical circumstances of our facticity.

(4) If we attempt somehow regarding the Other what Descartes attempted to do for God with that extraordinary "proof by the idea of perfection" which is wholly animated by the intuition of transcendence, then for our apprehension of the Other qua Other we are compelled to reject a certain type of negation which we have called an external negation. The Other must appear to the *cogito* as *not being* me. This negation can be conceived in two ways: either it is a pure, external negation, and it will separate the Other from myself as one substance from another substance—and in this case all apprehension of the Other is by definition impossible; or else it will be an internal negation, which means a synthetic, active connection of the two terms, each one of which constitutes itself by denying that it is the other. This negative relation will therefore be reciprocal and will possess a twofold interiority: This means first that the multiplicity of "Others" will not be a *collection* but a *totality* (in this sense we admit that Hegel is right) since each Other finds his being in the Other. It also means that this Totality is such that it is on principle impossible for us to adopt "the point of view of the whole." In fact we have seen that no abstract concept of consciousness can result from the comparison of my being-for-myself with my object-state for the Other. Furthermore this totality—like that of the For-itself—is a detotalized totality; for since existence-for-others is a radical refusal of the Other, no totalitarian and unifying synthesis of "Others" is possible.

•   •   •   •

It is not true that I first am and then later "seek" to make an object of the Other or to assimilate him; but to the extent that the upsurge of my being is an upsurge in the presence of the Other, to the extent that I am a pursuing flight and a pursued-pursuing, I am—at the very root of my being—the project of assimilating and making an object of the Other. I am the proof of the Other. That is the original fact. But this proof of the Other is in itself an attitude toward the Other; that is, I can not *be in the presence of the Other* without being that "in-the-presence" in the form of having to be it. Thus again we are describing the for-itself's structures of being although the Other's presence in the world is an absolute and self-evident fact, but a contingent fact—that is, a fact impossible to deduce from the ontological structures of the for-itself.

These two attempts which I am are opposed to one another. Each attempt is the death of the other; that is, the failure of the one motivates the adoption of the other. Thus there is no dialectic for my relations toward the Other but rather a circle—although each attempt is enriched by the failure of the other. But it should be noted that at the very core of the one the other remains always present, precisely because neither of the two can be held without contradiction. Better yet, each of them is in the other and endangers the death of the other. Thus we can never get outside the circle.

．　．　．　．

Everything which may be said of me in my relations with the Other applies to him as well. While I attempt to free myself from the hold of the Other, the Other is trying to free himself from mine; while I seek to enslave the Other, the Other seeks to enslave me. We are by no means dealing with unilateral relations with an object-in-itself, but with reciprocal and moving relations. The following descriptions of concrete behavior must therefore be envisaged within the perspective of *conflict*. Conflict is the original meaning of being-for-others.

OTHER PEOPLE AND THE HUMAN WORLD

MAURICE MERLEAU-PONTY

But the first need is to know how I experience my own cultural world, my own civilization. The reply will once more be that I see a certain use made by other men of the implements which surround me, that I interpret their behavior by analogy with my own, and through my inner experience, which teaches me the significance and intention of perceived gestures. In the last resort, the actions of others are, according to this theory, always understood through my own; the 'one' or the 'we' through the 'I.' But this is precisely the question: how can the word 'I' be put into the plural, how can a general idea of the *I* be formed, how can I speak of an *I* other than my own, how can I know that there are other *I*'s, how can consciousness which, by its nature, and as self-knowledge, is in the mode of the *I*, be grasped in the mode of Thou, and through this, in the world of the 'One'? The very first of all cultural objects, and the one by which all the rest exist, is the body of the other person as the vehicle of a form of behaviour. Whether it be a question of vestiges or the body of another person, we need to know how an object in space can become the eloquent relic of an existence; how, conversely, an intention, a thought or a project can detach themselves from the personal subject and become visible outside him in the shape of his body, and in the environment which he builds for himself. The constitution of the other person does not fully elucidate that of society, which is not an existence involving two or even three people, but co-existence involving an indefinite number of consciousnesses. Yet the analysis of the perception of others runs up against the difficulty of fundamental idea raised by the cultural

Reprinted from *The Phenomenology of Perception,* translated by C. Smith (New York: Humanities Press, 1962), pp. 348–357, 362 by permission of the publisher and Routledge & Kegan Paul.

world, since it is called upon to solve the paradox of a consciousness seen from the outside, of a thought which has its abode in the external world, and which, therefore, is already subjectless and anonymous compared with mine.

What we have said about the body provides the beginning of a solution to this problem. The existence of other people is a difficulty and an outrage for an objective thought. If the events of the world are, in Lachelier's words, a network of general properties standing at the point of intersection of functional relations which, in principle, enable the analysis of the former to be carried through, and if the body is indeed a province of the world, if it is that object which the biologist talks about, that conjunction of processes analysed in physiological treatises, that collection of organs shown in the plates of books on anatomy, then my experience can be nothing but the dialogue between bare consciousness and the system of objective correlations which it conceives. The body of another, like my own, is not inhabited, but is an object standing before the consciousness which thinks about or constitutes it. Other men, and myself, seen as empirical beings, are merely pieces of mechanism worked by springs, but the true subject has no counterpart, for that consciousness which is hidden in so much flesh and blood is the least intelligible of occult qualities. My consciousness, being co-extensive with what can exist for me, and corresponding to the whole system of experience, cannot encounter, in that system, another consciousness capable of bringing immediately to light in the world the background, unknown to me, of its own phenomena. There are two modes of being, and two only: being in itself, which is that of objects arrayed in space, and being for itself, which is that of consciousness. Now, another person would seem to stand before me as an *in-itself* and yet to exist *for himself*, thus requiring of me, in order to be perceived, a contradictory operation, since I ought both to distinguish him from myself, and therefore place him in the world of objects, and think of him as a consciousness, that is, the sort of being with no outside and no parts, to which I have access merely because that being is myself, and because the thinker and the thought about are amalgamated in him. There is thus no place for other people and a plurality of consciousnesses in objective thought. In so far as I constitute the world, I cannot conceive another consciousness, for it too would have to constitute the world and, at least as regards this other view of the world, I should not be the constituting agent. Even if I succeeded in thinking of it as constituting the world, it would be I who would be constituting the consciousness as such, and once more I should be the sole constituting agent.

But we have in fact learned to shed doubt upon objective thought, and have made contact, on the hither side of scientific representations of the world and the body, with an experience of the body and the world which these scientific approaches do not successfully embrace. My body and the world are no longer objects co-ordinated together by the kind of functional relationships that physics establishes. The system of experience in which they intercommunicate is not spread out before me and ranged over by a constituting consciousness. *I have* the world as an incomplete individual, through the agency of my body as the potentiality of this world, and I have the positing of objects through that of my body, or conversely the positing of my body through that of objects, not in any kind of logical implication, as we determine an unknown size through its objective relations to given sizes, but in a real implication, and because my body is a movement towards the world, and the world my body's point of support. If I experience this inhering of my consciousness in its body and its world, the perception of other people and the plurality of consciousnesses no longer present any difficulty. If, for myself who am reflecting on perception, the perceiving subject appears provided with a primordial setting in relation to the world, drawing in its train that bodily thing in the absence of which there would be no other things for it, then why should other bodies which I perceive not be similarly inhabited by consciousnesses? If my consciousness has a body, why should other bodies not 'have' consciousnesses? Clearly this involves a profound transformation of the notions of body and consciousness. As far as the body is concerned, even the body of another, we must learn to distinguish it from the objective body as set forth in works on physiology. This is not the body which is capable of being inhabited by a consciousness. We must restore to visible bodies those forms of behavior which are outlined by them and which appear on them, but are not really contained in them. How significance and intentionality could come to dwell in molecular edifices or masses of cells is a thing which can never be made comprehensible, and here Cartesianism is right. But there is, in any case, no question of any such absurd undertaking. It is simply a question of recognizing that the body, as a chemical structure or an agglomeration of tissues, is formed, by a process of impoverishment, from a primordial phenomenon of the body-for-us, the body of human experience or the perceived body, round which objective thought works, but without being called upon to postulate its completed analysis. As for consciousness, it has to be conceived, no longer as a constituting consciousness and, as it were, a pure being-for-itself, but as a perceptual consciousness, as the subject of a pattern of behaviour, as being in the world or existence, for only thus can another appear at the top of his phenomenal body, and be endowed with a sort of 'locality.' Under these conditions the antinomies of objective thought vanish. Through phenomenological reflection I discover vision, not as a 'thinking about seeing,' to use Descartes' expression, but as a gaze at grips with a visible world, and that is why for me there can be another's gaze; that expressive instrument called a face can carry an existence, as my own existence is carried by my body, that knowledge-acquiring apparatus. When I turn towards perception, and pass from direct perception to thinking about that perception, I reenact it, and find at work in my organs of perception a thought older than myself of which those organs are merely the trace. In the same way I understand the existence of other people. Here again I have only the trace of a consciousness which evades me in its actuality and, when my gaze meets another gaze, I re-enact the alien existence in a sort of reflection. There is nothing here resembling 'reasoning by analogy'. As Scheler so rightly declares, reasoning by analogy presupposes what it is called on to explain. The other consciousness can be deduced only if the emotional expressions of others are compared and identified with mine, and precise correlations recognized between my physical behaviour and my 'psychic events'. Now the perception of others is anterior to, and the condition of, such observations, the observations do not constitute the perception. A baby of fifteen months opens its mouth if I playfully take one of its fingers between my teeth and pretend to bite it. And yet it has scarcely looked at its face in a glass, and its teeth are not in any case like mine. The fact is that its own mouth and teeth, as it feels them from the inside, are immediately, for it, an apparatus to bite with, and my jaw, as the baby sees it from the outside, is immediately, for it, capable of the same intentions. 'Biting' has immediately, for it, an intersubjective significance. It perceives its intentions in its body, and my body with its own, and thereby my intentions in its own body. The observed correlations between my physical behaviour and that of others, my intentions and my pantomime, may well provide me with a clue in the methodical attempt to know others and on occasions when direct perception fails, but they do not teach me the existence of other people. Between my consciousness and my body as I experience it, between this phenomenal body of mine and that of another as I see it from the outside, there exists an internal relation which causes the other to appear as the completion of the system.

The *cogito* of another person strips my own *cogito* of all value, and causes me to lose the assurance which I enjoyed in my solitude of having access to the only being conceivable for me, being, that is, as it is aimed at and constituted by me. But we have learned in individual perception not to conceive our perspective views as independent of each other; we know that they slip into each other and are brought together finally in the thing. In the same way we must learn to find the communication between one consciousness and another in one and the same world. In reality, other people are not included in my perspective of the world because this perspective itself has no definite limits, because it slips spontaneously into the other person's, and because both are brought together in the one single world in which we all participate as anonymous subjects of perception.

•   •   •   •

There is one particular cultural object which is destined to play a crucial rôle in the perception of other people: language. In the experience of dialogue, there is constituted between the other person and myself a common ground; my thought and his are interwoven into a single fabric, my words and those of my interlocutor are called forth by the state of the discussion, and they are inserted into a shared operation of which neither of us is the creator. We have here a dual being, where the other is for me no longer a mere bit of behaviour in my transcendental field, nor I in his; we are collaborators for each other in consummate reciprocity. Our perspectives merge into each other, and we coexist through a common world.

· · · ·

The conflict between myself and the other does not begin only when we try to *think ourselves into* the other and does not vanish if we reintegrate thought into non-positing consciousness and unreflective living, it is already there if I try to live another's experiences, for example in the blindness of sacrifice. I enter into a pact with the other person, having resolved to live in an interworld in which I accord as much place to others as to myself. But this interworld is still a project of mine, and it would be hypocritical to pretend that I seek the welfare of another *as if it were mine*, since this very attachment to another's interest still has it source in me.

In the absence of reciprocity there is no alter Ego, since the world of the one then takes in completely that of the other, so that one feels disinherited in favour of the other. This is what happens in the case of a couple where there is more love felt on one side than on the other: one throws himself, and his whole life, into his love, the other remains free, finding in this love a merely contingent manner of living. The former feels his being and substance flowing away into that freedom which confronts him, whole and unqualified. And even if the second partner, through fidelity to his vows or through generosity, tries to reciprocate by reducing himself, or herself, to the status of a mere phenomenon in the other's world, and to see himself through the other's eyes, he can succeed only by an expansion of his own life, so that he denies by necessity the equivalence of himself with the other that he is trying to posit. Co-existence must in all cases be experienced on both sides. If neither of us is a constituting consciousness at the moment when we are about to communicate and discover a common world, the question then is: who communicates, and for whom does this world exist? And if someone does communicate with someone else, if the interworld is not an inconceivable *in-itself* and must exist for both of us, then again communication breaks down, and each of us operates in his own private world like two players playing on two chessboards a hundred miles apart. But here the players can still make known their moves to each other by telephone or correspondence, which means that they are in fact participants in the same world. I, on the other hand, share no common ground with another person, for the positing of the other with his world, and the positing of myself with mine are mutually exclusive. Once the other is posited, once the other's gaze fixed upon me has, by inserting me into his field, stripped me of part of my being, it will readily be understood that I can recover it only by establishing relations with him, by bringing about his clear recognition of me, and that my freedom requires the same freedom for others.

• • • •

We must therefore rediscover, after the natural world, the social world, not as an object or sum of objects, but as a permanent field or dimension of existence: I may well turn away from it, but not cease to be situated relatively to it. Our relationship to the social is, like our relationship to the world, deeper than any express perception or any judgment. It is as false to place ourselves in society as an object among other objects, as it is to place society within ourselves as an object of thought, and in both cases the mistake lies in treating the social as an object. We must return to the social with which we are in contact by the mere fact of existing, and which we carry about inseparably with us before any objectification.

FREEDOM

. . . every being that cannot act except under the idea of freedom is just for that reason in a practical point of view really free . . .

—Immanuel Kant THE FOUNDATIONS OF THE
METAPHYSICS OF MORALS

People rarely make use of the freedom which they have, for example, freedom of thought; instead they demand freedom of speech as compensation.

—Søren Kierkegaard, JOURNALS

Man is condemned to be free.

—Jean-Paul Sartre BEING AND NOTHINGNESS

INTRODUCTION

"Freedom" is the central concept and the central concern of the French existentialists. Presented here are analyses by Sartre, Merleau-Ponty, Marcel, and Frederick Olafson, an American interpreter of the existentialist movement.

FREEDOM

GABRIEL MARCEL

If I am to take into account my own living experience, it is apparent that the first question I must ask myself is: up to what point or within what limits can I or can I not assert that I am a free being. I have purposely put the question in the first person, because after all it is a question which can only be asked by me of myself. No outside answer will satisfy me, unless it coincides with my own answer, unless ultimately it *is my answer*.

At the same time it is impossible to overlook the difficulty in which I become involved as soon as I ask myself this question. Can I with all sincerity answer it by a comprehensive 'yes' or 'no'? To begin with, am I quite sure of the meaning which I am to attach to it? It is true that I can interpret it in a way which seems, at any rate, to be simple enough: am I conscious of doing what I want to do? The question would then revolve round the bond which unites will to action. But it is only too clear that there are countless instances in which I by no means do what I want to do; and we have the support of irrefutable evidence when we say that certain beings in captivity, in conditions, that is, which would involve the reduction to a minimum of what we commonly think of as independence, have nevertheless enjoyed a much deeper experience of their inner freedom than they would have been able to do in what we all call normal life. These considerations would lead us to presume that there is a freedom which is not concerned with *doing*; after all, the phrase 'do what I want to do', is at bottom ambiguous. To want, indeed,—I take this word in the sense of the French *vouloir*—is not to desire. The question with which we should now be concerned certainly cannot consist in asking ourselves whether or not I do what I

Reprinted from *The Mystery of Being*, vol. II (Chicago, Henry Regnery, 1951), pp. 122–127 by permission of the publisher.

desire. It might well be—the stoics first saw this, and all the subsequent thinkers who drew their inspiration from stoicism— that will is essentially opposed to desire. Do I not chiefly, if not exclusively, seem to myself to be free only when I succeed in using my will in opposition to my own desire—provided, of course, that it is not just a question of a mere whim, but that the will is embodied in acts which themselves form part of what I call reality? From this point of view one might say that the will appears as a resistance to the seductions to which desire exposes me, seductions which, if I yield to them, are quick to turn into compulsions.

We are still, however, I think, falling short of a reality which is much more complex and disconcerting. Let us suppose that I come to realize that in some particular circumstance I yielded to my desires, although I admit that I should not have done so. Would I be right in claiming that I did not act freely? It is a very delicate matter to answer such a question. In order to find some sort of self-justification, or to put it more exactly, in order to shift my responsibility, I should probably be inclined to say that the temptation was too strong for me to resist; that amounts to saying that a power independent of my will tyrannized me, and I was forced to obey. It may prove useful at this point to question what I shall call the legal force of such an assertion. We cannot just make a pure and simple affirmation of its truth or falsity. But I may be forced to conclude that the saving clause in which I took refuge against a particular accusation, does not provide me with the shelter on which I counted. Apart from any metaphor, it was meant to disarm the possible accuser within my own consciousness. Now, it may well be that it does not actually succeed in doing this. Here we meet again the inner plurality on which I laid such stress last year, and without which the very life of consciousness is completely unintelligible. I tried to excuse myself in my own eyes, but there is something in me which refuses to countenance this way of proving my innocence. The symptom of this refusal is a feeling of uneasiness, as though I had to admit that I have no right to locate in something internal (let us say in the circumstances themselves), the responsibility for what was in spite of every-thing my own act. What sort of a thing is this refusal or protest? If we examine it closely we cannot really focus it, unless we free ourselves from the categories which are nowadays our increas-ingly strict gaolers, the categories of power or efficiency. If I protest, it is because I have a vague feeling that I cannot win such an acquittal except at the expense of my own being. To put it in a much more concrete way, and in words whose meaning can be more readily grasped, if I allow to my desires, which are in some way detached from me, the power to reduce me to slavery, I put myself more and more at their mercy: almost as a man who has once yielded to the demands of a blackmailer finds that he is caught up in a web from which there is no escape. From the same point of view, we might say that the pro-test is tied up with the recognition of what I expose myself to if I make this plea of personal irresponsibility. The question then would not be whether the proposition is true or false, which is perhaps a meaningless question, but whether or not it entails consequences which will be fatal, not to what I am at the mo-ment, but to what I intend to be.

The true bearing of these remarks is evidently to enrich but also to obscure the idea I can form of my freedom. I have used the word obscure, but it is only an apparent obscurity. We can use the word in this connection only as opposed to a super-ficial clarity which is that of the understanding; but in fact this latter clarity is not the one which can throw light on freedom for us; to that extent one has probably good grounds for say-ing that it is *false* clarity; we can see things by its light, but it cannot be the clarity in which we see ourselves; in so far as we endeavour, I shall not say to think of ourselves, but to make a representation of ourselves which takes things as its model, we make it impossible for ourselves, by definition, to attach the least meaning to the word freedom; we have, accordingly, to take refuge in some determinist conception which implies an active misunderstanding of what we are, of the being which questions its own self when it examines itself as we did at the beginning of this chapter.

A sharply defined conclusion seems to me to emerge from
the above analysis. This conclusion is that my freedom is not
and cannot be something that I observe (*constater*) as I observe
an outward fact; rather it must be something that I decide and
that I decide, moreover, without any appeal. It is beyond the
power of anyone to reject the decision by which I assert my
freedom, and this assertion is ultimately bound up with the consciousness that I have of myself. Jaspers puts it extremely well
in his *Introduction to Philosophy* (pp. 61–62) ; 'We are conscious of our freedom when we recognize what others expect
from us. It is upon us that the fulfilment or shirking of these
obligations depends; we cannot, accordingly, deny with any
seriousness that we have thus to make a decision about something, and so about ourselves, and that thus we are responsible.
Further, anyone who refused to accept this responsibility would
ipso facto make it impossible for himself to exact anything from
other men'. I may add, however, that it will be fatal to try to
think of this freedom in terms of causality, though so far we
have not reached any precise definition; and as we have just
seen, in the whole history of philosophy there has been no more
tragic error than that of trying to think of free will in its opposition to determinism; in reality it lies in a completely different
plane. I would readily agree that it is meaningless from the
point of view of determinism, just as there would be no significance in trying to find a bond of cause and effect between the
successive notes of a melody.

FREEDOM AND FACTICITY: THE SITUATION

JEAN-PAUL SARTRE

The decisive argument which is employed by common sense
against freedom consists in reminding us of our impotence. Far

from being able to modify our situation at our whim, we seem to be unable to change ourselves. I am not "free" either to escape the lot of my class, of my nation, of my family, or even to build up my own power or my fortune or to conquer my most significant appetites or habits. I am born a worker, a Frenchman, an hereditary syphilitic, or a tubercular. The history of a life, whatever it may be, is the history of a failure. The coefficient of adversity of things is such that years of patience are necessary to obtain the feeblest result. Again it is necessary "to obey nature in order to command it"; that is, to insert my action into the network of determinism. Much more than he appears "to make himself," man seems "to be made" by climate and the earth, race and class, language, the history of the collectivity of which he is a part, heredity, the individual circumstances of his childhood, acquired habits, the great and small events of his life.

This argument has never greatly troubled the partisans of human freedom. Descartes, first of all, recognized both that the will is infinite and that it is necessary "to try to conquer ourselves rather than fortune." Here certain distinctions ought to be made. Many of the facts set forth by the determinists do not actually deserve to enter into our considerations. In particular the coefficient of adversity in things can not be an argument against our freedom, for it is *by* us—i.e., by the preliminary positing of an end—that this coefficient of adversity arises. A particular crag, which manifests a profound resistance if I wish to displace it, will be on the contrary a valuable aid if I want to climb upon it in order to look over the countryside. In itself— if one can even imagine what the crag can be in itself—it is neutral; that is, it waits to be illuminated by an end in order to manifest itself as adverse or helpful. Again it can manifest itself in one or the other way only within an instrumental-complex which is already established. Without picks and piolets, paths already worn, and a technique of climbing, the crag would be neither easy nor difficult to climb; the question would not be posited, it would not support any relation of any kind with the technique of mountain climbing. Thus although brute things (what Heidegger calls "brute existents") can from the start limit our freedom of action, it is our freedom itself which must first constitute the framework, the technique, and the ends in relation to which they will manifest themselves as limits. Even if the crag is revealed as "too difficult to climb," and if we must give up the ascent, let us note that the crag is revealed as such only because it was originally grasped as "climbable"; it is therefore our freedom which constitutes the limits which it will subsequently encounter. . . .

In addition it is necessary to point out to "common sense" that the formula "to be free" does not mean "to obtain what one has wished" but rather "by oneself to determine oneself to wish" (in the broad sense of choosing). In other words success is not important to freedom. The discussion which opposes common sense to philosophers stems here from a misunderstanding: the empirical and popular concept of "freedom" which has been produced by historical, political, and moral circumstances is equivalent to "the ability to obtain the ends chosen." The technical and philosophical concept of freedom, the only one which we are considering here, means only the autonomy of choice. It is necessary, however, to note that the choice, being identical with acting, supposes a commencement of realization in order that the choice may be distinguished from the dream and the wish. Thus we shall not say that a prisoner is always free to go out of prison, which would be absurd, nor that he is always free to long for release, which would be an irrelevant truism, but that he is always free to try to escape (or get himself liberated); that is, that whatever his condition may be, he can project his escape and learn the value of his project by undertaking some action. Our description of freedom, since it does not distinguish between choosing and doing, compels us to abandon at once the distinction between the intention and the act. The intention can no more be separated from the act than thought can be separated from the language which expresses it; and as it happens that our speech informs us of our thought, so our acts will inform us of our intentions—that is, it will enable us to disengage our intentions, to schematize them, and to make objects of them instead of limiting us to living them—*i.e.*, to assume a non-thetic consciousness of them. This essential distinction between the freedom of choice and the freedom of obtaining was certainly perceived by Descartes, following Stoicism. It puts an end to all arguments based on the distinction between "willing" and "being able," which are still put forth today by the partisans and the opponents of freedom.

It is nonetheless true that freedom encounters or seems to encounter limitations on account of the *given* which it surpasses or nihilates. To show that the coefficient of adversity of the thing and its character as an obstacle (joined to its character as an instrument) is indispensable to the existence of a freedom is to use an argument that cuts two ways; for while it enables us to establish that freedom is not invalidated by the given, it indicates, on the other hand, something like an ontological conditioning of freedom. Would it not be reasonable to say, along with certain contemporary philosophers: if no obstacle, then no freedom? And as we can not admit that freedom by itself creates its own obstacle—which would be absurd for anyone who has understood the meaning of spontaneity—there seems to be here a kind of ontological priority of the in-itself over the for-itself. Therefore we must consider the previous remarks as simple attempts to clear the ground, and we must take up again from the beginning the question of facticity. . . . The *situation*, the common product of the contingency of the in-itself and of freedom, is an ambiguous phenomenon in which it is impossible for the for-itself to distinguish the contribution of freedom from that of the brute existent. In fact, just as freedom is the escape from a contingency which it has to be in order to escape it, so the situation is the free coordination and the free qualification of a brute given which does not allow itself to be qualified in any way at all. Here I am at the foot of this crag which appears to me as "not scalable." This means that the rock appears to me in the light of a projected scaling—a secondary project which finds its meaning in terms of an initial project which is my being-in-the-world. Thus the rock is carved out on the ground of the world by the effect of the initial choice of my freedom. But on the other hand, what my freedom can not determine is whether the rock "to be scaled" will or will not lend itself to scaling. This is part of the brute being of the rock. Nevertheless the rock can show its resistance to the scaling only if the rock is integrated by freedom in a "situation" of which the general theme is scaling. For the simple traveler who passes over this road and whose free project is a pure aesthetic ordering of the landscape, the crag is not revealed either as scalable or as not-scalable; it is maintained only as beautiful or ugly.

Thus it is impossible to determine in each particular case what comes from freedom and what comes from the brute being of the for-itself. The given in-itself as *resistance* or as *aid* is revealed only in the light of the projecting freedom. But the projecting freedom organizes an illumination such that the in-itself is revealed by it *as it is* (*i.e.*, resisting or favorable) ; but we must clearly understand that the resistance of the given is not directly admissible as an in-itself quality of the given but only as an indication—across a free illumination and a free refraction—of an inapprehensible *quid*. Therefore it is only in and through the free upsurge of a freedom that the world develops and reveals the resistance which can render the projected end unrealizable. Man encounters an obstacle only within the field of his freedom. Better yet, it is impossible to decree *a priori* what comes from the brute existent and what from freedom in the character of this or that particular existent functioning as an obstacle. What is an obstacle for me may not be so for another. There is no obstacle in an absolute sense, but the obstacle reveals its coefficient of adversity across freely invented and freely acquired techniques. The obstacle reveals this coefficient also in terms of the value of the end posited by freedom. The rock will not be an obstacle if I wish at any cost to arrive at the top of the mountain. On the other hand, it will discourage me if I have freely fixed limits to my desire of making the projected climb. Thus the world by coefficients of adversity reveals to me the way in which I stand in relation to the ends which I assign myself, so that I can never know if it is giving me information about myself or about it. Furthermore the coefficient of adversity of the given is never a simple relation to my freedom as a pure nihilating thrust. It is a relation, illuminated by freedom, between the *datum* which is the cliff and the *datum* which my freedom has to be; that is, between the contingent which it is not and its pure facticity. If the desire to scale it is equal, the rock will be easy for one athletic climber but difficult for another, a novice, who is not well trained and who has a weak body. But the body in turn is revealed as well or poorly trained only in relation to a free choice. It is because I am there and because I have made of myself what I am that the rock develops in relation to my body a coefficient of adversity. For the lawyer who has remained in the city and who is pleading a case, whose body is hidden under his lawyer's robe, the rock is neither hard nor easy to climb; it is dissolved in the totality "world" without in any way emerging from it. And in one sense it is I who choose my body as weak by making it face the difficulties which I cause to be born (mountain climbing, cycling, sport). If I have not chosen to take part in sports, if I live in the city, and if I concern myself exclusively with business or intellectual work, then from this point of view my body will have no quality whatsoever.

Thus we begin to catch a glimpse of the paradox of freedom: there is freedom only in a *situation*, and there is a situation only through freedom. Human-reality everywhere encounters resistance and obstacles which it has not created, but these resistances and obstacles have meaning only in and through the free choice which human-reality *is*. . . . Human freedom precedes essence in man and makes it possible; the essence of the human being is suspended in his freedom. What we call freedom is impossible to distinguish from the *being* of "human reality." Man does not exist *first* in order to be free *subsequently;* there is no difference between the being of man and his *being-free.* . . . Freedom is total and infinite, which does not mean that it has no limits but that it *never encounters them.* The only limits which freedom bumps up against at each moment are those which it imposes on itself.

FREEDOM

Again, it is clear that no causal relationship is conceivable between the subject and his body, his world or his society. Only at the cost of losing the basis of all my certainties can I question what is conveyed to me by my presence to myself. Now the moment I turn to myself in order to describe myself, I have a glimpse of an anonymous flux, a comprehensive project in which there are so far no 'states of consciousness', nor *a fortiori*, qualifications of any sort. For myself I am neither "jealous', nor 'inquisitive', nor 'hunchbacked', nor 'a civil servant'. It is often a matter of surprise that the cripple or the invalid can put up with himself. The reason is that such people are not for themselves deformed or at death's door. Until the final coma, the dying man is inhabited by a consciousness, he is all that he sees, and enjoys this much of an outlet. Consciousness can never objectify itself into invalid-consciousness or cripple-consciousness, and even if the old man complains of his age or the cripple of his deformity, they can do so only by comparing themselves with others, or seeing themselves through the eyes of others, that is, by taking a statistical and objective view of themselves, so that such complaints are never absolutely genuine: when he is back in the heart of his own consciousness, each one of us feels beyond his limitations and thereupon resigns himself to them. They are the price which we automatically pay for being in the world, a formality which we take for granted. Hence we may speak disparagingly of our looks and still not want to change our face for another. No idiosyncrasy can, seemingly, be attached to the insuperable generality of consciousness, nor can any limit be set

Reprinted from *The Phenomenology of Perception,* translated by C. Smith (New York: Humanities Press, 1962) pp. 434–439, 442–443 by permission of the publisher and Routledge & Kegan Paul.

to this immeasurable power of escape. In order to be determined (in the two senses of that word) by an external factor, it is necessary that I should be a thing. Neither my freedom nor my universality can admit of any eclipse. It is inconceivable that I should be free in certain of my actions and determined in others: how should we understand a dormant freedom that gave full scope to determinism? And if it is assumed that it is snuffed out when it is not in action, how could it be rekindled? If *per impossible* I had once succeeded in *making myself into* a thing, how should I subsequently reconvert myself to consciousness? Once I am free, I am not to be counted among things, and I must then be uninterruptedly free. Once my actions cease to be mine, I shall never recover them, and if I lose my hold on the world, it will never be restored to me. It is equally inconceivable that my liberty should be attenuated; one cannot be to some extent free, and if, as is often said, motives incline me in a certain direction, one of two things happens: either they are strong enough to force me to act, in which case there is no freedom, or else they are not strong enough, and then freedom is complete, and as great in the worst torments as in the peace of one's home. We ought, therefore, to reject not only the idea of causality, but also that of motivation. [Cf. Sartre, BN, pp. 508ff.] The alleged motive does not burden my decision; on the contrary my decision lends the motive its force. Everything that I 'am' in virtue of nature or history—hunchbacked, handsome or Jewish—I never am completely for myself, as we have just explained: and I may well be these things for other people, nevertheless I remain free to posit another person as a consciousnes whose views strike through to my very being, or on the other hand merely as an object. It is also true that this option is itself a form of constraint: if I am ugly, I have the choice between being an object of disapproval or disapproving of others. I am left free to be a masochist or a sadist, but not free to ignore others. But this dilemma, which is given as part of the human lot, is not one for me as pure consciousness: it is still I who cause the other to be for me, and who cause us both to be as members of mankind. Moreover, even if existence as a human being were imposed upon me, the manner alone being left to my choice, and considering this choice itself and ignoring the small number of forms it might take, it would still be a free choice. If it is said that my temperament inclines me particularly to either sadism or masochism, it is still merely a manner of speaking, for my temperament exists only for the second order knowledge that I gain about myself when I see myself as others see me, and in so far as I recognize it, confer value upon it, and in that sense, choose it. What misleads us on this, is that we often look for freedom in the voluntary deliberation which examines one motive after another and seems to opt for the weightiest or most convincing. In reality the deliberation follows the decision, and it is my secret decision which brings the motives to light, for it would be difficult to conceive what the force of a motive might be in the absence of a decision which it confirms or to which it runs counter. When I have abandoned a project, the motives which I thought held me to it suddenly lose their force and collapse. In order to resuscitate them, an effort is required on my part to reopen time and set me back to the moment preceding the making of the decision. Even while I am deliberating, already I find it an effort to suspend time's flow, and to keep open a situation which I feel is closed by a decision which is already there and which I am holding off. That is why it so often happens that after giving up a plan I experience a feeling of relief: 'After all, I wasn't so very particular'; the debate was purely a matter of form, and the deliberation a mere parody, for I had decided against from the start.

We often see the weakness of the will brought forward as an argument against freedom. And indeed, although I can will myself to adopt a course of conduct and act the part of a warrior or a seducer, it is not within my power to be a warrior or seducer with ease and in a way that 'comes naturally'; really to *be* one, that is. But neither should we seek freedom in the act of will, which is, in its very meaning, something short of an act. We have recourse to an act of will only in order to go against our true decision, and, as it were, for the purpose of proving our powerlessness. If we had really and truly made the conduct of the warrior or the seducer our own, then we should *be* one or the other. Even what are called obstacles to freedom are in reality deployed by it. An unclimbable rock face, a large or small, vertical or slanting rock, are things which have no meaning for anyone who is not intending to surmount them, for a subject whose projects do not carve out such determinate forms from the uniform mass of the *in itself* and cause an orientated world to arise—a significance in things. There is, then, ultimately nothing that can set limits to freedom, except those limits that freedom itself has set in the form of its various initiatives, so that the subject has simply the external world that he gives himself. Since it is the latter who, on coming into being, brings to light significance and value in things, and since nothing can impinge upon it except through acquiring, thanks to it, significance and value, there is no action of things on the subject, but merely a signification (in the active sense), a centrifugal *Sinngebung*. The choice would seem to lie between scientism's conception of causality, which is incompatible with the consciousness which we have of ourselves, and the assertion of an absolute freedom divorced from the outside. It is impossible to decide beyond which point things cease to be ἐφ’ἡμιν. Either they all lie within our power, or none does.

The result, however, of this first reflection on freedom would appear to be to rule it out altogether. If indeed it is the case that our freedom is the same in all our actions, and even in our passions, if it is not to be measured in terms of our conduct, and if the slave displays freedom as much by living in fear as by breaking his chains, then it cannot be held that there is such a thing as *free action*, freedom being anterior to all actions. In any case it will not be possible to declare: 'Here freedom makes its appearance', since free action, in order to be discernible, has to stand out against a background of life from which it is entirely, or almost entirely, absent. We may say in this case that it is everywhere, but equally nowhere. In the name of freedom we reject the idea of acquisition, since freedom has become a primordial acquisition and, as it were, our state of nature. Since we do not have to provide it, it is the gift granted to us of having no gift, it is the nature of consciousness which consists in having no nature, and in no case can it find external expression or a place in our life. The idea of action, therefore, disappears: nothing can pass from us to the world, since we are nothing that can be specified, and since the non-being which constitutes us could not possibly find its way into the world's plenum. There are merely intentions immediately followed by their effects, and we are very near to the Kantian idea of an intention which is tantamount to the act, which Scheler countered with the argument that the cripple who would like to be able to save a drowning man and the good swimmer who actually saves him do not have the same experience of autonomy. The very idea of choice vanishes, for to choose is to choose *something* in which freedom sees, at least for a moment, a symbol of itself. There is free choice only if freedom comes into play in its decision, and posits the situation chosen as a situation of freedom. A freedom which has no need to be exercised because it is already acquired could not commit itself in this way: it knows that the following instant will find it, come what may, just as free and just as indeterminate. The very notion of freedom demands that our decision should plunge into the future, that something should have been *done* by it, that the subsequent instant should benefit from its predecessor and, though not necessitated, should be at least required by it. If freedom is doing, it is necessary that what it does should not be immediately undone by a new freedom. Each instant, therefore, must not be a closed world; one instant must be able to commit its successors and, a decision once taken and action once begun, I must have something acquired at my disposal, I must benefit from my impetus, I must be inclined to carry on, and there must be a bent or propensity of the mind. It was Descartes who held that conservation demands a power as great as does creation; a view which implies a realistic notion of the instant. It is true that the instant is not a philosopher's fiction. It is the point at which one project is brought to fruition and another begun [Sartre, BN, p. 544]—the point at which my gaze is transferred from one end to another, it is the *Augen-Blick*. But this break in time cannot occur unless each of the two spans is of a piece. Consciousness, it is said, is, though not atomized into instants, at least haunted by the spectre of the instant which it is obliged continually to exorcise by a free act. We shall soon see that we have indeed always the power to interrupt, but it implies in any case a power to *begin*, for there would be no severances unless freedom had taken up its abode somewhere and were preparing to move it. Unless there are cycles of behaviour, open situations requiring a certain completion and capable of constituting a background to either a confirmatory or transformatory decision, we never experience freedom. The choice of an intelligible character is excluded, not only because there is no time anterior to time, but because choice presupposes a prior commitment and because the idea of an initial choice involves a contradiction. If freedom is to have *room* in which to move, if it is to be describable as freedom, there must be something to hold it away from its objectives, it must have a *field*, which means that there must be for it special possibilities, or realities which tend to cling to being. As J. P. Sartre himself observes, dreaming is incompatible with freedom because, in the realm of imagination, we have no sooner taken a certain significance as our goal than we already believe that we have intuitively brought it into being, in short, because there is no obstacle and nothing *to do*. [Sartre, BN, p. 562] It is established that freedom is not to be confused with those abstract decisions of will at grips with motives or passions, for the classical conception of deliberation is relevant only to a freedom 'in bad faith' which secretly harbours antagonistic motives without being prepared to act on them, and so itself manufactures the alleged proofs of its impotence. We can see, beneath these noisy debates and these fruitless efforts to 'construct' us, the tacit decisions whereby we have marked out round ourselves the field of possibility, and it is true that nothing is done as long as we cling to these fixed points, and everything is easy as soon as we have weighed anchor. This is why our freedom is not to be sought in spurious discussion on the conflict between a style of life which we have no wish to reappraise and circumstances suggestive of another: the real choice is that between our whole character and our manner of being in the world. But either this total choice is never mentioned, since it is the silent upsurge of our being in the world, in which case it is not clear in what sense it could be said to be ours, since this freedom glides over itself and is the equivalent of a fate—or else our choice of ourselves is a genuine choice, a conversion involving our whole existence.

• • • •

The rationalist's dilemma: either the free act is possible, or it is not—either the event originates in me or is imposed on me from outside, does not apply to our relations with the world and with our past. Our freedom does not destroy our situation, but gears itself to it: as long as we are alive, our situation is open, which implies both that it calls up specially favoured modes of resolution, and also that it is powerless to bring one into being by itself.

We shall arrive at the same result by considering our relations with history. Taking myself in my absolute concreteness, as I am presented to myself in reflection, I find that I am an anonymous and pre-human flux, as yet unqualified as, for instance, 'a working man' or 'middle class'. If I subsequently think of myself as a man among men, a bourgeois among bourgeois, this can be, it would seem, no more than a second order view of myself; I am never in my heart of hearts a worker or a bourgeois, but a consciousness which freely evaluates itself as a middle class of proletarian consciousness. And indeed, it is never the case that my objective position in the production process is sufficient to awaken class consciousness. There was exploitation long before there were revolutionaries. Nor is it always in periods of economic difficulty that the working class movement makes headway. Revolt is, then, not the outcome of objective conditions, but it is rather the decision taken by the worker to will revolution that makes a proletarian of him. The evaluation of the present operates through one's free project for the future. From which we might conclude that history by itself has no significance, but only that conferred upon it by our will. Yet here again we are slipping into the method of 'the indispensable condition failing which . . .': in opposition to objective thought, which includes the subject in its deterministic system; we are setting idealist reflection which makes determinism dependent upon the constituting activity of the subject. Now, we have already seen that objective thought and analytical reflection are two aspects of the same mistake, two ways of overlooking the phenomena. Objective thought derives class consciousness from the objective condition of the proletariat. Idealist reflection reduces the proletarian condition to the awareness of it, which the proletarian arrives at. The former traces class-consciousness to the class defined in terms of objective characteristics, the latter on the other hand reduces 'being a workman' to the consciousness of being one. In each case we are in the realm of abstraction, because we remain torn between the *in itself* and the *for itself*. If we approach the question afresh with the idea of discovering, not the cause of the act of becoming aware, for there is no cause which can act from outside upon a consciousness—nor the conditions of its possibility, for we need to know the conditions which actually produce it—but class-consciousness itself, if, in short, we apply a genuinely existential method, what do we find? I am not conscious of being working class or middle class simply because, as a matter of fact, I sell my labour or, equally as a matter of fact, because my interests are bound up with capitalism, nor do I become one or the other on the day on which I elect to view history in the light of the class struggle: what happens is that 'I exist as working class' or 'I exist as middle class' in the first place, and it is this mode of dealing with the world and society which provides both the motives for my revolutionary or conservative projects and my explicit judgments of the type: 'I am working class' or 'I am middle class', without its being possible to deduce the former from the latter, or *vice versa*. What makes me a proletarian is not the economic system or society considered as systems of impersonal forces, but these institutions as I carry them within me and experience them; nor is it an intellectual operation devoid of motive, but my way of being in the world within this institutional framework.

FREEDOM AND CHOICE

FREDERICK OLAFSON

In an earlier chapter, in the course of a discussion of Kant's ethical theory, a distinction was made between two quite different senses that the term "freedom" may bear in ethical contexts. One of these was the freedom of causal indeterminacy, and the other was the freedom of autonomous moral legislation. When the existentialists say that man is free, they mean that he is free in both of these senses, and they hold that both kinds of freedom can be seen to follow from the general account they have given of human being. In this chapter, I propose to examine the views of Heidegger and Sartre with respect to both kinds of freedom. This review should then make it possible to gain a better understanding of the central existentialist thesis that *man makes himself,* as well as of the equally well known definitions of human being as "care" and as a "project." This in turn will lead to an inquiry into what Heidegger and Sartre mean by choice, and to a consideration of the much-vexed topic of the relation of choice to moral rules and principles. Here again I will argue that the doctrine of the existentialists has been largely misunderstood, and that their position is not correctly described as an extreme individualism that makes no place for general rules within the structure of the moral life. Instead, it is a view of the status of general rules in their relationship to particular acts of choice; and while this view breaks sharply with the Aristotelian interpretation of the relation of choice to rules, it should not be interpreted as denying the need for consistent policies in the conduct of the moral life.

Reprinted from *Principles and Persons,* (Baltimore, Johns Hopkins Press, 1967), pp. 145–150; 153–162 by permission of the publisher and the author.

I

When the existentialists discuss causal determinism, they usually treat it as a set of methodological assumptions distinctive of the scientific study of the natural world. Their main argument is that this mode of treatment of natural phenomena not only develops out of the quite different conceptual system of common sense, but also remains dependent upon that prior mode of construing the relationship of human being to "things," and cannot be used to suppress or eliminate the latter. The familiar prescientific understanding that we have of our relationship to the world implicitly recognizes the uneliminability of alternative possibilities of action. Its characterization of human beings is organized around the notions of responsibility and choice that presuppose the reality of such alternatives. Scientific determinism, by contrast, following in the path of Spinoza, undercuts this whole set of concepts by treating the belief in alternative possibilities as a product of our ignorance of the true mechanism of nature—human nature included—and it projects a reflexive application to human beings of causal and deterministic assumptions that were originally developed for the purpose of controlling physical nature. The existentialists' counterargument, in essence, is that this mode of self-objectification is one that human beings cannot really carry out in a thoroughgoing and consistent way, and that even when the attempt is made, the more primitive nondeterministic set of concepts reasserts itself. The profound sense of their defense of human freedom is accordingly that of the Kantian argument that human beings are so constituted as to be unable to think of themselves as being causally determined; and they go on to add (as Kant did) that to be unable to think of yourself except as free is in effect to *be* free.

While this assertion may sound strange to many ears, it does not proclaim any occult metaphysical doctrine. Indeed, it would be much more accurate to regard the existentialist defense of human freedom as antimetaphysical in intent than the reverse. It is antimetaphysical just in the sense that it refuses to undercut or devaluate our profound tendency to read the world in terms of

alternative possibilities of action in the interest of some preconception of what the real must be. It undertakes to show that no
scientific account of human action and behavior can ever, by itself, lay down the attitudes and perspectives of action that may
supervene upon it, and it goes on to point out that a determinism
that attempts this task must remain, as it were, a God's-eye-view
which leaves human beings to resolve exactly the same indetermi-
nacies as before. As such, determinism is perhaps irrefutable but
also gratuitous, since the assumption it makes is by no means necessary to the consistent carrying-on of scientific inquiry. While it
may satisfy some deep metaphysical craving, it has the positive
disadvantage of treating as a mere appearance what is in fact central to our understanding of the relation between action and
knowledge. There is a kind of paradox involved in the notion
that we are indissolubly committed to a concept—that of alternative possibilities—which we believe to be really inapplicable to
anything. The course taken by the existentialists is that of refusing to abandon the concept of alternatives, and of interpreting
scientific inquiry in such a way that it presupposes a relationship
to the world in which alternatives have a place, instead of trying
to fit human action into a conceptual world from which both alternatives and choice have been excised.

This way of arguing for the reality of human freedom has
certain obvious sources as well as some perhaps not-so-obvious
affinities with forms of argumentation that are current in the
English-speaking philosophical world.[1] Its primary inspiration is
clearly the transcendental point of view of Husserlian phenomenology; and from this point of view, as Merleau-Ponty has remarked, the only way an object can be said to influence human
consciousness is by serving as a point of departure for a new con-

[1] I have in mind here recent works like S. Hampshire, *Thought and
Action* (London: Chatto and Windus, 1959), and D. Pears (ed.), *Freedom
and the Will* (New York: St. Martin's Press, 1963), as well as a number
of articles like P. Herbst, "Freedom and Prediction," *Mind*, Vol. 66
(1957), pp. 1–27, and K. Popper, Indeterminism in Classical and Quan-
tum Physics," *British Journal of the Philosophy of Science*, Vol. 1 (1950),
pp. 117–33 and pp. 173–95.

figuration of meaning. [Merleau-Ponty, PP, p. 496.] Causal understanding of the world is only one such possible configuration of meaning; it cannot by itself give an account of the activity of conceptualization itself, or invalidate any competing set of concepts that may have presuppositions which conflict with its own. At the same time, it must be understood that in denying the reflexive applicability of deterministic modes of thought to human beings, the existentialists are not saying that the human organism and human behavior cannot be studied causally, but rather that there are other modes of conceptualizing the latter and that whatever its value in its own sphere, causal explanation cannot, without becoming explicitly and inadmissably metaphysical, claim to override or to absorb all other modes of conceptualizing our experience—in particular, the evaluative mode. Their primary interest—like that of many analytic philosophers of the "ordinary language" persuasion—is in maintaining the integrity of distinctions that are operative at the phenomenological level, rather than in establishing—as classical metaphysics undertook to do—either that freedom is a mysterious power resident in the noumenal self, or that there are real possibilities in the world quite apart from its relationship to human subjectivity. What the existentialist line of argument establishes, if it is successful, is not that from some external and absolute "God's-eye-point-of-view" man is free, but rather that within the human situation the notions of predictability and freedom are complementary and interdependent.

The way in which the existentialist argument against determinism proceeds is not difficult to grasp; it is essentially similar to forms of argumentation that have been used for the same purpose by nonexistentialists. The paradigm of all such arguments is given by the case of a prediction of the way the stock market will behave. If this prediction becomes known, speculators may well act differently from the way they would have acted if it had not; and the prediction may be falsified as a result of becoming known. If the example is changed so that the prediction not only concerns the action that some human being will take in certain circumstances but also is made in accordance with some scientific theory about human behavior, it becomes possible to make the existentialist point against determinism quite concisely. If I am informed of this prediction of my behavior, this knowledge will open up alternative possibilities of action in the situation in which it is predicted that I will act in a certain way. In existentialist parlance, the prediction as well as the theory from which it derives and the sequence of events which that theory projects, become elements in my situation to which I can react in a number of different ways that are not determined by the theory itself. But, if coming to know a predictive theory of some kind by itself modifies the situation in question in a way that is relevant to the possibilities of action in it, then the deterministic case can be saved only by expanding the original theory to take account of these modifications. There would, therefore, have to be a second law-based prediction in which my reaction to the circumstances specified in the first law, as well as to the prediction itself, would be taken into account. But the same issue arises with respect to this second law: does it predict what I will do in these circumstances if I also know of *this* new prediction? It appears that as long as I know what it is predicted I will do, a series of possibilities opens up that cannot be foreclosed by that prediction. Even if I went ahead and did what it was predicted I would do, knowing that it was so predicted, the case would be the same. Because this action that I thus perform is now only one among a number of alternative modes of reaction to my knowledge of the prediction, I will have to think of myself as having done this *rather than* something else; and this is to say that I would have chosen to do it.[2] Thus, when the prediction is known, even the course of action that confirms it does so in a way that offers no support to determinism. For I can not be sure that I will not use my knowledge of the law cited in the prediction for the pur-

---

[2] I may, of course, in a quasi-deliberate way, *avoid* thinking of what happens as my action and think of myself instead as passively awaiting an outcome. Heidegger calls this strategy of the inauthentic self *"Erwarten,"* or *"Gewärtigen."*

pose of intervening to forestall the predicted outcome. As a result, my predictive certainty must always remain at one remove from the point at which the question of action arises. Only after making a choice *without* any theory-based assurance of what that choice must be does it become possible to assess the "influence" of that knowledge upon the choices I make. And even if I succeed in expanding my original theory so that it incorporates that influence, the same kind of uncertainty as before will have reproduced itself at a higher level.[3]

The freedom human beings enjoy in structuring such situations with reference to action—the freedom of autonomy—consists negatively in the fact that a situation does not indicate by itself which of its features are criterial for what kind of action. . . . It makes sense to say that it is true that X is a feature of situation Y, but no sense at all to say that it is true that feature X of situation Y is reason for acting in a certain way. Positively, this notion of autonomy is intended to signify that the tranformation of a situation of fact into one that is oriented toward action is itself an act that individuals perform, and for which they alone are ultimately responsible. [Sartre, BN, pp. 522ff.] This is an act of conceptualization through which a particular situation is characterized by reference to selected features which are thus made to function as the springboard for action of a certain sort. Thus, to characterize another person's conduct as "disrespectful" or as "cruel" is to place it in a particular perspective of action, at the same time that it states a fact about that person. The autonomous character of this act naturally requires that it should have been possible for me to conceptualize the same situation differently, but this requirement which is closely connected with my *causal* freedom is not the whole story. The more important feature of autonomy is what I have called our logical freedom in evaluation, which results from the absence of any standard of truth to

---

[3] The existentialist argument is intended to show that it is impossible for me to predict what I will do. For a defense of the same thesis by an analytical philosopher, see C. Ginet, "Can The Will Be Caused?" *Philosophical Review*, Vol. 71 (1962), pp. 49–55.

which such acts of evaluative conceptualization should somehow correspond or by reference to which they might be justified.

The relationship between causal freedom and logical freedom or autonomy can now be stated. If human beings were not causally free in the sense that there always remain unreduced alternative courses of action in some sphere of their lives, there would clearly be no point in speaking of them as enjoying evaluative autonomy, since the notion of action would have lost its application. But the existentialists also contend that if human beings were causally free but not autonomous (i.e., not logically free), the concept of action would have been effectively subverted again. This is a more difficult thesis to accept because it is by no means clear that the concept of action, as ordinarily understood, by itself excludes the availability of objective moral truths. But while we may hesitate to make this logical freedom an element in the concept of action, the arguments of Chapter VI appear to show that in the full sense appropriate to human beings, action requires both a range of possible alternatives and an autonomous structuring of the action situation through which the latter is oriented toward some possible course of action as its appropriate resolution. What this comes to, in practice, is that all established and "impersonal" ways of tying situations of fact to projects of action (however natural and rationally compelling they may seem), are in principle decomposable into the elements of fact and evaluation. Stated in this way, the existentialist doctrine would take the form of a claim that it is always possible in principle to dismantle the whole structure of established evaluative concepts, and thereby to reach a kind of ground-zero of the moral life which will serve as a base-point for our understanding of the latter. It is to say that there is no association of an evaluative attitude with a type of situation that is so inveterate or so inevitable as to be able to resist permanently such analytic isolation and recombination of its elements. Of course it may be that no exact translation of an implicitly evaluative concept into factual and evaluative components will be possible because of the indefinitely large range of implications for action that such a concept may suggest, depending on the circumstances, but at least the general lines on which such a translation would proceed can be made clear. If human beings are, in principle, capable of carrying out this kind of analysis of what seem at first to be seamless unities of description and evaluation, they must also be capable of experiencing for themselves both the absence of logical controls over the way in which these unities are constituted and the act-character of the evaluative judgment by which factual premises are associated with conclusions that direct to action.

The preceding remarks suggest that we need to think of autonomy in two rather different ways. First, there is the logical freedom which consists simply in the absence of any independent standard of truth or validity governing the way in which evaluative premises are associated with factual premises. Still, a negative logical freedom of this kind might conceivably obtain without a person's ever recognizing it for what it is or finding any positive equivalent for it in his own moral experience. This possibility makes it necessary to consider autonomy as an attribute or capability of persons, rather than just as a feature of the language used for the formulation of moral judgments. Even if we accept the "decomposability-in-principle" of all concepts in which factual and evaluative claims are associated with one another, we may well wonder whether there are not people who are unable to make sense of this notion and who do not in fact experience any logical gap between the set of factual premises describing their situation and the course of action which they consider to be right. In what sense could such persons be said to possess a freedom that they are unable to recognize in their actual moral experience? It might be argued, too, that such an inability is not exceptional but typical of the familiar moral situation in which most of us find ourselves. This situation is one in which we more or less unthinkingly accept and employ a wide range of implicitly evaluative concepts for the purpose of identifying and describing persons, situations, objects, institutions, etc. To the extent that we do this—and all of us of course do—we live in a preevaluated world; and the more habitual our acceptance of an established way of tying situations of fact to certain specified modalities of action, the less sense we are likely to have of either the first-

personal act-character of evaluation, or of the absence of logical
limitations on the form that evaluation takes. Indeed, to the
moral consciousness that is firmly rooted in some operating moral
consensus of this kind, the claim that human beings are autonomous in either of these senses will seem not just problematic
but directly contrary to the plain testimony of common sense.
Here, then, is a situation in which the 'vulgar moral consciousness' appears to deny the applicability to it of the very conclusions with respect to autonomy which we have felt compelled to
accept. We are therefore forced to ask what features of ordinary
moral consciousness justify us in applying to it the very characterization which it rejects; and also, to what extent this rejection
itself might have the effect of limiting the relevance of the enriched existentialist concept of action to that ordinary moral
consciousness.

This issue of how the concept of moral autonomy is to be
meaningfully applied to persons who do not in fact recognize
themselves as autonomous has been the occasion of a rather serious disagreement among the existentialists themselves. [Merleau-
Ponty, PP, p. 496.] Briefly, this disagreement has turned on the
question whether freedom or autonomy can be said to be capable
of degrees, or whether it is necessarily absolute and total wherever it exists. In the existentialist idiom, this becomes the question whether the consciousness that confers the evaluative indeterminacy on natural events by virtue of which we are enabled to
set them in alternative perspectives of action is a special reflective
development of ordinary consciousness, or whether this function
is attributable to *all* states of consciousness. Sartre has defended
the latter view, and Merleau-Ponty and others have argued for
a conception of freedom as susceptible of degrees of realization.
They have argued that it is possible simply to *be*, e.g., a worker
or a bourgeois, without having the special form of self-consciousness that at once detaches us from our condition and communicates to it the volitional character of which I have spoken. This
amounts to saying that it is not only possible but normal for
human beings to remain almost entirely within a single mode of
evaluative conceptualization which they share with others, and

which they tend to treat as an unanalyzed whole without ever feeling a need to resolve it into its factual and evaluative components, and consequently without having any sense of autonomous activity on their own part in connection with the use of such concepts. As Merleau-Ponty puts it, these "public" evaluative concepts constitute a kind of *intermonde* between the evaluative indeterminacy of things and the self-conscious evaluative activity of the individual. [*Ibid.*, pp. 409, 410.]

Sartre, by contrast, has argued that there is, in addition to the explicit reflective form of self-consciousness which he concedes is by no means universally shared, a "nonthetic" form of self-consciousness which *is* a necessary structural feature of all conscious experience, and through which we all are aware of our own moral freedom. [Sartre, BN, p. 66ff.] It may be that this prejudgmental form of self-consciousness amounts to no more than the capability in principle of all human beings for the kind of explicit objectification of their situation that breaks down established fact-value unities. If such an analysis were permissible, then to say that a man is absolutely free would mean that there is no feature of his condition that could not be made a theme for self-conscious reflection and, thereby, the object of a range of possible attitudes and the point of departure for different courses of action. But it often seems that Sartre's categorical attribution of freedom to human beings goes well beyond any purely dispositional interpretation; and to the extent that it does, it has the disadvantage of making it sound as though the task of organizing our experience around foci of self-conscious reflection were accomplished *ab initio*. [*Ibid.*, p. 539.] By thus introducing the sophistication of more highly developed levels of self-consciousness into all states of mind, the illusion is created that *all* choices are made from the vantage point of an absolute self-consciousness that has surrounded its entire natural condition with the halo of evaluative indeterminacy that frees for action. Considered as a description of the state of mind that accompanies action in the great majority of cases, this account is, of course, simply false. Since a categorical attribution of total freedom will always tend to be understood in this way, it seems much wiser to guard against such a misrepresentation of ordinary consciousness by adopting the progressive and dispositional form of the theory of autonomy that is favored by Merleau-Ponty.

The advantages of this version of the theory are considerable and obvious. If freedom were always total and not susceptible of degrees, then everyone would be equally free; the slave who fought to free himself would enjoy no greater freedom than the slave who passively accepted his chains. In Merleau-Ponty's words, there would be no "natural analogue" to ontological freedom, since the latter would be equally compatible with all conditions of life. In order to account for actual progress from a condition of slavery to one of freedom, we would obviously have to assign much greater importance within our theory of freedom to those acts of reflective moral consciousness by which a gap is opened up between our situation and a range of possible alternatives. We would also have to de-emphasize correspondingly the role attributed by Sartre to nonthetic consciousness, on the ground that the freedom associated with the latter proves almost impossible to distinguish from the simple absence of logical restraints discussed above.

At the same time, in avoiding Sartre's error, we must be careful not to fall into its opposite. If it is a mistake to talk about human beings in such a way as to suggest that their relationship to their situation and themeslves is wholly in the volitional mode, and that they are always subtly detached from whatever positive characteristics they possess by the logical freedom with which they are endowed, it would be equally erroneous to conclude that the *only* sense of autonomy that is applicable to most human beings is the first one distinguished above, i.e., autonomy conceived as the mere absence of any logical obstacle to the dissolution of the specious unities of fact and value which are the common currency of the moral life. This would amount to saying that in most cases the application of the second sense of autonomy, which requires at least a measure of personal realization of this freedom, must remain entirely hypothetical. Now there certainly is an important hypothetical aspect to the existentialist attribution of autonomy to human beings, since its characterization of our condition takes the form of a number of implications which we would have to accept if we were to follow through to the end of a certain path of reflection on our moral experience. It may be freely conceded that most of us have not gone very far along that route, and as I have already remarked in connection with Sartre, one legitimate criticism of the existentialist doctrine of autonomy is that it seems to imply that we have moved much farther toward a condition of self-conscious moral freedom than many of us in fact have. At the same time, all of us in at least some area of our lives do think of ourselves as devising and choosing our own policies of action within a measure of logical freedom. This freedom may be thought of as operating only in the less important areas of our lives, and as limited in its range by objective norms over the validity of which we exercise no control. After all, autonomy does not have to be all-pervasive in order to be genuine. Just as causal freedom requires not that we be omnipotent but only that in some area of our lives there remain some unreduced alternative courses of action, so an attribution of autonomy should not be taken to imply that we have actually carried out an analysis into factual and evaluative components of all the action-directing concepts we employ, or even that we have recognized the possibility in principle of such analyses. It would imply merely that somewhere in our actual moral practice we reveal our ability to carry out this kind of analysis, and are aware of a hiatus between our situation and our projects of action. I do not think it it outrageously audacious to suggest that any human being who is capable of moral judgment at all is very likely to be capable of some form of such analysis. If so, the existentialist attribution of autonomy to such an individual would signify not just that there is no logical obstacle in the way of extending such an analysis to all fact-value concepts, but also that there is a positive presumption that he can raise the kinds of question that lead into such analyses of an indefinitely large class of these concepts. No doubt he may break off at some point, either because he no longer really knows how to perform the analysis at the level of generality that has been reached, or because he resists the demand for such analyses on philosophical grounds of his own. Even so, if we hold

that such philosophical objections must fail, then the "decomposability-in-principle" of all such concepts signifies simply our
justified presumption that human beings are in fact capable
of pressing that analysis at least some distance, and in any case
cannot *justify* their refusal to press it further. As in the case of
causal freedom, where even the most exiguous residue of alternative possibilities of action suffices to bring an element of uncertainty into the whole structure of our predictive knowledge, so a
very small amount of effectively realized autonomy sets us on a
track of moral interrogation on which there can be no turning
back.

EXISTENTIALIST ETHICS

It is a matter of living in that state of the absurd. I know on what it is founded, this mind and this world straining against each other without being able to embrace each other.

—Albert Camus THE MYTH OF SISYPHUS

Shall I make this promise? Shall I risk my life for so little? Shall I give up my liberty in order to save liberty? There is no theoretical reply to these questions. But there are these *things* which stand, irrefutable, there is before you this person whom you love, there are these men whose existence around you is that of slaves, and *your* freedom cannot be willed without leaving behind its singular relevance, and without willing freedom *for all*. Whether it is a question of things or of historical situations, philosophy has no function other than to teach us once more to see them clearly, and it is true to say that it comes into being by destroying itself as separate philosophy. But what is here required is silence, for only the hero lives out his relation to men and the world.

—Maurice Merleau-Ponty
THE PHENOMENOLOGY OF PERCEPTION (conclusion)

INTRODUCTION

Existentialism is best known for its ethical theses, and so we present a taste of them here. These ethical theses do not tell us what to *do*, so much as they construct a framework within which actions are to be viewed. The selection from Camus is from his "Myth of Sisyphus." The selection from Sartre is from *Being and Nothingness*, in which he presents one of the few explicitly ethical theses in that work. Simone de Beauvoir has written an admirable interpretation of Sartre's ethics, excerpts of which are reprinted here, and has developed lines of Sartrian thought into some of the best French novels of recent decades and the most insightful philosophical theory of being-a-woman ever written. The final selection is an excerpt from a recent interview with Sartre in which he briefly indicates the directions his thought has taken in the 25 years since he wrote the material discussed and included in this volume.

ABSURD WALLS

ALBERT CAMUS

At any streetcorner the feeling of absurdity can strike any man in the face. As it is, in its distressing nudity, in its light without effulgence, it is elusive. But that very difficulty deserves reflection. It is probably true that a man remains forever unknown to us and that there is in him something irreducible that escapes us. But *practically* I know men and recognize them by their behavior, by the totality of their deeds, by the consequences caused in life by their presence. Likewise, all those irrational feelings which offer no purchase to analysis. I can define them *practically*, appreciate them *practically*, by gathering together the sum of their consequences in the domain of the intelligence, by seizing and noting all their aspects, by outlining their universe. It is certain that apparently, though I have seen the same actor a hundred times, I shall not for that reason know him any better personally. Yet if I add up the heroes he has personified and if I say that I know him a little better at the hundredth character counted off, this will be felt to contain an element of truth. For this apparent paradox is also an apologue. There is a moral to it. It teaches that a man defines himself by his make-believe as well as by his sincere impulses. There is thus a lower key of feelings, inaccessible in the heart but partially disclosed by the acts they imply and the attitudes of mind they assume. It is clear that in this way I am defining a method. But it is also evident that that method is one of analysis and not of knowledge. For methods imply metaphysics; unconsciously they disclose conclusions that they often claim not to know yet. Similarly, the last pages of a book are already contained in the first pages. Such a link is inevitable. The method defined here acknowledges the feeling that all true knowledge is impossible. Solely appearances can be enumerated and the climate make itself felt. . . .

All great deeds and all great thoughts have a ridiculous beginning. Great works are often born on a streetcorner or in a restaurant's revolving door. So it is with absurdity. The absurd world more than others derives its nobility from that abject birth. In certain situations, replying "nothing" when asked what one is thinking about may be pretense in a man. Those who are loved are well aware of this. But if that reply is sincere, if it symbolizes that odd state of soul in which the void becomes eloquent, in which the chain of daily gestures is broken, in which the heart vainly seeks the link that will connect it again, then it is as it were the first sign of absurdity.

It happens that the stage sets collapse. Rising, streetcar, four hours in the office or the factory, meal, streetcar, four hours of work, meal, sleep, and Monday Tuesday Wednesday Thursday Friday and Saturday according to the same rhythm—this path is easily followed most of the time. But one day the "why" arises and everything begins in that weariness tinged with amazement. "Begins"—this is important. Weariness comes at the end of the acts of a mechanical life, but at the same time it inaugurates the impulse of consciousness. It awakens consciousness and provokes what follows. What follows is the gradual return into the chain or it is the definitive awakening. At the end of the awakening comes, in time, the consequence: suicide or recovery. In itself weariness has something sickening about it. Here, I must conclude that it is good. For everything begins with consciousness and nothing is worth anything except through it. There is nothing original about these remarks. But they are obvious; that is enough for a while, during a sketchy reconnaissance in the origins of the absurd. Mere "anxiety," as Heidegger says, is at the source of everything.

Likewise and during every day of an unillustrious life, time carries us. But a moment always comes when we have to carry it. We live on the future: "tomorrow," "later on," "when you have made your way," "you will understand when you are old enough."

Such irrelevancies are wonderful, for, after all, it's a matter of dying. Yet a day comes when a man notices or says that he is thirty. Thus he asserts his youth. But simultaneously he situates himself in relation to time. He takes his place in it. He admits that he stands at a certain point on a curve that he acknowledges having to travel to its end. He belongs to time, and by the horror that seizes him, he recognizes his worst enemy. Tomorrow, he was longing for tomorow, whereas everything in him ought to reject it. That revolt of the flesh is the absurd.[1]

Of whom and of what indeed can I say: "I know that!" This heart within me I can feel, and I judge that it exists. This world I can touch, and I likewise judge that it exists. There ends all my knowledge, and the rest is construction. For if I try to seize this self of which I feel sure, if I try to define and to summarize it, it is nothing but water slipping through my fingers. I can sketch one by one all the aspects it is able to assume, all those likewise that have been attributed to it, this upbringing, this origin, this ardor or these silences, this nobility or this vileness. But aspects cannot be added up. This very heart which is mine will forever remain indefinable to me. Between the certainty I have of my existence and the content I try to give to that assurance, the gap will never be filled. Forever I shall be a stranger to myself. In psychology as in logic, there are truths but no truth. Socrates' "Know thyself" has as much value as the "Be virtuous" of our confessionals. They reveal a nostalgia at the same time as an ignorance. They are sterile exercises on great subjects. They are legitimate only in precisely so far as they are approximate.

I want everything to be explained to me or nothing. And the reason is impotent when it hears this cry from the heart. The mind aroused by this insistence seeks and finds nothing but contradictions and nonsense. What I fail to understand is nonsense. The world is peopled with such irrationals. The world itself, whose single meaning I do not understand, is but a vast irra-

---

[1] But not in the proper sense. This is not a definition, but rather an *enumeration* of the feelings that may admit of the absurd. Still, the enumeration finished, the absurd has nevertheless not been exhausted.

tional. If one could only say just once: "This is clear," all would
be saved. But these men vie with one another in proclaiming that
nothing is clear, all is chaos, that all man has is his lucidity and
his definite knowledge of the walls surrounding him.

All these experiences agree and confirm one another. The
mind, when it reaches its limits, must make a judgment and
choose its conclusions. This is where suicide and the reply stand.
But I wish to reverse the order of the inquiry and start out from
the intelligent adventure and come back to daily acts. The experiences called to mind here were born in the desert that we must
not leave behind. At least it is essential to know how far they
went. At this point of his effort man stands face to face with the
irrational. He feels within him his longing for happiness and for
reason. The absurd is born of this confrontation between the
human need and the unreasonable silence of the world. This must
not be forgotten. This must be clung to because the whole consequence of a life can depend on it. The irrational, the human
nostalgia, and the absurd that is born of their encounter—these
are the three characters in the drama that must necessarily end
with all the logic of which an existence is capable.

I am taking the liberty at this point of calling the existential
attitude philosophical suicide. But this does not imply a judgment. It is a convenient way of indicating the movement by which
a thought negates itself and tends to transcend itself in its very
negation. For the existentials negation is their God. To be precise, that god is maintained only through the negation of human
reason.[2] But, like suicides, gods change with men. There are
many ways of leaping, the essential being to leap. Those redeem-
ing negations, those ultimate contradictions which negate the
obstacle that has not yet been leaped over, may spring just as
well (this is the paradox at which this reasoning aims) from a
certain religious inspiration as from the rational order. They
always lay claim to the eternal, and it is solely in this that they
take the leap.

---

[2] Let me assert again: it is not the affirmation of God that is questioned here, but rather the logic leading to that affirmation.

It must be repeated that the reasoning developed in this essay leaves out altogether the most widespread spiritual attitude of our enlightened age: the one, based on the principle that all is reason, which aims to explain the world. It is natural to give a clear view of the world after accepting the idea that it must be clear. That is even legitimate, but does not concern the reasoning we are following out here. In fact, our aim is to shed light upon the step taken by the mind when, starting from a philosophy of the world's lack of meaning, it ends up by finding a meaning and depth in it. The most touching of those steps is religious in essence; it becomes obvious in the theme of the irrational. But the most paradoxical and most significant is certainly the one that attributes rational reasons to a world it originally imagined as devoid of any guiding principle. It is impossible in any case to reach the consequences that concern us without having given an idea of this new attainment of the spirit of nostalgia.

I shall examine merely the theme of "the Intention" made fashionable by Husserl and the phenomenologists. I have already alluded to it. Originally Husserl's method negates the classic procedure of the reason. Let me repeat. Thinking is not unifying or making the appearance familiar under the guise of a great principle. Thinking is learning all over again how to see, directing one's consciousness, making of every image a privileged place. In other words, phenomenology declines to explain the world, it wants to be merely a description of actual experience. It confirms absurd thought in its initial assertion that there is no truth, but merely truths. From the evening breeze to this hand on my shoulder, everything has its truth. Consciousness illuminates it by paying attention to it. Consciousness does not form the object of its understanding, it merely focuses, it is the act of attention, and, to borrow a Bergsonian image, it resembles the projector that suddenly focuses on an image. The difference is that there is no scenario, but a successive and incoherent illustration. In that magic lantern all the pictures are privileged. Consciousness suspends in experience the objects of its attention. Through its miracle it isolates them. Henceforth they are beyond all judgments. This is the "intention" that characterizes consciousness.

But the word does not imply any idea of finality; it is taken in its sense of "direction": its only value is topographical.

At first sight, it certainly seems that in this way nothing contradicts the absurd spirit. That apparent modesty of thought that limits itself to describing what it declines to explain, that intentional discipline whence result paradoxically a profound enrichment of experience and the rebirth of the world in its prolixity are absurd procedures. At least at first sight. For methods of thought in this case as elsewhere, always assume two aspects, one psychological and the other metaphysical.[3] Thereby they harbor two truths. If the theme of the intentional claims to illustrate merely a psychological attitude, by which reality is drained instead of being explained, nothing in fact separates it from the absurd spirit. It aims to enumerate what it cannot transcend. It affirms solely that without any unifying principle thought can still take delight in describing and understanding every aspect of experience. The truth involved then for each of those aspects is psychological in nature. It simply testifies to the "interest" that reality can offer. It is a way of awaking a sleeping world and of making it vivid to the mind. But if one attempts to extend and give a rational basis to that notion of truth, if one claims to discover in this way the "essence" of each object of knowledge, one restores its depth to experience. For an absurd mind that is incomprehensible. Now, it is this wavering between modesty and assurance that is noticeable in the intentional attitude, and this shimmering of phenomenological thought will illustrate the absurd reasoning better than anything else.

For Husserl speaks likewise of "extra-temporal essences" brought to light by the intention, and he sounds like Plato. All things are not explained by one thing but by all things. I see no difference. To be sure, those ideas or those essences that consciousness "effectuates" at the end of every description are not yet to be considered perfect models. But it is asserted that they are

---

[3] Even the most rigorous epistemologies imply metaphysics. And to such a degree that the metaphysic of many contemporary thinkers consists in having nothing but an epistemology.

directly present in each datum of perception. There is no longer a single idea explaining everything, but an infinite number of essences giving a meaning to an infinite number of objects. The world comes to a stop, but also lights up. Platonic realism becomes intuitive, but it is still realism. Kierkegaard was swallowed up in his God; Parmenides plunged thought into the One. But here thought hurls itself into an abstract polytheism. But this is not all: hallucinations and fictions likewise belong to "extra-temporal essences." In the new world of ideas, the species of centaurs collaborates with the more modest species of metropolitan man.

For the absurd man, there was a truth as well as a bitterness in that purely psychological opinion that all aspects of the world are privileged. To say that everything is privileged is tantamount to saying that everything is equivalent. But the metaphysical aspect of that truth is so far-reaching that through an elementary reaction he feels closer perhaps to Plato. He is taught, in fact, that every image presupposes an equally privileged essence. In this idea world without hierarchy, the formal army is composed solely of generals. To be sure, transcendency had been eliminated. But a sudden shift in thought brings back into the world a sort of fragmentary immanence which restores to the universe its depth.

Am I to fear having carried too far a theme handled with greater circumspection by its creators? I read merely these assertions of Husserl, apparently paradoxical yet rigorously logical if what precedes is accepted: "That which is true is true absolutely, in itself; truth is one, identical with itself, however different the creatures who perceive it, men, monsters, angels or gods." Reason triumphs and trumpets forth with that voice, I cannot deny. What can its assertions mean in the absurd world? The perception of an angel or a god has no meaning for me. That geometrical spot where divine reason ratifies mine will always be incomprehensible to me. There, too, I discern a leap, and though performed in the abstract, it nonetheless means for me forgetting just what I do not want to forget. When farther on Husserl exclaims: "If all masses subject to attraction were to disappear, the law of attraction would not be destroyed but would simply remain without any possible application," I know that I am faced with a metaphysic of consolation. And if I want to discover the point where thought leaves the path of evidence, I have only to reread the parallel reasoning that Husserl voices regarding the mind: "If we could contemplate clearly the exact laws of psychic processes, they would be seen to be likewise eternal and invariable, like the basic laws of theoretical natural science. Hence they would be valid even if there were no psychic process." Even if the mind were not its laws would be! I see then that of a psychological truth Husserl aims to make a rational rule: after having denied the integrating power of human reason, he leaps by this expedient to eternal Reason.

Husserl's theme of the "concrete universe" cannot then surprise me. If I am told that all essences are not formal but that some are material, that the first are the object of logic and the second of science, this is merely a question of definition. The abstract, I am told, indicates but a part, without consistency in itself, of a concrete universal. But the wavering already noted allows me to throw light on the confusion of these terms. For that may mean that the concrete object of my attention, this sky, the reflection of that water on this coat, alone preserve the prestige of the real that my interest isolates in the world. And I shall not deny it. But that may mean also that this coat itself is universal, has its particular and sufficient essence, belongs to the world of forms. I then realize that merely the order of the procession has been changed. This world has ceased to have its reflection in a higher universe, but the heaven of forms is figured in the host of images of this earth. This changes nothing for me. Rather than encountering here a taste for the concrete, the meaning of the human condition, I find an intellectualism sufficiently unbridled to generalize the concrete itself.

It is futile to be amazed by the apparent paradox that leads thought to its own negation by the opposite paths of humiliated reason and triumphal reason. From the abstract god of Husserl to the dazzling god of Kierkegaard the distance is not so great.

Reason and the irrational lead to the same preaching. In truth the way matters but little; the will to arrive suffices. The abstract philosopher and the religious philosopher start out from the same disorder and support each other in the same anxiety. But the essential is to explain. Nostalgia is stronger here than knowledge. It is significant that the thought of the epoch is at once one of the most deeply imbued with a philosophy of the non-significance of the world and one of the most divided in its conclusions. It is constantly oscillating between extreme rationalization of reality which tends to break up that thought into standard reasons and its extreme irrationalization which tends to deify it. But this divorce is only apparent. It is a matter of reconciliation, and, in both cases, the leap suffices. It is always wrongly thought that the notion of reason is a one-way notion. To tell the truth, however rigorous it may be in its ambition, this concept is nonetheless just as unstable as others. Reason bears a quite human aspect, but it also is able to turn toward the divine. Since Plotinus, who was the first to reconcile it with the eternal climate, it has learned to turn away from the most cherished of its principles, which is contradiction, in order to integrate into it the strangest, the quite magic one of participation.[3] It is an instrument of thought and not thought itself. Above all, a man's thought is his nostalgia.

Just as reason was able to soothe the melancholy of Plotinus, it provides modern anguish the means of calming itself in the familiar setting of the eternal. The absurd mind has less luck. For it the world is neither so rational nor so irrational. It is unreasonable and only that. With Husserl the reason eventually has no limits at all. The absurd, on the contrary, establishes its

[3] A.—At that time reason had to adapt itself or die. It adapts itself. With Plotinus, after being logical it becomes æsthetic. Metaphor takes the place of the syllogism.

B.—Moreover, this is not Plotinus' only contribution to phenomenology. This whole attitude is already contained in the concept so dear to the Alexandrian thinker that there is not only an idea of man but also an idea of Socrates.

limits since it is powerless to calm its anguish. Kierkegaard independently asserts that a single limit is enough to negate that anguish. But the absurd does not go so far. For it that limit is directed solely at the reason's ambitions. The theme of the irrational, as it is conceived by the existentials, is reason becoming confused and escaping by negating itself. The absurd is lucid reason noting its limits.

Only at the end of this difficult path does the absurd man recognize his true motives. Upon comparing his inner exigence and what is then offered him, he suddenly feels he is going to turn away. In the universe of Husserl the world becomes clear and that longing for familiarity that man's heart harbors becomes useless. In Kierkegaard's apocalypse that desire for clarity must be given up if it wants to be satisfied. Sin is not so much knowing (if it were, everybody would be innocent) as wanting to know. Indeed, it is the only sin of which the absurd man can feel that it constitutes both his guilt and his innocence. He is offered a solution in which all the past contradictions have become merely polemical games. But this is not the way he experienced them. Their truth must be preserved, which consists in not being satisfied. He does not want preaching.

My reasoning wants to be faithful to the evidence that aroused it. That evidence is the absurd. It is that divorce between the mind that desires and the world that disappoints, my nostalgia for unity, this fragmented universe and the contradiction that binds them together. Kierkegaard suppresses my nostalgia and Husserl gathers together that universe. That is not what I was expecting. It was a matter of living and thinking with those dislocations, of knowing whether one had to accept or refuse. There can be no question of masking the evidence, of suppressing the absurd by denying one of the terms of its equation. It is essential to know whether one can live with it or whether, on the other hand, logic commands one to die of it. I am not interested in philosophical suicide, but rather in plain suicide. I merely wish to purge it of its emotional content and know its logic and its integrity. Any other position implies for the absurd mind deceit and the mind's retreat before what the mind itself has brought to light. Husserl claims to obey the desire to escape "the inveterate habit of living and thinking in certain well-known and convenient conditions of existence," but the final leap restores in him the eternal and its comfort. The leap does not represent an extreme danger as Kierkegaard would like it to do. The danger, on the contrary, lies in the subtle instant that precedes the leap. Being able to remain on that dizzying crest—that is integrity and the rest is subterfuge. I know also that never has helplessness inspired such striking harmonies as those of Kierkegaard. But if helplessness has its place in the indifferent landscapes of history, it has none in a reasoning whose exigence is now known.

FREEDOM AND RESPONSIBILITY

JEAN-PAUL SARTRE

Although the considerations which are about to follow are of interest primarily to the ethicist, it may nevertheless be worthwhile after these descriptions and arguments to return to the freedom of the for-itself and to try to understand what the fact of this freedom represents for human destiny.

The essential consequence of our earlier remarks is that man being condemned to be free carries the weight of the whole world on his shoulders, he is responsible for the world and for himself as a way of being. We are taking the word "responsibility" in its ordinary sense as "consciousness (of) being the incontestable author of an event or of an object." In this sense the responsibility of the for-itself is overwhelming since he is the one by whom it happens that *there is* a world; since he is also the one who makes himself be, then whatever may be the situation in which he finds himself, the for-itself must wholly assume this situation with its peculiar coefficient of adversity, even though it be insupportable. He must assume the situation with the proud consciousness of being the author of it, for the very worst disadvantages or the worst threats which can endanger my person have meaning only in and through my project; and it is on the ground of the engagement which I am that they appear. It is therefore senseless to think of complaining since nothing foreign has decided what we feel, what we live, or what we are.

Furthermore this absolute responsibility is not resignation; it is simply the logical requirement of the consequences of our freedom. What happens to me happens through me, and I can neither affect myself with it nor revolt against it nor resign myself to it. Moreover everything which happens to me is *mine*. By this we must understand first of all that I am always equal to what happens to me qua man, for what happens to a man through other men and through himself can be only human. The most terrible situations of war, the worst tortures do not create a non-human state of things; there is no non-human situation. It is only through fear, flight, and recourse to magical types of conduct that I shall decide on the non-human, but this decision is human, and I shall carry the entire responsibility for it. But in addition the situation is *mine* because it is the image of my free choice of myself, and everything which it presents to me is *mine* in that this represents me and symbolizes me. Is it not I who decide the coefficient of adversity in things and even their unpredictability by deciding myself?

Thus there are no *accidents* in a life; a community event which suddenly bursts forth and involves me in it does not come from the outside. If I am mobilized in a war, this war is *my* war; it is in my image and I deserve it. I deserve it first because I could always get out of it by suicide or by desertion; these ultimate possibles are those which must always be present for us when there is a question of envisaging a situation. For lack of getting out of it, I have *chosen* it. This can be due to inertia, to cowardice in the face of public opinion, or because I prefer certain other values to the value of the refusal to join in the war (the good opinion of my relatives, the honor of my family, *etc.*). Anyway you look at it, it is a matter of a choice. This choice will be repeated later on again and again without a break until the end of the war. Therefore we must agree with the statement by J. Romains, "In war there are no innocent victims." If therefore I have preferred war to death or to dishonor, everything takes place as if I bore the entire responsibility for this war. Of course others have declared it, and one might be tempted perhaps to consider me as a simple accomplice. But this notion of complicity has only a juridical sense, and it does not hold here. For it depended on me that for me and by me this war should not exist, and I have decided that it does exist. There was no compulsion here; for the compulsion could have got no hold on a freedom. I did not have any excuse; for us we have said repeatedly in this book, the peculiar character of human-reality that it is without excuse. Therefore it remains for me only to lay claim to this war.

But in addition the war is *mine* because by the sole fact that it arises in a situation which I cause to be and that I can discover it there only by engaging myself for or against it, I can no longer distinguish at present the choice which I make of myself from the choice which I make of the war. To live this war is to choose myself through it and to choose it through my choice of myself. There can be no question of considering it as "four years of vacation" or as a "reprieve," as a "recess," the essential part of my responsibilities being elsewhere in my married, family, or professional life. In this war which I have chosen I choose myself from day to day, and I make it mine by making myself. If it is going to be four empty years, then it is I who bear the responsibility for this.

Finally, as we pointed out earlier, each person is an absolute choice of self from the standpoint of a world of knowledges and of techniques which this choice both assumes and illumines; each person is an absolute upsurge at an absolute date and is perfectly unthinkable at another date. It is therefore a waste of time to ask what I should have been if this war had not broken out, for I have chosen myself as one of the possible meanings of the epoch which imperceptibly led to war. I am not distinct from this same epoch; I could not be transported to another epoch without contradiction. Thus *I am* this war which restricts and limits and makes comprehensible the period which preceded it. In this sense we may define more precisely the responsibility of the for-itself if to the earlier quoted statement, "There are no innocent victims," we add the words, "We have the war we deserve." Thus, totally free, undistinguishable from the period for which I have chosen to be the meaning, as profoundly responsible for the war as if I had myself declared it, unable to live without integrating it in my situation, engaging myself in it wholly and stamping it with my seal, I must be without remorse or regrets as I am without excuse; for from the instant of my upsurge into being, I carry the weight of the world by myself alone without anything or any person being able to lighten it.

Yet this responsibility is of a very particular type. Someone will say, "I did not ask to be born." This is a naive way of throwing greater emphasis on our facticity. I am responsible for everything, in fact, except for my very responsibility, for I am not the foundation of my being. Therefore everything takes place as if I were compelled to be responsible. I am *abandoned* in the world, not in the sense that I might remain abandoned and passive in a hostile universe like a board floating on the water, but rather in the sense that I find myself suddenly alone and without help, engaged in a world for which I bear the whole responsibility without being able, whatever I do, to tear myself away from this responsibility for an instant. For I am responsible for my very desire of fleeing responsibilities. To make myself passive in the world, to refuse to act upon things and upon Others is still to choose myself, and suicide is one mode among others of being-in-the-world. Yet I find an absolute responsibility for the fact that my facticity (here the fact of my birth) is directly inapprehensible and even inconceivable, for this fact of my birth never appears as a brute fact but always across a projective reconstruction of my for-itself. I am ashamed of being born or I am astonished at it or I rejoice over it, or in attempting to get rid of my life I affirm that I live and I assume this life as bad. Thus in a certain sense I *choose* being born. This choice itself is integrally affected with facticity since I am not able not to choose, but his facticity in turn will appear only in so far as I surpass it toward my ends. Thus facticity is every-where but in apprehensible; I never encounter anything except my responsibility. That is why I can not ask, *"Why* was I born?" or curse the day of my birth or declare that I did not ask to be born, for these various attitudes toward my birth—*i.e.,* toward the *fact* that I realize a presence in the world—are absolutely nothing else but ways of assuming this birth in full responsibility and of making it *mine.* Here again I encounter only myself and my projects so that finally my abandonment—*i.e.,* my facticity —consists simply in the fact that I am condemned to be wholly responsible for myself. I am the being which *is* in such a way that in its being its being is in question. And this "is" of my being *is* as present and inapprehensible.

Under these conditions since every event in the world can be revealed to me only as an *opportunity* (an opportunity made use of, lacked, neglected, *etc.*), or better yet since everything which happens to us can be considered as a *chance* (*i.e.,* can appear to us only as a way of realizing this being which is in question in our being) and since others as transcendences-tran-scended are themselves only opportunities and chances, the re-sponsibility of the for-itself extends to the entire world as a peopled-world. It is precisely thus that the for-itself apprehends itself in anguish; that is, as a being which is neither the founda-tion of its own being nor of the Other's being nor of the in-itselfs which form the world, but a being which is compelled to decide the meaning of being—within it and everywhere outside of it. The one who realizes in anguish his condition as *being* thrown into a responsibility which extends to his very abandon-ment has no longer either remorse or regret or excuse, he is no longer anything but a freedom which perfectly reveals itself and whose being resides in this very revelation. But as we pointed out at the beginning of this work, most of the time we flee anguish in bad faith.

THE ETHICS OF AMBIGUITY

SIMONE DE BEAUVOIR

From the very beginning, existentialism defined itself as a philosophy of ambiguity. It was by affirming the irreducible character of ambiguity that Kierkegaard opposed himself to Hegel, and it is by ambiguity that, in our own generation, Sartre, in *Being and Nothingness*, fundamentally defined man, that being whose being is not to be, that subjectivity which realizes itself only as a presence in the world, that engaged freedom, that surging of the for-oneself which is immediately given for others. But it is also claimed that existentialism is a philosophy of the absurd and of despair. It encloses man in a sterile anguish, in an empty subjectivity. It is incapable of furnishing him with any principle for making choices. Let him do as he pleases. In any case, the game is lost. Does not Sartre declare, in effect, that man is a "useless passion," that he tries in vain to realize the synthesis of the for-oneself and the in-oneself, to make himself God? It is true. But it is also true that the most optimistic ethics have all begun by emphasizing the element of failure involved in the condition of man; without failure, no ethics; for a being who, from the very start, would be an exact co-incidence with himself, in a perfect plenitude, the notion of having-to-be would have no meaning. One does not offer an ethics to a God. It is impossible to propose any to man if one defines him as nature, as something given. The so-called psychological or empirical ethics manage to establish themselves only by introducing surreptitiously some flaw within the man-thing which they have first defined. Hegel tells us in the last part of *The Phenomenology of Mind* that moral consciousness can exist only to the extent that there is disagreement between nature and morality. It would disappear if the ethical law became the natural law. To such an extent that by a paradoxical "displacement," if moral action is the absolute goal, the absolute goal is also that moral action may not be present. This means that there can be a having-to-be only for a being who, according to the existentialist definition, questions himself in his being, a being who is at a distance from himself and who has to be his being.

Well and good. But it is still necessary for the failure to be surmounted, and existentialist ontology does not allow this hope. Man's passion is useless; he has no means for becoming the being that he is not. That too is true. And it is also true that in *Being and Nothingness* Sartre has insisted above all on the abortive aspect of the human adventure. It is only in the last pages that he opens up the perspective for an ethics. However, if we reflect upon his descriptions of existence, we perceive that they are far from condemning man without recourse.

The failure described in *Being and Nothingness* is definitive, but it is also ambiguous. Man, Sartre tell us, is "a being who *makes himself* a lack of being *in order that there might be* being." That means, first of all, that his passion is not inflicted upon him from without. He chooses it. It is his very being and, as such, does not imply the idea of unhappiness. If this choice is considered as useless, it is because there exists no absolute value before the passion of man, outside of it, in relation to which one might distinguish the useless from the useful. The word "useful" has not yet received a meaning on the level of description where *Being and Nothingness* is situated. It can be defined only in the human world established by man's projects and the ends he sets up.

AMBIGUITY

The notion of ambiguity must not be confused with that of absurdity. To declare that existence is absurd is to deny that it can ever be given a meaning; to say that it is ambiguous is to assert that its meaning is never fixed, that it must be constantly won. Absurdity challenges every ethics; but also the finished rationalization of the real would leave no room for ethics; it is because man's condition is ambiguous that he seeks, through failure and outrageousness, to save his existence. Thus, to say that action has to be lived in its truth, that is, in the consciousness of the antinomies which it involves, does not mean that one has to renounce it. In *Plutarch Lied* Pierrefeu rightly says that in war there is no victory which can not be regarded as unsuccessful, for the objective which one aims at is the total annihilation of the enemy and this result is never attained; yet there are wars which are won and wars which are lost. So is it with any activity; failure and success are two aspects of reality which at the start are not perceptible. That is what makes criticism so easy and art so difficult: the critic is always in a good position to show the limits that every artist gives himself in choosing himself; painting is not given completely either in Giotto or Titian or Cezanne; it is sought through the centuries and is never finished; a painting in which all pictorial problems are resolved is really inconceivable; painting itself is this movement toward its own reality; it is not the vain displacement of a millstone turning in the void; it concretizes itself in each canvas as an absolute existence. Art and science do not establish themselves despite failure but through it; which does not prevent there being truths and errors, masterpieces and lemons, depending upon whether the discovery or the painting has or has not known how to win the adherence of human consciousnesses; this amounts to saying that failure, always ineluctable, is in certain cases spared and in others not.

It is interesting to pursue this comparison; not that we are likening action to a work of art or a scientific theory, but because in any case human transcendence must cope with the same problem: it has to found itself, though it is prohibited from ever fulfilling itself. Now, we know that neither science nor art ever leaves it up to the future to justify its present existence. In no age does art consider itself as something which is paving the way for Art: so-called archaic art prepares for classicism only in the eyes of archaeologists; the sculptor who fashioned the Korai of Athens rightfully thought that he was

producing a finished work of art; in no age has science considered itself as partial and lacunary; without believing itself
to be definitive, it has however, always wanted to be a total
expression of the world, and it is in its totality that in each age
it again raises the question of its own validity. There we have an
example of how man must, in any event, assume his finiteness:
not by treating his existence as transitory or relative but by
reflecting the infinite within it, that is, by treating it as absolute.
There is an art only because at every moment art has willed itself absolutely; likewise there is a liberation of man only if, in
aiming at itself, freedom is achieved absolutely in the very fact
of aiming at itself. This requires that each action be considered
as a finished form whose different moments, instead of fleeing
toward the future in order to find there their justification, reflect
and confirm one another so well that there is no longer a sharp
separation between present and future, between means and ends.

But if these moments constitute a unity, there must be no
contradiction among them. Since the liberation aimed at is not
a *thing* situated in an unfamiliar time, but a movement which
realizes itself by tending to conquer, it can not attain itself if it
denies itself at the start; action can not seek to fulfill itself by
means which would destroy its very meaning. So much so that
in certain situations there will be no other issue for man than
rejection. In what is called political realism there is no room
for rejection because the present is considered as transitory;
there is rejection only if man lays claim in the present to his
existence as an absolute value; then he must absolutely reject
what would deny this value. Today, more or less consciously in
the name of such an ethics, we condemn a magistrate who
handed over a communist to save ten hostages and along with
him all the Vichyites who were trying "to make the best of
things:" it was not a matter of rationalizing the present such as
it was imposed by the German occupation, but of rejecting it
unconditionally. The resistance did not aspire to a positive effec-
tiveness; it was a negation, a revolt, a martyrdom; and in this
negative movement freedom was positively and absolutely confirmed.

In one sense the negative attitude is easy; the rejected object is given unequivocally and unequivocally defines the revolt that one opposes to it; thus, all French antifascists were united during the occupation by their common resistance to a single oppressor. The return to the positive encounters many more obstacles, as we have well seen in France where divisions and hatreds were revived at the same time as were the parties. In the moment of rejection, the antinomy of action is removed, and means and end meet; freedom immediately sets itself up as its own goal and fulfills itself by so doing. But the antinomy reappears as soon as freedom again gives itself ends which are far off in the future; then, through the resistances of the given, divergent means offer themselves and certain ones come to be seen as contrary to their ends. It has often been observed that revolt alone is pure. Every construction implies the outrage of dictatorship, of violence. This is the theme, among others, of Koestler's *Gladiators*. Those who, like this symbolic *Spartacus*, do not want to retreat from the outrage and resign themselves to impotence, usually seek refuge in the values of seriousness. That is why, among individuals as well as collectivities, the negative moment is often the most genuine. Goethe, Barres, and Aragon, disdainful or rebellious in their romantic youth, shattered old conformisms and thereby proposed a real, though incomplete, liberation. But what happened later on? Goethe became a servant of the state, Barres of nationalism, and Aragon of Stalinist conformism. We know how the seriousness of the Catholic Church was substituted for the Christian spirit, which was a rejection of dead Law, a subjective rapport of the individual with God through faith and charity; the Reformation was a revolt of subjectivity, but Protestantism in turn changed into an objective moralism in which the seriousness of works replaced the restlessness of faith. As for revolutionary humanism, it accepts only rarely the tension of permanent liberation; it has created a Church where salvation is bought by membership in a party as it is bought elsewhere by baptism and indulgences. We have seen that this recourse to the serious is a lie; it entails the sacrifice of man to the Thing, of freedom to the Cause. In order for the return to the positive to be genuine it must involve negativity, it must not conceal the antinomies between means and end, present and future; they must be lived in a permanent tension; one must retreat from neither the outrage of violence nor deny it, or, which amounts to the same thing, assume it lightly. Kierkegaard has said that what distinguishes the pharisee from the genuinely moral man is that the former considers his anguish as a sure sign of his virtue; from the 'fact that he asks himself, "Am I Abraham?" he concludes, "I am Abraham"; but morality resides in the painfulness of an indefinite questioning. The problem which we are posing is not the same as that of Kierkegaard; the important thing to us is to know whether, in given conditions, Isaac must be killed or not. But we also think that what distinguishes the tyrant from the man of good will is that the first rests in the certainty of his aims, whereas the second keeps asking himself, "Am I really working for the liberation of men? Isn't this end contested by the sacrifices through which I aim at it?" In setting up its ends, freedom must put them in parentheses, confront them at each moment with that absolute end which it itself constitutes, and contest, in its own name, the means it uses to win itself.

It will be said that these considerations remain quite abstract. What must be done, practically? Which action is good? Which is bad? To ask such a question is also to fall into a naive abstraction. We don't ask the physicist, "Which hypotheses are true?" Nor the artist, "By what procedures does one produce a work whose beauty is guaranteed?" Ethics does not furnish recipes any more than do science and art. One can merely propose methods. Thus, in science the fundamental problem is to make the idea adequate to its content and the law adequate to the facts; the logician finds that in the case where the pressure of the given fact bursts the concept which serves to comprehend it, one is obliged to invent another concept; but he can not define *a priori* the moment of invention, still less foresee it. Analogously, one may say that in the case where the content of the action falsifies its meaning, one must modify not the meaning, which is here willed absolutely, but the content itself; however, it is impossible to determine this relationship between meaning and content abstractly and universally: there must be a trial and decision in each case. But likewise just as the physicist finds it profitable to reflect on the conditions of scientific invention and the artist on those of artistic creation without expecting any ready-made solutions to come from these reflections, it is useful for the man of action to find out under what conditions his undertakings are valid. We are going to see that on this basis new perspectives are disclosed.

In the first place, it seems to us that the individual as such is one of the ends at which our action must aim. Here we are at one with the point of view of Christian charity, the Epicurean cult of friendship, and Kantian moralism which treats each man as an end. He interests us not merely as a member of a class, a nation, or a collectivity, but as an individual man. This distinguishes us from the systematic politician who cares only about collective destinies; and probably a tramp enjoying his bottle of wine, or a child playing with a balloon, or a Neapolitan lazzarone loafing in the sun in no way helps in the liberation of man; that is why the abstract will of the revolutionary scorns the concrete benevolence which occupies itself in satisfying desires which have no morrow. However, it must not be forgotten that there is a concrete bond between freedom and existence; to will man free is to will there to *be* being, it is to will the disclosure of being in the joy of existence; in order for the idea of liberation to have a concrete meaning, the joy of existence must be asserted in each one, at every instant; the movement toward freedom assumes its real, flesh and blood figure in the world by thickening into pleasure, into happiness. If the satisfaction of an old man drinking a glass of wine counts for nothing, then production and wealth are only hollow myths; they have meaning only if they are capable of being retrieved in individual and living joy. The saving of time and the conquest of leisure have no meaning if we are not moved by the laugh of a child at play. If we do not love life on our own account and through others, it is futile to seek to justify it in any way.

AN INTERVIEW (1970)

JEAN-PAUL SARTRE

How do you envisage the relationship between your early philosophical writings, above all L'Etre et le néant, *and your present theoretical work, from the* Critique de la raison dialectique *onward? In the* Critique, *the typical concepts of* L'Etre et le néant *have disappeared, and a completely new vocabulary has taken their place. Yet when reading the passages of your forthcoming study of Flaubert, published in* Les Temps modernes, *one is struck by the sudden re-emergence of the characteristic idiom of the early work—thetic consciousness, ego, nihilation, being, nothingness. These notions are now juxtaposed in the text with the distinct set of concepts which derive from the* Critique. *What is the precise relationship between the two in your current thought?*

The basic question here, of course, is my relationship to Marxism. I will try to explain autobiographically certain aspects of my early work, which may help to clarify the reasons why my outlook changed so fundamentally after the Second World War. A simple formula would be to say that life taught me *la force des choses*—the power of circumstances. In a way, *L'Etre et le néant* itself should have been the beginning of a discovery of this power of circumstances, since I had already been made a soldier, when I had not wanted to be one. Thus I had already encountered something which was not my freedom and which steered me from without. Then I was taken prisoner, a fate which I had sought to escape. Hence I started to learn what I have called human reality among things: Being-in-the-world.

Reprinted from the *New Left Review*, 58 (1970), by permission of the *New Left Review*. Reprinted in *The New York Review of Books*, 14 (1970). These are the opening questions and replies of the interview.

Then, little by little, I found that the world was more complicated than this, for during the Resistance there appeared to
be a possibility of free decision. For my state of mind during
those years, I think that the first plays I wrote are very symptomatic: I called them a "theater of freedom." The other day, I
reread a prefatory note of mine to a collection of these plays—
Les Mouches, Huis clos, and others—and was truly scandalized.
I had written: "Whatever the circumstances, and wherever the
site, a man is always free to choose to be a traitor or not . . . ."
When I read this, I said to myself: it's incredible, I actually
believed that!

To understand how I could have done so, you must remember that there was a very simple problem during the Resistance
—ultimately, only a question of courage. One had to accept the
risks involved in what one was doing, that is, of being im-
prisoned or deported. But beyond this? A Frenchman was either
for the Germans or against them, there was no other option. The
real political problems, of being "for, but" or "against, but,"
were not posed by this experience.

The result was that I concluded that in any circumstances,
there is always a possible choice. Which is false. Indeed, it is so
false that I later wanted precisely to refute myself by creating a
character in *Le Diable et le Bon Dieu,* Heinrich, who cannot
choose. He wants to choose, of course, but he cannot choose
either the Church, which has abandoned the poor, or the poor,
who have abandoned the Church. He is thus a living contradiction, who will never choose. He is totally conditioned by his
situation.

However, I understood all this only much later. What the
drama of the war gave me, as it did everyone else who partici-
pated in it, was the experience of heroism. Not my own, of course
—all I did was a few errands. But the militant in the Resistance
who was caught and tortured became a myth for us. Such mili-
tants existed, of course, but they represented a sort of personal
myth as well. Would we be able to hold out against torture too?
The problem then was solely that of physical endurance—it was
not the ruses of history or the paths of alienation. A man is

tortured: what will he do? He speaks or refuses to speak: This is what I mean by the experience of heroism, which is a false experience.

After the war came the true experience, that of *society*. But I think it was necessary for me to pass via the myth of heroism first. That is to say, the prewar personage who was more or less Stendhal's egotistical individualist had to be plunged into circumstances against his will, yet where he still had the power to say yes or no, in order to encounter the inextricable entanglements of the postwar years as a man totally conditioned by his social existence and yet sufficiently capable of decision to reassume all this conditioning and to become responsible for it.

For the idea which I have never ceased to develop is that in the end one is always responsible for what is made of one. Even if one can do nothing else besides assume this responsibility. For I believe that a man can always make something out of what is made of him. This is the limit I would today accord to freedom: the small movement which makes of a totally conditioned social being some one who does not render back completely what his conditioning has given him. Which makes of Genet a poet when he had been rigorously conditioned to be a thief.

Perhaps the book where I have best explained what I mean by freedom is, in fact, *Saint Genet.* For Genet was made a thief, he said "I am a thief," and this tiny change was the start of a process whereby he became a poet and then eventually a being no longer even on the margin of society, someone who no longer knows where he is, who falls silent. It cannot be a happy freedom, in a case like this. Freedom is not a triumph. For Genet, it simply marked out certain routes which were not initially given.

L'Etre et le néant traced an interior experience, without any coordination with the exterior experience of a petty-bourgeois intellectual, which had become historically catastrophic at a certain moment. For I wrote *L'Etre et le néant* after the defeat of France, after all. But catastrophes have no lessons, unless they are the culmination of a praxis. Then one can say, my action has failed. But the disaster which overwhelmed the country had taught us nothing.

Thus, in *L'Etre et le néant,* what you could call "subjectivity" is not what it would be for me now, the small margin in an operation whereby an interiorization re-exteriorizes itself in an act. But "subjectivity" and "objectivity" seem to me entirely useless notions today, anyway. I might still use the term "objectivity," I suppose, but only to emphasize that everything is objective. The individual interiorizes his social determinations: he interiorizes the relations of production, the family of his childhood, the historical past, the contemporary institutions, and he then re-exteriorizes these in acts and options which necessarily refer us back to them. None of this existed in *L'Etre et le néant.*

In L'Etre et le néant, *you radically rejected the concept of the unconscious, saying that it was a philosophical contradiction. The model of consciousness in your early work effectively excludes any idea of it whatever. Consciousness is always transparent to itself, even if the subject creates a false screen of "bad faith." Since then, you have among other things written a filmscript on Freud—*

—I broke with Huston precisely because Huston did not understand what the unconscious was. That was the whole problem. He wanted to suppress it, to replace it with the preconscious. He did not want the unconscious at any price—

The question one would like to ask is how you conceive the precise theoretical stature of the work of Freud today? In view of your class position, it is not perhaps so surprising that you did not discover Marx before the war. But how did you miss Freud? Surely the opaque evidence of the unconscious, its resistances, should have been accessible to you even then? They are not exactly comparable to the class struggle.

The two questions are linked, however. The thought of both Marx and Freud is a theory of conditioning in exteriority. When Marx says: "It matters little what the bourgeoisie thinks it does, the important thing is what it does," one could replace the "bourgeoisie" by "a hysteric," and the formula would be one of Freud. Having said this, I must try to recount my relationship to Freud's work biographically.

I will begin by saying that I undoubtedly had a deep repugnance for psychoanalysis in my youth, which needs to be explained as much as my innocence of the class struggle. The fact that I was a petty bourgeois was responsible for the latter; one might say that the fact that I was French was responsible for the former. There would certainly be a lot of truth in this. You must never forget the weight of Cartesian rationalism in France. When you have just taken the *bachot* at the age of seventeen, with the "I think, therefore I am" of Descartes as your set text, and you open *The Psychopathology of Everyday Life*, and you read the famous episode of Signorelli with its substitutions, combinations, and displacements, implying that Freud was simultaneously thinking of a patient who had committed suicide and of certain Turkish mores, and so on—when you read all that, your breath is simply taken away.

Such investigations were completely outside my preoccupations at the time, which were at bottom to provide a philosophical foundation for realism. Which in my opinion is possible today, and which I have tried to do all my life. In other words, how to give man both his autonomy and his reality among real objects, avoiding idealism without lapsing into a mechanistic materialism. I posed the problem in this way because I was ignorant of dialectical materialism, although I should add that this later allowed me to assign certain limits to it—to validate the historical dialectic while rejecting a dialectic of nature, in the sense of a natural process which produces and resolves man into an ensemble of physical laws.

To return to Freud, however, I have to say that I was incapable of understanding him because I was a Frenchman with a good Cartesian tradition behind me, imbued with a certain rationalism, and I was therefore deeply shocked by the idea of the unconscious. However, I will not say *only* this because I must add that I remain shocked by what was inevitable in Freud—the biological and physiological language with which he underpinned thoughts which were not translatable without mediation.

Right up to the time of Fliess, as you know, he wrote physiological studies designed to provide an equivalent of the cathexes and equilibria he had found in psychoanalysis. The result is that the manner in which he describes the psychoanalytic object suffers from a kind of mechanistic cramp. This is not always true, for there are moments when he transcends this. But in general this language produces a *mythology* of the unconscious which I cannot accept. I am completely in agreement with the *facts* of disguise and repression, as facts. But the *words* "repression," "censorship" or "drive"—words which express one moment a sort of finalism and the next moment a sort of mechanism—these I reject.

Let us take the example of "condensation," which is an ambivalent term in Freud. One can interpret it simply as a phenomenon of association, as in your English philosophers and psychologists of the eighteenth and nineteenth centuries. Two images are drawn together externally, they condense and form a third: this is classical psychological atomism. But one can also interpret the term on the contrary as expressive of a finality. Condensation occurs because two images combined answer a desire, a need.

This sort of ambiguity occurs again and again in Freud. The result is a strange representation of the unconscious as a set of rigorous mechanistic determinations, in any event a causality, and at the same time as a mysterious finality, such that there are "ruses" of the unconscious, as there are "ruses" of history; yet it is impossible to reunite the two in the work of many analysts—at least early analysts. I think that there is always a fundamental ambiguity in them; the unconscious is one moment *another consciousness,* and the next moment *other than con-*

sciousness. What is other than consciousness then becomes simply a mechanism.

Thus I would reproach psychoanalytic theory with being a syncretic and not a dialectical thought. The words "complex," indeed, indicates this very clearly: interpenetration without contradiction. I agree, of course, that there may exist an enormous number of "larval" contradictions within individuals, which are often translated in certain situations by interpenetrations and not by confrontations. But this does not mean these contradictions do not exist. The results of syncretism, on the contrary, can be seen in the idea of the Oedipus complex, for instance: the fact is that analysts manage to find everything in it, equally well the fixation on the mother, love of the mother, or hatred of the mother, as Melanie Klein argues. In other words, anything can be derived from it, since it is not *structured.*

The consequence is that an analyst can say one thing and then the contrary immediately afterward, without in any way worrying about lack of logic, since after all "opposites interpenetrate." A phenomenon can mean this, while its contrary can also mean the same thing. Psychoanalytic theory is thus a "soft" thought. It has no dialectical logic to it. Psychoanalysts will tell me that this is so because there is no such thing as logic in reality. But this is precisely what I am not sure of: I am convinced that complexes exist, but I am not so certain that they are not structured.

In particular, I believe that if complexes are true structures, "analytic skepticism" would have to be abandoned. What I call the "affective skepticism" of psychoanalysts is the belief of so many of them that the relationship which unites two people is only a "reference" to an original relationship which is an absolute: an allusion to a primal scene, incomparable and unforgettable—yet forgotten—between father and mother. Ultimately, any sentiment experienced by an adult becomes for the analyst a sort of occasion for the rebirth of another.

Now, there is a real truth in this: the fixation of a girl on an older man may well come from her father, or the fixation of a young man on a girl may derive from a profusion of original relationships. But what is missing in conventional psychoanalytic accounts is the idea of dialectical irreducibility. In a truly dialectical theory, such as historical materialism, phenomena derive from each other dialectically: there are different configurations of dialectical reality, and each of these configurations is rigorously conditioned by the previous one, while preserving and superseding it at the same time. This supersession is, however, precisely irreducible. While one configuration may preserve another, it can never simply be reduced to its predecessor. It is the idea of this *autonomy* that is lacking in psychoanalytic theory. A sentiment or a passion between two persons is certainly highly conditioned by their relationship to the "primal object," and one can locate this object within it and explain the new relationship by it; but the relationship itself remains irreducible.

Thus there is an essential difference between my relationship to Marx and my relationship to Freud. When I discovered the class struggle, this was a *true* discovery, in which I now believe totally, in the very form of the descriptions which Marx gave of it. Only the epoch has changed; otherwise it is the same struggle with the same classes and the same road to victory. Whereas I do not believe in the unconscious in the form in which psychoanalysis presents it to us. In my present book on Flaubert, I have replaced my earlier notion of consciousness (although I still use the word a lot), with what I call *le vécu*—lived experience.

SELECTED BIBLIOGRAPHY

ABBAGNANO, NICOLA, *Critical Existentialism*, translated by N. Langiulli, New York: Doubleday, 1969.

ARON, RAYMOND, *Marxism and the Existentialists*, New York: Harper & Row, 1969.

ATWELL, JOHN E., "Signification and Object," *American Philosophical Quarterly*, 6 (1964).

BARNES, HAZEL, *An Existentialist Ethics*, New York: Knopf, 1968.

BARRETT, WILLIAM, *Irrational Man*, New York: Doubleday, 1958.

BECK, M., "The Last Phase in Husserl's Philosophy," *Philosophical and Phenomenological Research*, 2 (1941).

BERGMANN, GUSTAV, "Husserl's Ontology," in *Meaning and Existence*, Madison: University of Wisconsin Press, 1960.

BLACKHAM, H. J., *Six Existentialist Thinkers*, London: Routledge & Kegan Paul, 1952.

BOYCE-GIBSON, W. R., "The Problem of the Real and Ideal in the Phenomenology of Husserl," *Mind*, 34 (1925).

BRENTANO, FRANZ, *The True and the Evident*, translated by Roderick Chisholm, et. al., New York: Humanities Press, 1968.

CAIN, SEYMOUR, *Gabriel Marcel*, New York: Hillary House, 1963.

CAMUS, ALBERT, *The Myth of Sisyphus*, translated by J. O'Brien, New York: Knopf, 1961.

———, *Resistance, Rebellion and Death*, translated by J. O'Brien, New York: Knopf, 1961.

CHAPMAN, HARMON, in J. Wild, ed., *Return to Reason*, Chicago: Regnery, 1953.

CHISHOLM, RODERICK N., *Perceiving: A Philosophical Study*, Ithaca, New York: Cornell University Press, 1957.

———, ed., *Realism and the Background of Phenomenology*, Glencoe, Ill.: Free Press, 1960.

———, *Theory of Knowledge*, Englewood Cliffs, N.J.: Prentice-Hall, 1966.

———, "The Concept of a Person," *Monist*, 49 (1965). An American Philosophical Association Symposium with H. Spiegleberg and V. Chappell.

COLLINS, JAMES, *The Existentialists*, Chicago: Regnery, 1964.

CRANSTON, MAURICE, *Jean-Paul Sartre*, New York: Grove Press, 1962.

DAWES-HICKS, G., "The Philosophy of Husserl," *The Hibbert Journal*, 12 (1913–1914).

DE BEAUVOIR, SIMONE, *The Ethics of Ambiguity*, translated by B. Frechtman, New York: Philosophical Library, 1948.

———, *The Second Sex*, translated by H. M. Parshley, New York: Knopf, 1953.

DESAN, WILFRID, *The Marxism of Jean-Paul Sartre*, New York: Doubleday, 1966.

DESCARTES, RENÉ, *Philosophical Works*, translated by E. Haldane and G. Ross, London: Cambridge University Press, 1967.

DOWNES, CHAUNCEY, "On Husserl's Approach to Necessary Truth," *Monist*, 49 (1965).

DREYFUS, HUBERT L., *Husserl's Phenomenology of Perception: From Transcendental to Existential Phenomenology*. Dissertation, Harvard University, 1963.

DUFRENNE, MIKEL, "Existentialism and Existentialisms," *Philosophical and Phenomenological Research*, 26 (1965).

———, *The Notion of the A Priori*, translated by E. Casey, Evanston, Ill.: Northwestern University Press, 1966.

EARLE, WILLIAM, *Objectivity*, Chicago: Quadrangle, 1968.

EDIE, JAMES, ed., *Invitation to Phenomenology*, Chicago: Quadrangle, 1965.

———, ed., *New Essays in Phenomenology*, Chicago: Quadrangle, 1969.

———, ed., *Phenomenology in America*, Chicago: Quadrangle, 1967.

———, "Recent Work in Phenomenology," *American Philosophical Quarterly*, 1 (1964).

———, "Review of Ricoüer, *Husserl*," *Journal of Philosophy*.

———, "Traditional Phenomenology and Existentialism," *Philosophical and Phenomenological Research*, 25 (1964).

ELVETON, R. O., ed., *The Phenomenology of Husserl*, Chicago: Quadrangle, 1970.

FANON, FRANZ, *The Wretched of the Earth*, Preface by Jean-Paul Sartre, New York: Grove Press, 1968.

FARBER, MARVIN, *The Aims of Phenomenology*, New York: Harper & Row, 1966.

———, *The Foundations of Phenomenology*, Albany, N.Y.: State University of New York Press, 1969.

————, *Naturalism and Subjectivism*, Springfield, Ill.: Thomas, 1959.

————, ed., *Philosophical Essays in Memory of Edmund Husserl*, Cambridge: Harvard University Press, 1940.

FELL, J., *Sartre's Theory of the Passions*, New York: Columbia University Press, 1962.

FINDLAY, J. N., *Meinong's Theory of Objects and Values*, 2nd ed., Oxford: Clarendon, 1963.

————, "Phenomenology," *Encyclopedia Brittanica*, 1964.

————, *Values and Intentions*, London: Allen & Unwin, 1961.

FINK, EUGENE, *Studien Zur Phänomenologie, 1930–1939*, The Hague, Netherlands: M. Nijhoff, 1966.

FØLLESDAL, DAGFINN, *Husserl und Frege*, Oslo: Aschehoug, 1958.

————, "Phenomenology: A Link Between Analytic Philosophy and Existentialism," in *Contemporary Philosophy in Scandinavia*, R. Olson and A. Paul, eds., Baltimore: Johns Hopkins Press, 1971.

FREGE, GOTTLOB, *Philosophical Writings*, translated and edited by M. Black and P. Geach, Oxford: Blackwell, 1960.

————, "The Thought," *Mind*, 65 (1956).

FRINGS, MANFRED S., *Max Scheler*, Pittsburgh: Duquesne University Press, 1965.

————, ed., *Heidegger and the Quest for Truth*, Chicago: Quadrangle, 1968.

GENDLIN, EUGENE, *Experiencing and the Creation of Meaning*, New York: Free Press, 1962.

————, "Experiential Explication and Truth," *Journal of Existentialism*, 22 (1965).

————, "Expressive Meanings," in *Invitation to Phenomenology*, J. Edie, ed., *op. cit.*

GOLDMANN, LUCIEN, "Sartre in Theater," *The Drama Review*, (1970).

GOODMAN, NELSON, *The Structure of Appearance*, 2nd ed., New York: Bobbs-Merrill, 1966.

GORZ, ANDRÉ, *The Traitor*, Preface by Jean-Paul Sartre, translated by R. Howard, New York: Simon & Schuster, 1959.

GRENE, MARJORIE, *Martin Heidegger*, London: Bowes & Bowes, 1957.

GURWITSCH, ARON, *The Field of Consciousness*, Pittsburgh: Dusquesne University Press, 1964.

———, "Ontology, Existentialism and Phenomenology," *Journal of Philosophy, 58* (1961).

———, *Studies in Phenomenology and Psychology*, Evanston, Ill.: Northwestern University Press, 1966.

HARTMANN, EDWARD, *The Philosophy of the Unconscious*, New York: Harcourt, 1971.

HARTMANN, KLAUS, "Phenomenology, Ontology and Metaphysics," *Review of Metaphysics, 22* (1968).

———, *Sartre's Ontology*, Evanston, Ill.: Northwestern University Press, 1966.

HARTMANN, NICOLAI, *Ethics*, translated by E. Coit, New York: Macmillan, 1932.

———, *New Ways of Ontology*, translated by R. Kuhn, Chicago: Regnery, 1952.

HEGEL, GEORG WILHELM FRIEDRICH, *The Phenomenology of Spirit*, translated by J. Baillie, New York: Harper & Row, 1964.

HEIDEGGER, MARTIN, *Being and Time*, translated by John Macquarrie and Edward Robinson, New York: Harper & Row, 1962.

———, *Discourse on Thinking*, translated by J. Anderson and E. Freund, New York: Harper & Row, 1966.

———, *Hegel's Concept of Existence*, New York: Harper & Row, 1970.

———, *Introduction to Metaphysics*, translated by R. Manheim, New Haven: Yale University Press, 1958.

———, *Kant and the Problem of Metaphysics*, translated by J. Churchill, Bloomington, Ind.: University of Indiana Press, 1962.

———, "Letter on Humanism," translated by E. Lohner in *Philosophy in the Twentieth Century*, Aiken and Barrett, eds., vol. 2, New York: Random House, 1962.

———, "On the Essence of Truth," translated by A. Crick and R. Hull *in Existence and Being*, in W. Brock, ed., Chicago: Regnery, 1949.

———, *The Question of Being*, translated by Kluback and Wilde, New York: Twayne, 1958.

———, "The Way Back into the Ground of Metaphysics," in *Existentialism from Dostoyevsky to Sartre*, Kaufmann, ed., New York: Meridian, 1956.

———, *What Is Called Thinking?*, New York: Harper & Row, 1968.

————, "What Is Metaphysics?, translated by A. Crick and R. Hull in W. Brock, ed., *op. cit.*

————, *What Is Philosophy?*, translated by Kluback and Wilde, New York: Twayne, 1958.

HEINEMANN, FREDERICK H., *Existentialism and the Human Predicament*, New York: Harper & Row, 1954.

HUSSERL, EDMUND, *Cartesian Meditations*, translated by D. Cairns, The Hague, Netherlands: M. Nijhoff, 1960.

————, *The Crisis of European Sciences and Transcendental Phenomenology*, translated by D. Carr, Evanston, Ill.: Northwestern University Press, 1970.

————, *Erste Philosophie*, vol. 1, *Husserliana*, vol. 7, The Hague: M. Nijhoff, 1956. Vol. II, *Husserliana* VIII, 1959.

————, *Formal and Transcendental Logic*, translated by D. Cairns, The Hague, Netherlands: M. Nijhoff, 1970.

————, *Idea of Phenomenology*, translated by W. Alston and G. Nakhnikian, The Hague, Netherlands: M. Nijhoff, 1964.

————, *Ideen Zu Einer Reinen Phänomenologie Und Phänomenologischen Philosophie*, *Husserliana*, 3 vols. (III, IV, V) The Hague: N. Nijhoff, 1950, 1952, 1952.

————, *Ideas*, translated by W. R. Boyce-Gibson, New York: Macmillan, 1931/1962.

————, *Logical Investigations*, translated by J. N. Findlay, New York: Humanities Press, 1970.

————, *Paris Lectures*, translated by P. Koestenbaum, The Hague, Netherlands: M. Nijhoff, 1964.

————, *Phenomenologische Psychologie*, Husserliana, vol. 9, 1962.

————, "Phenomenology," *Encyclopedia Brittanica*, 14th ed., reprinted in *Realism and the Background of Phenomenology*, Roderick Chisholm, ed., Glencoe, Ill.: Free Press, 1960.

————, *The Phenomenology of Internal Time-Consciousness*, translated by J. Churchill, edited by Martin Heidegger, Bloomington, Ind.: University of Indiana Press, 1964.

————, "Phenomenology as a Rigorous Science," translated by Lauer in *Phenomenology and the Crisis of Philosophy*, New York: Harper & Row, 1965.

————, *Transcendentale Phänomenologie*, *Husserliana*, vol. 6.

INGARDEN, ROMAN, *Time and Modes of Being*, translated by H. Micheida, Springfield, Ill.: Thomas, 1964.

JASPERS, KARL, *The Philosophy of Existence*, translated by Grabau, Philadelphia: University of Pennsylvania Press, 1971.

———, *The Philosophy of Jaspers*, edited by Schlipp, New York: Tudor, 1957.

JOLIVET, R., *Sartre: The Theology of the Absurd*, translated by W. Piersol, Westminster, Md.: Newman, 1967.

KAELIN, EUGENE F., *An Existentialist Aesthetic (Sartre and Merleau-Ponty)*, Madison: University of Wisconsin Press, 1962.

———, "Merleau-Ponty: Fundamental Ontologist" *Man and World* 3 (Feb. 1970).

KANT, IMMANUEL, *The Critique of Pure Reason*, translated by N. Kemp-Smith, New York: St. Martin's Press, 1966.

KAUFMANN, FRITZ, "Phenomenology and Logical Empiricism," in *Philosophical Essays in Memory of Edmund Husserl*, M. Farber, ed., Cambridge: Harvard University Press, 1940.

KAUFMANN, WALTER, *From Shakespeare to Existentialism*, New York: Doubleday, 1959.

KERN, E., ed., *Sartre*, New Haven: Yale University Press, 1961.

KING, MAGDA, *Heidegger's Philosophy*, New York: Macmillan, 1964.

KLEMKE, E. D., ed., *Essays on Frege*, Urbana: University of Illinois Press, 1968.

KOCKLEMANS, JOSEPH J., *First Introduction to Husserl's Phenomenology*, Pittsburgh: Dusquesne University Press, 1967.

———, *The Phenomenological Psychology of Edmund Husserl*, Pittsburgh: Dusquesne University Press, 1967.

———, ed., *Phenomenology*, New York: Doubleday-Anchor, 1967.

KWANT, R. C., *From Phenomenology to Metaphysics*, Pittsburgh: Dusquesne University Press, 1966.

LAING, R. D., *The Politics of Experience*, New York: Ballantine, 1967.

——— and D. G. Cooper, *Reason and Violence*, London: Tavistock, 1964.

LANGAN, THOMAS, *The Meaning of Heidegger*, New York: Columbia University Press, 1959.

LAUER, QUENTIN, *Phenomenology: Its Genesis and Prospect*, New York: Harper & Row, 1958.

LAWRENCE, N. and D. O'CONNER, eds., *Readings in Existential Phenomenology*, Englewood Cliffs, N.J.: Prentice-Hall, 1967.

LEE, E. and M. MANDLEBAUM, eds., *Phenomenology and Existentialism*, Baltimore: Johns Hopkins University Press, 1967.

LEVIN, DAVID M., *Reason and Evidence in Husserl's Phenomenology*, Evanston, Ill.: Northwestern University Press, 1970.

————, "Induction and Husserl's Theory of Eidetic Variation," *Philos. Phen. Res. 29* Sept. 1968.

LEVINAS, EMANUEL, *Totality and Infinity*, translated by A. Lingis, Pittsburgh: Dusquesne University Press, 1969.

LEWIS, C. I., *Mind and World Order*, New York: Scribners, 1929.

LUIJPEN, W. A., *Existential Phenomenology*, Pittsburgh: Dusquesne University Press, 1969.

LÖWITH, KARL, *Nature, History, and Existentialism*, Evanston, Ill.: Northwestern University Press, 1966.

MACQUARRIE, JOHN, *An Existentialist Theology*, London: SCM, 1955.

MANDLEBAUM, MAURICE, *The Phenomenology of Moral Experience*, Baltimore: Johns Hopkins University Press, 1969.

MANSER, ANTHONY, *Sartre: A Philosophical Study*, London: Oxford University Press, 1966.

MARCEL, GABRIEL, *Being and Having*, translated by K. Ferrer, Boston: Beacon, 1951.

————, *The Mystery of Being*, 2 vols., translated by Fraser and Hague, Chicago: Regnery, 1951.

————, *The Philosophy of Existence*, translated by M. Harari, New York: Philosophical Library, 1949.

MARITAIN, JACQUES, *Existence and the Existent*, translated by Galantiere, New York: Vintage, 1966.

MAY, ROLLO, with E. ANGEL and H. ELLENBERGER, *Existence*, New York: Basic Books, 1958.

MAY, ROLLO, *Love and Will*, New York: Norton, 1969.

————, *Man's Search for Himself*, New York: Norton, 1953.

MEINONG, ALEXUS, "The Theory of Objects," in *Realism and the Background of Phenomenology*, Roderick Chisholm, ed., Glencoe, Ill.: Free Press, 1960.

MERLAN, P., "Time Consciousness in Husserl and Heidegger," *Philosophical and Phenomenological Research, 8* (1947).

MERLEAU-PONTY, MAURICE, *Humanism and Terror*, translated by J. O'Neill, Boston: Beacon, 1969.

————, *In Praise of Philosophy*, translated by J. Wild and J. Edie, Evanston, Ill.: Northwestern University Press, 1964.

————, *The Phenomenology of Perception,* translated by C. Smith, London: Routledge & Kegan Paul, 1962.

————, *The Primacy of Perception,* translated by J. Edie, Evanston, Ill.: Northwestern University Press, 1964.

————, *Signs,* translated by R. McCleary, Evanston, Ill.: Northwestern University Press, 1964.

————, *The Structure of Behavior,* translated by A. Fisher, Boston: Beacon, 1963.

MOHANTY, J. *Edmund Husserl's Theory of Meaning,* The Hague, Netherlands: M. Nijhoff, 1964.

MOLINA, FERNANDO, *Existentialism as Philosophy,* Englewood Cliffs, N.J.: Prentice-Hall, 1962.

MORRIS, PHYLLIS, "Sartre and the Existence of Other Minds," *Journ. Brit. Soc. Phen.* Vol. I, (May 1970).

MORRISON, JAMES C., "Husserl and Brentano on Intentionality," *Philos. Phen. Res. 31* (Sept. 1970).

MURDOCH, IRIS, *Sartre: Romantic Rationalist,* London: Collins, 1953.

NATANSON, MAURICE, *A Critique of Jean-Paul Sartre's Ontology,* Lincoln, Nebraska: University of Nebraska Press, 1951.

————, "Empirical and Transcendental Ego," in *For Roman Ingarden,* Tymieniecka, ed., The Hague, Netherlands: M. Nijhoff, 1959.

————, ed., *Essays in Phenomenology,* The Hague, Netherlands: M. Nijhoff, 1966.

————, *Literature, Philosophy and the Social Sciences, Essays,* The Hague, Netherlands: M. Nijhoff, 1962.

————, "Phenomenology and Existentialism: Husserl and Sartre on Intentionality," in *Phenomenology,* J. A. Kocklemans, ed., New York: Doubleday-Anchor, 1967.

NOVACK, GEORGE E., ed., *Existentialism vs. Marxism,* New York: Dell, 1966.

O'BRIEN, CONOR CRUSE, *Camus,* New York: Fontana, 1970.

OLAFSON, FREDERICK A., *Principles and Persons,* Baltimore: Johns Hopkins University Press, 1967.

OSBORN, A., *The Philosophy of Husserl,* New York: Columbia University Press, 1934.

PFÄNDER, ALEXANDER, *Phenomenology of Willing and Motivation,* translated by H. Spiegleberg, Evanston, Ill.: Northwestern University Press, 1967.

RABIL, A., *Merleau-Ponty: Existentialist of the Social World*, New York: Columbia University Press, 1967.

READ, HERBERT, *Existentialism, Marxism and Anarchism*, London: Freedom Press, 1949.

RICHARDSON, WILLIAM J., *Heidegger: From Phenomenology to Thought*, The Hague, Netherlands: M. Nijhoff, 1963.

RICOUER, PAUL, *Freedom and Nature: The Voluntary and the Involuntary*, translated by E. Kohâk, Evanston, Ill.: Northwestern University Press, 1966.

————, *History and Truth*, translated by C. Kelbley, Evanston, Ill.: Northwestern University Press, 1965.

————, *Husserl: An Examination of His Philosophy*, translated by E. Ballard and L. Embree, Evanston, Ill.: Northwestern University Press, 1967.

————, *The Philosophy of Will*, translated by C. Kelbley, Chicago: Regnery, 1965.

ROUBICZEK, PAUL, *Existentialism for and Against*, Cambridge: Cambridge University Press, 1964.

RYLE, GILBERT, Reviews of M. Farber, *Foundations of Phenomenology*, in *Philosophy* Vol. XXI, pp. 263–69 and Martin Heidegger, *Sein und Zeit*, in *Mind* Vol. XXXVIII, pp. 355–70.

SALMON, C. V., "The Starting Point of Husserl's Philosophy," *Procedures of the Aristotelean Society*, 30 (1930).

SANBORN, PATRICIA, *Existentialism*, New York: Pegasus, 1968.

SARTRE, JEAN-PAUL, *Being and Nothingness*, translated by H. Barnes, New York: Philosophical Library, 1956.

————, *Critique de la Raison Dialectique*, Paris: Gallimard, 1960. Translated in part by H. Barnes as *Search for a Method*, New York: Knopf, 1963.

————, *The Emotions-Outline of a Theory*, translated by B. Frechtman, New York: Philosophical Library, 1948.

————, *Existentialism Is a Humanism*, translated by Mairet, London: Methuen, 1948.

————, *Imagination*, translated by F. Williams, Ann Arbor, Mich.: University of Michigan Press, 1962.

————, "Intentionality: A Fundamental Idea of Husserl's Phenomenology," *Journ. Brit. Soc. Phen. 1* (May 1970).

————, "Situations I and III," translated by A. Michelson, in *Literary and Philosophical Essays*, New York: Collier, 1962.

————, "Portrait of an Anti-Semite," in *From Shakespeare to Existentialism*, W. Kaufmann, ed., New York: Doubleday, 1959.

————, *Psychology of the Imagination*, translated by B. Frechtman, London: Philosophical Library, 1948.

————, *Saint Genet: Actor and Martyr*, translated by B. Frechtman, New York: Braziller, 1963.

————, *The Transcendence of the Ego*, translated by F. Williams and R. Kirpatrick, New York: Noonday, 1957.

————, *The Words: An Autobiography*, translated by B. Frechtman, New York: Braziller, 1964.

SCHELER, MAX, *The Nature of Sympathy*, translated by P. Heath, London: Routledge & Kegan Paul, 1954.

————, *Philosophical Perspectives*, translated by A. Haag, Boston: Beacon, 1958.

SCHRAG, CALVIN O., *Existence and Freedom*, Evanston, Ill.: Northwestern University Press, 1961.

————, "Phenomenology, Ontology, and History in the Philosophy of Martin Heidegger," *Revue Internationale Philos.* XII, 1958.

SCHMITT, RICHARD, *Heidegger On Being Human*, New York: Random House, 1969.

————, "Husserl's Transcendental-Phenomenological Reduction," *Philosophical and Phenomenological Research*, 20 (1959–1960).

————, "Phenomenology and Analysis," *Philosophical and Phenomenological Research*, 23 (1962–1963).

————, "Phenomenology and Metaphysics," *Journal of Philosophy*, 59 (1962).

SCHRADER, GEORGE, ed., *Existential Philosophers*, New York: McGraw-Hill, 1967.

————, "Heidegger's Ontology of Human Existence," *Rev. Metaphysics*, X, 1956–57.

SCHÜTZ, A., *Collected Papers*, 3 Vols., edited by M. Natanson, The Hague, Netherlands: M. Nijhoff, 1962.

————, *Phenomenology of the Social World*, translated by G. Walsh and F. Lehnert. Evanston, Ill.: Northwestern Univ. Press, 1967.

SINHA, D., "Phenomenology and Positivism," *Philosophical and Phenomenological Research*, 23 (1962–1963).

SOKOLOWSKI, ROBERT, *The Formation of Husserl's Concept of Constitution*, The Hague, Netherlands: M. Nijhoff, 1964.

SOLOMON, ROBERT C., *From Rationalism to Existentialism: The*

Existentialists and Their Nineteenth-Century Background, New York: Harper & Row, 1972.

SONTAG, FREDERICK, *The Existentialist Prolegomena,* Chicago: University of Chicago Press, 1969.

SPIEGLEBERG, HERBERT, *The Phenomenological Movement,* 2 vols., The Hague, Netherlands: M. Nijhoff, 1960.

———, "Husserl's Phenomenology and Sartre's Existentialism," *Journal of Philosophy,* 57 (1960). Reprinted in J. A. Kocklemans, ed., *Phenomenology,* New York: Doubleday-Anchor, 1967.

STERN, ALFRED, *Sartre,* New York: Liberal Arts, 1953.

STRASSER, STEPHEN, *Phenomenology and the Human Sciences,* Pittsburgh: Dusquesne University Press, 1963.

THÉVANEZ, PIERRE, *What Is Phenomenology?,* translated by Courtney, edited by Brockelman and J. Edie, Chicago: Quadrangle, 1962.

TILLICH, PAUL, *The Courage to Be,* New Haven: Yale University Press, 1952.

TILLMAN, FRANK, "Phenomenology and Philosophical Analysis," *International Philosophical Quarterly,* 6 (1966).

TYMIENIECKA, A. T., ed., *For Roman Ingarden,* The Hague, Netherlands: M. Nijhoff, 1959.

———, *Phenomenology and Science in Contemporary European Thought,* New York: Farrar, Strauss, 1962.

VAN PEURSEN, C. A., "Edmund Husserl and Ludwig Wittgenstein," *Philosophical and Phenomenological Research* 20 (1959).

WAHL, JEAN, *Philosophies of Existence,* translated by F. Lory, New York: Schocken, 1969.

WALRAFF, CHARLES, *Karl Jaspers,* Princeton: Princeton University Press, 1970.

WANN, T. W., ed., *Behaviorism and Phenomenology,* Chicago: University of Chicago Press, 1964.

WARNOCK, MARY, *Existentialism,* London: Oxford University Press, 1970.

———, *The Philosophy of Sartre,* London: Hutchinson, 1965.

WELCH, E. PARL, *Philosophy of Edmund Husserl,* New York: Octagon, 1965.

WILD, JOHN, *The Challenge of Existentialism,* Bloomington, Ind.: University of Indiana Press, 1955.

———, *Existence and the World of Freedom,* Englewood Cliffs, N.J.: Prentice-Hall, 1963.

WILL, FREDERICK, "Sartre and the Question of Character in Literature, *Modern Language Association,* 76.

WILLARD, DALLAS, "Husserl's Refutation of Logical Psychologism," *American Philosophical Quarterly,* (1971).

WILLIAMS, FORREST, "Doubt and the Phenomenological Reduction," *Philosophical and Phenomenological Research,* 18 (1957).

WILSON, COLIN, *Introduction to the New Existentialism,* London: Hutchinson, 1966.

ZANER, RICHARD M., *The Problem of Embodiment,* The Hague, Netherlands: M. Nijhoff, 1964.

——, *The Way of Phenomenology,* New York: Pegasus, 1970.

72 73 74 75   10 9 8 7 6 5 4 3 2 1